Legal Foundations of Russian Economy

Edited by Juha Tolonen and Boris Topornin

KIKIMORA PUBLICATIONS

Series B : 14 Helsinki 2000

Legal Foundations of Russian Economy

ISBN 951-45-9276-X
ISSN 1455-4828

Aleksanteri Institute
Graphic design: Vesa Tuukkanen

Gummerus Kirjapaino Oy
Saarijärvi 2000

Contents

List of authors

Topornin, Boris Nikolajevich
Academician, Director of the Institute of State and Law
Russian Academy of Sciences

Ikonitskaya, Irina Aleksandrovna
Vice Director of the Institute of State and Law,
Russian Academy of Sciences
Doctor of Law, Professor
Honoured Scientist in Russia

Andrejev, Vladimir Konstantinovich
Main Legal Researcher in the Institute of State and Law,
Russian Academy of Science,
Professor, Doctor of Law

Andrejeva, Ljubov Vasiljevna
Docent, Assistant Professor of Moscow State Academy of Law
Candidate of Legal Science (PhD)

Bardina, Marina Petrovna
Senior Legal Researcher in the Institute of State and Law,
Russian Academy of Science
Candidate of Legal Science (PhD)

Kabatova, Elena Vitaljevna
Senior Legal Researcher in the Institute of State and Law,
Russian Academy of Science
Candidate of Legal Science (PhD)

Salisheva, Nadeshda Georgijevna
Leading Legal Researcher, Docent, Assistant Professor
in the Institute of State and Law,
Russian Academy of Science,
Honoured Lawyer of the Russian Federation,
Candidate of Legal Science (PhD)

Vinogradova, Elena Aleksandrovna
Senior Legal Researcher in the Institute of State and Law,
Russian Academy of Sciences
Candidate of Legal Science (PhD)

Zaharova, Raisa Fedotovna
Director of the Sector of Tax Law in the Institute of State and Law,
Russian Academy of Science;
Candidate of Legal Science (PhD)

Co-discussants:

Fogelklou, Anders
Doctor of Law
Professor of Law,
University of Uppsala

Jakushev, Valeri
Licentiate of Business Administration
Business University of Turku

Knoph, Jan
Doctor of Law
University of Uppsala

Kärkkäinen, Mika
Master of Business Administration
Teacher of Commercial Law
University of Vaasa

Lehtinen, Leena
Doctor of Law
Docent of Law,
University of Tampere
Legal Consultant

Nystén-Haarala, Soili
Doctor of Law
Acting Professor of Private Law
Faculty of Law, University of Lapland

Juha Tolonen
Doctor of Law
Professor of Law
University of Vaasa

Introduction

Juha Tolonen and Boris Nikolajevich Topornin

This book contains description and analysis of several branches of Russian law. As the title of the book reveals relevant branches relating to Russian economy have been chosen. The aim of the authors´ collective is to state the official legal rules governing the economic activity in Russia after the collapse of the Soviet Union.

There are several books in Western Europe and in the USA on the Russian legal system in general or on some of its branches in particular. Mostly they have been written by experts living outside Russia. Therefore, the text of those works has a western point of view. In this book, in contrast to the others, the viewpoint of the articles is Russian. The book has been written by legal experts in Russia. It has been the intention of the editors and authors of this book to get the reader acquainted with the way Russian lawyers themselves think and interpret the law. This is the valid law in Russia. It is to be noted that the difference between these two perspectives (Western and Russian) is considerable. From the Western point of view, everything divergent from their legal model is negative and it is described accordingly. It is useful to read the interpretation of the legal situation in Russia as described by Russian experts themselves.

The Russian law, as it stands now, has a long history. All past history is, in one way or another, to be seen in the present system. Already during the Russian Empire, before the World War I, there was a very strong German tradition in Russian law. From the time of Peter the Great German experts have exerted influence on the formation of Russian law and its concepts, and the way of thinking of law in general. This feature did not vanish during the Soviet period, quite on the contrary, the German conceptual thinking continued to live in new circumstances. One has to remember that the socialist doctrine, prevalent in the Soviet Union, was originally German. To combine Marxist thinking with German legal concepts was not so difficult, because Marx and Engels themselves expressed their legal ideas through German notions.

Legal development typical of the Soviet period had its starting point in the early twenties, when Soviet authorities introduced the "New Economic Policy" which meant only moderate changes in the economic system: big enterprises were nationalised, but small and medium sized private firms continued to exist; the co-operative movement in agriculture was favoured, but on a voluntary basis. The real radical change started at the end of the twenties with the introduction of the centralised planned economy. The first five year plan started to function in 1929. Changes of the legal system ensued. The plan economy created its own institutions and solutions to various economic problems. They all were reflected on the legal system where the economic plan itself was the central legal concept.

The central idea of the plan economy was to accelerate the economic progress in general and to avoid the capitalistic way of development. This meant in practice that the market system of the exchange economy was, by and large, replaced by economic plans which defined to enterprises what and how much to produce and how to distribute the products. The market was only of secondary importance in the relations between enterprises. The economic one-year and five-year plans were legally binding acts which were (at the top level) accepted by the Soviet Parliament, i. e. The Supreme Soviet of the USSR. They were made concrete by administrative acts through ministries giving directives to the enterprises under their control. Enterprises had their horizontal relations with other enterprises mostly determined by distribution plans. The role of contracts in this context was only secondary.

In this system the economic entities (enterprises) were controlled by the state. Most of them were also formally owned by the state. The legal form of these enterprises was that of a "state enterprise". Only in agriculture (kolhozes) and retail trade were there also co-operative units. The proprietary rights of all these units had to be regulated accordingly. The state enterprises did not have any "own property". They used the property of the state on the basis of the so called right of "operative management". Moreover, all land and natural resources belonged to the state according to the 1936 Constitution of the Soviet Union, which was replaced by the new Constitution in 1977.

This socialist economic order, which in itself was totally logical and consistent, was constructed through vertical and horizontal relations. Vertical (administrative) relations meant the relations of state enterprises to administratively superior bodies, in the last instance to the ministries. Horizontal relations were the relations of state enterprises to other state enterprises They were in principle governed by contracts, but these contracts had to be consistent with the distribution plans, otherwise the contract was legally invalid. Administrative law was, thus, predominant in the legal system of the Soviet economy. In the last decades of its existence there was, however, continuous theoretical discussion concerning the role of private law and administrative law. This discussion was conducted under the theme "Plan and Contract" which meant how to combine contractual relations with administrative plans. Discussion was especially intense in the academic discipline of "economic law" (hozjaistvennoje pravo). There was an idea within this discipline to combine the administrative and contractual relations into a new type of legal relations, i.e. relations of economic law. The administrative functions of an economic complex (such as ministry, intermediary administration and enterprises under this ministry) should, according to this idea, operate on a self-financing (so called "hozraztset") principle where revenues are collected from the administrative services given to the enterprises. This idea is astonishingly similar to the western tendency to privatization of state functions like public services etc. Unfortunately the Soviet Union collapsed before these new models were put into practice.

The administrative system of the Soviet Union followed the principle of "democratic centralism". According to it, state power was used on various levels: on the level of the Soviet Union (so called all union -level), on the level of the republics and on the local level. The power on all these levels was state power. There was, thus, no independent local self-government. The power either belonged exclusively to one level (for example the all-union level) or the power was used jointly. Administration of any economic branch was either all-union or union-republican. All-union administration meant that the branch was under a ministry of the Soviet Union and the administrative lines from basic units (enterprises) went upwards (vertical subordination). Local or republican administration had nothing to do with all union branches even if enterprises of the branch concerned may have been situated on their territory.

The union-republican branches had two ministries, one on the union level and the other on the level of the republics. In these cases the republican ministry and the enterprises under it were in "dual subordination". On the one hand, they were under the Government and the Supreme Soviet of the republic where they were situated (vertical subordination). On the other hand, they were subordinated vertically to the ministry of the Soviet Union. The first subordination represented democracy and the other centralism, whence the term: democratic centralism. This model repeated itself also on the local level and was thus the leading idea of the whole administrative apparatus of the Soviet Union. The dialectics of the administration were in principle here. Theoretically it was an excellent idea, in practice, however, it did not function, because the vertical ordination was too dominant and the horizontal too weak.

The economic branch administration was thus organised under Ministries. There was, however, also so-called functional economic state administration. This meant administration of a certain specific function over all branches. This administration was run by state committees. The State Planning Committee and The State Price Committee were good examples. All this functional administration worked on the union-republican basis.

The legislative power over all union branches, accordingly, lay only with the Supreme Soviet of the Soviet Union. The union-republican model was, however, more important. As far as private law, criminal law and law of procedure were concerned, the legislative power was according to this dual model. The Supreme Soviet of the Soviet Union enacted the so called "Fundamentals of Legislation" (e.g. Fundamentals of Civil Law Legislation). On the basis of it the republics enacted more detailed laws (e.g. Civil Code). This inferior law could never be in controversy with the superior law. It only contained more detailed rules than "Fundamentals".

The third variation of the use of public power was the so-called republican administration. This meant that the powers were exclusively in the republics. This variation was, however, of minor significance only. As a rule there was only one republican branch: local industries like production of children toys or tourist souvenirs. For this purpose there was in several republics the Ministry of Local Industry.

The court system in the former Soviet Union had, from the economic point of view, one peculiarity. There existed two court systems: the General Courts and the State Arbitration. Under the jurisdiction of the last-mentioned courts (which were permanent) were the disputes between state bodies, either administrative bodies or state enterprises. The idea behind this distinction was that disputes within the state sector had their own character. Behind both litigants was only one subject, the state. Therefore, in this procedure certain general aspects have to be taken into consideration which were not relevant in regular dispute settlement. These special aspects were implied in the fact that all state bodies have to fulfil the general objectives of the State as expressed in established economic plans.

All this information of the former Soviet system has been expounded on here because it forms the necessary background to understand the legal problems and solutions in today's Russia. No society can once get rid of its past. There is always historical continuity.

The articles of this book are written by Russian legal experts, who have written one article each. In addition, the authors have been invited to seminars where Scandinavian experts have expressed their views. The list of these co-discussants is above. The intention was not to interfere with the contents of the articles. The Scandinavians only pointed out issues which they had difficulties in understanding or issues they wanted more information on.

This book reflects, thus, Russian legal thinking and doctrine. The doctrine is, of course, based on the social, political and economic history of Russia. Typical features of the Russian doctrine are as follows:

– The *legal doctrine* is based on legislation and inferior legal acts (Decrees of the President, Resolution of the Government, etc). References to the legal tradition and classical works are, on the contrary, quite rare. The same may be said about court practice. The reasons for this are quite obvious. The Russian society and legal system in this century has been exposed to several radical shocks and changes. In the early twenties there was a civil war and war communism. Then later on, in the same decade the economic system was organised according to Lenin´s "new economic policy". After Lenin´s death in 1924 there was an internal battle within the Communist Party leading to the victory of Stalin. He introduced from 1929 a centralised planned economy. Then the World War II followed. After the war Hrutsev attempted to realise his economic ideas where the regional administration of economy (sovnarhoz-system) was central. The branch administration of economy was restored after the Hrutsev´s dismissal. In the middle of eighties Gorbatshev started the economic reform called "perestroika". Soviet Union collapsed in 1991 and the market economy reforms commenced in 1992. It is accordingly, natural that no stable legal tradition could be developed, and classical legal text books have lost their significance. The same applies to court practice. Cases from the Soviet period have lost their actuality due to fundamental changes in the social structure. Also in the last decade new laws and their amendments have been made all the time.

Times are, however, gradually changing. Russian legal journals have started to publish important cases. So, there will probably be more reference to cases in the future, but it takes time and presupposes stable development in Russian society in general.

– When one analyses *legal argumentation* in the Russian legal doctrine, the paradigm of legal (legislative) positivism is conspicuous. The argumentation is mostly based on the text of the law and only on it. The idea that behind the legal solution there would be a more fundamental social structure and so-called stable legal principles almost never appears in Russian juridical texts. The new Constitution admittedly contains a long list of basic human rights. References to these rights are quite frequent and this is a new phenomenon in Russian thinking. However, they are referred to only insofar as these rights are mentioned in the Constitution.

The legal dogmatics in any country always reflects in one way or another the social reality of the country concerned. This held true in the Soviet Union, and the same is the case in Russia of today. A keen reader analysing the text of this book and reflecting on it can understand the social reality behind the legal argumentation of the authors.

The texts in this book were completed in the beginning of 1999. The translation has taken some time. The texts have been first translated by Dr. Marina Roumjantseva from the University of Petrozavodsk and by Dr. Valeri Jakushev from Turku School of Economics and Business Administration. After the translation the undersigned have checked all the special legal terms, which also took quite a lot time. There have been minor changes in legislation during the past year. In principle, however, the chapters describe the legal situation in Russia at present. Moreover, the texts express the legal thinking and tradition in Russia. This has been the main goal of this book.

I Constitutional Foundations of the New Russian Economy

Boris Nikolajevich Topornin

1. Background

Post-socialist transformation of the Russian society has involved practically all aspects of its development. The essence of the economic system has been radically changed, the state power has been built on the new principles, the rule of one ideology has been replaced by the ideological variety. The majority of the old political and legal institutions have been replaced by the new ones, while the remaining ones have been radically changed. It means that the attempts which were undertaken during the years of perestroika to improve socialism, to cure it from the diseases tormenting it and at the same time to preserve its foundations, were insufficient. The crisis of socialism turned out to be deeper and more serious than it had looked in the beginning. The course of the events led to the reforms of the 90s which had a systemic character. Their results from the point of view of law were basically summarized in the Constitution of the Russian Federation of 1993.The Constitution says that the new Russian state is based on the principles which are universal and are fixed in the constitutional legislation of the countries of the modern world: sovereignty of the people, law-gov-erned state, wide range of rights and freedoms of man, division of powers. It should be emphasized that the Russian economy is develop-ing on the basis of market relations, recognition, support and protec-tion of private property and freedom for entrepreneurship.

The transition from the strictly planned regulation of the economy to the market economy would be impossible without cardinal re-evalua-tion of the original approaches to law, its purpose and character. It is well-known that the Soviet state was not just the bearer of the political power, but also the owner of the means of production. According to the socialist guidelines, the state directly performed economic activity. The unity of the political and economic leadership performing eco-nomic activity on the basis of the state ownership and central planning were the major foundations of the legal regulation of socialist economy. The constitution of 1977, which was in force up to the disintegration of the USSR, fixed that governing of the economy was carried out on the basis of the state plans of the economic and social development with consideration of branch of industry and territorial principles. At the same time, it mentioned a need to combine central planning and economic independence and initiative of enterprises, associations and other organizations (art.16) which reflected the influ-ence of the time. But in reality strict centralism obviously prevailed. Both state enterprises and state farms as units functioning under the conditions of the socialist economy, were very dependent on superior administrative state bodies.

With the beginning of the economic reforms in Russia the necessity to create a new system of the legal regulation of the economic activity was clear. It would be in principle different from the command-admin-istrative mechanism which characterized the Soviet power. Even to the people inexperienced in politics it was clear that old law was an obstacle to the formation of the market relations. But creation of new law was not an easy task. It required big efforts and took certain time. It was necessary not only to develop the general structure of the new legal system, but also to outline its content and stages of its implemen-tation. The idea was to create a well developed and coordinated system. It was important to prevent chaotic development of the legislation and accidental choice of concrete decisions which would lead to decreasing efficiency of legal regulation.

In general, it was clear that management of the economy had to be brought to compliance with the requirements of the period of transition to the market economy. It meant, first of all, taking decisive and large-scale measures aimed at separate political power and ownership, creating for the economy the "rules of the game" which would ensure equality for the participants and prevent bureaucracy from interfering into economic processes. It was necessary in a short time to work out and adopt a great number of legislative acts in the sphere of private business.

This particular sphere had enormous gaps. They did not appear accidentally but were a consequence of the old approach which can be expressed in a short formula summarizing the essence of the state policy in economy: "we do not recognize anything private; everything in the economy is publicly-legal, not private". The state character of the economy under the Soviet power resulted in the situation when the civil legislation had a restricted character and many branches of the private law practically did not exist. Bank law, for example, just regulated organization and performance of the Central bank and several other state banks since commercial banks at that time did not exist.

How well were the judicial theory and practice prepared to the legal reform, to the introduction of the new categories (private type of ownership, stockholding form of ownership, regulation of the flow of goods according to the market demands, rejection of the old views on speculative activity, voluntary non-participation in the public economy, etc.) into the legislation and legal practice? The answer is quite complicated. We should recognize that jurisprudence was badly infected with dogmatism and saturated with ideological cliches and schemes. A grave problem of the old practice consisted in governing not by law but by instructions, administrative orders, telephone directives. Above law were the party bodies decisions, and directives of the party apparatus. And yet, the Russian judicial community including the participants of the law-making process, judges and scholars was able to cope with the really historical task quickly and on good professional level.

Certainly, the process of adoption by jurisprudence of the new approaches and categories of the market economy was not easy. It was necessary for the lawyers to change orientation and to educate the society by bringing in a new legal culture. But it should be remembered that starting from the 60s and especially during the years of perestroika lawyers had laid good foundation for the future. They worked out the problems of democracy, legality, law-governed state, increasing efficiency of managing the economy. Though they were talking about socialist democracy, socialist legality and socialist law-governed state, in fact, they were studying and discussing universal values.

Study of the foreign experience, development of international legal cooperation and especially academic connections considerably contributed to the formation of new Russian law. Scholars in the field of law from the USSR actively participated in international associations and societies formed in the modern world on the different branches of law and on the complex problems of jurisprudence. Publishing in the USSR of translated foreign literature on law has definitely acquainted the Soviet reader with the development of law abroad.

Study and adoption of the foreign experience makes it possible to use the results of universal development, to make a period of search shorter, and to choose the most appropriate models of state and legal organization as well as the instruments necessary for the reforms. Respectful attitude to foreign achievements has nothing to do with blind copying or thoughtless imitation. It should be mentioned because a variety of legal systems exist in the world.

It is well known that the two systems – the continental law and the common (precedent) law play the most important role in the world. The former has been spread on the European continent, the latter – in the USA, Great Britain and some other countries. Though lately the tendency to harmonize the legal systems has been increasing, which reflects the processes of integration in the world economy and trade, major differences between the legal systems stay. The advantage of the common (precedent) law is its relatively stronger attention to the specific precedent (in a sense a stronger orientation at the individual). It is a direct result of the fact that the common law was developing gradually from precedent to precedent which, however, required more time. The continental law developed in a different way by means of uniform regulation of large groups of social relations. Such qualities enable to facilitate the regulation process and to deal with the society as a whole or its big parts.

Reference to the history of the Russian law, especially to the beginning of this century has also played its role. It should be mentioned that at that time Russia rapidly developed along with industrial countries. Legal regulation of the economy was getting a special attention on behalf of the state authorities. Thorough studies of the concept of legal entity both in the public law (treasury, departments, institutions) and private law (societies, partnerships, etc.) appeared in jurisprudence at that time. Among the types of partnerships were defined complete partnership, limited partnership, joint-stock partnership. Pre-revolutionary Russian law knew not only the concept of enterprise, but also its types – trusts, syndicates, concerns, joint-stock companies.

Thus, the general level of the advanced part of Russian lawyers and first of all law professors, was rather high. They understood the essence of current changes and the vector of modern history. The leading position in the development of the judicial thought in new Russia occupies now the Institute of the State and Law of the Russian Academy of Sciences (the former USSR Academy of Sciences). Its employees actively participate in renovation of the legal system. Practically all branches of law are being developed at the Institute by 400 highly qualified specialists including 200 professors.

Among the first market-oriented laws passed in post-Soviet Russia are the RSFSR Law "On property in RSFSR" of December 24, 1990" and the RSFSR Law "On enterprises and entrepreneurial activity" of December 25, 1990. According to the first of these laws, the property can be in private ownership. Private property was introduced with preservation of the state and municipal property. It is fixed that the state has no right to introduce any kind of limitations or privileges on exercising the property rights depending on the type of property – private, state, municipal or public organisations property.

The right for private property envisages that citizen's property is created and multiplied by means of income from participation in production and other use of his/her abilities to work, from entrepreneurial activity, from having one's own farm, as well as income from the money invested in the credit institutions, shares and other securities, inheritance of the property and other legal sources.

The Law "On property in RSFSR" eliminated previous limitations of the right for personal property, especially its derivative nature the public property and its consumer orientation. Personal property of the citizens was preserved but not as restricted category of property right, but rather as one of its types. Citizen as the owner received an opportunity to use his/her property not only for consumption, but also for performing entrepreneurial activity.

The significance of the latter law (On enterprises and entrepreneurial activity) consisted in opening the way to entrepreneurship which was interpreted as independent activity of citizens performed on their behalf, at their risk and their own property responsibility. Entrepreneurship has the purpose of making profit or personal income. It is stated that as an entrepreneur the citizen has a right to acquire as one's property state enterprises and other enterprises and organisations including property complexes; to participate with one's property in the activity of other economic subjects; to open bank accounts; to participate in due order in foreign economic relations; to perform currency transactions; to freely dispose of the profit and get unlimited amounts of personal income. At the same time entrepreneurs are endowed with certain obligations.

The Law "On enterprises and entrepreneurial activity" reflected conditions of the time. First of all, it contributed to the development of the small and medium-size business. As for the large-scale private entrepreneurial activity, it was just outlined. The law spoke about economic partnerships and companies, but very briefly and without specifying their types.

The new Russian legislation developed also in other directions. But nevertheless, Russia kept living according to the old constitution. The Constitution of RSFSR, which was one of the former USSR republics, it was adopted in 1978. In full compliance with the rules of that time, it was an exact copy of the USSR Constitution of 1977. It should be mentioned, however, that among the Soviet constitutions the last one was the most developed. The Constitution of 1977 declared many general democratic principles and contained an extensive catalogue of basic rights and freedoms of the person and citizen. At the same time, it fixed one-party political system in which political power was concentrated in the hands of the Communist Party, and more specifically, in the hands of its apparatus. The Constitution was based on the state-governed economy and counted on administrative methods of its management. Obviously, it excluded private ownership and private business. A market economy was out of the question.

The Soviet state was considered federative. Federalism was treated mainly as an instrument of regulating national relations and determining nation-state structuring of the country. The Soviet Union consisted of the union republics named after the nation of the core population. Declarations of federalism and sovereignty of the union republics did not eliminate strict centralisation in governing the whole country which was similar to that in unitary states. USSR was built on the command-administrative system which prevailed over the elected representative bodies of power, the Soviets, both on the local level in the cities, districts, regions, and on the level of the union republics, as well as in the centre. The USSR Supreme Soviet which had been declared by the Constitution the supreme body of state power, dealt mainly with passing decisions worked out by the party apparatus.

After the collapse of the USSR and transition of the RSFSR into the independent state, and especially with the beginning of the reforms in the Russian society, the RSFSR Constitution of 1978 started falling behind the time. In order to prevent it from being outdated and inconsistent with the changing society, amendments were gradually introduced into the Constitution which influenced its content. For example, the right for private property, as well as a market economy, were recognised, the institute of the President was introduced, the principle of division of powers was fixed, the character of federalism was changed, and the provisions of the Declaration of Human Rights and Freedoms, adopted in 1991 recognized. In some years about 300 amendments were introduced in the Constitution of 1978. However, this did not sufficiently renovate the Constitution.

Difficulties were connected with the fact that massive and hasty amendments introduced in the text of the Constitution resulted in discordance of norms and contradictory approaches. The comparison of the Constitution with a patchwork quilt was justified. Critical situations were quite common. It was impossible to define the form of governing in Russia for, on the one hand, the Constitution fixed the principle of division of powers, and on the other hand, it contained the norm giving the Congress of the People's Deputies the right to accept for consideration and pass a decision on any issue within RSFSR jurisdiction. The Supreme Soviet of RSFSR which unlike the Congress of the People's Deputies, convening for sessions from time to time, had to work on a permanent basis (the Supreme Soviet was elected at the Congress of the People's Deputies from the deputies). The Supreme Soviet was still called not just representative and legislative, but also administrative body. Inevitable confrontations also resulted from the fact that the introduction of the President's institution was not accompanied by a cardinal revision of the article about the functions of the Presidium of the RSFSR Supreme Soviet. It was bad even in cases when political positions of the President and of the Presidium coincided. But in cases when these institutes of the supreme power had different interests and intentions, the situation was even worse. Numerous examples could be given here, and the conclusion is obvious: the state and the society did not have an institutional and legal mechanism meeting requirements of the serious transformation of the economy and all other major spheres of life in the country.

The constitutional development more and more reflected the political struggle around the reforms and choice of the main road for the future. Though at the first RSFSR Congress of the People's Deputies the Constitutional commission was formed headed by B.N.Eltsin, then Chairman of the RSFSR Supreme Soviet, there was little progress made. The milestones of confrontation were sittings of the Congress of the People's Deputies and sessions of the Supreme Soviet. Consensus could not be achieved. Goals and tasks were too contradictory. The conflict could be settled only by means of replacing the old Constitution with the new one based on new foundations. The need for constitutional reform was getting more and more obvious and urgent.

Russia needed a new Constitution not just for legislative confirmation of the changes that had already taken place in the state and in the whole society, but also for making a foundation for new changes that would be equally important. It was extremely important to lay them down systematically. It was necessary to provide support on the constitutional level for the judicial reform which had been outlined in the early 90s. New courts had been already formed – constitutional and arbitration. There were discussions about forming courts with juries. The criminal and criminal-procedural legislation were under reconsideration. Economic reforms were under way. They drastically changed property relations. Privatisation started to develop.

The support rendered by the Russian society at the referendum of April 1993 to President B.N.Eltsin, who was willing to drastically reform the country, served as a stimulus to speeding-up preparation of the draft Constitution. The initiative came directly from the President. According to his decree, in order to complete this work, a Constitutional meeting was held in Moscow in June 1993. Its work was organised mainly in five sections formed of the 1) representatives of the federal bodies of state power; 2) representatives of the bodies of state power of the republics within the Russian Federation, territories, regions, autonomous regions, autonomous areas, Moscow and St.Petersburg; 3) representatives of local self-government; 4) representatives of political parties, trade unions, youth and other public organisations, mass movements and religious confessions; 5) representatives of commodity producers and entrepreneurs. Representatives of the Constitutional Court, Supreme Court, Supreme Arbitration Court, Procurator's Office of the Russian Federation also participated in the work of the Constitutional meeting.

In June-July 1993 the Constitutional meeting basically finished preparation of the draft Constitution, but the October crisis in Moscow interrupted this process. After settling the crisis the additional work was done. It consisted in considering amendments and corrections offered by the subjects of the Russian Federation, public organisations, and experts. The revision of the draft constitution was carried out by the Commission formed by the President. It consisted of the representatives of Russia's regions, leading scholars and practitioners. Many issues were discussed at the meetings of the State and Public chambers of the Constitutional meeting formed on the basis of the previous five sections. It should be noted that the Commission of the Constitutional Arbitration Court was formed for considering disputes arising in the process of preparation of the draft Constitution. This commission consisted of highly qualified lawyers/jurists. On December 12, 1993 the final draft of the new Constitution was presented for the Russian referendum. Its results meant that instead of the Constitution of 1978 the Constitution of 1993 had become the basic law of Russia.

2. New constitution of the Russian Federation. General aspects.

The new Constitution of the Russian Federation is a document which definitely reflected the characteristic features of the time and the situation in the country. It could be seen, for instance, in the choice of the form of government and especially in the division of authority among the branches of power. But specific solutions do not contradict the conclusion that the Russian Constitution is also a part of the world constitutional process. It has realigned the leading tendencies of the modern constitutionalism and contains generally accepted answers to some urgent questions in the field of theory of state and law and social relations.

If we compare the 1993 Constitution with analogous constitutions of other countries, and first of all of the countries considered most democratic and economically strong, we can say that the Russian basic law deserves to be mentioned among the newest, most advanced and progressive ones. Provisions on the rights and freedoms of man and citizen demonstrate it especially well. Provisions on Russia's federative structure should be also noted. It is important to mention that the Constitution of 1993 marked the transition from the state economy and its management based on centralised administration to the variety of the forms of property. It meant among other things recognition, protection and support of private property and the development of market relations. It will not be an exaggeration to say that the first post-Soviet Constitution found a decent place in the new generation of the constitutions in the world.

The Constitution of 1993 was adopted in the transitional period and is criticised because of a declarative character of some of its provisions which are just being introduced. Among them are provisions of the law-governed state, social rights of people and some others. Such constitutional provisions are qualified as the ones which fix principles and goals rather than existing realities. The criticism has certain grounds. But accepting justified criticism we should not undervalue what has been done in accordance with the Constitution.

Probably, its makers did not take into account the obstacles that may occur in the process of cardinal restructuring of the society. It should be said, however, that the main problems lie not in the Constitution itself, but in the economic and social situation in the country. The gap between the constitutional norm and practice is predetermined by the fact that the parameters set up in the economy have not been achieved. This causes difficulties for people. It cannot be otherwise with the production level not increasing as it was expected and the state not having enough money to pay wages, salaries and pensions. Should the constitutional development in Russia move backwards in such a difficult situation? Never! The prestige of the Constitution is a good tool for achieving high goals set by the society. This prestige is used for providing general rules, principles, concrete thesises which are obligatory for the whole society and first of all for state agencies and officials on all levels of state power and all its branches. The Constitution envisages democratic mechanisms for implementation of its provisions. These mechanisms must be fully used. This will help to overcome difficulties and facilitate the planned progress of the society. The state agencies, public organisations and all the citizens have a duty to act according to the Constitution and to implement its norms.

The Constitution of 1993 had another important task. It was necessary to clarify the basics of the development of the whole legal system of Russia. This task resulted from the supremacy of the Constitution in this system and its mission as the main and basic law of the state. The supremacy of the Constitution is correctly understood in the sense that its provisions are primary, basic and fundamental. All other legal acts passed in the state including federal laws, constitutions of the republics, charters of the regions, cities of federal importance, autonomous regions and autonomous areas must be consistent with the Constitution of the Russian Federation. No other law can change or cancel a norm of the Constitution or be placed on the same level with it.

This led to the task of bringing all other previously passed legal acts into compliance with the federal Constitution. In the second section of the Constitution of 1993 it is specified that the laws and other legal acts, which had been in force on the territory of the Russian Federation before the current Constitution came into legal force, are applied only in the part which does not contradict the Constitution. With the adoption of the Constitution of 1993, the function of the legal norms preventing formation of market economy ceased automatically.

On the other hand, the Constitution gave directions and dictated basic principles for the development of all branches of law on the new foundations. Trying to make a preliminary summary of this development we should recognize that, for example, the constitutional, financial and bank law have been renovated as much as possible. Among the unfavorable factors hindering the development of the Russian law are the phenomena of the economic crisis, opposition of the regions against the center, confrontation of the dominant political power and the opposition, difficult inheritance of the past in different spheres of life. It should be mentioned that the formation of the new Russian law was affected by the mistakes made in governing the country, especially in the process of elaboration and implementation of the strategic course of the economic reforms.

The Constitution of the Russian Federation of 1993 differs from its Soviet predecessors both in its approach to regulating the economy, the extent of such regulation and their position in the structure of the Constitution. The basics of the economic system are discussed in several places. It was planned to define the basics of the economic system both in the general provisions of the Constitution (Chapter 1 "The Basics of the Constitutional System») and along with the rights and freedoms of man and citizen (Chapter 2 "Rights and Freedoms of Man and Citizen"). This leads to the structural differences of the new Russian Constitution. While the previous RSFSR Constitution of 1978 contained a separate chapter "Economic System" which basically fixed the foundations of the state, planned-command economy, according to the general approach to structuring of the 1993 Constitution, a separate chapter on the economic system of the Russian state does not exist.

Does this fact mean that the importance of the economy is underestimated or that there is an intention to avoid the issues of its formation? Certainly not. It is enough to say that the forms of property and especially introduction of the private property are discussed in the very first chapter of the Constitution which serves as a carcass of the legal construction of the political and social system. It is in this chapter named "The Basics of the Constitutional System" that the fundamental principle is fixed: "In the Russian Federation recognized and equally protected are the private, state, municipal and other forms of property" (Article 8, paragraph 2). In the next article this principle is extended also on the land and other natural resources (Article 9).

The lack of a separate chapter on the economic system should not be misunderstood as weakening of the constitutional influence on the economic sphere. There are not enough grounds for such a conclusion. The main and decisive criteria are the complete constitutional coverage of social relations and the content of the existing norms. Structuring of the Constitution and the position of the specifically "economic" articles is a secondary consideration. Moreover, the external differences of the Constitution of 1993 from the previous Russian and Soviet constitutions have certain grounds.

Under the Soviet power the Constitution emphasized that it was the state that instituted and established the economic system according to the ideology. The Constitution of 1993 is based on different assumptions. Economy as a basic part of the civil society is produced by it and is created by people in the process of their activity and as a result of such an activity. People should be given all necessary freedom of activity according to the possibilities and needs of the free development of the economy and its self-regulation. Participants of the economic activity should be provided guarantees against arbitrary intervention of the state. We are not talking about unrestricted liberalisation of the economy and complete separation of the state from this sphere of social development. Such understanding would be in disagreement with the objective approach to defining the economic role of state nowadays. The criticism of the total governmentalisation of the economy could easily become extreme and lead to the equally dangerous apology of market anarchy.

Separation of property and power is definitely necessary for the Russian economy. The country objectively needs further economic reforms aimed at the stabilization of the market relations in their most civilized forms. However, the state remains a most important factor of the economic development, its guarantor and stimulator. The economy cannot successfully develop without state regulation. The problem is to correctly determine the directions and content of the economic role of state. The medical commandment "Do not harm" can be very well applied to economy. The self-regulation and free decision-making by the person is rather wide. The Constitution is supposed to establish principles, forms and methods, as well as limits of state regulation and to point out what state has to do under the market conditions.

Foreign experience shows that the economic role of state has been interpreted in different ways throughout the history. When capitalism was just being formed, liberal ideas were very strong. They reflected the interests of the new bourgeoisie struggling against absolutism and feudal rules. The originating market needed space for its development. It required protection from the arbitrary actions of the authorities. This led to the concept of state as a night warden in the economic sphere.

The mission of state was restricted to providing free development of private property itself and of other social and state institutes related to it. Respective functions were attributed to law. Its main function was protection.

It is clear that state seemed to stay quite far from the economy and was to play a modest role in it. Since that time the ideas of the liberal economy, non-admittance of the state to the market has been quite widely spread in the world. In some countries these ideas predetermined the content of state policy. At the same time, they were applied with consideration of the reality. In practice the state could not stay away from economy in its activity or to eliminate all influence on its development. Life itself did not allow state to give up its regulating role, for example in protecting its market or introducing obligatory rules of trade.

It is interesting that liberal understanding of the economic role of state thrived under the conditions of successful development of capitalism. On the contrary, in the situations of the economic crisis the conceptions of the increasing role of state dominated. Mechanisms of self-regulation did not allow to overcome such phenomena of crisis as inflation, unemployment, interrupted production rhytm, breakdown of market mechanisms etc. "The Great Depression" in the USA in the 20–30-s can serve as a good example.

The military economy of the II World War was quite firmly governed by state using administrative methods. After the end of the war the state involvement in economy was naturally declining. But the state did not go in to the shadows completely. Under the influence of Keynes' views, a certain extent of state involvement in economy was considered a necessary condition for normal development of capitalism. It included, first of all, interest of providing normal development of economy, its protection from crisis, and stability of market relations. The state was supposed to support the key branches of the national production, to contribute to the formation of the social infrastructure and to maintain social peace.

But by the end of the 70s Western countries had increased the mood in favour of reducing state interference in the economy. Quite popular were the appeals to "deregulation" and "minimized state". In the 80s in some major countries of Western Europe there was a wave of privatization embracing major branches of industry, finances and the sphere of services. The state was acquiring methods of indirect economic regulation which turned out to be very effective. Of special importance was state support to the most promising directions of economic growth. In many countries there was used a policy of giving priority to new technologies, structural changes in production and progress of science.

The world experience teaches that the economic role of state is a flexible category reflecting concrete historical conditions in a particular country in a wide international context. In Russia the general approach was determined to a large extent by the negative conclusions from the recent past of the country and by the desire to put an end to a command-administrative economy. In the period of preparation and adoption of the Constitution there were strong opinions oriented at the state's abandoning economy or, at least, diminishing the economic role of state to the minimal number of functions. The market was expected to help in getting rid of all difficulties. Later, when the economic crisis in the country dragged on and the situation became worse, many illusions of the early 1990s were dispelled. The market "romanticism" was beaten by the hard reality giving way to a more balanced approach to state and to the possibilities of using its potential for overcoming the crisis phenomena.

The question of the economic role of state has up to now been a focus of heated discussions which sometimes got sharp political character. Evidently, it is a consequence of the lack of a well developed and clear conception of the transition to market economy. Very few people question the necessity and vital importance of such a transition or its main goals. But in history there is no analogy of establishing a market economy in the country where for decades the economy was state-governed and organized according to the dogmas of the communist ideology. The role of state was made a fetish and absolute. There was a rule of order and planning. Finally, the economy lost its flexibility and ability to self-regulation and development. In such conditions it is impossible to act according to available historical patterns or hope that it would be enough to destroy the old mechanism and proclaim new principles. Establishing a market is a complicated and complex task.

The Constitution of 1993 does not define the concrete policy of state in the sphere of economy. It is interesting to note that it does not even use the term "market economy". At the same time, it cannot go unnoticed that the Constitution does not leave any doubts in this respect. It clearly fixes the basics of the market relations in economy and defines the tasks of state in this sphere, as well as the main parameters of the state activity. It can be definitely stated that the Constitution of 1993 is a document claiming that Russia should be a country with a market economy.

At times, the Constitution of 1993 is reproached in that it does not offer a definition of the economic system of the country. It is especially noticeable when comparing the acting Constitution with the Soviet ones which many times proclaimed the socialist nature of the state and its ideological set up. Quite recently the USSR Constitution of 1977 declared that the developed socialist society had been built in the country and the supreme goal of the Soviet state was the building of a classless communist society. The supreme goal of public production under socialism was determined as the most complete satisfaction of the growing material and spiritual needs of the people (Article 17). There is nothing like that in the Constitution of 1993. It just declares universal values and talks about ensuring the well-being and prosperity of Russia.

This can be explained as follows. In the period of its preparation there were opinions in favour of telling in the Constitution about the nature of the system that had been established and was still being established in Russia as a result of economic, social and political transformations. It was even proposed, though very timidly, to mention capitalism or capitalist relations in the Constitution. As it follows from the text of the adopted Constitution, such proposals were not accepted.

Definitely, the prejudice against the concept of "capitalism" itself, which had been inherited from the state ideology of the Soviet times, played its role. It had to be taken into consideration. But the main and defining argument had nothing to do with the level of mass thinking.

There was something else. The Constitution had basically to be, first of all, a legal document having nothing to do with the ideological sphere. Reconsideration of values which took place in the post-Soviet time showed that the previous constitutions adopted both on the level of the USSR and in the Union republics, were saturated with non-judicial provisions. Discrepancy between ideological declarations and reality in the Constitution, especially in the description of the advantages of the so-called "mature socialism", diminished the prestige of the Constitution and placed it in the same line with pretentious but unrealistic political documents.

Furthermore, another important issue was the concept of "capitalism" in the minds of many people, has been closely connected with the course of history. It tends to symbolize the social system which was established in many countries at the end of the 19th–early 20th centuries. Since then great changes have taken place in the world. That is why the concept of the "post-industrial society" has become popular in research papers. In such a society the state is characterized by a number of new features reflecting changing imperatives of history. On the one hand, we can speak about a certain regulatory influence of state on the economy. This is especially noticeable in the policy aimed at the support of promising directions, such as technological and structural changes in production, strengthening of its scientific base, and informatization of society. Ecological functions of state have become of special importance. The state enhances activity aimed at the protection of national business and simultaneously at the extension of the international economic cooperation including formation of inter-state economic unions. On the other hand, it still continues the process of privatization involving the branches of production and enterprises in the state sector. Market mechanisms are more and more used for regulating economic relations. This substantially changes the methods of state activity.

It should be mentioned that the modern and economically developed state has acquired certain features which were first introduced to the world by socialism. First of all, we are talking about a social predestination of state and expansion of respective functions of state. The state care of the quality of life is reflected in the programs supporting health, education and social security. The state control over the quality standards of consumer goods, ecological conditions and medical care is getting stricter. In this connection, a certain symbiosis, or a mixed social system, is sometimes discussed. But a different conclusion can also be made: mankind is eager to get useful lessons from its own development which may be characterized by searching for the best solutions connected sometimes with great losses and sacrifices.

Especially important are the state efforts aimed at preservation of civil peace and smoothing of social contradictions. In some countries there have been formed different conciliatory commissions. The forms of interaction between state and the private business are developing. The state reacts faster and much more flexibly to changing social conditions including the growth of regional and national movements. This results in numerous changes in the state system, special legislative decisions, state programs of rendering support to regions and various groups of population.

The Constitution of 1993 reflects a desire of the Russian society to be up-to-date and to assimilate the lesson of the history. The lack of a declaration about market economy in the Constitution may even be symbolic, since it does not only reflect an orientation at the de-ideologization of the Constitution, but also an attempt to give the Constitution a working character. What other type of economy except a market economy can exist in the state where private property, freedom of entrepreneurship and economic unity of the territory have been fixed? Is it not enough? The Constitution is also free of provisions about centralized planning, governing the economy, priority of state property, or the monopoly of state in foreign trade. The Constitution is really not very wordy, sometimes even scanty with regard to economy, but at the same time, it contains necessary and a sufficient number of provisions pertaining to the market economy in particular.

At the same time, the Constitution of 1993 preserves certain "neutrality" towards the different conceptions of the economic role of state in the concrete market conditions being formed in Russia. A degree of economy liberalization, the extent of privatization, a necessity to have a more or less substantial state sector are the issues which the Constitution leaves to be solved by the current legislation. The state authorities got an opportunity to determine aims, guidelines and steps of the state economic policy in view of the concrete circumstances and accumulated experience. They are tied only by major provisions fixed on the constitutional level. There are not too many of those provisions, but they are of a fundamental character and of special importance for understanding the nature of the economic system determining concretely state economic policy.

3. Constitutional regulation of property relations

Now let us refer to the provisions of the Constitution on property. Their significance is determined by the fact that they actually determine the economic system of the society. It goes without saying that the recognition of private property as one of the legitimate forms of property, which is a real revolution in the economic life, plays the leading role in the development of the Russian state. The Constitution placed private property on the same level with state, municipal and other forms of property existing in the country. The monopoly of property (state and cooperative) which consisted of the quintessence of the socialist system, as it was fixed in all Soviet constitutions, was put an end to. What is also important is that the list of the forms of property in the prevailing Russian Constitution starts with private property.

It is possible that the necessity of introduction and constitutional fixation of private property in Russia, which can be compared in importance only with the revolutionary breakthrough in the system of social relations, somehow predetermined the character and content of the corresponding articles. The Constitution of 1993 declares the legitimacy of private property without posing restrictions. Nothing is said, for example, about a possibility of nationalization if the interests of the society will require it. In the chapter about rights and freedoms of man and citizen it is only said that nobody can be deprived of property otherwise than by a court decision (Article 35, p.3). The explanation should be sought in the fact that at the moment of adopting the Constitution of 1993 there was a task of instituting private property. Compared to that, all other issues were less important. The current legislation was supposed to take care of them.

Introduction of the private property, or more precisely, returning to it, since the economy of the pre-revolutionary Russia was based on the private property, did not imitate the pattern of introduction of socialist property. Private property has not become the only one, a predetermined or a leading form of property in Russia. The ultimate constitutional fixation of private property can not serve as a foundation for placing it juridically above state, municipal, or other forms of property. It is specifically indicated in the Constitution that all forms of property – state, municipal and others are equally recognized and protected. Russia is a country with a variety of forms of property.

Constitutional regulation of the forms of property does not have an exhaustive character. It is being developed and specified by other laws among which the Civil Code of the Russian Federation should be mentioned first of all. It is effective only in part, since the third part has not yet been adopted and chapter 17 "The property and other right to land" has not been yet applied. It will come in force with the new Land Code. This Code is under preparation. The Civil Code was officially published on December 8, 1994.

The adoption of the new Civil Code played a very important role in enforcing the legal foundation of market economy. It is well known that the Civil Code of the RSFSR of 1964 reflected the conditions of a different period of history when the state was simultaneously the owner and the manager of the country's economy. The amendments made at the end of the 1980s and early 1990s were not able to overcome the initial conception reflected in hundreds of its articles. The current Russian Civil Code is a document of the new time. Its structure and content are built on such principles as equality of the participants of the economic relations, immunity of property, freedom of contract, inadmissibility of arbitrary interference into private matters, free use of civil rights, ensured reinstitution of violated rights and their judicial protection.

The Civil Code complements the Constitution revealing the content of the property right. It is done in the spirit of the pre-revolutionary law traditions which had worked out a well-known triad of powers of the property holder: possession, use and disposition. This triad, which has become a classic of Russian law, was fixed already in the Code of Laws of the Russian Empire. The Soviet civil law did not reject it and the civil codes adopted in 1922 and 1964 exactly reproduced it. It should however be said that the Russian judicial doctrine has been treating the property right in its own way which is different from other countries'. In the civil codes of foreign countries, also other definitions of the property right can be found. The Russian solution of the problem can be compared with the French civil code or the German civil code.

What are the constituents of the property right? Possession is usually treated as a real possibility to administer certain property. Use is understood as a possibility of economic utilization of the property, extracting its useful features, its consumption. Disposition is basically a possibility of changing property holder, its condition or purpose. Obviously, in each case we are talking about the legal nature of these constituents and, first of all, about their legal protection.

It is worth mentioning that the owner by his own will can endow another person with certain power with regard to his/her property. A possibility of passing to another person the whole triad of powers is not excluded. But a necessary condition is an expression of the owner's will. Without it neither power or the whole triad can be received by another person. The owner's decision dictated by his/her interests determines the use of certain powers or the whole triad.

This is the direction in which the modern Russian legislation develops. According to the prevailing Civil Code, the owner has rights to possession, use and disposition of one's property. It can be seen that the triad of powers has been preserved in full. But the legislator did not stop here. The possibilities contained in the triad of powers have been explained. It has been fixed that the owner has a right to perform by his/her own will any action with regard to his/her property which is not prohibited by law or other legal act and does not violate rights and interests of other people protected by law. The powers of the owner may include alienation of one's property for other persons' possession, passing to them the rights of possession, use and disposition of property while remaining the owner, pledging property, etc.

The Constitution of 1993 contains not only general declarations about a variety of property rights. It contains the basics of the legal regulation of each. However, it should be taken into account that the constitutional lexicon in many cases includes not only purely judicial, but also economic concepts without making clear distinctions. Even the concept "the form of property" is closer to the economic theory than jurisprudence. In this connection, the way of defining private property is important.

This was necessary to do not only in order to make the existence of private property legitimate on the supreme legislative level, but also to reveal its major features. The specific historical background for establishing this form of property should be remembered. Quite recently the Soviet law rejected private property while recognizing and supporting so-called personal property as a sort of compensation. According to the USSR Constitution of 1977, a citizen could have any property for consumption or production. It was determined that such property could be acquired for the earned money or by other legitimate ways. The Constitution introduced some restrictions: personal property could not include the types of property which were not allowed to be acquired by citizens. All the economy which was in the hands of state or state farms' property was beyond personal property. It was allowed, though, to perform "individual labour activity" in the sphere of handicrafts, agriculture, consumer services, and other types of activities based exclusively on the personal labour of citizens and members of their families. But only a few people were engaged in such activities.

Private property incorporates everything that had been earlier understood as personal property. The main advantage of private property, however, consists in the fact that it incorporates not only the property necessary for the purposes of personal consumption, but also the property which was in the forbidden zone before – the zone of the state, state farm and cooperative economy. While personal property symbolized the Socialist understanding of economy, private property has become the forerunner of the market economy. The objects of private property are, for example, industrial enterprises, banks and other financial institutions, commercial organizations, farms and other agricultural enterprises, etc.

In the Constitution of 1993 the right to private property is explained in the following way, "Everyone has the right to have property, possess, use and dispose of it both personally and jointly with other people»(Article 35, p.2).

The indication that "everyone" can have property means that the right to private property can be exercised not only by a citizen of the Russian Federation, but also by foreign citizens and stateless persons. Furthermore, it is important that everyone can have property both personally and jointly with other people. The second possibility seems to be especially important under the conditions of market economy. It incorporates not only the common property accumulated in the family, joint property of houses and even the joint property in the form of farm enterprises, but also such types of joint property as joint-stock companies, production cooperatives, etc. The property owner can use his property for participation in state and municipal enterprises.

Of special importance is the question of possessing land as private property. The general principle proclaimed by the Constitution of 1993 reads, "Citizens and their associations have the right to possess land as private property. Possession, utilization and management of land and other natural resources are exercised by the owners freely if it is not detrimental to the environment and does not violate the rights and lawful interests of other people. Terms and rules of the use of land are fixed by federal law" (Article 36).

These provisions are developed in Chapter 17 of the new Civil Code. It has been specified that persons possessing a plot of land as private property have a right to sell it, give it as a gift, pledge, lease, or dispose of it in another way. However, the Civil Code specifies that according to law and in due order the land is allotted for agricultural or other purposes. It cannot be used otherwise or its use is restricted.

Utilization of a plot of land qualified in this way can be realized within these limits (Article 260).

This chapter of the Civil Code, however, has remained on paper. It does not work. A federal law on introducing into action the first part of the Civil Code of the Russian Federation adopted together with the first part of the Civil Code, specified that Chapter 17 would enter in to force together with the new Land Code of the Russian Federation. This condition has not been fulfilled as yet. The Land Code, which had been passed through the State Duma and the Council of Federation, was not signed by the President of the Russian Federation. The main motif of the President's veto consisted of the fact that the Land Code in some of its provisions contradicted the Constitution of 1993, especially concerning the right to possessing land as private property. After long political controversies the question of the new Land Code was submitted for consideration to the Round Table – a mechanism of civil conciliation representing major political forces in modern Russia. According to the recommendation of the Round Table, the positions are being brought into agreement. It can be expected that the problem of possessing land as private property will be soon successfully resolved. Without it, stabilization of a market economy would be problematic.

Considering the issues of the protection of the right to private property, it should be said that this right is ensured and protected practically by all branches of Russian law including civil, criminal, administrative and other. Crimes against property and private property in particular are covered in a number of articles of the prevailing Criminal Code. Among them are, first of all, different types of illegal appropriation of property including theft, deceit, embezzlement, plundering, and robbery. Infliction of property damage, as well as destruction of property committed intentionally or negligently, are subject to criminal punishment.

For Russia of special importance is the question of the private property guarantees. Memories of nationalization and other kinds of confiscation of property from the private property owners after October 1917 are still fresh. Foreign owners were involved in the process along with Russian citizens. Today, at the time when new Russia shows great interest in attracting foreign investments, guarantees of the right to private property are important for foreign trade. Considering all this the Constitution of 1993 pays close attention to the guarantees of the right to private property. The Constitution clearly expresses two principal statements developed and specified by other laws and subordinate acts (decrees of the President of the Russian Federation, resolutions of the Government, etc.).

First, it is stated in the Constitution of 1993 as a general rule that nobody can be deprived of property otherwise than by a court decision (Article 35, p.3). It means that the administrative order of termination of the right to property existing under the Soviet power is not allowed. Any references to expedience cannot be a ground for administrative bodies' forced termination of the right of property against the owner's will. Only by a court decision in the cases stated by law the owner can be deprived of this property. In the Civil Code there is a list of such cases: 1) distrain on the property for debts; 2) seizure of the property which cannot legally belong to the possessor; 3) expropriation of the real estate; 4) redemption of the mismanaged cultural values, pets; 5) requisition; 6) confiscation; 7)alienation of property in case of a) division of property being in participatory share ownership and apportionment of participatory share (Article 252, p.4); b) loss by the real estate owner the right of using the plot of land (Article 272, p.2); c) redemption of the plot of land for the state and municipal needs by a court decision (Article 282); d) confiscation of the plot of land used with violation of the legislation (Article 285); termination of the right of property of the mismanaged dwelling place. (Article 293).

It should be mentioned that Russian legislation envisages both confiscation and requisition. From the judicial point of view the difference between them is rather substantial. Confiscation takes place in cases of violation of law on behalf of the owner and it is performed without compensation. Requisition is performed in cases of natural calamities (floods, earthquakes, hurricanes, etc.) and other extraordinary circumstances when national, regional and other such needs are at stake. It is important to take into account that requisition is a measure taken for compensation.

It is written in the Constitution of 1993 that forced alienation of property for state needs can be performed only on the condition of preliminary full compensation (Article 35, p.3). It is the second general rule of such alienation of property. It is also reflected in the new Civil Code which reads that expropriation – turning property possessed by citizens or legal entities into state property – is performed according to law with compensation of the value of this property and other damages in the order fixed by article 306 of the Civil Code (Article 235, p.2).

It should be said that this formulation and the content of article 306 cause different interpretations by the specialists. Article 306 of the Civil Code reads, "In case of adoption by the Russian Federation the law terminating the right of property, losses caused to the owner as a result of adoption of such an act, are compensated by the state. Disputes on compensation of losses are resolved by the courts". The statement of the compensation being paid by the state is certainly not disputed. It is absolutely consistent with the Constitution. But further on, the Civil Code digresses from the Constitution and replaces the concept of the "full compensation" with the civilistic term "compensation of losses". Is the language of civil law adequate in this case? Probably not, since the concept used in the Constitution is more complete and precise. It means that full compensation of property is a general and necessary condition and, besides, combines the condition of full compensation with the requirement that compensation precedes alienation of property. At the same time, when defining the losses civilists usually determine causative relations between cause and effect which in our case means determination of such relations between the act of forced alienation of property and the following losses. This example once more confirms the necessity of strict observation of the principle of the supremacy of the Constitution over other laws without any exemptions for codes.

The most important guarantee of the right to private property is right of inheritance. The Constitution of 1993 contains the following words, "The right of inheritance is guaranteed" (Article 35, p.4). The constitutional provision about the right of inheritance is thoroughly regulated in the Civil Code which contains a chapter "Inheritance Law". Inheritance is treated as transition of the property of the deceased to heirs or other successors. Inheritance takes place according to law or will. Heirs or other successors can be physical entities, legal entities and the state. Fulfillment of the owner's will is basically guaranteed, but freedom of the will is restricted with the purpose of protecting the interests of minor or disabled heirs of the dead.

Emphasizing the role and significance of the constitutional provisions on the right to private property we should not run to extremes and think that an utterly liberalized economy almost excluding state property has been established in Russia. Far from it! The private sector in the Russian economy produces a little more than one third of the gross national product. This figure demonstrates the extent of privatization in Russia. The rest comes from the state sector of economy and constitutes a considerable amount. State property is recognized, protected and supported in the Constitution of 1993 along with other forms of property. It is also established that certain kinds of property according to law can be only in state property.

Under the conditions of market economy the essence of governing state property is drastically different from that of the Soviet times. Such governing should be based on the assumption that state and its agencies should not be direct subjects of economic activity. Such role is not appropriate for state. At the same time, the efficiency of state property should be constantly raised. This property should not be a burden for the state budget. In this connection, measures directed at stronger control over governing state property are being discussed at present.

The Constitution of 1993, the new Civil Code and other recent laws create legal conditions for differentiating competence and responsibility between the bodies of state administration performing regulatory, control and supervisory functions and disposing of the federal budget funds, on the one hand, and bodies (persons) representing interests of the state as owner, on the other hand. At the same time, a lot of work is to be done in order to adopt legal acts determining the powers and responsibilities of the persons representing the state-owner.

It should be noted that the privatization process in Russia is not yet complete. But it has already reached the level of "saturation". Considering the sharp criticism of serious drawbacks and faults, which took place at the previous stages of privatization, the authorities claim their readiness to correct their future actions in this sphere. Basically, the privatization is not considered as the preferential means of increasing revenues to the state budget. The effectiveness of the Russian economy as a whole is emphasized. The investments necessary for the production, technological and social development of the privatized enterprises and improvement of the environment should be attracted to production. As for the future owners of the privatized property, the orientation is made at the owners having strategies of the enterprise development and aimed at the accumulation and renewal of the capital. As a result of privatization, expenses on the economic management and support of the unprofitable enterprises must be reduced without causing harm to national interests.

The concept of "municipal property" refers to relatively new form of property, which was introduced in early 1990s. Before that the municipal property had been spoken about when considering issues of the foreign state and rights. In the USSR, where the local bodies of state power constituted a part of one state mechanism, their property was a part of state property. In post-Soviet Russia, which had chosen the route of developing local self-government, separate from the state, municipal property was isolated as a separate form of property not included in the concept of state property. Without this it would have been difficult to realize the institution of the local self-government and its efficiency, which is important.

For the first time in Russian law, the concept of "municipal property" was fixed by the RSFSR Law of December 24, 1990 "On Property in RSFSR" (Article 23). The Constitution of 1993 specified municipal property twice: first, when it was named in the list of the forms of property (Article 8), and second, when the right of the bodies of local self-government to independent management of municipal property was defined (Article 132). In more detail, municipal property is discussed in the new Civil Code and the Federal law of August 28,

1995 "On general principles of organization of the local self-government in the Russian Federation".

If we turn to the Civil Code we should note that it treats municipal
property as the property possessed by urban and rural communities and
other municipal units (Article 215). The fact that such property is
owned by municipal units, is very important for understanding municipal property. Bodies of local self-government are not the owners of
municipal property. They can only manage such property on behalf of
a municipal unit. It should be added that in cases provided by the laws
of the subjects of the Russian Federation, the management of municipal property can be performed directly by the population of a municipal unit.

According to the prevailing legislation, the municipal property consists of two parts. The first is the property attached to municipal
enterprises and institutions. They are vested only with the right of
economic management or operative administration. The second incorporates the rest of the property including the local budget. It is a
municipal treasury of a city, rural or other municipal unit.

The concept of municipal property is treated rather broadly in the
legislation. As it follows from the Federal law "On general principles
of organization of the local self-government in the Russian Federation", such a concept includes:
  • local budget funds, municipal extra-budget funds;
  • property of the bodies of local self-government;
  • municipal lands and other natural resources being municipal
    property;
  • municipal enterprises and organizations;
  • municipal housing fund and non-living premises;
  • municipal educational, health-care, culture and sport institu-
    tions;
  • other movable and immovable property (Article 29).

The development of self-government in Russia is not an easy process.
The subjects of the Russian Federation which have achieved and are
still trying to achieve more independence, sometimes act in the spirit

of the worst traditions of the centralized state with regard to local self-government. The non-state nature of local self-government fixed by the Constitution is sometimes perceived by Subject of the Russian Federation as a criterion of their having a status of association. This results in a desire to weaken economic potential of the local self-government and in a lack of interest to render financial or other material aid to it. Thus, we should recognize that actual rights of local self-government remain insufficient. Legally, the organizational side of local self-government activity has been developed better than the financial, material and technical basis.

This results in many difficulties dealing with implementation of the constitutional provisions on local self-government. Ideas of its independence in practice perish in the process of constant search of finances for schools, local medical institutions, local transport and the whole local infrastructure. That is why, improvement of the legal base of local self-government and especially the sphere of municipal property remains one of the most important goals of the development of Russian law.

Taking into account all weaknesses and drawbacks of legal regulation, we can, nevertheless, argue that, on the whole, considerable progress in creating a system of legal norms instituting and confirming a market economy with its specific forms and methods of economic organization has been reached. Basic provisions of the Constitution of 1993 are being further developed and specified. But we cannot leave unnoticed a necessity for further reforms of Russian law.

4. Rule of law/ Legal state

The future process of legal reforms in the country in all spheres is tied to the implementation of the constitutional provision defining Russia as a law-governed state. This statement is located in the first lines of the Constitution of 1993 (Article 1) but without specification. This may be explained by the fact that the definition of a law-governed state has not yet been worked out in theory. It still remains a subject of many discussions. A law-governed state means not only recognition of the priority of law and emphasis of the fact that the state and all its agencies and officials are bound by legal norms and, first of all, constitutional ones. This is, certainly, the basis of a law-governed state, but it does not provide its complete definition. A law-governed state is characterised by giving priority to human rights and freedoms and considering human beings as the supreme value in the society. Furthermore, for a law-governed state it is typical to have an effective judicial system with many branches and an independent court system. Finally, modern legal state recognises the priority of international law.

A law-governed state implies an active regulation of the process of establishing and developing a market economy. In this connection we can pose the following question. To what extent does the legislation forestall real establishment of new economic relations, to what extent does it directly provide for their establishment, or to what extent does it restrain it by preserving the old legal order? Can it be said that the legal system should possess a certain degree of conservatism to stabilise social progress and not to allow imposing on the society something that it would inevitably reject?

Obviously, fast revolutionary destruction of the old legal order was objectively necessary. But it is important to escape a legal vacuum in the process. Besides, one aspect should be taken into account. Certainly, law has its own autonomy of development, its own rules and logic. But it cannot be separated from politics. In one way or another it would inevitably reflect compromises of different political forces and economic groups. This can be one of the reasons of instability and inconsistency of legislative foundations and even of their violations in the legislation. In current conditions it is especially important to increase the role of the Constitution. Basically, we are talking about the new understanding of the Constitution which influences the content of the whole constitutional law. The Constitution is transforming from a declarative political document of the kind it often used to be in the past.

The Constitution is supposed to become a stimulus for the development of law in the spirit of high criteria of law-governed state. One of such criteria is the supremacy of law. Unfortunately, it is often violated. In the practice of norm-making activity it often happens that economic or other relations, which according to the Constitution can be regulated only by law, become subjects of regulation in the President's decrees and resolutions of the Government. In the subjects of the Russian Federation they sometimes are regulated by the legal acts of the executive power and the governments of the subjects of the Russian Federation. To some extent, such practice is determined by an insufficient activity of legislative bodies beginning with the State Duma. But this does not change the general negative picture. It would be enough to say that many economic reforms were performed on the basis of the subordinate acts without waiting for laws. In the process of conducting reforms it was clear that many important spheres of economic activity did not have proper legal regulation.

Probably, moods of legal nihilism having certain roots in Russian society have played their role. It should be noted that legal nihilism was supported by the extreme attacks against the economic role of state common since the first years of the reforms. The fight against the state socialism sometimes turned into negation of positive possibilities and objective necessity of legal regulation under the conditions of a market economy. A market economy, however, cannot be established without the new rules of the game. Economic relations under market conditions are getting more complicated. It concerns reforms in the sphere of property, wide use of financial and tax tools, extent of economic subjects' independence, development of contract relations and especially provisions of state protection of the interests of the participants of the economic relations including judicial defence.

Governing by means of legislation and not by means of subordinate acts is important not only because of the hierarchy of legal acts, but also due to the logic of economic efficiency. The entrepreneur is basically interested in having equal opportunities in the market. Subordinate acts do not always follow this principle giving privileges to some entrepreneurs to the detriment of others. In theory it is called an expanded sphere of administrative discretion, but practically it means introduction of subjectivity into the process of decision-making.

Increasing of the role of law in its turn means higher requirements to the participants of the legislative process. The situation in this sphere cannot be considered satisfactory. The major problem is that laws are not always effective. A difficult economic situation in the country can explain many things, but not everything. Laws are often declarative without having a mechanism of implementation. They leave many decisions on the level of instructions and other subordinate acts.

It is difficult to give a simple answer to the question, how far the legislation has advanced in solving core problems of the market economy progress. There are certain results, especially adoption of the first and second parts of the Civil Code. Many problems have been solved in these parts including the problems of property, those of obligation relationships. Among federal laws can be mentioned the following ones: "On Companies", "On Budget Classification in the Russian Federation", "On the Securities Market", "On Non-commercial Organisations" and some others. Economic issues are well presented in the new Criminal Code. But even with positive evaluation of what has been done, it would not be honest to claim that the problems of legal order in the economy have been solved. The course of economic reforms implies further substantial renewal of Russian law.

A cardinal reform of the tax law is forthcoming. The draft Tax Code proposed by the Government was rejected by the State Duma first of all because it did not contribute to the growth of entrepreneurship, attraction of investments into the sphere of production. The tax system remained basically intact having primarily a fiscal character. In the sphere of the budget law the first task is to create in the Russian Federation a rational relationship among budgets of all levels. In other words, we are talking about formation of the system of the budget federalism. The draft Budget Code is likely to be prepared soon.

We can see that the work on law codification continues and is getting more intensive. There is a question, if it will enable the setting up of a legal system for a long period of time or if it just reflects the current transitional period. In any case it is not advisable to hurry. If the codes will contain temporary norms (and this is at times impossible to prevent), in the near future numerous amendments and corrections will have to be made. They will probably make useless the job done by the codifiers and, what is most important, will complicate legal regulation. The achieved systemic character and other positive features of the code would be impaired.

5. Social aspects of the Constitution

The Constitution of 1993 is notorious for proclaiming Russia a social state. This feature is not unique for Russia. Similar statements can be found in a number of foreign constitutions. For example, the basic law of the Federative Republic of Germany of 1949 carries a statement that FRG is a social state. As a rule, such are constitutions adopted after the Second World War when it was evident that state accepted certain social functions. Otherwise, even the developed capitalist society would not be able to cope with many serious and complicated problems, which arise in the course of its development. Among them are such problems as stratification of the society into different layers and groups, conflicts between labour and big property, interests of protection and support of "the weak" and disadvantaged groups of population. In order to keep social peace and civil conciliation, to smooth and prevent social conflicts which may undermine foundations of the social order, the state could not but become an active participant of social relations. This was an objective necessity, a new challenge of the time.

What does the statement about social state in the Constitution of 1993 mean related to the conditions of market economy? Very generally we can say that it means a necessity to provide social orientation in the economic development of Russia and to conduct a social policy adequate to new conditions. The Constitution serves as a major milestone for the authorities, business community and all society. Due to its mission and judicial nature the Constitution does not contain and should not contain a concrete social program. Such a program should be worked out by the state in co-operation with private business, trade unions and other organisations uniting working people. Today in Russia a principle of "three-party commissions" is applied, though not enough.

But though the Constitution does not contain concrete norms concerning social policy, it is easy to find an answer to the question of the main goals and tasks of such policy. Many articles of the Constitution deal with this, and first of all, those devoted to the rights and freedoms of man and citizen. A lot of laws directly or indirectly related to social policy issues and have been adopted according to the Constitution.

By the Constitution, the state policy is aimed at creating conditions ensuring a worthy life for a man. It is a broad concept which should meet modern standards of well-being accepted in the civilised world. The state is supposed to set a guaranteed minimum wage which is very topical for Russia. Today, for example, the fixed minimum wage is not equivalent to the minimum subsistence wage. It has turned into a certain conventional unit used in economic calculations and payments. This task is closely related to the next one – to create conditions stimulating the growth of employment of the population and restriction of unemployment.

A social state must be characterised by ensuring support of weakly socially protected layers of the society, paying special attention to the protection of family, maternity, fatherhood and childhood, handicapped and elderly people. Pensioners and children have turned out to be in a difficult situation in modern Russia. Additional tasks in Russia are connected with rendering help to Russian migrants, and first of all, refugees and forced migrants from the former union republics and Russia's regions with continuous national conflicts.

For the social state is typical active participation in such vitally important spheres of life as education, health care and culture. Without it would be impossible to guarantee constitutional rights and free development of man.

A social state should not be identified with a paternal state which, according to the traditional views dating back to Confucius, is supposed to play the role of a kind and rich farther of the family who cares for it. We cannot rely on the state taking full responsibility of man and providing for all the needs. A social state simply cannot do this because it does not perform substantial direct entrepreneurial activity and the extent of the state property in the country's economy is minor. However, the state must do everything it can to organize all the system, including the budget, tax, pension, health care, educational and other ones, for the solution of social problems. The state has effective tools for conducting social policy reflecting the needs of the society.

If we look back at the recent past of Russia, we can hardly consider the Soviet state paternal, though it claimed in its official ideology that it was taking care of all people. The conditions in which the state functioned and, first of all, the state governing of the economy, prohibition of private property, strict centralised administration in the field of economy including the budget and tax spheres, ensured that the state received and redistributed practically all the results of labour in the society.

However, technological lagging of production, low labour productivity, restrained initiative and entrepreneurial endeavors on the level of enterprises, barriers for integration of the Soviet economy into the world economic system and other weaknesses of socialism led to the situation where the concentration of the distribution functions in the hands of the state did not produce desired results. The level of life in the USSR remained rather low. Participation of the country in the arms race, enforcement of the military – industrial complex at the expense of the other industry branches aimed at the satisfaction of the direct human needs, contributed to this.

Pseudo-paternalism in the Soviet times was characterized by raising big social expectations among the population. They were enforced by the official propaganda which used to substitute concepts and emphasize not what had been taken from people, but rather what had been returned to them. There was created an impression that the state gave welfare to people from its own pocket. This made the influence of the state and its mobilizing functions stronger but did not guarantee proper standards of well-being or flourishing of the social sphere. According to the tradition, the needs of the social sphere were the last to be financed from what had been left in the budget. In other words, the social sphere was provided by material means according to the so-called remainder principle.

However, we should mention that Socialism entered the history of mankind as a system which had proclaimed broad social rights of people and declared the obligation of the state to guarantee them. The ideas, unlike their practical implementation, found understanding and recognition in the world, added popularity to Socialism and, moreover, played a positive role in the process of global development.

It is in this focus that we should assess the provisions of the Soviet constitutions concerning social protection of citizens. Even though this protection was low, it was real and systemic. People are sensitive to this now, at the time when many have confronted current hardships in post-Soviet Russia, especially those living on state subsidies, pensioners and employees in the sphere of education, science, culture, health care, all of which are financed from the budget.

Free education, health care, housing and many other things are a realization of the social progress and a serious achievements of mankind. That is why today people, who are unable to preserve their previous social security and who are in a poor situation due to circumstances, experience nostalgia towards past times. We should try to understand these people. They expected that democratization of the state life, transition to the market economy and other new conditions of social development would improve their life both spiritually and materially. On behalf of the new authorities there were promises of rapid rises in standards of well-being. But the social sphere is in an extremely difficult situation.

How should the Russian state respond to the challenge of the time? The conditions of market economy are different from those during the Soviet power. Reformation of the social sector cannot be postponed anymore. Such reformation is only possible on the condition that it is coordinated with the development of the economic system and, first of all, with the established market relations. Such approach is even more important because the situation in the social sphere is very contradictory.

The analysis of the social policy shows that originally it counted on the idea that transition to market relations would, on the one hand, enable the state to ensure the socially oriented course of the economic development and, at the same time, to solve a considerable portion of social problems; on the other hand. It would enable to find non-state sources which would complement and support state efforts having more and more social functions which are objectively necessary for the state to fully develop. Unfortunately, the Russian state due to economic problems cannot fully cope with social tasks and the private business has not become an alternative to the state as it was expected.

A social orientation of the forming market economy in Russia needs to be seriously corrected. This is a general opinion. But how can this be achieved? First of all, special constituents ensuring development of social problems should be inserted in the mechanism of the market economy. For example, we can speak about combining effective production and especially the profitability of enterprises with expenses on the social sphere. We mean expenses on the improvement of employees' living conditions, their training, formation of additional pension funds, adaptation of workers to changing working conditions, etc.

But we cannot hope that the market alone will deal with social problems. We can observe limitations of self-regulation of a market economy. Foreign experience demonstrates that even in the economically developed countries social conflicts persist. They are most commonly connected with payment for labour, unemployment, transfer of enterprises to other regions, etc. Thus, a social role of the state should be enforced and further developed.

6. Human rights in the new Constitution

A major condition for institutions and strengthening of the market economy in Russia is the confirmation in the Constitution of 1993 a broad specter of basic rights and freedoms of man. This is a summary of the world experience. Only a free person whose dignity is respected in the society, only a person who is able to actively participate in the life of the society, only a person who is endowed with a variety of rights and who is sure that his/her rights will be observed and protected, only a person whose initiative and business activity are supported by state, can demonstrate his/her abilities under the conditions of market relations and achieve economic results. Therefore, the provisions of the Constitution of 1993 on basic rights and freedoms of man have important economic implications. It refers to the whole catalogue of rights and freedoms of man, not only to the economic ones.

Today Russia is a part of the world community. It recognizes the Universal Declaration of Human Rights, UN Charter, international conventions on human rights (civil, political, economic, social and cultural). Russia's joining the Council of Europe was an important step. In this connection Russia took certain obligations on bringing its legislation in accordance with principles and standards of the Council of Europe. Russia has, thus, become a participant of all major international conventions on human rights and freedoms.

It should be noted that the Constitution of the Russian Federation confirms rights and freedoms of man as it is done in the constitutions of the democratic and economically developed countries. Russia is characterized by a transitional character of its economy; its economy has not been stabilized and transition to it has not been completed; many social and political problems have not been solved. These are the features of the transformational process. None of them became, however, a reason for reducing a list of rights and freedoms of man or instituting a temporary moratorium on some of them. Thus, the Constitution emphasizes that in spite of serious difficulties in its development, Russia will do everything possible for the full and consistent implementation of the declared ideas of humanism and democracy. This must be the main direction of various activities of the Russian State and of the Russian law development.

A separate chapter is devoted to rights and freedoms of man in the Constitution of 1993. It is Chapter 2 which deals with the basics of the constitutional system. Chapter 2 is called "Rights and Freedoms of Man and Citizen". Though placed in a separate chapter, rights and freedoms are not considered as an independent institution functioning in isolation from the rest of the constitutional regulation. On the contrary, the whole chapter and its articles are supposed to work in harmony and coordination with the whole text of the Constitution. Implementation of human rights and freedoms and their protection are closely connected with the development of all spheres of life of the Russian society. Such a connection is a pre-condition of the progress in economy, social sphere, politics and culture. The social progress enriches the content of rights and freedoms of man and creates conditions for further humanization of the Russian life.

Before classifying human rights and freedoms, we should note that the Constitution proclaims equality of all before the law and the court.

Rights and freedoms fixed in the Constitution of 1993 may be divided into three large groups: 1) personal (civil) rights and freedoms, 2) political rights and freedoms, 3) economic, social and cultural rights and freedoms. Each group forms a relatively independent constitutional institution embracing a certain sphere of life. There are no barriers among them, because these groups work as a complex and sometimes as a combination of certain rights and freedoms from different groups. Basically, it is difficult to speak about a hierarchy of these groups, since each of them is important and necessary. It is impossible to remove one institution from the list of rights and freedoms. If this happens, the whole system of coordinated rights and freedoms will be ruined.

At the same time, it is symptomatic that consideration of rights and freedoms in the Constitution of 1993 starts with personal (civil) rights and freedoms. Such a priority results from their purpose: to provide the autonomy of a person, individual personality development and self-determination. Personal rights and freedoms are supposed to protect a person from any interference into the sphere of his/her personal freedom. They protect people from the falsely understood collectivism, forced socialization and forced standardization of the personality.

Economic, social and cultural rights and freedoms of man and citizen are inseparable from other rights and freedoms. At the same time, they have specific features. Under the conditions of market economy they are implemented according to the available resources of the state. That is why the degree of protection of economic, social and cultural rights and freedoms for the objective reasons is not as high as that of other groups. It resulted in the following division of rights and freedoms in theory of constitutional law. The first have a legally obligatory character and must be provided by the state; the second can be compared to certain standards or programme statements which the state recognizes and accepts but cannot fully implement in practice. Their implementation depends on the economic prosperity of the state and can be done step by step.

By the way, such is the situation not only in Russia, but in other countries of the modern world including the most developed ones and in international practice. It would be sufficient to look into international human rights conventions adopted under the aegis of the United Nations Organization. While the Convention on civil and political rights says that its provisions should be applied immediately and without any reservations, the Convention on economic, social and cultural rights says only that the states must take maximal measures within available resources in order to provide complete gradual implementation of these rights. The conventions have also different mechanisms aimed at their fulfillment.

The articles of the Constitution on basic rights and freedoms of man and citizen in the sphere of economy, basically do reflect conditions and needs for the transition to market economy. The principle of the freedom of economic activity is proclaimed in the chapter on the basics of the economic system. It is further developed in the chapter of rights and freedoms of man and citizen which says, "Everyone has the right for a free use of his abilities and property for entrepreneurial and other activities not prohibited by law (Article 34, p.1). The Constitution does not define the concept of entrepreneurship, which it really does not have to do. It is done in the Civil Code which says that entrepreneurial activity is any independent activity performed at risk and aimed at receiving systematic profit from using property, selling goods, performing work or service by persons registered in this capacity in due legal order. (Article 2, p.1).

The freedom of economic activity is protected by the Constitution from misuse. First of all, not allowed is economic activity aimed at monopolization of production, trade and services and unfair competition. (Article 34, p.2). On the contrary, honest entrepreneurs are provided with proper protection of their lawful interests. Provisions fixed in the Constitution are reflected in the prevailing legislation. For example, a new wording of the RSFSR Law of March 22, 1991 "On competition and restriction of monopolistic activity at commodity market" was passed in 1995.

The development of entrepreneurship requires paying special attention to the legal provision of the right to private property. Establishing the basics of the constitutional system, the Constitution legalizes the private property giving to it the same status with other types of property including state property. The next chapter discusses the rights and freedoms of man and citizen, private property is treated from the point of view of the individual. The Constitution of 1993 fixes four important provisions related to private property (Article 35).

First, the right to private property is protected by law. It means that it is allowed to make amendments dealing with the right to private property only by means of enacted law. We are talking not just about federal law, but about the Constitution. Its revision can be made only in accordance with a complicated procedure. The Constitution of 1993 belongs to the "rigid" ones. For introducing amendments into it, a qualified majority is required. As for the first two chapters of the Constitution, to change something or insert additions to the provisions there is as difficult as to adopt a new constitution. These provisions cannot be reviewed by the Federal Assembly. If a proposal on their revision were backed up by the three fifths of votes of the total number of the Council of Federation members, according to the federal constitutional law a special body would be convened – the Constitutional Assembly. It would either confirm immutability of the Constitution or develop a new draft Constitution to be adopted by the two thirds of votes of the total number of its members. Then it would be submitted to a nation-wide referendum.

Secondly, all necessary attributes are given to the right to private property. This right can be enjoyed by "everyone", which means not only citizens of the Russian Federation, but also foreigners and stateless persons. The Constitution does not impose any age limits with regard to the right to private property. All the powers of the owner are fixed. He/she has a right to possess, use and dispose of his/her property. It is possible to possess property personally or jointly with other people. However, there is one reasonable restriction: exercising the right to private property should not result in violating rights and lawful interests of other people or be detrimental to the citizens' health or the environment.

Thirdly, the right to private property is protected. Nobody can be deprived of property otherwise than by a court decision. Forced expropriation of property for state needs can be carried out only upon conditions of a preliminary and complete compensation.

Fourthly, the right of inheritance is guaranteed.

Under the conditions of the market economy, the rights contributing to the formation of the legal status of the owner/proprietor and to the protection of the owner's rights are especially important. We should admit that the evident weakness of the new legislation consists in the preference given to big business and insufficient attention to the interests and rights of small and medium-size enterpreneurship/business. It should be also mentioned that there is a tendency to the excessive governing of the small and medium-size business accompanied by another tendency to give more independence to the big business. Sometimes, the legal status and real possibilities of managers dominate over the status and options of owners/proprietors. In some spheres of activity the owners'/proprietors' rights remain unguaranteed with regard to the state agencies. This is especially noticeable in the regions. Small and medium businesses suffer first of all.

It can be expected that a reform of labour law will be carried out. It is getting more and more urgent. The current legal regulation in the sphere of labor relations and, first of all, the Code of Laws on Labour is lagging behind the realities of the establishment of a market economy. It is bad both for employers and employees. The employees suffer from not being paid on time, from curtailing production, from shutting down of enterprises and from other unfavourable circumstances characterizing current times.

Employers confront difficulties in performing entrepreneurial activity. It is explained by the fact that the legislation does not provide for reducing the number of employees or other personnel composition changes. Market relations stipulate, on the one hand, taking measures aimed at the stronger legal protection of employees and, on the other hand, clear definition of their duties under new conditions. Labour conflicts become a feature of market reforms.

Contract relations in the labour sphere need to be reviewed. At present they are too complicated being based on the criteria of the plan-based economy. It is necessary to realize that now sometimes it is impossible to provide people with jobs at the same enterprise. The structure of employment is changing and will continue to do so. The discretion of the employer is getting more important than before.

The labour law reform causes hot discussions in the Russian society. There are supporters of bringing the labour law closer to the civil law. This would make employees and employers two equal parties in case of disputes between them. For considering labour disputes special courts are going to be created (courts on labour disputes, or labour courts). On the other hand, there are quite a few supporters of preserving as many as possible of the ideas and provisions found in the current Code of Labour Laws.

7. Russian Federation

The fact that Russia is a federal state also has an economic dimension. In the process of transition from the state-governed planned economy strictly administered from the centre to the market relations based on the institution of private property, a demand in using the instruments of federalism became evident. It seems that economic factors are so interwoven with others – historical, geopolitical, national, etc., that the onesided economic perception of the Russian federalism would distort not only its general picture, but the role it is expected to play in a market economy. Federalism in Russia has many foundations explaining its complex structure and its mission in certain spheres of social development. This results in the need of the complex approach to the analysis of its nature and main functions.

First of all, one important consideration should be kept in mind. Specification of the principle of federalism in the Constitution of 1993 has not been done as a part of a world-wide fashionable trend or as a repetition of the previous state structure, but as a balanced conclusion from the national history, the experience of foreign states and the analysis of current Russian realities. Such a conclusion was not easy to make. It was formed in the process of long sharp discussions, the comparison of different approaches and proposals. Supporters of the strong central power, as well as those of the weak one, expressed their opinions as did those supporting unitarian models or almost complete autonomy of the regions.

Various standpoints and views did not appear accidentally. Let me remind you that during the centuries the Russian society experienced different models of state organization from the "united and indivisible empire" to the Soviet models of federalism. That is why so significant is the basic decision of the federative organization of the Russian state. It is proclaimed in chapter 1 of the constitution "The basics of the Constitutional System" of the Constitution of 1993. The problems of federalism are dealt with in a separate chapter which is called "The Russian Federation" (Chapter 3).

So, Russia did not choose unitarism, but rather federalism for its development. Readers familiar with the history of the state can ask why it is considered as something new. The Soviet Union as a predecessor of Russia was formally defined as a federative state. The USSR consisted of 15 union republics with RSFSR among them and was called a federation. But actually, the Soviet Union was governed strictly as a centralized unitary state. Constitutional features of federalism were not backed up by the system of real relations between the powerful center and the subordinate union republics. The Communist party had a unitary structure and headed the whole mechanism of the state leadership.

From the point of view of law, the Soviet federalism had one more distinction. It was considered as an instrument for solving national problems. Each union republic presented a state. The name was determined by the title nation living in each republic. It was characteristic that one of the parts of the 1977 Constitution was called "National-state structure" (Part III). RSFSR being the largest of the republics had the same status as other republics. Its regions with the economic potential prevailing over that of many other union republics had even fewer rights. This showed a lack of balance in the administrative system which produced negative influence on the development of Russian regions.

RSFSR remained a unitary state. A tendency of decentralization and regionalization, which were becoming more and more popular, could not overcome the barriers of the party and administrative governing. The name RSFSR itself (Russian Soviet Federative Socialist Republic), especially the indication of its federative nature, was explained by historical circumstances. It is a well-known fact that in the first years of the Soviet power there were plans of uniting all union republics which had appeared on the territory of the former Russian Empire. It was to be done by means of their incorporation into RSFSR on the principles which were closer to autonomy rather than to federalism. Later, the unification of the union republics was performed within the framework of the USSR, but the name RSFSR stayed.

The Russian federalism of today is not limited by the national-state structure which was typical of the Soviet model of federalism. At the same time, it has not chosen the way of a strictly territorial structure which is typical of the majority of the contemporary federative states. It is well-known that at present federalism is winning new positions internationally. Certainly, Russian federalism uses international experience which contains numerous interesting ways of solving similar problems. It helped to identify most advanced tendencies of the world development and use them as a foundation. Besides Russia, six more federative states exist in Europe; their total number all over the world is 24, including such countries, as the USA, Germany, Australia, Mexico, Brazil and Switzerland.

The world has known various forms of federalism. At the same time the experience shows that the national-state form applied not only in the former Soviet Union, but also in Yugoslavia and Czechoslovakia, has not turned out to be viable enough in modern conditions. The prevailing tendency in the world now is a territorial foundation of the federative organization. However, the national factor should not be disregarded. The example of Belgium tells that this factor can play a significant role in the development of state organizations, for example, in determination of the powers of the centre and the constituent parts of the federation.

The Russian federalism today is in many ways unique. The attempts to copy or automatically reproduce in Russia the experience of the USA, Germany and other countries having everywhere subjects like American states or German lands, which was typical of many constitutional Russian projects in early 1990s, did not have chances for success for a simple reason that they did not suit Russian realities. Theoretically consistent conceptions with all their attractiveness and similarity to the models already tested in the West, could not help to solve Russian problems.

The constitutional formula "Russia is a federative state" reflects conditions and needs of the country's development today. Russia is one of the largest countries not just in Europe, but in the world. Governing such a country cannot be effective without taking into account its territory, the population, a variety of the regions differing on many important indicators including economic ones. A federative state model when used properly can help to integrate regions with different economic characteristics into a united economic space. It should not be forgotten that the national composition of Russia is not homogeneous. Besides Russians, many other peoples live there. The principle of federalism is extremely important for providing successful development of the Russian state in all spheres of life.

A market economy adds its requirements to the development of the state structure. According to the world experience, the formation of market relations and the development of federalism are an inter-related phenomena. While in the past the federative structure was built on the priority of political and national interests with the economic factor neglected, now the situation has drastically changed. Economic and social interests more and more determine the basics of federalism and the solution of the problems dealing with the division of powers between the centre and the parts of the federative state.

Recently, federalism has left political and national framework. It is interesting to note, that such concepts as economic federalism, budget federalism, tax federalism are used not only by scholars, but can also be found in official documents. A real share of the members of the federation depends on sharing powers amongst them and the centre in the sphere of property, investments, budget relations and taxes. The economic potential of the regions becomes a strong weapon in defending their interests in relations with the centre.

Russian federalism has not become an exception to the general rule. On the contrary, due to many reasons the problems of the formation of a market economy have determined both the basic guidelines of the development for the constitutional foundations of the Russian Federation and the solutions of some questions related, first of all, to the sphere of the powers of the center and subjects of the Federation. When the market economy formation was accompanied by the creation of the legal grounds of federalism, it was beneficial. If such correlation was weakened or ignored, the general course was damaged. Attempts to solve economic problems apart from the problems of state structure were doomed to failure.

It should be remembered that in early 1990s in Russia there was a danger of the collapse of economic integrity which was connected with separatist tendencies in some regions. The economic separatism was not restricted to the nationalism and was pronounced not only in the republics. The slogans of the economic separatism could be seen also in the territories and regions, especially in those with a good economic potential. It led to such extremes as the opening of customs imitations and other agencies preventing the flow of goods from one region to others and the introduction of their own duties.

It is possible to explain such tendencies and actions. The subjects of the Russian Federation were eager to get rid of the former centralized system, to implement their own initiative and entrepreneurship and to use their own sources of income in view of the interests of the regions. They suffered from the effects of a general hard economic situation and of the fact that the centre had been weakened both politically and economically. On the whole, there was a danger of economic disinte-gration in Russia. This would inevitably lead to the situation where the country was a sum of separate economic units different in qualitative and quantitative indexes instead of a unified market. Advantages of market economy were minimized.

The Constitution of 1993 had to accept challenges of the time. It formulated the rules which can seldom be found in other constitutions, but are typical of the inter-state formations such as the European Union. Though in Western Europe these are the rules providing for the integrity of the economic space created on the basis of the economies of the sovereign states – members of the new formation. In other words, for them it was a transition from the economic independence to the close economic unity marked by creation of the single/common market. In Russia the situation was different. It was necessary to preserve the uniform economic space within the federative state. It would seem that Russia had an easier task to solve compared to the task which confronted Western-European countries which had chosen the route of economic integration. It should not be forgotten, however, that the European community and later the European Union were from the beginning built by the countries with market economies, while in Russia the transition from the planned and command economy to the market was still to be performed.

The requirements of market economy were clearly put in the follow-ing provisions of the Constitution of 1993: 1) in the Russian Federa-tion the integrity of the economic space is guaranteed, 2) in the Russian Federation is guaranteed a free flow of goods, services and financial resources (Article 8, p.1). These are the main characteristic features of the single economic space fixed in Chapter 1 "The Basics of the Constitutional System". But there are other references to the single economic space. Especially important is the provision that establish-ment of legal foundation for a single market economy is within the jurisdiction of the Russian Federation (Article 71).

An important guarantee of the single economic space is the constitu-tional provision which reads that within the territory of the Russian Federation it is not allowed to establish customs borders, duties or any other barriers to a free flow of goods, services and financial resources (Article 74, p.1). It is certainly a real barrier for those who would try to separate a certain subject of the Russian Federation and to isolate its economy from the single Russian internal market. There cannot be any custom union between the subjects of the Russian Federation. Russia pursues a single federal customs policy aimed at the ensuring interests of the whole Russian market, support of the Russian economy development and at the same time of foreign trade contacts, and Russia's integration into the world economic system. The customs agencies of the Russian Federation act according to the Federal Customs Code adopted on June 18, 1993.

The Constitution allows for certain restrictions in the transfer of goods and services. But such restrictions may be introduced only according to federal law and only in case when it is necessary to ensure security, protect life and health, and protect nature and cultural values (Article 74, p.2). Such restrictions do exist which is confirmed by the provisions of federal laws "On sanitary and epidemiological well-being of the population", "On the weapons" and others.

Thus, economic interests in their modern market understanding also prove the tendency of the predominantly territorial approach to the federative state system. But the new approach does not mean that the sphere of national relations has been neglected in Russia. It would be unreasonable to do so in a multi-national state from the point of view of both theory and practice. Achievement of the civil peace in Russia implies constant attention and respect towards many nations and ethnic groups comprising the population of Russia. A constant concern of the multi-national state should be the creation of the conditions preventing international complications and conflicts threatening the integrity of the whole society. Sometimes it involves measures aimed at the improvement of the difficult heritage left by old regimes. The Russian state has to solve numerous problems relating to the restoration of historical justice towards it´s people who were the victims of repressions in past decades.

On the whole, the Russian federalism has acquired a universal character. It combines advantages of the territorial approach and national-state needs. Federalism started to determine relations not only between the centre and republics within Russia, but also between the centre and other regions. Among them are territories, regions and cities of federal importance which were previously considered as purely administrative units and were governed on the unitary grounds. The new approach to the understanding of federalism eliminated dissatisfaction of regional with their previous position.

It should be noted that there were grounds for such dissatisfaction. Territories, regions, cities of federal importance, many of which superseded republics in terms of territory, population and other indexes, were well behind them in terms of the amount of powers and the autonomy from the centre. Territories, regions and cities of federal importance often used economic arguments in favor of leveling their status with that of the centre. Such regions determined the state of the Russian budget, the level and amount of production and the material potential of the whole country. Autonomous regions and areas were also involved in the leveling of the status of the Russian Federation subjects. According to the Constitution of 1993, in relation with federal bodies of state authority all subjects of the Russian Federation are equal among themselves (Article 5, p. 4).

The Russian federalism is characterized by the fact that the republics within Russia have proclaimed their sovereignty. This provision was originally passed in the Federative Treaty of 1992 preceding the Constitution of 1993 and practically completely incorporated in its text. Sovereignty of the republics is fixed in their constitutions, in a number of agreements on dividing powers among the federal bodies of state authority and bodies of state authority of the subjects of the Russian Federation and in other important documents. For example, "The Treaty on delimitation of the objects of jurisdiction between the bodies of state authority of the Russian Federation and the bodies of state authority of the Republic of Bashkortostan" (August 3, 1994) reads in the very first article, "The Republic of Bashkortostan is a sovereign state within the Russian Federation". Such statements can be found in other treaties concluded by federal authorities and republics of Russia.

Thus, the situation in Russia is characterized by the combination of two sovereignties within one state. The sovereignty of the federal state somehow envelopes, covers the sovereignty of the incorporated republics which have also proclaimed their sovereignty. At times, such situation reminds me of a Russian matryoshka which holds a number of smaller ones. Such a construction is quite applicable on the condition that it does not break a historically formed state integrity of the Russian Federation or cast doubt on its sovereignty. These requirements, which basically meet the interests of all peoples and all subjects of the Russian Federation, require a special attention on behalf of the centre and the subjects of the federation. State institutions and legal means, especially the Constitutional Court of the Russian Federation are to play their role in this.

The principles of federalism fixed in the Russian Constitution of 1993 are not just general declarations. It must live and work. It is very important that their stability is combined in various forms and by methods which have dynamic and flexible application. On the one hand, we are talking about establishing firm guarantees preventing from restoration of unitary and authoritarian grounds in the activity of the center. On the other hand, federalism should have enough potential to withstand separatism and excessive regionalism. As our own experience and the world experience show, weakening of federalism brings along numerous hardships for people. Especially harmful is disruption of the settled economic ties and destruction of the single market. That is why it is so important to take care of the preservation of the single legal space in Russia, to overcome tendencies towards regional economic separatism, not to allow the substitution of the regional interests by self-interests of the regional elite. At the same time it is important to take into account regional specific features, to encourage the economic initiative of the regions and the development of their resources and reserves of growth.

The object of the most serious attention is correlation of the Russian Constitution and constitutions and charters of the subjects of the Russian Federation. Though this problem is not new being a heritage of the first post-Soviet years, this heritage can be felt today as discrepancy between certain provisions and concrete norms. We can suppose that the leading politicians do not want to make sharp movements which may aggravate the situation at this difficult time. They believe that the time itself and processes of self-regulation will improve the situation and eliminate legal discrepancies. But inaction may have negative consequences. Good examples can be found in history. From this point of view, the passivity of the agencies and officials at the top is at least surprising. The impression is that legal mechanisms providing the supremacy of the federal Constitution either run free or do not work at all. It is not appropriate for the state, which according to the constitution is law-governed.

Equality of all subjects of the Russian Federation in their relations with federal bodies of state authority does not mean that the constitutional and legal status of all the subjects is the same. The Constitution itself envisages existence of several kinds of subjects of the Russian Federation and allows for the status of a certain subject to be specified upon agreement. Grouping of the subjects in the Constitution shows three basic statuses given to the a) republics; b) administrative-territory units (territories, regions, cities of federal importance); c) autonomies (autonomous regions, autonomous areas).

The core problem for any really federative state is the division of powers between the federation and its constituents. Russia is not an exception. The Constitution of 1993 fixes the following approach: on the federal level there are powers in two ways. The first comprises issues of exclusive jurisdiction of the Russian Federation, and the second – objects of joint jurisdiction of the Russian Federation and its subjects. All other issues are left with the subjects of the Russian Federation. They are not represented in the federal Constitution and can be found in the constitutions and charters of the subjects of the Russian Federation.

According to the Constitution, the state property has two forms: 1) federal property and 2) property of the subjects of the Russian Federation – republics, territories, regions, cities of federal importance, autonomous regions and areas. The principles of delimitation of state property are determined in the Constitution of 1993. Both the Russian Federation and each subject are independent as owners of their property and are not responsible for each other's obligations.

Federal state property is included in the jurisdiction of the Russian Federation (Article 71). The content of this formula which may seem repetitive, is explained in a number of legislative acts. As early as December 27, 1991 the following Decree of the Supreme Soviet of the Russian Federation was adopted "On dividing state property of the Russian Federation into federal property, state property of the republics within the Russian Federation, territories, regions, autonomous areas, cities of Moscow and St.Petersburg and municipal property". Amendments to this Decree were introduced by a similar act on May 23, 1992. According to the Decree, federal property includes objects referring to five groups:

1) Objects consisting of the foundation of the national wealth of the country. These are resources of the continental shelf of the territorial waters and maritime/sea economic zone of the Russian Federation; protected or specifically used natural objects such as reserves, national parks, resorts, preserves; objects of historical and cultural heritage and artistic values, institutions of culture of national importance.

2) Objects necessary for ensuring the functioning of the federal state bodies. The list of such objects includes the State Treasury of the Russian Federation including the resources of the federal budget, pension fund, social security fund and other state federal extra-budget funds, the Central bank; gold reserves, diamond and currency funds. Here belongs the property of the armed forces, border troops, security agencies, internal affairs agencies. Further on the list names higher educational institutions, research institutes, enterprises and objects of geological and hydrometeorological services, enterprises and objects of sanitary and epidemiological and veterinary services, service of plants protection, agencies of patent, standardization and metrology services. State reserves and mobilization reserves should be also mentioned.

3) Object of defence production. They include all the enterprises producing systems and elements of weapons, explosives and poison

gases, fission and radioactive materials, missile carriers, space crafts and equipment and aviation equipment, military ammunition, enterprises and objects performing research work in these areas.

4) Objects of the branches providing viability of Russia's economy as a whole and development of other branches of economy. This group comprises enterprises of the mining industry (excluding mining local resources), enterprises of fuel and energy complex, enterprises and objects of power engineering, enterprises and objects of the railway and air transport, marine and inland water transport, gasification enterprises, federal automobile roads of general use.

Many of the enterprises mentioned above have up to now been privatized.

However, the division of state property has not been completed. This is a barrier for creating an efficient mechanism of the state property management. Remaining uncertainty in redistribution of the property rights in the state sector of the economy results in making individual decisions with regard to a certain object. Eventually, investment and other commercial risks go up complicating the situation in the state sector, while its effectiveness falls.

The division of powers and tasks between the Federation and the subjects of Federation has basically repeated what was agreed upon in the Federative Agreement in 1992. The signing of the agreement was an important step in the process of Russia's integration at the time when it was pervaded by "parades of sovereignties" proclaimed in a number of national regions of the country. It should be noted that the Federative agreement itself is the proof of "different calibre" of the Russian Federation subjects. It is not a single document, but rather a sum of three separate agreements on dividing spheres of jurisdiction and powers signed, on the one side, on behalf of the Russian Federation, and on the other side, on behalf of a) republics, b) administrative-territorial units, c) autonomies. Actually, the Constitution of 1993 adopted the classification elaborated in the process of preparation of the Federative agreement.

If we consider only constitutional differences in the status of the subjects of the Russian Federation, we will see that they are, first of all, seen in the sphere of the sources of law. The federal Constitution in all cases is the basic law for all the subjects without any exceptions. Along with it and in accordance with it, republics can adopt their own constitutions and other subjects – charters. With regard to the autonomy, a federal law on the autonomous region and autonomous area can be adopted. It is important that the state language on the whole territory of the Russian Federation is Russian. But along with it, republics have a right to set their own state languages. Noticeable distinctions are seen in the systems of the bodies of state power in the subjects of the Russian Federation. There can be found one-chamber and two-chamber supreme representative bodies. The system of bodies of the executive power may be headed by presidents, heads of the administration, mayors, heads of governments, etc. As for the sphere of economy, the Constitution of 1993 does not fix any distinctions among the subjects of the federation based on their affiliation with a certain group of subjects.

Agreements on the specification of the division of powers between the centre and the subjects is not an necessary feature of Russian federalism, but it is very important. Such agreements are supposed to complement and develop provisions fixed in the Constitution especially in cases when certain questions of jurisdiction among the centre and a subject remain unsettled. First of all, it refers to objects of so-called "joint jurisdiction" requiring additional clarification. The Constitution does not always give a complete answer. At the same time, the concept of "joint jurisdiction" implies that the center and a subject of the Federation should know their positions and limits of their governing. A need for an agreement may also arise when conditions of the development of a certain subject of the Federation are so specific that the general norm fixed by the Constitution is insufficient. It needs to be specified and clarified considering specific features of the geographic location of the subject, its history, ethnic composition, economic indexes, etc.

Considering the problems of these agreements forming the relations among the centre and the subjects of the Federation, we should take into account that from the very beginning and until now major difficulties have consisted in ensuring consistency of the agreements to the Constitution of the Russian Federation. Theoretically, all the problems should be solved without complications. The supremacy and supreme juridical force of Russia's Constitution in the legal system of the country is unquestionable. The Constitution expresses the will of the multinational Russian people, the bearer of sovereignty and the only source of power in the Russian Federation.

Any intra-federal agreement is a document of a lower rank and cannot introduce norms inconsistent with the Constitution of the Russian Federation. This rule is valid in cases of the provisions related to the status of the subjects of the Federation, hierarchy of their relations with the centre, objects of federal or joint jurisdiction. Deviation from this rule is sufficient ground for recognizing a agreement legally void. Otherwise, agreements lose their meaning – to contribute to the consolidation of the integrating ties among the centre and the subjects of the Federation. They may even introduce disintegrating elements into the all-Russian legal system.

Unfortunately, the seemingly evident situation is sometimes inadequately interpreted. The sources of discrepancies in understanding relationships between the Constitution and federative agreements date back to the first years of the post-Soviet Russia. At that time in a number of republics there were strong separatist and nationalist tendencies. At the moment of signing the Federative agreement there were statements that Russia had become a contractual federation. That was why the constitutions of the republics adopted before the Constitution of the Russian Federation of 1993 emphasize the provisions about state sovereignty of the republics. But such legal uncertainty could not continue for a long time. It was harmful to the interests of the Russian society in general and weakened the unity of the Russian state.

Enforcement of the Constitution of the Russian Federation of 1993 was of major importance in this respect. The Constitution has supremacy over all other norms of the Russian law. All important issues of building and functioning of the federative state are covered by this constitution. As for the contractual regulation, it can be qualified as a lower, sub-constitutional level in the system of the Russian law. Only within these limits norms of intra-federal agreements can be recognized as having proper legal force.

There is no rule without exceptions. The treaty with Tatarstan which contains some specific norms is one of those. It could be expected that legal settlement of relations between the centre and Chechnya will also involve non-standard decisions.

8. Division of powers among the President, the Federal Assembly and the Government

For the development of Russian economy it is very important to create a rational mechanism for exercising state power. In post-Soviet Russia the principle of division of powers, according to classical political doctrine (Montesqieu), was used as the foundation of such mechanism. But world experience shows that the division of powers is not a pattern which can be applied in the same way in all countries. Its implementation is determined by concrete local conditions and by concrete historical experience. The original understanding of this principle is typical of the USA where the degree of the organizational separation of powers is very high, and the institute of the President is one of the strongest institutes of executive power in the world. Modern interpretation of the division of powers in Great Britain is based on slightly different foundations. There are closer ties between legislative and executive powers, and the government plays a big role, with the Prime Minister being a dominant political figure. The development of the constitutional system in France led to the establishing of the institute of the strong President. On the whole, France is a typical semi-presidential republic, where the head of the state is above the Prime Minister, with the latter performing important functions in the system of the executive power. The institute of the President in Germany is built into the parliamentary republic.

In the Constitution of 1993 the principle of the division of powers is fixed in its classical, traditional way. But practically Russia has chosen the way reminiscent of the French version. Russia's features, though, determined its specific decisions. Russia has become a sort of a semi-presidential republic. This concept should not, however, be associated with under-developed presidential power or its weakness.

The President is not just proclaimed the head of state in the Constitution. His/her role is not limited by the representation of the Russian Federation within the country and in international relations. The Russian President is endowed with important powers placing him in the centre of the system of the federal bodies of power. He is a guarantor of the Constitution, of rights and freedoms of man and citizen. The President adopts measures to protect the sovereignty of the Russian Federation, its independence and state integrity, ensures coordinated functioning and interaction of all state bodies. The Russian President is rightly considered one of the strongest heads of the state in the world.

The Constitution of 1993 gives the President important instruments for influencing the course of governing the country. Especially it refers to the organization and activity of the Government. The President presents to the State Duma a candidate of the Chairman of the Government, appoints (upon the nomination by the Chairman of the Government) deputy chairmen and federal ministers. The programme of the Government should be based on the basic guidelines determined by the President.

In relations with the Federal Assembly two powers can be singled out. First, the right of legislative initiative, and second, the right of veto which can only be overcome by the second approval of the lawbill in the State Duma and this time not by simple majority, but by qualified majority in both chambers. It is important that the President has a right to dissolve the State Duma. This rule is applied after the State Duma has three times declined candidates presented by the President for the appointment to the post of the Chairman of the Government or after the State Duma has given a vote of no-confidence to the government.

The President's role in law-making is quite important. The President has a right to issue decrees and resolutions. They are obligatory for fulfillment on the whole territory of the Russian Federation. Decrees may be of normative character, which gives the President an opportunity to settle by his decrees issues referred to the sphere of legislative regulation in cases when a there is no appropriate law or acting laws do not contain necessary norms. In this way the President has made decisions of principal importance for the country. It is especially significant for the sphere of economy where market relations in many cases were introduced by the President's decrees. As a rule, introduction of new norms has been accompanied by the indication that provisions of the decree lose their force with adoption of an appropriate law.

Thus, the Russian version of division of powers is based on the strong President. It is not accidental. The Constitution of 1993 was a product of the historical process. The course of events does not stop, and the situation in the country is constantly changing. We can suppose that stabilization of the new social system, overcoming of the crisis in economy and social life, establishing of market relations and other good changes will influence the practice of division of powers. Concrete powers among the basic branches of power may be redistributed.

Changes in the relations between the President and the Government can serve as a good example. These changes are not drastic, but quite illustrative. The role of the Government has slightly increased. This is consistent with the mission of the Government and its place in the system of the federal bodies of power. According to the Constitution of 1993, the Government exercises executive authority in the Russian Federation (Article 110, p.1). The constitutional status of the Government under new conditions was further developed and specified by the Federal Law of December 17, 1997 "On the Government of the Russian Federation". It was the document which was discussed in long debates by the President and the State Duma before its final adoption. It should be noted that the Law specifies that the Government heads the unified system of executive power in the Russian Federation.

The authorities of the Government in the sphere of economy are determined as quite wide. In this sphere the Government fulfills the following functions:

- regulates economic processes;
- ensures integrity of the economic space and freedom of economic activity, free flow of goods, services and financial resources;
- forecasts social-economic development of the Russian Federation, develops and implements programs of developing priority branches of economy;
- works out state structural and investment policy and takes measures to implement it;
- works out and implements state policy in the sphere of international economic, financial and investment cooperation;
- performs general management of customs administration;
- takes measures to protect interests of domestic producers of goods;
- forms plans of mobilizing the economy of the Russian Federation, provides functioning of defense production in the Russian Federation.

In the sphere of the budget, financial, credit and monetary policy the Government:

- ensures single financial, credit and monetary policy;
- works out and presents to the State Duma federal budget and ensures its fulfillment;
- presents to the State Duma a report on fulfillment of the federal budget;
- works out and implements tax policy;
- ensures improvement of the budget system;
- takes measures to regulate securities market;
- manages state internal and foreign debt of the Russian Federation;
- performs currency regulation and currency control;
- heads financial activity between the Russian Federation and foreign states;
- works out and implements measures on a single price policy.

Thus, the potential of the Government is quite substantial. There is consequently potential for improvements in Government performance and an increase of its prestige in the society. The economic situation in the country remains a basic parameter. The key to success in modern conditions can only be found by means of skillful use of instruments of the market economy.

A number of new laws have been passed, but does it mean that this task has been fulfilled? Further modernization of the legislation remains a major condition of social-economic development. The adequate legal normalization of the factors of a rising economy potential for renewed economic growth.

There is an opinion that at present the task of law-making gives the way to the more urgent task of providing control over the observance of legal norms and especially activation of judicial bodies.

The Russian economy has tread a long difficult path of immersion into a market economy in a short time. But the situation has not stabilized enough as it was planned. Establishing of market economy has turned out to be a more complicated and difficult task. Its successful fulfillment demands more active application of the legal potential and resources of the state. Goals and further development of legal regulation guidelines of the development, basics of creating a mechanism of governing the country are prescribed by the Constitution of the Russian Federation. Observance of the constitutional prescriptions is the primary condition of the further development of legal regulation.

II Main Institutions of the Russian Administrative Law in the Sphere of the Administration of Economy

Nadeshda Georgijevna Salischeva

1. General

The contemporary administrative law of Russia as a complex of the administrative legal institutions stands in close connection with the functioning of the complicated and diversified structure of the public administration under the totally new conditions of the relationships between the state and the civil society.

The basic principles of the public administration are enshrined in the Constitution of the Russian Federation of 1993. The most important of them are the principles of the organization of the public authorities, specifically, the enunciation of Russia as a democratic, federative, law abiding and socially oriented state, where a person's rights and freedoms are of paramount importance. The protection of these rights and maintenance of decent living conditions for free development of the individual is the duty of the state. The starting point for the organization of the public administration are the constitutional principles of the division of powers with independence of the legislative, executive and judicial powers. This does not exclude, however, close interaction among all three branches of power.

The principle of the Constitution on recognition and equal protection of all forms of property – private, state, municipal and other forms, as well as the principle on recognition and on safeguarding of independence of local self-government, plays a very significant role in the development of the administrative legal institutions in the Russian legislation.

In this an attempt has been made to present the main institutions of Russian administrative law which have an immediate impact on the regulation of the economy.

Here the author defines the term "legal administrative institutions" as a totality of legal norms regulating:

a) system of bodies of the executive power in the administration of the economy – the competence of the executive bodies and of local bodies of self-government in the regulation of the economic sphere; interaction of the federal bodies of the executive power, of the bodies of the executive power of the subjects of the Federation and the bodies of the local self-government in the process of administration, coordination and control in the economic sphere;

b) specific features of the state service;

c) legal status of the citizens and of the non-state owned organizations in the economic sphere;

d) administrative responsibility of legal and private persons in the economic sphere.

e) administrative responsibility of legal and physical persons in the economy

We will examine further the main features of these legal institutions.

2. System of bodies of the executive power in the administration of the economy

For the time being in Russia there exist two structures of the executive power – *the federal system and the system of the subjects of the Federation*. The final adjustment of their activities is not yet completed as far as the system of the federal bodies of executive power itself is continuously transforming, though the new federal constitutional law "On the Government of the Russian Federation" has been accepted by the Federal Assembly in December 1997. From August 1996 until now the President of the Russian Federation has been modifying and amending by his decrees the structure and in certain cases the competence of the federal executive bodies – of the ministers, of the state departments and committees. One can easily see, however, the tendency towards the shifting of the public administration from the principle of the branch administration to the principle of the functional administration, particularly in the economic sphere.

The Government of the Russian Federation is at the head of *the federal system of the executive bodies.* Its competence and methods of organization are regulated in chapter 6 of the Constitution of the Russian Federation (art.110–117) and in federal constitutional law "On the Government of Russian Federation".

In Russia, which one can easily qualify as a republic with strong presidential powers, the formation of the Government depends mainly on the President. According to the art.111 of the Constitution of the Russian Federation, the head of the Government shall be nominated by the President upon approval of the State Duma. In case if the State Duma turns down thrice the candidates for the head of the Government, introduced by the President, the latter may dissolve the State Duma, call new elections and appoint the head of the Government at his own discretion.

The Government of the Russian Federation is at head of the federal executive bodies: the federal ministries, state committees, federal commissions, federal services, agencies and inspection offices. They effectuate the implementation of the laws and other normative acts of the President and of the Government of the RF within their competencies. It should be mentioned that the President of the RF determined a new structure of the executive power (federal ministries, state committees and federal services) in may–august 1999. This change was relevant also for the administrative bodies in the economy sphere.

The following federal executive bodies bear relation to the economic sphere.

Among the ministries of the Russian Federation: the Ministry of Nuclear Energy; the Ministry of Trade; the Ministry of Science and Technology; the Ministry of Natural Resources; the Ministry of Transport; the Ministry of Agriculture and Food; the Ministry of Fuel and Energy; the Ministry of Labour and Social Development; the Ministry of Finance; Ministry of Taxes and Public Fees; the Ministry of Economy; the Ministry of State Property, the Ministry of Antimonopoly Policy and of Support of the Business and some other Ministries.

Among the state committees of the Russian Federation: the State Committee on the Development of the Northern regions; the State Committee on Protection of the Environment; State Committee on Land Policy; the Customs State Committee.

Among the federal commissions: the Federal Commission on the Market of Securities; the Federal Commission on Energy.

Among the federal services of the Russian Federation: the Federal Service on Currency Exchange and Export Control; the Federal Service on Restructuring of Companies and Bankruptcy; the Federal Service on Forestry; the Federal Service of Taxation Police.

Among the agencies: the Russian Agency on Space; the Russian Agency of Ship Building, Russian Agency of Administration Systems (Decree of the president of RF 17.8. 1999)

Among the federal inspection offices: the Federal Inspection in Mining and Industry; the Federal Inspection on the Nuclear and Radiation Safety.

The system of *the executive bodies of the subjects of the Russian Federation* may be subdivided into several groups: the executive bodies of the republics, of the territories ("krai" in Russian), of the regional ("oblast") and of the autonomous district ("avtonomnyi okrug"). Each group has its own features, stipulated in their constitutions and charters.

According to the art.77 of the Constitution of the RF each subject of the Federation is entitled to decide independently on the system of its public administration. This system should comply with the fundamentals of the Constitution of the RF and with the general principles on the organization of representative and executive offices of public authorities, stipulated by the federal law. This federal law "On the principles of the organising the legislative and executive powers of the subjects of the Russian Federation" has been enacted on November 6, 1999. It defines the basic tasks and powers of the supreme organs of the executive of the subjects of the RF and their relation to the legislature. Part two of the art.77 of the Constitution of the RF requires, however, the unified principles, methods and patterns of implementation of the state administration on a national scale. It stipulates that in the spheres, where the federal authorities and the subjects of the Federation have joint competence, the federal executive bodies and the executive bodies of the subjects of the Federation shall form the unified system of the executive power.

The executive power of the subjects of the Federation may be of two kinds.

First of all, there are bodies of general competence, as governments of the republics (in certain republics the presidents, elected directly by the inhabitants, are the heads of the governments), administrations of territories, regions, autonomous regions, autonomous districts, led by the heads of administrations (sometimes called governors), elected, as a rule, by the inhabitants. There is no uniform federal legislation on the procedure of election of the heads of administrations. In the years 1996–1999, the governors were elected in all subjects of Federation on the basis of their regional legislative acts. In Moscow, simultaneously with the city municipal office, the Government of Moscow, lead by the Mayor of Moscow, functions.

Secondly, executive bodies in the subjects of the RF are composed of the ministries, committees and other departments in the republics, territories, regions and districts, subordinated to the governments of the republics to administrations of territories, regions and districts. They administer directly socio-cultural, political, economic and police issues.

These executive bodies, organized according to the branch or functional principle, are set up by the acts of the president or of the government of the republic, head of administration (governor) of the region, territory or district.

For example, the Constitution of Karelia stipulates that the President of the Government of the Republic, being the head of the executive power, appoints the heads of the public administration bodies: ministers, heads of the state committees of the republic, heads of departments and other chief executive officers in the public administration.

Further on, the Constitution of the Republic pronounces that the public administration bodies are free to resolve the problems within their competence according to the Constitution. The heads of these offices are responsible for the matters within their competencies.

The specifics of the public administration require *the sensible division of powers* grounded on objective criteria between the different bodies of the executive power. The problem of centralization and decentralization of the functions in administration is here important.

The basis for the resolution of this problem is laid down in the art.71 and art.72 of the Constitution of the RF. These articles distinguish between the items which belong to the exclusive jurisdiction of the Russian Federation and the items which belong to the joint jurisdiction of the Federation and of the subjects of the Federation. In the latter case the division of powers between federal organs and those of the subjects of federation, is provided.

Thus, in the economic sphere the following issues belong to the exclusive federal jurisdiction: foreign economic relations; federal transport, communications, information technology and telecommunications; standards; state statistics and bookkeeping; defence industry; issues on the procedure of sale of arms and of ammunition; nuclear energy, etc.

The following issues belong to the joint jurisdiction of the federal authorities and of the subjects of the Federation: issues on possession, use and disposal of the land, mineral resources, water and other natural resources; division of the state property; establishment of the uniform principles for taxation and other public fees in the Russian Federation; coordination of the foreign economic relations of the subjects of the Russian Federation; use of nature, environmental issues and ecological security.

The division of the powers, mentioned in the art.71 and 72, provides for the centralized system of the executive bodies in the spheres like foreign economic relations, federal transport, communication and nuclear energy. In the same time, there is a need to set up regional branches of the corresponding federal ministries, state committees and federal services. Such regional organs already operate within certain areas of the economy, for example, in order to ensure the coordination of policies in nature protection activities, the pursuance of the consolidated financial, credit and taxation policies, the administration of the state property and implementing the federal programmes, etc.

For the time being the issues on *the organization of the regional branches of the federal ministries and departments* are stipulated in the federal laws and in the statutes of these ministries and departments, approved by the President of the RF (regarding the bodies, subordinated directly to the President as an extension of his constitutional powers) or, more often, by the Government of the RF (regarding the majority of the executive bodies).

Thus, for example, the Law of the RF "On nature protection" provides for the establishing of regional bodies.

The statute of the Ministry of Economy declares that it is entitled to set up its regional branches according to the established procedure in order to ensure proper interaction with the executive bodies of the subjects of the Russian Federation and to be able to prepare programmes of development of these regions.

The Ministry on state property, the State Committee of Standardization, and Metrology and the federal inspections have their branches on
the regional level as well.

The decision to establish the regional branches of the federal executive bodies and the appointment of their directors shall be made taking
into consideration the opinions of the corresponding public bodies of
the subjects of the Russian Federation.

For the time being the system of *the local self-government* in the
economic sphere is yet under its stage of formation and very much
depends on the concrete economic circumstances of the self-government bodies in the regions.

Speaking about the system of local self-government, it should be
taken into consideration that art.130–133 of the Constitution of the
Russian Federation declare that local self-government, not being a part
of the system of the state power, shall ensure independent decision
making of problems of local importance as well as of issues about
possession, use and disposal of the municipal property.

The basic law in this sphere of the administrative activities is the
Law "On the general principles of the organization of the local self-
government in the Russian Federation", dated 28 April 1995. The Law
defines the status of municipality as an urban or rural area, or several
residential areas united in one unit, or a part of a residential area as
independent local unit. Self-government units have their own local
self-government, municipal property, local budget and elected bodies
of the local self-government. The new federal law plays an important
role in this context "On financial basis of local self-government",
1997.

Art.131 of the Constitution of the Russian Federation proclaims that
the inhabitants of the municipality have the rights to decide independently on the structure of the local self-government. Under "the structure" both the representative and the executive bodies of the local self-
government are included. The executive bodies may be elected by the
local residents directly or be appointed by the representative bodies.
The powers of the executive bodies should be determined in the statute

of each municipality. It is advisable to define the exclusive competence of the representative body and to work out the list of the issues which needs to be approved at the general assembly of all inhabitants of the municipality. Thus, for example, the conditions and procedure of the privatization of the municipal property may be determined by the inhabitants directly or by the representative bodies of the municipality (art.29 of the Law "On the general principles of the organization of the local self-government in the Russian Federation"). However, day-to-day administration of the municipal property is effectuated by the executive body. In a similar way the specialized administrative structures in the spheres of the municipal economies, communal services and the control on the use of natural resources may be organized.

According to the legislative acts of the Russian Federation and of the subjects of the Federation the statutes of the municipalities should regulate the issues of the local importance, for example, on the local roads management, on the municipal housing stock, on the management of the shops and other service enterprises.

The meaning of self-government lies in its ability to bear the responsibility for the autonomous solutions of local problems. Thus, the Constitution of Karelia stipulates that the bodies of local self-government dispose independently of the municipal property, they work out, approve and carry out the local budget, establish local taxes and other dues, ensure public policy, decide on other matters of local importance.

The structure of the executive bodies of local self-government plays a crucial role. Besides the representative bodies, elected on the basis of universal, equal and direct suffrage, other institutions include the head of the municipality and other elected executive officers as well as other bodies of local self-government and municipal employees, formed or appointed by the head of the municipality.

One of the existing problems in the organization of the executive power in Russia is the co-existence of the local executive state bodies with the bodies of local self-government in cities and in country side areas.

In a number of subjects of the Federation (Iakutia, Komi, Moscow and a few others) the local state executive bodies on a certain level are considered to be as bodies of the self-government simultaneously.

For example, the statute of Moscow stipulates that both the representative and the executive bodies of Moscow are "simultaneously the institutions of city self-government and bodies of state power subject to the Russian Federation (Moscow), and possess all the legitimate competences of the said bodies" (art.6 of the Statute).

In the Republic of Bashkotorstan, according to its Constitution, in the cities (towns) and the areas of republican significance the administration is a part of the executive (state) power; other territorial units have the bodies of self-government. In the Iaroslavl region all the local administration bodies are under self-government. In the Khabarovsk region, according to its statute, cities and bigger municipal local administrative bodies belong to the state + administrative, villages and smaller towns have local bodies representing self-government. The heads of the administrations of the cities and of bigger municipal areas are appointed by the head of the administration of the region (subject of Federation). In the Moscow region surrounding the city of Moscow the head of the local administration is appointed by the head of the regional administration after approval of the elected representative body of the local self-government.

Considering the above-mentioned, the conclusion may follow that the structure of the regional state executive power and of the local self-government mainly depends on the discretion of the subject of the Russian Federation. It shall respect the federal legislation of the local self-government and at the same time take into consideration the local economic, social, demographic and other conditions of its territory.

3. Powers of the Government of the RF in the sphere of administration of the economy

The powers of the Government of the Russian Federation in the economic sphere is defined in general in the art.114 of the Constitution of the RF. The new federal constitutional law "On the Government of the Russian Federation" was accepted in 1997. Articles 13, 14 and 15 of this law define the powers of the Government in regulation of economic life. There is stated inter alia that the Government has to ensure the unity of economic space in Russia, the freedom of economic activity and free circulation of goods, services and capital throughout the whole territory of the RF. The Government has, moreover, to work out a structural and investment policy of the RF and to take measures to implement it. Further, the Government has the duty to prepare and implement the state policy concerning international financial and investment policy. The Government has also to direct the customs policies. The law finally obligates the Government to take measures for the defence of the interests of domestic producers of goods and services.

The Government of the RF is responsible for working out, organizing and implementing the federal budget as well as for presenting the budget and for reporting its implementation before the State Duma. The procedure of the composition of the budget, the sources of its revenues section and the general directions for the expenditure section should be determined according to the legislation on budget, taxation and other acts of the Russian Federation, taking into consideration the relationships between the Federation and its subjects as well as the approved federal programmes for economic and social development.

According to the Constitution, the Government has to ensure the uniform financial, credit and monetary policy within the RF and the administration of the federal property.

The analysis of the legislation and of the practice of the Government of the RF during the recent years allow us to make an assumption that the major change in the sphere of the public administration and regulation in the economic sphere had taken place. From the chaotic attempts to administer the economy the state went over to the planned social and economic development, rejecting totalitarian and voluntaristic methods based on centralistic administration. Now, all decisions are taken with the consideration of foresight and applying market-oriented programmes based on scientific criteria of expediency. Independency in decision-making of the subjects of the Federation is taken into consideration. This concerns some important questions about the economical sphere.

One of the most important activities of the Government of the RF is to organize the work of making a prognosis of the economic and social development in Russia, as well as the federal target programmes.

The federal Law "On state prognostication and on programmes of social and economic development of the Russian Federation", dated 20 July 1995, obliged the Government to develop short-term, middle-term and long-term official prognostications for the Russian Federation in the social and economic sphere.

The task of the Government is to provide the scientific basis of the prognostications, using the comprehensive analysis of the scientific and technical potential, of the demographic situation, of the conditions of natural resources, of social structure, of foreign-policy factors, etc.

Federal specific programmes are considered as a very important tool in the implementation of the structural policy of the state in the social and economic sphere. As a rule, federal specific programmes and the bodies who are working them out, are appointed by the state. The programmes should represent a system of well balanced (regarding resources, performers and durations) activities in the economic, social, industrial, managerial, scientific and other spheres which ensure the solution of the problems in the public, economic, ecological, social and cultural development of the Russian Federation.

Besides the specific federal programmes for certain branches of the economy and social spheres, the Government conducts such global national programmes,, for example, as "The development of reforms and the formation of the Russian economy".

One of the most important duties of the Government in the economic sphere is to provide for effective state administration in order to ensure the beneficial economic conditions for the stabilization of various branches of the national economy. Examples of these are perhaps the resolutions of the Government of the RF in the last years on the development of national textile and light industry and on the measures for the stabilization of the economic basis of industry, etc. The Government of the RF is continuously working at the solutions of the problems connected with the fuel and energy industry, transport, communications, formation of financial and industrial associations, etc.

The Government of the Russian Federation, being the main body of the federal executive power, is carrying out the uniform financial, credit and monetary policies in order to ensure the sovereignty of the Russian Federation, indivisibility of the economic space and maintenance of the conditions for decent living and free development of the individual.

At the same time, the Government has to take into consideration the necessity of ensuring the conditions for free entrepreneurship, a socially oriented economy, rational use of the natural resources, protection of the health and labour conditions of the citizens. The powers of the Government in these spheres are reflected in the legislation on taxation, on banking activities, on customs and on currency exchange. For example, the federal Law "On the Central Bank of the Russian Federation (Bank of Russia)", dated 26 April 1995, mentions that the Government of the RF and the Bank of Russia shall "keep each other informed of the anticipated activities which have the national importance".

In order to ensure the uniform financial policy in Russia the Government of the RF recently took a number of important decisions on the development of the security market, on the detailed elaboration of the competencies of the taxation authorities and tax collection office, on the improvement of the work of the customs administration.

One can add to the above-mentioned list the state control over the prices (tariffs) on certain products, primarily, on the products of the natural monopolies.

At present a number of organizational and legal measures has been taken by the Government of the Russian Federation to ensure the fulfillment of the federal budget, the creation of necessary conditions for the reform of housing and communal services, radical improvement of the administration of the enterprises of different forms of ownership, support and development of the small entrepreneurship.

The main goals of the Government in the sphere of the foreign economic activities are to stimulate the export of the manufactured goods, to promote the Russian export to the foreign countries, to create mechanisms of support for the exporters.

The Constitution and the law on the Government of the RF empowers the Government to *administer the federal property*. This property include i.a. federal energy system, nuclear energy, federal transport, information and telecommunication, space activities and other objects, classified as federal property by the federal legislation and the federal agreements between the Russian Federation and its subjects.

Day-to-day administration of the federal property is carried out by the corresponding federal bodies of the executive power (the Ministry on State Property, the Ministry of Fuel and Energy, the Ministry of Transport, the Ministry of the railways, the Ministry of Nuclear Energy, etc.)

The Government of the RF delegates to the federal ministries and departments its powers on the administration and the rights on disposal of the objects of the federal property, specifying these powers and rights in the statutes on each of these bodies of federal power.

The Government of the RF, acting in accordance with federal laws, concludes international intergovernmental agreements in the economic sphere and takes necessary measures for the fulfilment of the international obligations of the Russian Federation. Within its competence, the Government of the RF issues the regulations on export and import, establishes the procedure for the granting of licenses for export, import and for engaging in certain business activities, stipulates customs fees and tariffs.

To illustrate the activities of the Government of the RF in the economic sphere, we can refer to the issues, dealt with by the Government by analysing some of its resolutions.

First of all, the Programme on the structural changes and on the economic growth in the years 1997–2000, approved by the Government, should be taken into account. This voluminous document deals with the problems of the development of the national economy and of its branches.

In the sphere of administration of the federal property the Government of the Russian Federation decided on the issues of holding in the federal ownership a part of the shares of privatized state enterprises, as well as, on the auction sales of another part of these shares.

The Government approved the statutes of a number of state-owned enterprises with the special legal regime. The conditions for the allotment of financial support for the reformed state and municipal enterprises were elaborated. A lion share of the acts of the Government dealt with the transfer of the property or of the shares of property in possession of the federal authorities into the ownership of the subjects of the Federation.

In the sphere of administration of the industrial, agro-industrial and transport branches the Government of the RF continuously dealt with the problems of state support to the enterprises and organizations (among them the enterprises of the timber industry, of the financial enterprises, of heavy and engineering industry and of defence industry).

The Government approved the specific federal programmes for the development of sources of raw material for the metallurgy; for the development of farming holdings and agricultural co-operatives for the years 1996–2000. Particular attention was paid to the regulation of the activities of the natural monopolies. The Programme on the structural changes, privatization and the strengthening of the state control over the natural monopolies, the General rules on the pricing of the electric and fuel energy and a few other decisions were approved by the Government.

A considerable place in the activities of the Government of the RF occupied the issues on the use of the natural resources, of the environment protection, of the ecological security and of the people's health protection.

In order to comply with the stipulations of the Forest Code of the RF, approved in January 1997, the Government of the RF worked out the resolution "On accountancy in the field of forestry"; "On the state administrative bodies with the special competence on the use, protection of the forest stock and on reproduction of forest"; "On elaboration and approval of the regional rules (instructions) on timber logging"; "On the increase of the protection of the animals and their habitat on the territory of the forest stock in the Russian Federation".

In order to implement the rules of the Water Code the Government of the RF approved the Rules on the granting of the use of the waters under the state property, the Regulation on the procedure of the state control over the use and protection of the water reservoirs, the Procedure of the use of the water reservoirs.

The Government of the RF approved the Regulation on the Government Commission on the environment and the use of nature and appointed its members.

To ensure the ecological safety and the health protection of the population of the RF the Government of the RF set up the Joint Commission on the protection of the internal consumer market from inferior and dangerous goods. The Government stipulated the rules for the export and import of the medicines and on the mandatory translation into the Russian language of all important information on the goods. The Government issued the list of the goods and services which require mandatory state certification. As far as the state monopoly on production and sale of spirits is concerned the Government undertook a number of measures on excise marking, state registration and control in this sphere.

In the financial sphere the Government of the RF dealt with the problems on the issue of the government bonds, on the use of the credits extended by the foreign banks and organizations for financing of the concrete projects, and on working out the uniform system for the administration of the state debt of Russia. The main problems in the financial sphere were the problems of the implementation of the federal budget, of the paying off the unpaid wages, pensions and allowances to the employees, and the military and other categories of workers financed from the budget.

In the sphere of foreign economic relations a number of international intergovernmental agreements were concluded. The Government issued resolutions about the use of international financial resources, on the regulation of export of certain types of goods, on protective measures in relation to foreign trade, and on the customs tariffs, etc.

It is also worth mentioning that the Government of the RF paid considerable attention to the social and economic development of the subjects of the Russian Federation. A number of the specific federal programmes on the social and economic development of the Republic of Udmurtia, Republic of Tchuvaschia, Republic of Kalmykia, Republic of Buriatia, the region of Briansk and also certain other regions have been approved.

To ensure control over the illegal export-import and currency exchange operations, a specific Commission of the Government of the RF was formed.

4. A short description of the powers of some federal bodies with executive power in the economic sphere

At present the role of the ministries and departments which effectuate the functional (specific tasks over all branches) administration on the federal level has augmented. The objective of the functional administration of different branches consists in the coordination and supervision of the directly subordinated objects of the administration.

For example, while working out the competence of *the Ministry of Finance*, the Government of the RF emphasized that the ministry should ensure the uniform financial, budget, tax and currency exchange policy throughout the country as well as coordinate the activities of the other federal public authorities in this sphere.

The Statute on *the Ministry of Economy* stipulates that the ministry should pursue a uniform social and economic policy, determine the methods for efficient development of the economy, launch the strategy of the social and economic development and analytical and prognostic activities, and work out the comprehensive measures to influence the development of the economy. The Ministry of the Economy should work out the fundamentals for the restructuring policy for the state, should organize and coordinate the state policy on investment and on innovation, to formulate the proposals for price policies, for the improvement of the regulation of the foreign economic relations. The Ministry of Economy prepares the joint financial balance of the state, ensuring the economic basis of various items of the federal budget. The Ministry is in charge of the methodological administration and of the coordination to work out and implement the federal and international specific programmes. The Ministry of Economy supervises the state military defence contracts and other private law contracts of the state.

The Ministry of Economy presents to the Government of the RF economically founded conclusions on the issues of the development of various branches of the economy and of the regions. The regional aspect of the activity of the Ministry of Economy has direct impact on the interests of the subjects of the Federation since the Ministry analyses the economic situation in the regions and upon its results works out the regional programmes for social and economic development, strategy of the localisation of the productive forces and the proposals for the improvement of the territorial structures.

The competence of the Ministry of Economy includes the coordination of the activities of the economic services of the executive bodies on the level of the Federation and on the level of the subjects of the Federation. The Ministry of Economy has to analyse and to generalize the experience of the activities of the local self-government bodies in the social and economic sphere. In order to be able to perform these tasks the Ministry have to take into consideration the tendencies in the development of the local self-government.

In order to be able to carry out its functions the Ministry of economy is entitled to work out the legal regulations, mandatory for the executive bodies, enterprises and organizations. Quite often the Ministry takes joint decisions with other executive bodies or coordinates the decision-making process with them.

The Statute of *the Ministry of Natural Resources* of the RF stipulates that the Ministry pursues the state policy in the sphere of research, reproduction, use and protection of natural resources and coordinates within certain limits the activities of other federal executive bodies. This Ministry administers the mineral resources. It also controls the use and protection of water stock; and, within the certain limits, this ministry takes care of the nature protection.

The structure of the Ministry includes its regional offices, among them the water basin offices. Being a ministry with coordinative functions among other bodies of the federal executive power, the Ministry effectuates the function of the public administration regarding the mineral resources stock, the use and protection of the water stock, issues and registers the licenses for the use of water, etc.

The Ministry on *State Property* of the RF pursues the state policy in the sphere of privatization, administration and disposal of the federal property; coordinates the activities of other federal executive bodies in this sphere. The Ministry of State Property ("Mingosimuschemtvo" is its abbreviation in Russian) is working out and implementing the state programme of the privatization of the industrial and other objects of immovable property under federal ownership, including the land plots; transfers the federal state property into the specific legal regimes of "economic administration" and "operational management" for state enterprises. The Ministry is a holder of the shares in privatized companies belonging to the Federation.

It is the duty of this Ministry to supervise the proper use and security of the federal property as well as to carry out the state register of this property. The Ministry is carrying out a number of functions on control, as well as the functions on administration within its powers; issuing legal regulations on privatization, administration and disposal of the federal property, approving the statutes of the state-owned enterprises with the special legal regimes, issuing licenses for the performance of certain activities, working out the state programmes of privatization of the state and municipal enterprises. At present the Government of the RF and on its command the Ministry on state property are taking necessary measures in order to implement the recently adopted federal laws on the privatization of state and municipal enterprises, on the state registration of the rights on immovable property and on transactions with it. The structure of the Ministry on State Property includes its regional offices (agencies) on privatization and administration of the federal property.)

The Ministry of Anti-Monopoly Policy and on Support of the Business and its offices are entitled to take compulsory measures: to decide on

the compulsory division of the enterprises; on the annulation or modification of contracts; on the confiscation of the profit, in violation of the
anti-monopoly legislation; to impose administrative fines upon the legal
persons and their executive officers for the violation of anti-monopoly
legislation and of the non-performance instructions of the Committee.

State Committees fullfil coordinating functions between branches
(organs of functional administration)

The State Committee on Protection of the Environment was set up in
1996. The Committee has to implement coordination between different
branches and functional administration of the environment, ensuring
the ecological security and the preservation of the biological diversity.
This body effectuates also the state ecological control and the state
ecological expertise. The State Committee on protection of the environment ("Goskomekologia" is its abbreviation in Russian) has its
regional offices and specialized inspection agencies. Conjointly with
other executive bodies the Committee administers the use of nature,
guided by the interests of the protection of the environment. The
Committee provides for the dissemination of the ecological information. In the Statute on the State Committee on Protection of the Environment, approved by the Regulation of the Government of the RF on
26 May 1997, the powers of the Committee were defined. Amongst
them are the powers to issue licenses, for example, for utilization,
stock, transportation, burying, liquidation of industrial and other
wastes, of all materials and substances, except for the nuclear wastes;
for release of waste into the environment, etc. The Committee also
approves the instructive and technical documents (rules) on the protection of the environment and on the other spheres of its activities;
examines the reports of the heads of the organizations on compliance
with the requirements of the legislation on protection of the environment, on the implementation of the corresponding programmes and
measures. The Committee is entitled to restrict or to suspend economic
or activity; to decide on the administrative misdemeanor cases within
its sphere of activities; to revoke the licenses; to forbid putting into
operation, enterprises and installations; to forbid the import and the
transit of ecologically dangerous products in case the ecological stand-

ards are infringed; to bring the legal actions in tort for the compensation for environmental damages. The decisions of the Committee and of its regional offices are mandatory for all the executive bodies, legal and private persons, but may be disputed in court.

The executive officers of the Committee and its regional offices are entitled in their office hours to bear and use the arms and special equipment in the cases, provided for in the legislation according to the official regulations on the arms.

In the economic sphere also *the federal commissions, the federal services and the federal agencies* are operational. Analysis of the statutes of these bodies leads to the assumption that they are in charge of the implementation of the specific functions on execution, control, authorization and a number of other functions in certain branch of the administration of the economy. In a number of cases the powers of these bodies are defined by legislation. For example, the Forest Code specifies that the forest stock and the forests, situated on the territories of the military organizations belong to the federal property and that federal law permits the transfer of part of the forest stock into the property of the subjects of the Federation (art.19). In this connection the Code specifies the powers of the federal body on the administration of the forestry and of its territorial offices (art.27, 29, 51 and 53).

For the time being the body, authorized to effectuate the public administration in the sphere of forestry is *the Federal Service on Forestry* of the RF. According to its Statute the Federal Service effectuates the state administration and the state control in the sphere of use, reproduction and protection of forests, and works out the main features of the state policy in this sphere.

The Federal Service on Forestry and its regional branches have the right to enact the mandatory prescriptions for private and legal persons, working in forest, to eliminate the infringements of the forest legislation and the rules on the land use; to decide on the administrative misdemeanor cases and to impose administrative fines. Besides, these bodies have the right to decide on the stoppage of work, restrictions of the activities and termination of work of the enterprises, violating the rules of the forest legislation.

The Federal Road Agency effectuates the specific, executive, authorizing and controlling functions in the sphere of the motor-car road economy as well as the operational management of the resources of the motor-car road fund, federal motor-car roads, coordinates with the subjects of the Federation the activities on the development of the network of the motor-car roads and performs corresponding functions. This body has the right to initiate and implement instruction letters, rules, regulations, standards and other legal acts within its own competence which are mandatory for every legal and private person; to decide on the termination or interruption of the financing of the objects, subsidized from the federal motor-car road fund of the RF; to initiate the proposals to the Government on the interruptions of the subsidies to the subjects of the RF from the federal motor-car Road fund in case the subjects do not use the subsidies according to their initial purposes.

The Federal Road Agency approves the statutes of the enterprises and organizations of the road economy which belong to the federal property and has the right to appoint and to dismiss their superiors and to conclude the employment contracts with them.

The possibility of *delegation of powers* from the federal executive body to the executive body of the subject of the Federation, stipulated by the Constitution of the RF (art.78) is of paramount importance in the sphere of administration of the state property. This delegation may only take place on the basis of mutual consent of the corresponding bodies. The Constitution allows only partial transfer of powers and only in case when this transfer will not run counter to the rules of the Constitution and of the federal laws. Article 11 of the Constitution says that division of powers between the federal organs of state powers and the organs of state power of the subjects of Federation will be realised on two conditions: This division of powers cannot be against the Constitution of the RF and it must be made by the means of agreements between the parties. The agreements may in some cases give good results because it offers the opportunity to balance the interests of the federal centre and the region concerned and in this way weaken the existing tensions in their mutual relations.

The most common practice is to transfer by these agreements federal property to the subjects of Federation. In some cases this property may be transfered – with the acceptance of the subject to municipal property. In this connection we should mention the Decree of the President of the RF "On the approval of the Regulation on the procedure of work on delimitation of the powers between the federal bodies of public administration and the bodies of public administration of the subjects of the Federation, and on the mutual delegation of the parts of powers of the federal bodies of public administration and the bodies of public administration of the subjects of the Federation", dated 12 March 1996. The Regulation provides for the establishing of a specific commission by the President and defines its competence. This commission monitors, in particular, the agreements on the transfer by the federal executive bodies of part of their powers to the executive bodies of the subjects of the Federation. The commission gives its conclusions on these agreements and submit them to the Government of the RF for final approval. The agreements on the delegation of the powers are signed by the head of the Government of the RF or by the authorized Government representative of the federal executive body, as well as by the representative of the subject of the Federation.

These agreements come into force after their official publication. The control for their implementation is effectuated by the Administration of the Government of the RF.

It is mentioned in this Regulation that the transfer of the powers of the federal bodies of public administration is forbidden in the spheres which ensure the implementation of the constitutional order of the Russian Federation, the equality of the subjects of the Federation, the equality of the rights and freedoms of the individual and of the citizen throughout the territory of the RF, as well as other powers, in case their transfer may create the threat to the territorial integrity of Russia, the supremacy of the Constitution of the RF and the federal laws on the territory of the Russian Federation.

As a rule, the agreements on the transfer of powers between the bodies of the executive powers were concluded on the basis of the agreements on the delimitation of powers, signed by the President of the RF and by the supreme public official of the subject of the Federation (for example, by its president, the head of the government or the governor). Agreements on the transfer of powers are concluded, for example, on the basis of the agreements on the delimitation of powers between the federal bodies of the state power and the bodies of the state power of Tatarstan, Buriatia, Tchuiivashia, of the Kaliningrad, Sverdlovsk, Nizhii Novgorod, Sakhalin, Tver, Rostov and Altai region, etc.

Part 3 of the art.78 of the Constitution of the RF regulates the procedure for the possible transfer of powers from the executive bodies of the subjects of the Federation to the federal executive bodies. It provides for the partial transfer of powers on the basis of agreement with the assumption that such transfer does not run counter to the basic rules of the Constitution of the Russian Federation and of the constitution or the charter of the subject of the Federation. Such agreement shall be signed by the supreme public official of the subject of the Federation, authorized by the provisions of the constitution or of the charter to represent this subject. The procedure of the preliminary examination of this agreement on the level of the federation is stipulated in the above-mentioned Decree of the President of the RF, dated 12 March 1996 (amended by the Decree, dated 25 November 1996).

The paragraph 4 of the art.78 of the Constitution of the RF obliges the President and the Government of the RF to ensure the federal executive power on the territory of the Russian Federation.

An important role in the strengthening of the cooperation between the Government of the RF and executive bodies of the subjects of the RF plays the Governmental Commission for strengthening economic foundations of federal relations and for implementation of regional policy. This commission has to coordinate between the organs of executive power, in the sphere of joint competence. A new federal law "On the principles and order of the delimitation of the powers between the state organs of the Russian Federation and the state organs of the Subjects of Russian Federation" has been enacted on July 24, 1999. It defines the order in implementing the powers of different organs in the area of joint competence, the procedure of concluding agreements in this issue between the Federation and the Subjects of the Federation.

5. Powers of the executive regional bodies and of the subjects of the Russian Federation and of the bodies of self-government in the economic sphere

The first basis of determination of the powers of the executive bodies of the subjects of the Russian Federation is the division of the state property into federal property and property of the subjects of the Federation. Initial delimitation of the property was made in the Regulation of the Supreme Soviet of the Russian Federation on 27 December 1991. The objects exclusively in the federal ownership are:

- resources of the continental shelf, of the territorial waters and of the maritime economic zone of the RF; safeguarded territories or areas with specific use (natural parks, resorts, etc.);
- state treasury, the property of the military forces and of the police; sanitary service offices; the environment protection offices; patent offices; standardization and metrology service offices; state reserves and other objects, necessary for the functioning of the federal public service;
- objects of the military industry;
- objects of the industries which provide for functioning of the economy by large (enterprises of the energy industry, of the air, railway and maritime transport and some other branches).

In Annex no.2 of the Regulation a number of objects in federal ownership were listed which may be transferred to the state property of the subjects of the Federation. These objects include the enterprises of all branches of the economy which have the dominating position at the regional or local level, objects of machine-building for the energy industry; for motor-car transport, for building and maintenance of the hydrotechnical installations, for the building industry, etc.

The further subsequent division of property and powers in the administration of the economic sphere between the federal bodies of public administration of the Federation and the subjects of the Federation was the result of the implementation of the art.71 and 72 of the Constitution (see above).

It goes without saying that the fact of possession of the state property in the jurisdiction of the subjects of the Federation imposes on them the duty to organize the administration of these objects and requires the establishment of specific bodies of the executive power. The constitutions of the republics and the charters of other subjects of the Federation mirror this process. For example, the Statute of Moscow, approved by Moscow City Duma on 28 June 1995, stipulates that the branch and functional bodies of the city administration effectuate functions of administration of the property of the city.

These bodies implement the public administration in the sphere of conjoint competence of the Russian Federation and Moscow (according to the art.72 of the Constitution of the RF) and in the sphere of the competence of the city. The latter includes: city property and the right to dispose of it; city budget, non-budget and hard currency funds, taxation matters (excluding the federal taxes); establishment of city enterprises and their management; the housing fund of the city, engineering and communication services; energy services; other city services and utilities; gross and detail trade; building and renovation. The city departments effectuate administration of the issues under their powers. The heads of these departments (ministers) are the members of the Government of Moscow, headed by the Mayor of Moscow. The structure of these departments has been defined and their statutes concerning each department approved.

The Regulation of the Supreme Soviet of the RF, mentioned above, gives also the list of *the objects under the municipal ownership* to be administered by the bodies of local self-government. These objects are: housing fund; housing and communal enterprises; repair and building enterprises; auxiliary objects of the municipal property; objects of the engineering infrastructure of the city, of the city communal transport; communal services, etc.

The bodies of local self-government are entitled to set up the municipal enterprises for the implementation of economic activities, to decide on their restructuring and liquidation, to regulate prices and tariffs on the products of these enterprises, to approve the statutes of the municipal enterprises, to appoint their directors. Besides, the bodies of the local self-government are entitled to coordinate the activities of non-municipal enterprises on municipal territory, in order to comply with the comprehensive social and economic development of the territory, to satisfy the demands of its inhabitants. The bodies of self-government may, thus, decide on the siting of enterprises taking into consideration environmental factors, ecological security and the health protection of the inhabitants.

In the sphere of agriculture and of land use the bodies of local self-government decide on the matters, related to the registration of the ownership on land plots, of allotment of land plots under municipal control to heritable tenancy or on a lease; effectuate the state control over the use of land; raise the fees on land.

In the sphere of housing and communal services the bodies of self-government organize the maintenance of the municipal housing fund, the objects of the communal and road economy, decide on the issues of the sale of houses and apartments, the use of the residential premises, decide on the planning and building activities on their territory, etc.

The bodies of the local self-government administer the transport enterprises and organizations under the municipal ownership; effectuate the control over the municipal passenger transport; decide on the routes and schedules for the local transport; organize the work of the communication services and of the road services.

In the sphere of the use of nature and of the environment protection the bodies of the local self-government effectuate the state control over the protection and use of land, over the compliance with the rules on hunting and fishing; regulate the use of the water objects of the local importance and of the deposits of generally used mineral resources;

effectuate other functions of the state control over the use of nature.

The bodies of local self-government organize the maintenance of the enterprises of trade and public catering under the municipal ownership, effectuate the control over other enterprises within this branch; coordinate the plans of the retail trade, organize the fairs and markets, work out the rules of trade and control the sanitary condition of the trade places.

The bodies of the self-government decide on the issues of the local financing, namely: approve and implement local budgets; impose local taxes and other payments; set up specific non-budget funds; regulate prices on the products or services of the municipal enterprises and effectuate certain other activities in the sphere of budget and finance.

At present the reform of the system of local self-government is taking place in Russia, on the basis of the Decree of the President of the RF, dated 11 June 1997. The Government of the RF in its turn set up the Council of the heads of the local self-government as a consultative body to prepare recommendations on the implementation and adjustment of the policy of the Government in the sphere of the social and economic reform, taking into consideration the particularities of the local self-government.

6. State service

One of the most important institutions in administrative law is the institution of the state service as the structure of rules of administrative law that regulates the status of the state employee, the principles of the state service, the procedure of the holding of a position in public office, the procedure for the carrying out of the state service, the responsibility of the state employees.

The principal act in this sphere in Russia is federal Law "On the Fundamentals of the state service of Russian Federation", dated 31 July 1995. On the basis on this Law certain subjects of the federation approved their own legal acts on the state service.

According to the Fundamentals (art.2), state service represents the professional activity concerned with the powers of the public bodies. It consists of the federal state service and of the state service of the subjects of the Federation. It is worth mentioning that the institution of the state service comprehends by its legal regulation both the state employees of the executive branch and the state employee of the legislative (representative) branch of power. The category of the state employees overall includes military employees, public prosecutors, investigators and the judicial staff. That is why fundamental principles concern all categories of employees although peculiar features of various kinds of services are governed by specific federal laws.

Let us examine closer the so-called civil service. There is a fundamental principles distinction generally between the two groups of state employees, depending on the content of their functional duties. The first, relatively small category of the state employees occupy the positions designed to be in service of the persons who, not being "state employees" according to the art.1 of the Fundamentals, are holding exceptional official positions according to the Constitution of the RF, the federal laws, constitutions of the republics and charters of the subjects of the Federation (the President of the RF, the Head of the Government of the RF, the Heads of the Chambers in the Federal Assembly, the heads of the legislative and executive power of the subjects of the Federation, the ministers, the judges, etc).

The second category of the state employees serves the positions, established by the bodies of the public administration for fulfilment of their powers (persons who occupy the positions in the administration of the Government, ministries, state committees and other federal departments, in the administrations of the subjects of the Federation, etc.). It is not yet clear how to classify the employees who occupy the positions of the auxiliary character in the above mentioned bodies. Art.1 of the Fundamentals stipulates that "in order to provide technical assistance for the functioning of the state bodies it is possible to include into their regular office list the positions which are not qualified as official positions". It would be logical if the State Committee on

Labour and Social Development of the RF will work out a list of these non-official positions. Nowadays, speaking about the federal state service and the service of the subject of the Federation one should mean only official positions (i.e., according to the art.1 of the Fundamentals, the official position in the public bodies, is established in accordance with the Constitution of the RF, within certain area of duties on the performance and safeguarding of the powers of the corresponding public body and having responsibility for the fulfilment of these duties).

The classification of the official positions, according to art.6 of the Fundamentals, is the following. There are five categories (groups) of the official positions in the state service: principal, superior, leading, senior and junior. For each of these groups qualification requirements on specialization and level of education are established. There is also a system of qualification rating. This is established on the basis of the examinations and of the demands of the office. Thus, the person who occupies the superior official position may be given the title of "real state counsellor" (second or third class).

The President of the RF issued the following decrees: "Conjoint list of the official positions in the Russian Federation", "The Register of the positions of the federal state service", "Qualification requirements on the state positions of the federal state service", "Regulation on the attestation of the federal state employee", "Regulation on the procedure of conferment and retaining of the qualification ratings to the federal state employees", "List of the state offices for the federal state service".

The list of the rights and duties of state employees and of restrictions, connected with the performance of the state service, are stipulated in the art. 9–11 of the Fundamentals. In particular, the state employee may not: carry out any other paid job except his official work (exception is made only for pedagogical, scientific and other creative activities); be a deputy of any representative body of power; carry out business activity personally or through intermediaries; make working visits abroad on the account of private or legal persons (except for the visits, effectuated in accordance with international treaties or other official agreements); use his/her official position for the interests of political parties. According to art.12 of the Fundamentals the state employee has the duty to inform the state taxation office on incomes and on taxable property annually.

The state employees are the subjects of disciplinary responsibility in order of subordination. There exists the following types of disciplinary sanctions: remark, reprimand, strict reprimand, warning on the incomplete conformity to the position and dismissal.

State employees are also subject to the labour legislation (Labour Code) with the details, stipulated by the Fundamentals.

According to federal Law "On appeal in the court of the actions and decisions, violating the rights and freedoms of the citizens", from actions (or inactions) of the state employees may be lodged an appeal by the citizen, including a foreign citizen, to the court of general jurisdiction according to the procedure defined by the rules of the chapter 24 of the Code of the Civil Procedure of the RSFSR.

The new Criminal Code of the Russian Federation stipulates the stricter responsibility for state employees who occupy an official position (art.285–293 of the Criminal Code of the RF).

7. Administrative regulation of the activities of commercial enterprises

The principal legislative act that regulates the legal status of the state and municipal enterprises ("unitarnye predpriatia" in Russian) and other commercial enterprises is the Civil Code of the Russian Federation. At the same time these economic subjects, which effectuate different tasks in the spheres of production and of services in order to satisfy the consumers' demands and to earn profit, become very often participants in the administrative relationships. These relationships have emerged in the process of the state administration of the economy and of its particular branches. Administrative law regulation methods have their own distinct features compared to civil law regulations. One of these features is the presence of the public body (or of the executive officer) using state power. Therefore, these kind of relationships may be considered as founded on subordination. Certainly, it does not mean the inclusion of an enterprise or a commercial organization into the structure of the public administration nor the direct subordination of the enterprise to the state body. Under the new conditions of a market economy the so-called administrative-economic methods of the administration are replacing the old methods. The new methods limit or prevent the intervention of the state or of its bodies into the activities of economic subjects. However, in order to protect the interests of the society in respect of all kinds of commercial enterprises, the legislation provides for a number of mandatory administrative rules. These rules are the following.

- The state registration of all legal persons; the definition of the due state offices for the registration, the procedure of registration, the reasons for refusal to register an enterprise.
- The law establishes for all types of enterprises and organizations a duty to carry out bookkeeping. The federal Law "On bookkeeping", dated 21 November 1996, determined the competence of the chief bookkeeper of an organization, the main requirements for the bookkeeping, the composition of the bookkeeping and a number of other rules. One of the tasks of bookkeeping is the formation of complete and credible information on the activities of the organization and of its assets.
- Mandatory statistical accounts are to be presented according to the requirements of the Federal Agency of Statistics.
- The legislation imposes on the organization the duty to submit specified information to the state bodies according to the established procedure. The powers of the corresponding executive bodies to demand the data from the commercial organizations in order to be able to perform its functions are stipulated in the legislation and in particular, in the statutes on the corresponding executive bodies. For example, to ensure the collection and processing of

economic data on national level, the Ministry of Economy of the RF is entitled to demand the corresponding information from commercial subjects, state executive bodies on the level of Federation and from subjects of the Federation.

- Every legal person, created for the purpose to earn profit from its commercial activities as its main goal, has the duty to pay taxes and other public fees; to submit information to the taxation office on its financial accounts. The legislation on the tax system, on the taxation service and on the tax police office stipulates the relationships between the enterprises and the official bodies, mentioned above, the administrative and other types of responsibility for non-compliance with the duty to pay taxes.
- All enterprises, regardless of forms of their ownership, are obliged to comply with the requirements of the land legislation, other rules in the sphere of the use of nature and of the protection of the environment; sanitary and veterinary rules.
- All enterprises have the duty to undergo the procedure of industrial safety certification in order to be able to ensure the safe conditions of work, health protection of the population, prevention of industrial accidents and other dangerous situations.
- The state regulates the conditions of industrial safety and of labour protection, enacting the rules, implemented by the laws and legal regulations of the Government of the RF. The state executive bodies effectuate the inspection on the implementation of the rules on labour protection. For the violation of these rules administrative, criminal and civil law responsibilities of executive officers and employers are stipulated.
- The legislation of the RF stipulates the fire safety rules, mandatory for commercial organizations and the rules for the maintenance of motor-car transport and other sources of the augmented danger as well as responsibility for violation of these rules.

This list could be completed by specific lists of the mandatory rules, established for individual enterprises, depending on their particular activities or on the type of ownership.

On the basis of a legal act of the Government or within the competent federal body *state-administered enterprises* in the specific legal regime ("unitarnye i kazennye predpriatia") can use state property under the regime of "economic administration" and "operational management". On behalf of the owner (i.e., of the state in case if it is federal property or of the subject of the Federation in case it is a property of a subject of the Federation) the competent executive body effectuates the control and supervision over the activities of the enterprise, approves its statute, and appoints its director on a contractual basis.

The state-administered enterprises (organizations) with the rights of "operational management" (i.e., "kazennye predpriatia"), financed from the budget, receive from the state executive bodies the so-called plan-order, obligatory for implementation. The director of this enterprise is also appointed by the state executive body. The director is responsible for the management of the enterprise, for the safety of the property of the enterprise, and submits annually to the administrative state organization the report on the economic activities of the enterprise, on the actual condition of the property and finances of the enterprise.

Companies, the shares of which are partly owned by the state, are to a certain extent subjects of the control from the state executive bodies. These functions are effectuated by the representatives of the state in the executive bodies of the companies. These representatives are appointed by the Government of the RF, which determines their duties.

The state does not interfere in the economic, managerial and financial activities of state owned enterprises or into other forms of enterprise ownership, allowing them to operate at their own risk. The only exception to this rule are state enterprises with the right of "operational management" (i.e., "kazennoe predpriatie"). However, in particular cases within certain limits the state effectuates the control over the activities of the enterprises and in necessary cases initiates the procedure on bankruptcy or takes the decision to wind up the enterprise (for example, an inefficient coal mine).

During the initial transition of Russia to a market economy the particular emphasis was placed on the working out of the legal and administrative rules for the transformation of the ownership of the enterprises by way of privatization of the state and municipal enterprises. Nowadays this process is regulated by federal Law "On the privatization of state property and on the basis of the privatization of the municipal property in the Russian Federation", dated 21 July 1997. This law also contains typical administrative legal regulations. For example, the power of the Government of the RF in the privatization process is specifically identified use of the exclusive right of the Russian Federation to participate in the management of certain privatized companies of specific profiles including the representative of the Government into the council of directors of the company. The Law specifies the powers and duties of these representatives (art.5).

The Law stipulates the powers of the federal body on the administration of state property (art.7) and of the bodies on the administration of the property of the subjects of the Federation (art.8) under the privatization process (nowadays these bodies are the State Committee on the administration of the state property and the corresponding bodies of the subjects of the Federation). The Law regulates the procedure and the methods of the privatization process.

It is worth mentioning that these days the rights of commercial organizations are guaranteed in the legislation. The powers of public administration have been limited accordingly. For example, the refusal to register an enterprise with reference for expediency is forbidden; the period for the registration procedure is strictly limited.

An enterprise or other commercial organization may require judicial review of an act of the state administration or of the local self-government in court, if the acts of the above-mentioned executive bodies infringe the rights and lawful interests of the enterprise.

8. Issues on the administrative responsibility

The principal legislative act concerned with administrative penalties, and the principles and procedure of their application in respect of natural persons, is the Administrative Misdemeanors Code of the RSFSR.

At the same time, starting from the 1990′s, in Russia the principle of administrative responsibility of the legal persons for the misdemeanors in the sphere of the use of nature and of environmental protection, building legislation, protection of the continental shelf, unfair competition, tax legislation, trade legislation, etc., has been introduced. The rules on administrative responsibility are included into a number of the federal laws.

Art.72 of the Constitution of the Russian Federation classifies the issues of the administrative legislation and consequently, the issues of the administrative responsibility as joint competence of the Russian Federation and its subjects. In this connection the subjects of the Russian Federation via legislation provide for administrative responsibility in cases of violation of communal and sanitary rules, rules on the keeping of pets, of public order, of the trade, of protection of the historical monuments. In the variety of cases administrative responsibility of the legal persons, together with the responsibility of the natural persons, is provided.

At present the federal law stipulate the administrative responsibility of the legal persons in the economic sphere for the violation of the following rules:

- the Customs Code of the RF;
- the federal Law "On the continental shelf of the Russian Federation";
- rules on taxation and on procedure of the money transfer;
- rules on procedure of payment of fees into the state nonbudgetary funds;
- the Law "On commodity exchange and on the trade on the commodity exchange";

- anti-monopoly legislation;
- sanitary rules;
- legislation on the use of nature and on the environment, including legislation on land, water, mining and forests;
- rules on standardization and certification;
- rules on consumer trade;
- legal requirements in connection with the state monopoly on spirits;
- fire safety; certain other rules of the federal legislation and of the legislation of the subjects of the Federation.

As an administrative sanction, in the majority of cases for the violation of legislation by the legal person the fine is appropriate, in certain cases, however, the legal person may face the confiscation of his/her property.

The current Administrative Misdemeanors Code of the RSFSR provides for the specific responsibility of the executive officers. In comparison with the sanctions for the similar misdemeanors, made by private persons, the sanctions for executive officers are stricter.

The Administrative Misdemeanors Code, for example, establishes the responsibility of the executive officers in the form of a fine (sometimes in the form of warning) for the following misdemeanors in the economic sphere:

- for violation of labour legislation and of rules on labour protection (the fine is up to 100 times of the minimum monthly salary),
- for the nonfulfillment or breach of the collective agreement (the sanction is analogous to the previous);
- for the violation of sanitary rules;
- for the violation of state property on mineral resources and forests;
- for the non-rational use of land, damage to agricultural and other lands;
- for illegal grant of the licenses to carry out work on continental shelf of the RF (the fine is up to 1000 times the minimum monthly salary);

- for the violation of rules on the use and protection of water resources;
- for the violation of the procedure on the use of wood-cutting stock,
  of the purchase and transportation of timber, for the damage to
  saplings or the violation of other rules of forest legislation;
- for excessive air pollution, for putting into operation enterprises
  without considering the requirements relating to air pollution;
- for violation of rules on industrial safety;
- for violation of rules on the safety relating to railway and maritime
  transport, safety of air flights, fire safety on all modes of transport;
- for unauthorized cutting down and damage to trees in the urban
  area;
- for violation of the mandatory requirements of official standards.

The legislation stipulates the possibility of simultaneous sanctions to
the legal person and to its executive officers.

III Tax Law of the Russian Federation

Raisa Fedotovna Zaharova

1. Tax legislation of the Russian Federation. General

Russian Federation tax legislation was introduced at the end of 1991 and enacted at the beginning of 1992. The basic conception which was used as a basis for the tax legislation consisted in making laws on direct taxes directly applicable and eliminating a possibility of issuing subordinate acts specifying and developing them. Only the legislative tax foundation ruling out various interpretations could create necessary conditions for real protection of taxpayers' rights.

1.1. Concept of the tax legislation

The concept of the "tax legislation" should encompass only the laws of the Russian Federation and of the republics within the Russian Federation, decisions of the Federation and subjects of Federation bodies of authority which have been issued based on the Constitution and laws of the Russian Federation and within the authority granted to these bodies by the Constitution of the Russian Federation.

It should be noted that an attempt made in 1991 in the process of adopting a new system of taxation to create a body of laws on direct taxes, which would eliminate a possibility of subordinate acts, failed. For example, a possibility of departmental regulation of tax relations results from Article 25 of Russian Federation Law "On the Foundations of the Tax System in the Russian Federation" according to which instructions and manuals on application of the tax legislation are published by the State Taxation Service of the Russian Federation in agreement with the Ministry of Finances of the Russian Federation.

Norms regulating tax relations in different ways may be found not only in the special taxation laws, but also in the financial laws and laws of the taxation character. For example, the necessity of taking into consideration norms contained in financial laws can be very well illustrated by the article 54 of the Federal Law of February 1997 "On the Federal Budget for the year 1997". In accordance with this Law, the introduction of respective changes into the Law of the Russian Federation "On the Road Fund in the Russian Federation", new tax rates have been adopted for the users of motor roads, as well as for miscellaneous connected activities.

Only the officially published acts of the tax legislation, effective on the day of occurrence of the circumstances connected with the fulfillment of tax obligations, must be used in taxation.

The prevailing legislation contains a rule according to which laws and other acts of the tax legislation introducing new taxes or deteriorating the situation of the taxpayer, do not have retroactive force. At the same time, laws and other acts of the tax legislation (norms, theses) canceling taxes, reducing tax rates, eliminating or reducing responsibility for violation of the tax legislation or otherwise improving the situation of the taxpayer, may have retroactive force if it is provided for by the above mentioned acts.

Departmental normative acts occupy a special place in regulating tax relations in Russia. Quite often they cause a negative attitude to taxpayers because the instructions distort the contents of the laws and infringe rights and lawful interests of taxpayers.

1.2. Tax legislation system in the Russian Federation

The tax legislation system is composed of a considerable number of legal acts.

The general principles of taxation, the competence of the Russian Federation and the subjects of federation, the bodies of power and administration of the Russian Federation are secured in the Constitution of the Russian Federation adopted on December 12, 1993.

In article 57 of the Constitution it is specified that "each individual must pay legally established payments and duties. Laws adopting new taxes or deteriorating the situation of taxpayers do not have retroactive force." Thus, the Constitution of the Russian Federation secures the principle of universal taxation, as well as legality of adopting and introducing tax payments.

Issues of dividing the competence between the Russian Federation and its subjects in the field of taxation are dealt with in the articles 71, 72 and 75 of the Constitution of the Russian Federation.

The establishing of general principles of levying taxes and duties belongs to the joint jurisdiction of the Russian Federation and the subjects of the Russian Federation. The issue should be regulated in detail by a federal law.This law has not yet been adopted. A leading position in the tax legislation system is occupied by Russian Federation Law "On Foundations of the Taxation System in the Russian Federation". This law establishes the general principles of the taxation system in the Russian Federation giving a list of taxes, duties, fees and other payments, as well as defining rights, duties and responsibilities of taxpayers and tax authorities.

The Russian Federation laws regulating legal taxation relations are not homogenous in their content. They consist of general laws and certain tax laws.

The general laws include the laws regulating issues dealing with the status of taxation agencies or performance of taxation proceedings.

Such laws as the RSFSR Law of March 21, 1991 "On the State Taxation Service of the Russian Federation", the Russian Federation Law "On the Simplified System of Taxation, Registration and Accounting for the Subjects of Small Enterprises" and others can be qualified as the general laws.

At the same time, laws on particular taxes regulate the order of calculation and payment of one kind of taxes. There are 15 laws of this type in the system of tax legislation (for example, the "Law on the profit tax", the "Law on the excise tax", the "Law on income tax", etc.)

The federal budget, as well as the federal taxes and duties is within the jurisdiction of the Russian Federation. The system of taxes levied to the federal budget is established by the federal law as well.

In accordance with the Article 73 of the Constitution of the Russian Federation, the subjects of the Russian Federation have complete state power beyond the jurisdiction of the Russian Federation and the authority of the Russian Federation on the issues of joint jurisdiction. It should be noted that the Constitution of the Russian Federation does not directly establish the principles of taxation. It refers this issue to the joint jurisdiction issues of the Russian Federation and its subjects.

Federal laws are adopted by the State Duma, one of the two chambers of the Federal Assembly. Draft laws on adopting and canceling taxes, or on tax exemption can be submitted to the State Duma in accordance with part 3, article 104 of the Russian Federation Constitution only if there is a statement by the Government of the Russian Federation.

A certain role in the system of the tax legislation is played by the normative acts of the former Supreme Soviet of the Russian Federation and of the Federal Assembly.

First of all, it concerns decrees on the implementation of enacted tax laws:

– Decrees containing independent taxation norms. A decree of the Supreme Soviet Russian Federation of July 10, 1992 "On certain issues of the Russian Federation tax legislation" which established a principle of the priority of the tax law over the non-tax law, can serve as an example.

- Decrees explaining the order of application of the norms contained
  in the tax laws. For example, the decree of the Supreme Soviet of
  the Russian Federation of January 29, 1993 "On application of the
  Law of the Russian Federation "On the Value Added Tax" explains
  the order of levying payments on delivery of goods (work or services) among the economic subjects in the territory of the CIS countries

The Russian Federation President's decrees on taxation have double
significance. On the one hand, these decrees establish independent
legal norms sometimes introducing quite substantial corrections of the
taxation system. For example, the Russian Federation President's decree of December 22, 1993 "On some changes in taxation and the
relationship between budgets of different levels" adopted new taxes,
canceled some of the taxes, established new tax rates, new tax privileges and provided for responsibility. On the other hand, the President's decrees have a character of commission to the bodies of the
federal administration to work out normative acts on taxation. They
may also determine the main directions of the financial work of the
executive power bodies. The President's decree of May 8, 1996 "On
main directions of the taxation reform in the Russian Federation and
measures on improving taxation and payment discipline" can serve as
an example.

It should be noted that the authority of the President of the Russian
Federation in the field of taxation has not been finally determined,
despite the fact that since 1991 the President has adopted more than 30
decrees. Dealing with this issue we should refer, first of all, to article
73, clause 5 of the Russian Federation Constitution, according to
which the system of federal taxes and the general principles of taxation
are established only by the federal law. Thus, all normative tax acts
must have force of law, and introducing changes and additions by
means of inferior normative acts is inadmissible. The President of
Russia has authority to adopt normative acts on taxation only in cases
where such an authority has been directly provided for in the federal
law, or if the President as the leader of the state, in accordance with

clause 1, article 90 of the Russian Constitution, adopts a certain decree in case some taxation issue has not been regulated by the law. At the same time, in accordance with clause 3, article 90 of the Constitution of the Russian Federation, decrees and orders of the Russian President should not contradict the Constitution or the federal laws.

The Russian Government establishes and regulates the issues of collecting, first of all, non-tax payments. In accordance with article 8 of the "Law on the foundations of the taxation system" the Russian Government establishes the excise tax rates and custom duties. In accordance with article 4 of the "Law on the profit tax" The Government determines the composition of production and sales expenses to be applied in the taxation of profits. Furthermore the Russian Government adopts regulations dealing with taxation issues. For example, on April 23, 1994 the Russian Government adopted the Regulation "On approval of the list of the property sold belonging to military units, enterprises, organizations and offices of the Ministry of Defence and the services being rendered by them to be exempt of VAT and profit tax."

A special place in the system of the Russian tax legislation is occupied by the normative acts of the State Taxation Service of the Russian Federation and the Ministry of Finance of the Russian Federation. In accordance with article 25 of the "Law on the foundations of the taxation system", instructions and manuals on application of the tax legislation are published by the State Taxation Service of the Russian Federation in agreement with the Ministry of Finance of the Russian Federation. The purpose of the departmental instructions is to regulate uniform ways of practical activity of the administrative bodies dealing with correct and timely levying of taxes but not to impose or change the duties of taxpayers.

Instructions of the State Taxation Service are issued, basically, for specific calculation and collection of the taxes and for regulation of the organizational relations within the tax administration.

It is common to receive joint letters from the State Taxation Service and the Ministry of Finance. They generally concern complicated cases of tax collection and implementation of the concrete norms of the tax legislation. The letter of the Ministry of Finance of the Russian Federation and the State Taxation Service of the Russian Federation of July 18, 1996 "The order of calculation and payment of transportation tax by foreign legal entities" is a good example example.

Letters, directives and explanations from the State Taxation Service of the Russian Federation mostly concern particular taxation problems. Explanations, as a rule, summarize the practice of the taxation. It is not the responsibility of the State Taxation service of the Russian Federation to explain and/or interpret general questions of tax legislation application nor can it be a means for making taxpayers responsible. In the process of resolving disputes, such documents are evaluated by the courts of arbitration along with other materials on the case. (see Annex to the Letter of the Supreme Arbitration Court of the Russian Federation of May 31, 1994).

Telegrams of the State Taxation Service of the Russian Federation which have a normative character, are, as a rule, applied in operative regulation of certain relations after adoption of the new tax legislation or changing the order of imposing a certain tax before the instructions are issued, for example, the telegram of the State Taxation Service of the Russian Federation of April 18, 1996 "On re-calculation of the payments to the budget for the accounting period of 1996 in the connection with the changed order of applying VAT.»

Normative acts of the bodies of the subjects of the Russian Federation and of the bodies of local self-government regulate relations in the sphere of adopting and collecting regional and local taxes and duties. The competencies of these bodies is secured in articles 20 and 21 of the "Law on the foundations of the tax system".

1.3. Principles of the tax policy of the member states of the CIS

The creation of the Commonwealth of Independent States inevitably resulted in the coordination of the economic and financial policy of the new sovereign states.

On March 13, 1992 an agreement was signed among the states – members of the CIS on the coordinated principles of the tax policy. Realizing the necessity of coordinated radical reform in economics, taking into consideration in this connection the increasing role of taxes under the conditions of the developing real market mechanisms and trying to withhold from the actions bringing economic damage to one another, the governments of the states – members of the CIS pledged to carry out a coordinated tax policy on the basis of the unified principles and rules of taxation and to apply a single list of basic taxes equally important for all the states of the CIS.

Among the direct taxes, the member states of the CIS agreed to apply within their territory the profit tax on enterprises, associations, organizations and their branches irrespective of the form of ownership, as well as income tax from the physical entities. Among the indirect taxes are VAT and excise duties.

Besides, in accordance with this agreement, the member states of the CIS pledged to coordinate on the basis of rapprochement and unification at least the following forms of tax legislation:
– in the area of profit tax on enterprises, associations, organizations and their branches the rules of defining subjects and objects of taxation and the order of accounting production and sales costs for the product;
– in the area of income tax on physical persons – the principles of defining taxable and non-taxable income;
– in the area of VAT – the application of the single tax rate and the unified order of its calculation and payment.

On the basis of the Agreement on formation of the CIS of December 1991, the member states' intention was to guarantee the fulfillment of the treaties previously signed by the Soviet Union with the foreign states in order to avoid double taxation of income and property. But as for the new treaties on these issues signed between the CIS states and with other states, each country – member of the CIS will act independently.

In order to implement the Agreement of February 13, 1992, it was planned to create joint groups of experts which would make proposals to the Council of the Heads of Governments. This agreement was signed by the representatives of the Russian Federation, Republic of Armenia, Republic of Tadjikistan, Republic of Belarus, Republic of Kazakhstan, Republic of Uzbekistan, Republic of Kirghistan, and Republic of Moldova.

Later, on May 15, 1992, in Tashkent, the Council of the Heads of Governments signed the protocol on unification of the approach to make agreements on avoiding double taxation of income and property. In accordance with the document, Heads of the Governments of the states-members of the CIS agreed to use among themselves and with third countries model agreements on this issue. The model agreement determines unified approaches and conditions for the preparation of the respective agreements. It is regarded as a provisional recommendation.

1.4. Enactment of the tax laws

The general conditions of enacting of the tax laws are determined in the Constitution of the Russian Federation. Article 15 (clause 3) of the Constitution provides for obligatory official publishing of all laws (without any exceptions). The same article contains the consequences of non-observance of the requirements of obligatory publishing of laws and other normative legal acts concerning rights, freedoms and obligations of citizens. In case they have not been officially published, they are not applied and thus do not result in any legal consequences since they are not in force. They cannot serve as a legal foundation for regulating relations or applying any kinds of sanctions to citizens, officials or organizations for non-observance of the orders contained in them either.

The law comes into legal force as indicated in the law itself or in the decree on the enforcement of the law. In case of absence of such an indication, the time of entry into legal force for the law is determined according to the procedure provided for in the prevailing legislation. The Constitution of the Russian Federation contains, however, an important stipulation concerning the procedure of enacting the tax laws, "laws imposing new duties or deteriorating situation of taxpayers have no retroactive force." A new tax legislation contains a similar norm.

The Law of the Russian Federation of October 10, 1991 "On the foundations of the budget structure and budget process in RSFSR" determines the order of changes in tax legislation. According to this law, proposals on the tax reform are lodged to the supreme representative body at least 3.5 months before the beginning of a respective financial year and will be considered when adopting the budget.

The Decree of the Supreme Soviet of the Russian Federation of July 10, 1992 "On some issues of tax legislation" contributes to the stability and systematic character of tax legislation. The decree determines that legislative proposals of the Russian Federation regulating issues are not connected with taxation, and should not contain stipulations on taxation.

1.5. International treaties incorporated within the tax law sources of the Russian Federation

For the first time in the history of our country the Constitution contains a statement proclaiming principles and norms of the international law and international treaties of the Russian Federation as a part of its legal system (part 4, article 15). Thus, a new opportunity has been opened to act directly and apply norms of international law by the bodies of state power including the courts. Interested individual or legal entities can directly refer to the norms of international law in disputes with taxation agencies.

Article 15 of the Constitution introduces two categories of the international legal norms into the Russian legal system. Firstly, it refers to the generally accepted principles and norms of international law. These are the norms established and accepted by the international community of states and being, thus, obligatory for all its members.

Secondly, part 4 of article 15 mentions international treaties of the Russian Federation. Despite the fact that the Constitution does not mention the treaties ratified by the Russian Federation, such treaties are intended in the first place. At the same time, the wording of article 15 in principle also allows the application of the treaties which were concluded on behalf of the Russian Federation by its competent bodies, which need not to be lodged to the Federal Assembly for ratification. It should be kept in mind that part 4 of the article 15 does not contain a requirement to publish international treaties officially as a necessary condition of their applicability.

In accordance with part 4 of article 15, rules of international treaties have a priority over contradicting rules of the internal laws. It means that in case of revealing a contradiction between an international treaty and the law, judicial bodies must follow not the law, but rather the norms contained in the treaty. The international treaty has a priority over any laws both federal and those of the subjects of the Russian Federation adopted either before or after signing of the treaty. At the same time, it is clear from part 4 of article 15 of the Constitution of the Russian Federation, that international treaties have a priority only over the laws and cannot prevail over the stipulations of the Constitution of the Russian Federation.

There exist the following types of international treaties on tax issues:

Acts establishing general taxation principles, for example, the Final Act on Security and Cooperation in Europe of 1975, European Social Charter enacted in 1965 and others. Principles contained in them are implemented in internal legislation.

Bilateral and multi-lateral tax agreements concluded with the purpose to avoid double taxation, to prevent discrimination of taxpayers performing business activity in the territory of foreign states and tax evasion. They exist in the form of general tax agreements which embrace all the issues concerning relations between contracting states in terms of direct taxes (taxes on income and property) or indirect taxes (for example, the value added tax). Russia has concluded about 30 agreements concerning direct taxes. There are negotiations now in progress on concluding more agreements in order to avoid double taxation with a number of countries. There are restricted tax agreements dealing with specific taxes (for example, agreements on taxes on social security or taxes on inheritance etc.) or with taxation of certain types of activity (for example, agreements on elimination of double taxation concerning the carriage of goods by sea and air). The USSR concluded about 20 agreements with foreign states on the issues of cargo transportation. Russia is a successor of these agreements. Agreements on rendering administrative assistance on taxation issues are also considered as tax agreements. Such agreements are concluded between taxation agencies of different countries with the purpose of exchanging information, enforcing tax control, etc.

Different international agreements which along with other issues consider issues of the tax law should be especially emphasized. Among such agreements are those establishing diplomatic and consular relations, trade agreements which establish the most favoured regimes with respect to the custom duties.

Article 23 of the law of the foundations of the tax system envisages that in case international treaties of the Russian Federation or the former USSR contain rules different from those contained in the tax legislation of the Russian Federation, the rules of the international treaty shall be applied.

1.6. Conception of the idea of the new tax legislation

The basic conceptual ideas of the draft Tax Code of the Russian Federation are the following:
- further decreasing of the tax burden and simplifying of the tax system by means of deleting ineffective taxes and assignments to the departmental extra-budget funds;
- extension of the tax base by means of eliminating unjustified tax privileges, extension of the range of taxpayers, income and of the sources to be taxed;
- gradual shifting of the major part of the tax burden from enterprises to the income and property of individuals;
- taking measures to improve the effectiveness of tax collection.

A number of less important and less effective taxes are being reduced and new taxes are being established such as the capital tax which is not going to aggravate the tax burden on all taxpayers, since it will be applied only to certain types of income which before the adoption of the new Taxation Code are taxed within the profit tax of enterprises or income tax of individuals.

At the same time, under way is a legal mechanism which would, first, make it possible to increase the amount of collected taxes by means of creating the effective bookkeeping of taxpayers, second, to determine quite precisely the moments of receiving income and carrying out expenses for accounting, and third, to enlarge a scope of possibilities for temporary reduction of the tax burden (payment by installment, deferred payment, and investment tax credits).

One of the solutions to the tax federalism problem is the establishment in the draft Tax Code of the legal boundaries for the sphere of authority given to federal and regional bodies and local self-government on the regulation of tax relations based on the idea that all federal, regional and local taxes and public fees are parts of the single tax system which is one of the most important factors to favour the development and functioning of a unified market of the RF.

The draft Tax Code pays significant attention to the rights and obligations of taxpayers, tax agencies and other participants of tax relations. In the draft Tax Code, rules for all the participants of tax relations have been elaborated. Such regulations will facilitate quick and effective resolution of disputes.

The draft Tax Code determines grounds and rules of transferring tax obligations from one taxpayer to other persons/entities, for example, during the process of restructuring of an enterprise or in connection with a heavily indebted taxpayer.

A new draft Taxation Code introduces a concept of the "tax secret", increases responsibility of taxation agencies for disclosure of the information about taxpayers containing tax secrets, as well as for the loss of documents containing tax secrets.

A new approach to refunding taxpayers for overpayment of taxes or for erroneously levied fiscal charges (taxes, fees and fines) has been provided. Such sums must be returned to the taxpayer with the interest calculated from the time appointed for refunding overpaid sums, or from the moment of erroneous actions by the tax authority.

The draft Taxation Code provides for the establishment of consolidated group of enterprises for paying tax on profit. In this case, enterprises act as a single taxpayer on tax obligations of all the participants of the group. A Russian enterprise and its subsidiaries can form a consolidated group.

The stipulations of the new Tax Legislation separate tax accounting from regular accounting. The major method of determining the moment of receiving income or of incurring expenses will be the "method of charging" which is similar to the "on shipment" method but more flexible, since it enables to take into account different nuances of the contracts concluded between the partners. The application of the so-called "cash method" close to the method of "on earnings" is allowed by the new tax legislation only to a minor range of taxpayers.

Unlike the current procedure of bringing responsibility for violating tax legislation it is effective until the adoption of the new Tax Code, the draft Tax Code provides for separating violations of the tax legislation as an independent type of violations – tax violations. The draft Tax Code determines principles and independent grounds for the responsibility for tax violations, tax sanctions, order and terms of their imposition, it establishes essential characteristics of the tax violations in connection with specific details of the tax legislation, as well as the procedure for hearing cases on tax violations.

1.7. Legal aspects of interconnections between taxes and budgets

In accordance with article 106 of the Constitution of the Russian Federation, adopted by the State Duma, federal laws on questions of the federal budget, federal taxes and public fees, financial, currency, credit, and tax regulation, as well as money emission are subject to obligatory consideration in the Council of Federation.

To provide control over the fulfillment of the state budget, the Council of Federation and State Duma organize an "Auditing Chamber". Its composition and activity are determined by federal law. The

Auditing Chamber is supposed to render help to the Federal Assembly to exercise control over the observance of all financial laws including tax laws and, first of all, of the state budget.

Budget law and tax law interact, but the priority should be given to the tax law which directly regulates relations connected to entry to the budget of the main sources of revenue. For example, in accordance with article 10 of the RSFSR Law of October 10, 1991 "On the foundations of the budget structure and budget process in RSFSR", revenues of budgets on every level are formed in compliance with tax legislation. At the same time, according to article 9 of the "Law of the foundations of the tax system", entry of taxes in the budget is regulated by the budget legislation which demonstrates the correlation and inter-dependence of the two laws.

2. Taxes paid by individuals

This group of taxes includes: income tax, property tax on individuals, inheritance tax and tax on the property received as a gift, real estate tax and miscellaneous taxes.

2.1. Income tax on the individuals

Individual income tax is a federal tax adopted by the Russian Federation Law of December 7, 1991 "On individual income tax " (with later changes). The following parties are recognized as taxpayers of personal income tax:
- individuals having permanent residence in Russia (residents); residents are individuals living in Russia at least 183 days a year;
- individuals not having residence in the Russian Federation (non-residents), in case of receiving income within the territory of Russia;

    Individuals include citizens of the Russian Federation, foreign citizens and stateless persons.

- foreign sole proprietorship companies – their incomes are considered as incomes of the owners. The owner of a sole proprietorship company is an individual who owns any economic unit the income of which is not taxed in the country of registration of the sole proprietorship company with corporate profit tax or other similar tax.

  The individuals´age does not affect his/her responsibility as an income tax payer.

Taxation for individuals covers their aggregate income received in a calendar year:

  for residents – from sources in the Russian Federation and abroad;

  for non-residents – from sources in the Russian Federation.

While specifying an aggregate annual income as a source of taxation, the legislator does not clarify this concept. At present, the lack of legislative definition of the income results in disputes concerning income tax payments.

It should be noted that uniform terms of calculation and payment of income tax have been secured in the prevailing legislature for the whole territory of the Russian Federation. This concerns such issues as tax deduction at source (when tax is withheld at source with further calculation according to the real results of the passed year), the existence of a single standard non-taxable minimum income for all taxpayers at an amount of one annual minimum monthly labour payment specified by law. The following deductions are preserved: deductions of sums paid to the Pension Fund (pension/retirement deduction), deductions of the sums paid for maintenance of children and dependents (deduction for children and dependents), deductions of charity sums and part of property sales income (property deductions), as well as deduction for production costs.

The law provides for the preservation of additional discounts for specific categories of individuals for example in the amount of two-, four-, and nine-fold yearly amount of the minimum monthly payment for labour, and application of several tax discounts for the category in need of special social support on behalf of the state.

The law regulates the process of submitting tax declarations on the income received by taxpayers. Submission of a tax declaration is established as obligatory for all persons except those who have no other income besides earnings from one substantial place of employment. The tax legislation allows submission of tax declaration not only personally, but also by mail.

The tax amount is calculated on the basis of the following tax rates: with the tax base up to 12 million rubles, the tax amount is 12 %, with the tax base from 12 million to 24 million, the tax amount is 1 440 000 rubles plus 2 % of the sum exceeding 12 000 000 rubles. With the tax base from 24 000 000 to 36 000 000 rubles, the tax amount will be 3 840 000 rubles plus 25 % of the sum exceeding 24 000 000 rubles. With the person's income from 36 000 000 rubles to 48 000 000 rubles, the established tax is 6 840 000 rubles plus 30 % of the sum exceeding 36 000 000 rubles. On the sums exceeding 48 000 000 rubles, the due tax is 35 %.

The prevailing tax legislation provides a consistent net to cover taxpayers' expenses and incomes. The net or jurisdiction covers:
- acquisition by a taxpayer including via third party the following kinds of property:
    a) residential/non-residential buildings, constructions or their parts;
    b) plots of land;
    c) water (except row boats), air or land (except bicycles) vehicles subject to registration;
- donating sums of money to other persons by a taxpayer including loans.

Acquisition by a taxpayer of such property is the ground for exercising tax jurisdiction under the condition that the market value of such property on the day of acquisition constituted at least 1 000-fold minimum monthly payment for labour established by federal law. In the case of acquisition several objects of this kind within one calendar year, the ground for exercising control would be exceeding the mentioned standard of their total market value.

Donating/lending sums of money by a taxpayer to other people is a ground for jurisdiction under the condition that the total sum of the money given within one calendar year constituted at least 1 000-fold minimum monthly payment for labour established by the federal law on the day the money was donated/lent.

In the process of a tax audit, the taxation agency has a right to demand submission of a special tax declaration if the taxpayer has not submitted one for the previous taxation period or if the income stated in the tax declaration is not enough for acquisition of such property.

On receiving a demand to submit a special tax declaration, a taxpayer is obliged to submit to the tax agency at the place of registration a special tax declaration indicating all income and its source or other circumstance providing for acquisition of the property indicated in the demand and the price of the property.

If the results of the tax audit confirm the authenticity of the information submitted by the taxpayer and the correctness of the tax payment for the respective taxation period, the special tax declaration is returned to the taxpayer with the note "passes, no violations revealed". In case of non-fulfillment of declaration duty, taxpayers are brought to responsibility for violation of tax law.

2.2. Individual property tax

Individual property tax is specified as a local tax. Payers of this tax are individuals having as their property objects defined by the Russian Federation Law of December 1991 "On the property tax of individuals". On the basis of the law, the Instruction of the State Taxation Service of the Russian Federation was published on May 30, 1995 "On the order of calculation and payment of the property taxes of individuals".

Taxpayers are individuals – owners of the property irrespective of the place of the person's residence or of the manner of exercising ownership, usage or disposition of the property. If the immovable property or vehicle are under joint ownership of several persons, every one of these persons will be recognized as a taxpayer in accordance with his/her share of the property. If the immovable property or vehicle are in the common joint ownership of several persons, one of these persons will be recognized as a taxpayer according to their mutual agreement. But all the owners will carry joint responsibility concerning the fulfillment of tax obligations.

According to the stipulations of the tax legislation, the following items may be considered as taxation objects if they are located within a city or district territory where a legal act, adopted respectively by the city or district body of local self-government is effective: residential buildings, flats, country houses, garages and other buildings or constructions; vehicles, with some exceptions.

The tax base is determined on each object as the value of this object. Tax rates are determined by the local self-governing body. However, despite the fact that extensive rights have been given to the bodies of local self-government, the federal legislation has defined limitations according to which the tax on buildings, premises and constructions is paid annually at the amount not exceeding 0.1 % of their inventory value, and in case when it has not been determined, of their value defined on obligatory insurance.

Transport vehicles tax is levied depending on the engine power. The amount of the tax should be defined by taxation agencies at the location of the taxable property and the taxpayer should be informed about it according to the procedure determined by the tax act.

2.3. Tax on purchasing currency

The federal law "On the tax on purchasing foreign money and payment documents expressed in foreign currency" was adopted in July 1997. The purpose of this law is to receive additional revenue and to reduce the profitability of the citizens' investments in foreign currency. On August 25, 1997, the Ministry of Justice of the Russian Federation registered the Instruction of the State Taxation Service of the Russian Federation of August 7, 1997 "On the order of calculation and payment to budget of the tax on purchasing foreign money and payment documents expressed in foreign currency".

According to article 2 of the law, a taxable base is determined as the sum in rubles paid while purchasing foreign cash, as well as sums withdrawn from deposits opened in rubles if they are paid in foreign currency. Taxpayers (see articles 2,3 of the law) are any subject carrying out transactions on purchasing foreign currency, except the Central Bank of the Russian Federation and organizations financed only from the budgets of all levels and credit organizations in cases when they buy foreign currency from other credit organizations.

Analyzing the law we can conclude that the legislator provides for levying the tax both for purchasing foreign currency and carrying out transactions considered equal to purchasing foreign currency.

3. Taxes paid by enterprises

3.1 Value added tax

Value Added Tax (VAT) is one of the most important taxes. Since the burden of paying VAT is transferred to the final consumer, it is considered an indirect tax. But in cases when goods (work, services) are sold within the enterprise for its own needs, when construction is carried out based on self-financing and in some other cases, VAT can obtain features of a direct tax.

The major document determining the procedure of levying VAT is the Law of the Russian Federation of December 6, 1991 "On the value added tax) with later changes.

Value added tax is a form of budget collection a part of the added value created at all stages of production and defined as a difference between the value of sold goods, works and services and the value of the material costs for production of the sold goods, works and services (article 1 of the Law).

Since VAT has two objects of taxation – sale of goods (works, services) on the territory of the Russian Federation and goods imported to the territory of the Russian Federation, it is reasonable to discuss the legal position of taxpayers concerned with these two objects, separately.

Among those who pay VAT when selling goods (works, services) within the country, are any organizations (both commercial and non-commercial) having according to the legislation of the Russian Federation a status of a legal entity and performing economic or other commercial activity. This covers all commercial organizations (including enterprises with foreign investments); economic partnerships and companies, production cooperatives, state and municipal unitary enterprises for which according to clause 1, article 50 of the Civil Code of the Russian Federation, making profit is the major goal of activity. VAT payers are also industrial and financial organizations, insurance companies, banks etc.

Non-commercial organizations, public or religious associations performing entrepreneurial activity according to part 2, clause 3, article 50 of the Civil Code of the Russian Federation are also considered VAT payers. The major problem here relates to non-commercial organizations and to determine what is commercial activity, because only in this case do the organizations become VAT payers.

Enterprises are a special group which have not got an organizational and legal structure consistent with the new Civil Code of the Russian Federation. It should be noted that individual (family) enterprises and enterprises set up by private and public organizations on the basis of complete economic management are subject to transformation into business partnerships, societies, cooperatives or to liquidation by July 1, 1999 (clause 5, article 6 of the Federal Law of the Russian Federation of November 30, 1994 "On introduction into effect of the first part of the Civil Code of the Russian Federation". Stipulations based on unitary enterprises based on the right of operative management are applied to these enterprises until they are transformed or liquidated.

These enterprises are VAT payers. In case they are not transformed or liquidated by the date mentioned above, they are subject to compulsory liquidation upon the demand of the tax agency.

VAT payers include subsidiaries and branches of the organizations and other separate units which are not legal entities, but are selling goods (works, services).

The tax legislation does not specify the order of determining independent distribution, but according to the rules of the Civil Code, for a separate unit to be able to sell goods (works, services) independently, it must be established in the form of a subsidiary or a branch; and act on the basis of its own statute fixing their right on independent distribution; have an independent bank account; and carry on separate accounting.

Among the VAT payers are also international organizations and foreign legal entities performing production or other commercial activity within the territory of the Russian Federation. The law on the value added tax does not specify in what form the above mentioned organizations should perform their activity and how the problem should be solved in case of inconsistency in the definition of a legal entity concept in Russian and foreign legislation.

Concerning the goods imported to the territory of the Russian Federation, VAT payers are enterprises and other entities determined in accordance with clause 3, article 2 of the "Law on the value added tax". Application of VAT is carried out on the basis of the Customs Code of the Russian Federation of June 18, 1993 and of the "Law on the value added tax" (article 112, Customs Code of the Russian Federation). The Instruction of the State Customs Committee of the Russian Federation and State Taxation Service of the Russian Federation of January 30, 1993 "On the order of applying VAT and excise tax with regard to the goods imported to the territory of the Russian Federation" stipulates that VAT is paid by the declarant or other person determined by legislation relating to the customs duties. Thus, VAT payers at the customs are usually enterprises importing goods to the territory of Russia.

At the same time, in accordance with the letter of the State Taxation Committee of the Russian Federation of July 4, 1995 "On levying VAT from physical entities performing entrepreunerial activity without establishing a legal entity", citizens-entrepreneurs must pay VAT when they fulfill imports obligations. It should be emphasized that neither in the Customs Code of the Russian Federation, nor the "Law on the value added tax" do indicate that individuals are VAT payers at the customs.

The objects of VAT taxation are:

- turnover of goods (works, services) within the territory of the Russian Federation;
- turnover of goods (works, services) within the enterprise for its own production needs when expenses are not considered as production costs;
- goods imported to the territory of the Russian Federation

VAT relief are granted by means of a tax exemption for certain categories of payers and by means of withdrawal of certain elements of the taxation object from taxation.

20 % tax rate is applied to all objects which are not subject to a reduced VAT rate. For selling food and goods for children (the list has been approved by the Russian Federation Government) a reduced 10 % rate is applied.

3.2. Tax on enterprise profit

The tax on profit, along with VAT, is the major tax of enterprises and organizations. Levying of this tax is carried out in accordance with the Russian Federation Law of December 27, 1991 "The tax on profit of enterprises and organizations" (with later changes) and the instruction of the State Taxation Service of the Russian Federation of August 10, 1995 "On the order of calculation and payment of the tax on profit of enterprises and organizations".

Payers of the tax are enterprises and organizations including the budget (unitary) enterprises which are legal entities according to the Russian legislation; their subsidiaries and branches having a separate balance and account; as well as companies, firms and any other organizations performing business activity in the Russian Federation through permanent representation (foreign legal entities). A permanent representation of a foreign legal entity for taxation purposes is a subsidiary, bureau, office, agency, any other place for performing activity connected with exploration and development of mineral resources, performing of construction, installation, assembling, adjustment works, providing equipment service, rendering services and performing other works, as well as organizations and citizens empowered by foreign legal entities to perform representation functions in the Russian Federation.

The object of taxation is the profit of the enterprise which consists of the amount of profit from sales of products (works, services), of fixed assets or other property of the enterprises and revenue from non-sale transactions reduced by the sum of expenses on these transactions.

The tax rate on the profit of enterprises and organizations paid to the federal budget has been established at the amount of 13 %. The budget of the subjects of the Russian Federation the tax on the enterprise profit (including foreign legal entities) is paid at the rates established by the legislative (representative) bodies of these subjects at the amount not exceeding 22 %. The profit received from mediatory/ intermediary transactions and deals by exchanges, broker offices, banks and other credit organizations and insurers is taxed at the rates not exceeding 30 %. These tax rates may be changed during by the federal budget for the new fiscal year.

The "Law on profit tax" provides for tax relief in the form of reducing the taxable base by the sums used for specific legal purposes.

Besides the profit tax, enterprises pay taxes from the incomes:
- in the form of dividends received on shares belonging to the enterprise-shareholder, as well as incomes in the form of the interest received by the owners of the Russian Federation state securities, state securities of the subjects of the Russian Federation and securities of the local self-government bodies;
- income from participation in other enterprises created on the territory of the Russian Federation (at the 15 % rate);
- income (including income from renting and other ways of using casinos, other gambling houses (places) and other gambling business, videotecs (from video demonstration), from renting video and audio cassettes and recordings defined by the difference between

the revenue and expenses included in the product (works, services) cost, considered in taxation of the profit except for the expenses on payment for labour. The above mentioned income is taxed at 70 % rate except for the income from the casino and other gambling business are taxed at the 90 % rate.

In cases of foreign legal entities, only the part of the profit received in connection with their activity in the Russian Federation is taken into consideration for taxation purposes. For taxation purposes, the profit of a foreign legal entity is not considered if it is received from foreign trade transactions carried out exclusively on its behalf and connected with buying products (works, services) in the Russian Federation, as well transactions on export in the Russian Federation of products (works, services) when the legal entity becomes the owner of the product (works, services) before crossing the state border. Profit received from selling goods from warehouses located on the territory of the Russian Federation and belonging to or rented by a foreign legal entity is subject to taxation.

In cases when a foreign legal entity performs activity not only in the Russian Federation, but also beyond its territory and does not separately register profit from the activity of the permanent representation in Russia, the tax amount may be determined on the basis of the calculation agreed by the taxpayer and by the tax agency supervising tax payments to the budget. If it is not possible to determine directly the profit received by the foreign legal entity from its activity in Russia, the taxation agency can calculate it on the basis of the turnover or production costs on the basis of the 25 % profitability rate.

Specific rules of taxation of foreign legal entities income and profit are presented in the Instruction of the State Taxation Service of the Russian Federation of May 16, 1995 "On taxation of foreign legal entities income and profit". It should be noted that this instruction has become an independent act because it contains many important rules not included in the law on profit tax.

3.3. Excise duties

Excise duties – are indirect taxes included in the price of a product. These taxes were adopted by Russian Federation Law of December 1991 "On excise duties". By the Federal Law of the Russian Federation of March 7, 1996 "On changes in the Russian Federation Law On excise duties" this law was presented with a new wording. The State Taxation Service published the Instruction of July 22, 1996 "On the order of calculation and payment of excise taxes".

Payers of excise duties are enterprises and organizations producing and selling goods subject to excise duties.

An object of charging the excise duty is the value of the self-produced goods. The taxable turnover is determined from their value calculated on the basis of the sales price without VAT.

A list of goods subject to excise duties and the excise duty rates are established by the Russian Federation law "On excise duties" and in some cases – by the Government of the Russian Federation. Goods subject to the excise duty include many kinds of alcoholic drinks, sturgeon and salmon caviar, tobacco products, cars and trucks, jewelry, oil and oil products etc.

Excise duties are not charged on exported goods (except certain kinds of mineral raw materials) because for the purpose of the excess profit recovery in this case a mechanism of collecting customs duties is applied. When intermediate organizations sell goods for export, the amounts of paid excise taxes are returned to these organizations by taxation agencies.

The amount of the excise duty is defined by the taxpayer on the basis of the value of the sold goods and effective rates. Payment of excise duties to the budget takes place depending on the kind of the product – every ten days or monthly. For the control purposes taxpayers must submit special calculations to the taxation agencies at the place of their location. They carry responsibility for the payment being correct and on time.

On the goods imported to Russia, excise tax payers are their declarants. The purpose of taxation in this case is the customs value of the goods plus the sum of customs duties and fees.

The Law "On excise taxes" provides for a relief. For example, goods used for producing other products are exempt from excise duties.

3.4. Tax on the property of enterprises

This type of tax is regulated by the Russian Federation Law December 13, 1991 "On the tax on the property of enterprises" with changes and additions made in the Russian Federation Laws of July 16, 1992 "On changes and additions to the tax system of Russia»; of December 22, 1992 "On changes and additions to certain Russian Federation Laws on taxes»; of March 6, 1993 "On changes and additions to the Russian Federation Laws On state pensions in RSFSR", "On the tax on the inherited property or property received as a gift", Russian Federation Laws "On the State duty", "On tax on the property of enterprises", "On the value added tax", "On income tax of physical entities; of June 3, 1993 of "On changes and additions to the Russian Federation Law "On the tax on the property of enterprises»; of April 25, 1995 "On changes and additions to the Russian Federation Law "On the tax on the property enterprises".

The tax is calculated on property belonging to the enterprise (including main assets, production stocks, long-term investments, production costs which are in the process of being turned into some kind of property except monetary resources on the accounts of the enterprise, as well as the property exempt from taxation.

The Law establishes the procedure of assessing average yearly value of the taxable property. For taxation purposes the average yearly value of the taxable property is determined by means of adding the value of the property at the beginning of each month and dividing the result by the number of the months the enterprise has been functioning.

The law establishes only the upper limit of the tax rate. Depending on the type of the enterprise activity, a real tax amount is determined by the bodies of the subjects of the RF.

3.5. Taxes – sources of road funds

Taxes paid to road funds are regulated by the Russian Federation Law of October 18, 1991 "On the road funds in the Russian Federation". According to this law, levying of the following taxes has been provided:
- on selling fuel and lubricants
- on motor roads users
- on vehicles owners
- on acquisition of motor vehicles

The tax on selling fuel and lubricants and 0.25 of the motor roads users tax goes to the Federal road fund. Other taxes (including 0,75 of the tax on motor roads users) go to the territory road funds.

– The amount of the **tax on motor roads users**, the tax on vehicles owners and the tax on acquisition of motor vehicles are included by the taxpayers into the composition of expenses on production and sales of the product (works, services). The source of payment of the tax on selling fuel and lubricants is the profit of the enterprise before the calculation and payment of the profit tax.

The order of calculation of taxes imposed by the Law "On the road funds in the Russian Federation" is determined by the Instruction of the State Taxation Service of the Russian Federation of May 15, 1995 "On the order of calculation and payment of taxes entering the road funds". It should be emphasized that this Instruction has determined many issues which are not presented in the Law (for example, the order of calculation, time of payment, etc.) which is not justifiable from the point of view of the law.

Payers of the tax on selling fuel and lubricants are associations, organizations and enterprises irrespective of the form of ownership, departmental affinity or organizational and legal forms, as well as individual entrepreneurs. The object of taxation for enterprises producing fuel and lubricants is their sales turnover based on the real selling prices without considering VAT. In resale of fuel and lubricants the object of taxation is the sum of the difference between sales revenue (without VAT) and the cost of purchasing (without VAT).

The tax is paid at the 25 % rate every ten days, monthly or quarterly depending on the amount of the taxable turnover.

The tax on motor roads users is paid by enterprises and organizations which are legal entities. Non-commercial/non-profit organizations are taxpayers when they have income from some business activity.

The object of taxation is : in production of goods and providing services (works, services) sales earnings (gross income); in resale of the purchased goods – the turnover.

In calculating the tax, VAT, the excise duty, and the tax on selling fuel and lubricants are excluded from the tax base. For some organizations (exchanges, religious organizations, banks and other credit organizations, investment funds etc.), special features for determining a taxable base have been established.

In accordance with article 54 of the Russian Federation Law of February 27, 1997 "On the federal budget for the year 1997" in 1997 (until the changes introduced into the Russian Federation Law "On road funds in the Russian Federation») the following tax rates on the motor road users were adopted:

– 2.5 % from the product (works, services) sales revenue;
– 2.5 % of the sum of the difference between the selling price and the price of purchasing of goods sold as a result of the procurement, supply and trade activity.

The amount of the tax on motor roads users is determined on the basis of independent reporting and accounting is paid to the road funds monthly or quarterly on the basis of the tax calculations.

Tax relief has been determined for the enterprises providing maintenance of the motor roads for public use (out-of-town motor roads being the property of the Russian Federation).

The tax from owners of vehicles is paid by persons possessing vehicles (cars, motorcycles, buses) and other pneumatic self-propelled machines and mechanisms at the rates adopted depending on the power of the engine.

This tax is imposed on the vehicles which are subject to proper registration at the state Auto-Inspection and in other similar agencies which give the state registration signs for participation in the traffic in accordance with the Decree of the Russian Federation Government of August 12, 1994 "On the state registration of the auto-motor-vehicles and other types of the self-propelled vehicles within the territory of the Russian Federation". Registration, and technical inspection of the vehicles is not performed without submitting proof of payment.

The tax rates are adopted depending on the type and power of the engine.

Disabled persons of all groups, enterprises providing maintenance of motor roads of public use, public transport enterprises and other categories are exempt from this tax. Bodies of state power of the subjects of the Russian Federation have a right to establish additional privileges for certain categories of taxpayers.

Payers of the tax on acquisition of motor vehicles are enterprises, organizations and individual entrepreneurs acquiring motor vehicles by means of sale and purchase, barter, leasing and installments.

The object of taxation is the selling price (without VAT and excise duty. Taxable cost is determined based on :
– selling price without VAT and the excise duty;
– current market prices – in barter terms;
– balance value – in leasing;
– customs value – in purchasing outside Russia.

The tax on acquisition of motor vehicles is calculated at the following rates: trucks, pickups, vans, buses, specialized automobiles and cars – 20 %, trailers and semi-trailers – 10 %.

Motor vehicles acquired for further resale are not subject to the tax on acquisition of motor vehicles (if the organization has a license for automobile trade).

Registration and re-registration of motor vehicles is not performed without submitting proof of tax payment to the agency performing registration or re-registration. The tax is paid within five days from the day of acquisition of a motor vehicle. For enterprises and organizations the day of acquisition is the day when the vehicle becomes a fixed assets, and for individual entrepreneurs – the day of actual acquisition.

A relief in the form of exemption from the tax payment exists for citizens acquiring cars for personal use, public associations or disabled persons, and enterprises providing maintenance of motor roads for public use.

3.6. Tax on transactions with securities

In accordance with the Russian Federation Laws of December 12, 1991, of October 18, 1995 payers of the tax on transactions with securities are legal persons – emitents of securities.

The purpose of taxation according to law is the nominal amount of the securities issue announced. The nominal amount of the securities issued by the company realizing the increase of the authorized capital by re-evaluation of assets is not an object of this kind of taxation according to the decision of the Russian Federation Government.

Civil law relations connected to securities are regulated by articles 142–149 of the Civil Code of the Russian Federation which is extremely important for defining legal content of the security in the process of selecting a type of securities taxation. At present, there are many problems with security taxation due to the large and frequent emissions of securities (trade and investment ones) performed through banks.

In the Law on the tax of securities transactions only one object of taxation is actually mentioned – the amount of the securities issue. In accordance with article 3 of the law, the tax rate is adopted at 0.8 % of the nominal amount of the issue. In case of refusal to register the issue, the tax is not refunded.

The payer calculates the tax amount independently based on the nominal amount of the issue and the corresponding tax rate. The tax on transactions with securities performed in hard currency is calculated in rubles at the exchange rate determined by the Central Bank of the Russian Federation and effective on the day of the issue registration.

The tax is paid by the payer simultaneously whilst submitting documents for issue registration and it is transferred to the federal budget.

4. Taxation agencies and tax control

In accordance with the Decree of the USSR Council of Ministers of January 24, 1990 "On the State Taxation Service", the State Taxation Service of the USSR was established. The legal status of this agency was determined by the USSR Law of May 21, 1990 "On the rights, duties and responsibility of the state tax inspections". The structure and issues of subordination, as well as functions of the tax inspections of different levels were determined by the Statute of the State Taxation service approved by a decree of the USSR Council of Ministers of July 26, 1990.

On March 21, 1991 Russian Federation Law "On the State Taxation Service of the RSFSR" changed the legal status of this service. The Decree of the Russian Federation President of December 31, 1991 "On the State Taxation Service of the Russian Federation" approved the Statute of the State Taxation Service of the Russian Federation and the Statute of the Employees Ranks at the State Taxation Service of the Russian Federation. The Russian Federation Law "On foundations of the State Taxation service of the Russian Federation" also determines some issues related to the rights, duties and responsibility of the taxation service and its officials.

In accordance with the prevailing legislature, the State Taxation Service of the Russian Federation has a unified system of control over the observance of the tax legislation. Its authority covers both state and local taxes. The State Taxation Service of the Russian Federation has an independent system of control over the observance of the tax legislation. Independence is understood as, first of all, independence from local bodies of power and administration.

This is a permanent realization of the principle of the division of powers: the right of the local bodies of power to introduce local taxes, to adopt tax rates, and to determine tax relief as opposed to the duty of the taxation inspection to act in strict consistency with law. Taxation inspections implement only those decisions and decrees of the local bodies of power on taxation issues which have been passed in consistency with law and within their powers. Local bodies have no right to change or cancel the decisions of taxation agencies or give operative directions to them. All state tax inspections are legal entities; they have their own operating budget, current accounts in banks and a stamp containing the state coat-of-arms of the Russian Federation and the name of the inspection.

A tax audit of enterprises and organizations is a major means of state control over taxpayer's activity. At the same time, it should be noted that the prevailing tax legislature does not define the status and procedure of conducting such audits which may result in legal arbitrariness and violation of taxpayers' rights and interests.

According to article 14 of the "Law of the foundations of the taxation system" taxation agencies have a right to audit all the documents related to the calculation and payment of taxes and to receive necessary explanations and information on the questions arising in the process of audits. These issues are regulated in clause 1, article 7 of the RSFSR Law of March 21, 1991 "On the state taxation service of RSFSR" where all subjects and objects of tax audits are listed.

More detailed regulation of tax audits is presented in internal administrative rules. For example, Temporary Directions of the State Taxation Service on the order of conducting documentary audits of legal entities irrespective of the types of activity and the form of ownership (including enterprises with a special regime of work), on consistency with tax legislation, correctness of calculation, complete and timely payment of the profit tax to the budget (a letter of the State Taxation Service of the Russian Federation of August 28, 1992 and the letter of the State Taxation Service of the Russian Federation of April 30, 1993). It should be noted that such documents are only of persuasive authority and do not apply to taxpayers.

Tax audits are divided into cameral and documentary which, in their turn, are divided into planned and unplanned, complete and thematic (selective), as well as counter audits.

Subjects of tax audits include:
- ministries, departments, state offices and organizations including judicial bodies;

- commercial/business enterprises and organizations based on any forms of ownership;
- non-state and non-commercial enterprises and organizations;
- citizens of the Russian Federation, foreign citizens and stateless persons.

The objects of a tax audit are financial documents, accounting books, reports, plans, budgets, tax returns, agreements, contracts, orders, business correspondence and other documents connected to the calculation and payment of taxes and other obligatory payments to the budget.

The State Taxation Service of the Russian Federation in a letter of September 14, 1993 explained that the documentary audit, first of all, applies to the documents prepared by the taxpayer and must be conducted at the enterprises premises. It is not lawful to make any conclusion about a taxpayer's honesty or apply any financial sanctions only on the basis of certain observations of the activity, for example, in the process of auditing observation of the movement of money in the bank account. In the process of auditing, the taxation agencies have a right to require necessary explanations and information which arise questions, except information connected with commercial secrets defined in the order specified by the legislation.

Taxation agencies have a right of inspection (according to the present rules) any production, warehouse, trade or other premises of the taxpayer connected with the making of profit (income) or covered by tax grounds. In case of absence or neglect of keeping an account of the taxation object, the tax agencies have a right to determine the tax amounts due to be paid to the budget by means of calculations based on the information on similar enterprises (clause 6 of the Russian Federation President's Decree of May 23, 1994 "On taking complex measures on timely and complete payment of taxes and other obligatory charges to budget»).

5. Responsibility for violation of the tax legislation

Responsibility for violation of the tax law is provided for in articles 13 and 15 of the "Law on the foundations of the tax system" and article 22 of the "Law of the income tax from individuals".

Responsibility envisaged by article 13 of the "Law on the foundations of the tax system" can be applied both in the case of violation of the tax legislation in calculation and payment of taxes and duties included in the Russian Federation tax system.

The subject of tax violation having committed the violation is usually the taxpayer. At the same time, the concept of the taxpayer and the subject of responsibility are not identical because in the legislation there may be specific cases when tax violation may be committed by another person (for example, the tax collector).

The prevailing legislation names the following subjects of responsibility:
– taxpayers (legal and individual entities);
– tax collectors (legal entities and entrepreneurs);
– banks and other credit organizations responsible for transferring taxes to the budget and non-budget funds.

Major kinds of tax violations and measures of responsibility for them have been determined in clause 1, article 13 of the "Law on the foundations of the tax system" according to which the taxpayer who has violated the tax legislation in the cases specified by law carries responsibility in the form of:
a) recovery of the whole amount of the concealed or reduced income (profit), or of the amount of tax for other concealed (or left out of account) required for tax purpose and a fine for a similar amount. In case of repeated violation – a due amount and the double-fold amount of fine. If the court establishes there has been intentional concealment or a reduction of income (profit), a fine at the five-fold amount of the concealed or reduced amount of income (profit) may

be recovered to the federal budget according to the court judgment or court decision on the lawsuit brought by the taxation agency or prosecutor.

b) A fine for each of the following violations:

> absence of accounting taxation objects and for keeping account of the taxation object with violations of the determined procedure which have resulted in concealing or reducing of income for the examined period – in the amount of 10 % of the additionally charged tax amounts;

> for non-submission or late submission to the tax agency of the documents necessary for calculation and payment of tax – to the amount of 10 % of the tax amount due to be paid for a certain period;

c) recovery of a fine from the taxpayer in case of a delayed tax payment at the amount of 0, 30 % of the unpaid tax amount for every day of the delay starting from the due date of payment of the discovered delayed tax amount if the law does not provide for other fine amounts. Recovery of a fine does not free the taxpayer from other kinds of responsibility.

d) other sanctions provided for by legislation.

Moreover, the tax legislation contains specific details applied with regard to persons promoting a tax payment. For banks and other credit organizations responsibility in the form of fine has been established under article 15 of the "Law on the foundations of the tax system.»

Responsibility for violations of the tax legislation applies to all taxpayers irrespective of the form of ownership, organizational and legal forms, departmental affinity etc.

In the prevailing tax legislation of the Russian Federation, the procedure in cases dealing with tax violations or general rules of imposing sanctions are practically missing. That is why conditions and procedure of applying responsibility for violations of the tax legislation have been developed by the norm-making of the State Taxation Service of the Russian Federation, as well as by the legal practice of taxation agencies and courts.

The taxpayer who has violated tax legislation may be released from responsibility even if his/her actions have violated tax law. For example, the taxpayer is released from responsibility from financial sanctions provided for in sub-clauses "a" and "b", clause 1, article 13 of the "Law of the foundations of the tax system" in case he/she:

–   makes mistakes resulting in non-payment or incomplete payment of taxes and other obligatory payments;
–   voluntarily/independently corrected mistakes before the taxation agency audit;
–   in due order entered corrections to the accounting reports and to the calculations on taxes and payment.

However, because of the delay in paying taxes to the budget, a fine for non-punctual tax payment is recovered from the taxpayer.

These conditions of releasing responsibility for violation of the tax legislation have been provided for not in legislation, but in the letters of the State Taxation Service of the Russian Federation of May 10, 1995 "On non-application to the taxpayer of financial sanctions for violation of the tax legislation in case of voluntary/independent correction of mistakes in the accounting documents" and of October 30, 1995 "In addition to the letter of the State Taxation Service of the Russian Federation of May 10, 1995."

The Russian Federation President's Decree of May 8, 1996 "On main directions of the tax reform in the Russian Federation and measures on enforcing tax and payment discipline" also established that technical mistakes in preparing and calculating tax payments which are independently disclosed by the taxpayer and in due time passed to the tax agencies are not considered as tax violations. The State Taxation Service of the Russian Federation in its letter of June 28, 1996 "On realization of certain rules of the Russian Federation President's Decree of May 8, 1996 "On main directions of the tax reform in the Russian Federation and measures on enforcing tax and payment discipline" also explained that in this case the fine for untimely tax payment and other obligatory payments is not recovered. Besides, in the opinion of the State Taxation Service, any reductions of financial results in calculation of the taxable base and taxes made by taxpayers may be considered technical mistakes if they have not been a deliberate tax violation (Letters of the State Taxation Service of November 22, 1996; of December 10, 1996; of December 14, 1996).

6. Tax disputes

The prevailing legislation provides for two ways of resolving tax disputes between taxation agencies and taxpayers.

An administrative way means that the whole procedure of resolving disputes takes place only at the taxation agency. The taxpayer whose rights have been violated has a right to appeal to the tax authorities. But the practice shows that such a way does not fully protect the taxpayer's rights. Sometimes, consideration of taxpayers' arguments in the taxation agencies and higher taxation instances is not impartial. Taxpayers prefer therefore to appeal to the independent judicial bodies.

The russian judicial system includes courts of general and specialized jurisdiction. The latter includes the Constitutional Court – a judicial body of the constitution which has independent control exercising judicial power in the form of constitutional court proceedings (article 1 of the Federal constitutional law "On the Constitutional Court of the Russian Federation"). This body considers disputes of a financial/legal nature. Its decisions in this field:
- provides exclusion from prevailing tax laws on the basis of unconstitution of applicable tax regulations;
- contributes to restoration of the violated rights of citizens;
- actively influences the legislative process. Many decisions of judicial bodies of the constitution control contain important directions resulting from the interpretation constitutional rules;
- contributes to elaboration of general criteria of the constitutionality of tax laws and other acts which can be used by the courts of general jurisdiction and other judicial bodies. For example, on August 5,

1996, a decision of the Judicial Board on civil cases of the Kursk regional court entered into legal force. It invalidated clause1.3. of the Kursk regional Duma decision "On regional taxes" of August 12, 1994 envisaging adoption of the tax in excess of gross income received by enterprises and individuals in a calendar year. This according to court opinion, contradicted federal legislature and eventually prevented the realization of constitutional principles on the freedom of entrepreneurship and other economic activity not forbidden by law.

Thus, the Constitutional Court of the Russian Federation together with other judicial bodies solves and controls problems of providing legality in the financial field.

7. New Tax Code of the Russian Federation

According to Federal Law "On carrying into effect of the first part of Tax Code of the Russian Federation "this part of the Tax Code has come into force on January 1, 1999.

This Tax Code is the first codified legislative act where the rights and duties and responsibilities of tax agencies and tax payers are regulated. It reflects the basic legal and economic principles of taxation. They are amongst others the following:

– The principle of equality of the tax burden. This means a liability to pay taxes and an equality of all tax payers in terms of tax legislation. The principle follows for directly from art. 8,19 and 57 of the Constitution of the RF. The principle implies,first, that it is not permitted to impose additional taxes or taxes or public fees with higher than normal rates or tax relief in dependency of the form of property, nationality of physical persons or the territory of the source of capital (clause 3 art. 3 of Tax Code); second, everyone´s liability to pay legally imposed taxes or public fees (clause1 art. 3 of Tax Code).

- The principle of legislating taxes only by laws. This principle is, as a matter of fact, confirmed in the art. 57. 75 and 76 of the Constitution of the RF. The principle means that taxes and public fees have to be imposed by competent bodies of state power and only in stipulated forms i.e. federal laws. (clause 5, art. 3 of Tax Code of RF).
- The principle of inadmissibility of retroactive tax legislation. This principle follows directly from art. 57 of the Constitution of the RF according to which legislation on new taxes or implying the worsening of the tax payer´s position cannot have a retroactive effect (clause 2–4, art 3 of the Tax Code).
- The principle of the priority of tax law over the non-tax law; This means that in case the non-tax law contains rules concerning tax issues, these rules may be applied only if they are consistent with corresponding principles of tax legislation.
- The principle that all issues of taxes ought to be in tax laws. This means that all details needed for tax calculation have to be defined in the law. Even if only one detail is missing in the law the taxpayer has the right to non-payment of the tax (clause 6 art. 3 and art.17 of Tax Code).

The tax legislation has been in this way made consistent with the Constitution of the RF. The whole system of tax legislation of the RF includes, thus, following sources of legal regulation of tax relations: the Constitution of the Russian Federation as a basic principle being the foundation for all branches of law; federal laws, among others, the Federal Law "On carrying into effect the first part of the Tax Code of the Russian Federation"; laws and other fundamental acts adopted by representative bodies of the subjects of the RF; international treaties; acts of federal executive bodies, executive bodies of subjects of the Federation, bodies of local self-government and bodies of non-budgetary funds.

The system of various taxes and public fees in the Russian Federation, according to art 12 of the Tax Code of the RF, consists of federal taxes and public fees, taxes and public fees of the subjects of the Russian Federation (also called "regional" taxes and fees) and local taxes and public fees. The list of federal, regional and local taxes and fees is defined in the art. 13–15 of the Tax Code. This system of the forms of taxes and fees in the Russian Federation will, however, be carried into effect simultaneously with the second part of the Tax Code of the RF (art 3 of the Law "On the carrying into effect the first part of the Tax Code of the RF). Therefore, according to the art 2 of the above mentioned Law the system of taxes and public fees determined by the clause 2 art 18 and art 19–21 of the Law 27.12. 91 "On the foundation of the Taxation System in the Russian Federation" is still valid.

It has to be noticed that in spite of the adoption of the Tax Code in consistency with the Constitution of the RF, the Tax Code defines more in detail the guarantees of the rights of the tax payer. For example all controversies, not yet corrected and all unclear rules of tax laws shall be interpreted in favour of the tax payer (or payer of public fees) according to the clause 7 of the art.3 of the Tax Code. There has also been enacted a presumption of innocence of a tax payer. Some changes have also been made concerning the rules of the tax payer´s responsibility. All these innovations and changes notwithstanding one has to admit that the Tax Code contains several clear failures of a legal-technical nature leading in several cases to making it impossible to apply some fundamental principles of the Tax Code. Thus, some alterations have to be made to the Tax Code.

On 17 August 1999 Federal Law "On carrying into effect of alterations and additions into the first part of the Tax Code of the RF" from 9.7.1999 came into force. This Law provides for alterations and additions to more than 120 articles (the total number of articles in this law is 142). It is, as a matter of fact, question of a new redaction of the first part of the Tax Code : a new publishing of the whole law text is presumed (art. 3 of the Federal Law 9.7.99, mentioned above). This Law corrects legal-technical mistakes, makes some issues more permanent and has some additions compared with the old version of the first part of the Tax Code. It is, however, evident that very big change of this part, made in less than half a year from the day of entering into force of the part first of the Tax Code, is not justified from point of view of implementation of law.

Evaluating generally the changes and additions to the Tax Code, introduced to this Code by the Law from 9.7. 1999, one may state that the changes did not remove all evident deficiencies of the Tax Code, but on the contrary, made them deeper, introduced some new obscurities and confusions to tax legislation. In some cases, keeping the general principles of taxation corresponding to the Constitution of the RF, the new Law of 9.7.1999 worsens, however, essentially the position of a law-abiding tax payer, deprives him/her of some guarantees against arbitrary acts of the tax authorities, granted by the first redaction of the first part of the Tax Code. Moreover, some rules of the new federal Code contradict private law and some other branches of law. It is, thus, not excluded that new corrections and additions to the first part of the Tax Code of the RF will be enacted in the future.

IV Land Law of the Russian Federation

Irina Aleksandrovna Ikonitskaya

1. Introduction

The land law has been emerged as an independent branch within the system of the Russian law following the October Revolution 1917, namely, the Decree on Land, was adopted in October 1917, which abolished the private ownership on land. The nationalisation of the land and the consequent consolidation of the ownership on land within the realm of the state meant, from the legal point of view, the withdrawal of the land from the commercial exchange and the redistribution of it by administrative methods.

Nowadays the private ownership on land in Russia has been reintroduced, the land market is in its stage of formation. This means that the land is again object of commercial exchange. Despite of these changes, the fact, that, the land law appears as a specific branch of the law, is still to be justified. The argument for it is the following. Notwithstanding the art.130 of the Civil Code of RF, that classifies the land as immovable property (i.e., the property which is impossible to relocate), it is immovable property with the very specific particularities.

The land represents natural resources of any country and constitutes an important material basis for the prosperity of any society. Therefore, the land fulfills a very important social function. The fundamental function of the land according to the art.9 of the Constitution of the RF is that it is the basis for life and prosperity for the people who populate it.

The above mentioned feature as well as the argument that the land has its own natural attributes, give the reason to establish for the government institutions, legal and natural persons a set of specific legal rules, designed for the socially and economically justified distribution, rational use and protection of the land. Taking into consideration the multitude of the subjects, who have the right to own land, the land law at present establishes the rules on the transfer of land, on the use and protection of land irrespective of the category of the rights on the use of land plots as well as it regulates the activities of the state institutions on the control of the rational use and the protection of land.

The land law is under process of transformation and constitutes one of the most important instruments in the land reform in Russia at present.

2. Land reform and its legal foundations

The agrarian reform in Russia aims to restructure agricultural economy in general and agricultural enterprises (collective and state farms) in particular. The land reform originally was conceived as a constituent part of the agrarian reform. However, for the time being, the land reform surpassed the limits of the agrarian reform and became a basis for the economic reform in general.

Main goals and general features of the land reform in Russia can be understood, by comparing the older legal acts since 1917, and the newer legal acts in force since 1990 until the present time.

The substantial legal acts at present that lay the basis for the land reform in Russia are the following:

- Constitution of the RSFSR;
- Resolution of the Congress of the People's Deputies of RSFSR "On the programme of regeneration of the Russian village and of the development of the agricultural sector", dated 3 December 1990;
- Law "On the land reform", dated 23 November 1990 with amendments, dated 27 December 1990;
- Law "On property in the RSFSR", dated 24 December 1990;
- Law "On the peasant's (farmer's) household", dated 22 November 1990;
- Land Code of the RF, dated 25 April 1991;
- Law "On public fee for land", dated 11 October 1991;
- Law "On the rights of the citizens of the RF to own as a private property and to sell the land plots for the subsidiary small-holdings, gardening and building of the dwelling-houses", dated 23 December 1992;
- Resolution of the Government of the RF 4.9.1992.708 "On the procedure of the privatization and the reorganization of the enterprises and organisations in the agricultural sector", dated 4 September 1992;
- Decree of the President of the RF "On sale of the land plots to citizens and to legal persons under the privatization of the state and municipal enterprises", dated 25 March 1992;
- Decree of the President of the RF "On approval of the Procedure of the sale of the land plots under privatization of the state and municipal enterprises, under enlargement and additional construction of these enterprises as well as of the land plots at the disposal of the citizens or of their organizations for the entrepreneurial activities", dated 14 June 1992;
- Decree of the President of the RF "On regulation of the land market and on the development of the agrarian reform in Russia", dated 27 October 1993;
- Constitution of the Russian Federation, dated 12 December 1993;
- Decree of the President of the RF "On bringing of the land legislation of the Russian Federation to conformity with the Constitution of the Russian Federation", dated 24 December 1993;

- Decree of the President of the RF "On implementation of the constitutional rights of the citizens on land", dated 7 March 1996.

The analysis of these legal acts allows to disclose three main trends in
the land reform if the Russian Federation.

The first trend was the redistribution of land. It was needed for the
restructuring process in the agricultural sector, namely, when side-by-
side with the existing forms of agricultural enterprises, as state and
collective farms, new enterprises, as individual farms and agricultural
co-operatives, appeared. New enterprises needed the land, but there
was no vacant land in Russia for agricultural use. That is why the
redistribution of the lands in the possession of the old enterprises has
been taking place in Russia. The art.1 of the Law "On the land reform"
stated:

"The land reform has for its goal the redistribution of the land in
order to create the favourable conditions for the development of the
alternative forms of the agricultural businesses on an equal footing, for
the formation of multistructural economy, the rational use and the
protection of land on the territory of the RSFSR. Under the land reform
the land shall be allocated to citizens, enterprises, organizations and
institutions, associations and partnerships and their rights on land will
be specified according to the legislation of the RSFSR".

The second trend and one of the goals of the land reform was the
transformation of the forms of ownership. It is well known that, according to the Decree "On the land", adopted in 1917, the private
ownership on land had been abolished in Russia "forever" and the land
had been let at the disposal of all the people, cultivating it. The state
had the exclusive rights of ownership on land until the end of the 1990.
The law "On the land reform", dated 23 November 1990, granted the
possibility of the ownership on land to the citizens, side by side with
the state. The right to possess agricultural land under private ownership was reintroduced in the art.12 of the Constitution of the RSFSR
by the Second Congress of the People's Deputies. The right of private
ownership on land for the citizens was recognized by the Law "On the
ownership in the RSFSR" and in the Land Code of the Russian Federa-

tion. Recently the right of private ownership on land was confirmed in the art.9 and art.36 of the Constitution of the Russian Federation.

The third trend of the land reform was the introduction of the payment for the use of land in the form of land tax and of rent payment. The principle of rent-free use of land was the guiding principle from 1917 until 28 February 1990, when the "Fundamentals on the land of the Union of the SSR and the Republics" introduced the principle of payment for the use of land. This latter principle was adopted by the subsequent legislation of the Russian Federation, as, for example, by the Land Code of the RF, by the Law "On rent payment for land" and was specified in the acts of the Government of the Russian Federation.

The realization of the first trend of the land reform, i.e., of the redistribution of the land or of the allotment of land to the citizens, who wish to set up agricultural enterprises, is realized in two ways, depending on the fact whether the applicant was already working at the agricultural enterprise (usually, at the state or collective farm) or not. In case, if the applicant is a member of a collective farm or a employee of a state farm, the land for his new farm shall be allotted from his former enterprise. If the applicant is a newcomer, the allotment shall take place from the specific stock of land which, in its own turn, is formed out of the allotments, taken from the existing agricultural enterprises.

The realization of the second and third trends will be specified in the chapters on ownership of the land and on payments on land.

3. System of the land legislation of the Russian Federation

Contemporary land legislation of the Russian Federation is a system of the legislative and subordinate acts which regulate complex social processes in connection with: the rights of ownership and other rights on the land; the activities of legal and natural persons and government agencies for the rational use and protection of land on all areas of social life.

The Constitution of the Russian Federation, the supreme legislative act on land, introduces the most important principles of the protection of land resources within the Russian Federation and of the ownership of these resources. According to the art.9 of the Constitution, the land is used and protected in the Russian Federation as the basis for life and activities of the people, populating it. This principle is forming the basis for every legislative and administrative act on land. For example, the land legislation contains a system of rules on the protection and the regeneration of the land in agricultural use, a system of rules on the allocation of land for building purposes, etc.

By the reintroduction of the right of private ownership on land in the Russian Federation, the Constitution confirms this right to be one of the basis of the legal status of persons and lays down its protection.

The Land Code stands apart from the other legislative acts within the system of the land legislation in the RF. A code of law is a fundamental act of the corresponding branch of law, which establishes the most important principles and regulates all the issues of the said branch of law. All the succeeding subordinative legal and administrative acts, made within the said branch of law, shall correspond to the rules of the code. Current Land Code of the RF was adopted on 25 April 1991 and embraces a considerable range of the issues on land. It refers as well to the subordinate acts and to the acts of the subjects of the Russian Federation. The Land Code consists of 15 chapters and of 127 articles. It deals with the general issues of the land law, as, for example, with the rights of ownership and other rights on land; allotment of land plots; rights and duties on use and protection of land; payment for the use of land; the basic idea and general principles of the carrying out the state land cadastre and of the exercising of the state control for the use and protection of land; liability for infringement of the land legislation. Specific part of the Land Code deals with the different types of lands: lands in agricultural use, lands of municipalities; lands for industrial use, lands for the needs of transport, infrastructure, telecommunications, for military defense and specific use; lands of the nature reserve, of the medicinal, recreational and historical significance; lands under forest and water areas. A specific chapter deals with the international treaties, setting the priority of the rules of the international treaties over those of the national legislation of Russia.

After the Land Code was adopted, a number of considerable political, economic and legal changes have taken place in Russia. Among them are: the dissolution of the Soviet Union; the extension of the presidential powers to amend the laws in economic sphere, following the dramatic events in October 1993; the approval of the new Constitution of the Russian Federation on 12 December 1993. All these changes left their marks on the development of the land legislation. First of all, a number of decrees of the President of the Russian Federation, mentioned above, was approved; these acts triggered the evolution of the land market by extending the rights of the private ownership on land to all sectors of the economy and not only to agricultural sector as it was stipulated in the legislative acts of the beginning of the 1990-ies. Secondly, as it was already mentioned, the new Constitution of the Russian Federation was adopted on 12 December 1993, which abrogated all the restrictions for the private ownership on land in the Land Code. Therefore, the Decree of the President of the Russian Federation "On bringing land legislation of the Russian Federation in conformity with the Constitution of the Russian Federation", dated 24 December 1993, made a considerable number of the articles of the Land Code of the RF invalid, mainly from its first chapters, as well as certain articles of the Law "On the land reform". In particular, the articles on the types of rights on the land plots, on the conditions for transfer of the land plots in the ownership of the legal and natural persons, on the procedure of the allotment of the land plots to the citizens, etc., were abrogated. This situation created legal vacuum in the land law. The need for the enactment of the new Land Code of the RF became evident. The new draft Land Code was approved by the State Duma on 11 June 1997 and by the Federation Council on 3 July 1997. But the President of the Russian Federation vetoed the new law on 21 July 1997.

The new Civil Code of the Russian Federation was approved on 21 October 1994 and came into force on 1 January 1995. It contains rules on the land issues as well. Therefore the problem of correlation between the civil and land legislation in the land questions emerged. This problem has not merely theoretical, but also an important practical impact on the enactment of the new Land Code. It is very important to determine clearly to what extent the norms of the Land Code should correspond to those of the Civil Code and vice versa. This problem unsolved on the theoretical level and aggravated by the disagreements among the deputies of the Russian parliament on this issue lead to the situation, that the chapter 17 of the Civil Code on the ownership on land and other rights on land, will come into force only after the adoption of the new Land Code.

It is possible, however, to determine the correlation of the land and civil legislation by analysing the corresponding articles of the Civil Code. The art.2 of the Civil Code (part I) classifies, among the others, the legal status of the participants of the commercial exchange, the origins and the way of using the property rights and other rights in immovables, as well as the regulation of the contractual and non-contractual obligations as civil law issues. Regarding the property rights and other rights on land, the Civil Code only mentions that the land may be in the ownership of the state, of a municipality or of a legal person (art.214), and that the rights on the land plots can be of the various categories: the estate of inheritance, the right of the permanent use of land, and the easement (art.216) etc. What concerns the issues of transfer of the rights on land from one person to another, the Civil Code leaves it for the specific land legislation (art.129, 209).

The art.218 of the Civil Code on the grounds of the acquisition of the property rights through the conclusion of corresponding agreements explains to the origins of the rights of the private ownership on land only partially because the rights on the private ownership on land can emerge, among other grounds, as a consequence of an administrative act or in the process of privatization of the state lands according to the land legislation.

Regarding the origins of the other rights on land besides ownership, the right of the estate of inheritance, according to the art.265 of the Civil Code, come into being on the grounds, set by the land legislation; the right of the permanent use of land, according to the art.268 of the

Civil Code, appears upon the decision of the state or municipal body whichever have the competence to allot the land plots. Both above mentioned articles may come into force only after the approval of the new Land Code of the RF. The analysis of these articles gives reasons to make the conclusion that the procedure of the acquisition of the above mentioned rights on estate should be determined by the land legislation.

The art.260 (chapter 17) contains an important principle on the use of the land plots, the principle of use for specific purposes. But the procedure of the determination of the specific purposes for the land plots and the potential alteration of them has not been specified in the Civil Code.

The part 2 of the Civil Code deals with the specific types of contracts. According to the art.13 of the Law "On the introduction of the second part of the Civil Code of the Russian Federation", dated 22 December 1995, the rules of the second part of the Civil Code in the sections, concerning the contracts on the land plots, are applicable to the extent the land legislation allows. Therefore, from the analysis of the rules of the civil legislation, mentioned above, the conclusion follows that the latter relate to the rules of the land legislation as rules of lex generalis. In other words, it is necessary to apply the basic concepts and the principles of the civil law to the issues, connected with the ownership on land and with related rights on land, different from ownership. In the same time, the land legislation shall convey the specific attribute of the land, i.e., the fact that the land is not merely the immovable property, but the most important part of the natural resources, the feature, which justifies the presumable restrictions on the free transfer of land by way of enactment of specific regulations with particularly strict rules.

In case if the land legislation allows to conclude certain agreements on the land plots, the conclusion of the agreement, its realization and all consequences of the agreement shall conform the civil law rules. This idea is based on the art.3 of the Civil Code. According to this article, the rules of the civil law nature, included into non civil law legislative acts, shall conform the Civil Code.

The system of the land legislation includes, besides the legislative and subordinate acts of the Russian Federation, the legislative and subordinate acts of the subjects of the Russian Federation. According to the art.72 (k) of the Russian Constitution, the land legislation belongs to the joint competence of the Russian Federation and its subjects. This situation creates the problem of division of the concrete competencies between the central and regional authorities in the matters of the land legislation. This problem has not a purely theoretical but also a significant practical impact, since the solution of it influences directly on the content of the new Land Code of the Russian Federation.

The Constitution of the Russian Federation plays the primary role in the resolution of this problem by asserting in its art.36 that the conditions and the order of the use of land shall be regulated by the federal law. In the same time, the Constitution do not specify what one should understand under "the conditions" and "the order" of the use of land. It is only possible to interpret these terms at present by analysing the current Land Code, as well as the project of the new draft Land Code. The analysis may suggest the following. "The conditions" embrace the categories of the rights on land; payments for the allotment and the use of land (or no payments at all, in case the land was granted for free and no rentals were stipulated); concomitant duties for the user of land, in case the law specifies them; the conditions for the deprivation of the rights for the use of land. "The order" of the use of land includes the more detailed rights and duties on the use of land, designed for a number of specific purposes; the procedure of the control of the implementation of the law by the state bodies; the issues on the management of the land by the state bodies, e.g., setting out the plan for the use of the stock of land, carrying out the state land cadastre, the issues on the organization of the use of land.

Taking into consideration that according to the art.71 of the Constitution of the Russian Federation, the civil legislation is in the exclusive competence of the Russian Federation, the rules on the land issues, included into the Civil Code, may not be changed or specified in the legislation of the subjects of the Russian Federation.

Thus, for example, the list of the grounds for termination of the ownership under the Civil Code is exhaustive and cannot be supplemented with legislative acts of the Subjects of the Russian Federation. What concerns the termination of the other rights on land, the list may be complemented by the legislative acts of the subjects of the Russian Federation, unless the federal authorities make the exhaustive list on these rights in the federal land legislation as well.

4. Land ownership law within the Russian Federation

Art.9 of the Constitution of the Russian Federation asserts that the land in the Russian Federation may be in private, state, municipal and other forms of ownership.

The process of formation of the law of private ownership in contemporary Russian land legislation has undergone several stages.

Private ownership of land in the Russian Federation, was introduced by the Law "On the land reform", dated 23 November 1990, it concerned the private persons only, who were engaged in agriculture. According to the legislation of that period, private persons had the rights to come into possession of the land plots for the purpose of subsidiary small-holdings, gardening and building of dwelling-houses. Besides that, the lands of the reorganized state and collective farms were transferred into common ownership of their employees and of the people, engaged in all kinds of auxiliary services within relevant areas of habitation, where the farms were located.

In 1992 the circle of persons, who had the right to come into possession of land plots, was extended. A number of private persons, among them persons who posessed land plots for the building of summer cottages without using them for gardening (as was previously required) and persons engaged in private business in the non-agricultural sector were allowed to own the land. The individual acquired also a possibility to own the land. According to the Decree of the President of the RF "On sale of the land plots to citizens and to individuals under the privatization of the state and municipal enterprises", dated 25 March 1992, individuals were entitled to acquire the land plots which belonged to the enterprises under privatization and the land plots, necessary for the extension of their economic activities. However, the question remained unanswered as to whether individuals had the rights to take into possession the land for new enterprises, not connected with the privatization, as well as the land for any other business activity. Unfortunately, even today we do not have answer to this question. Nevertheless, taking into consideration the abrogation of art.7 of the Land Code, which laid down the list of the categories of persons and of the categories of activities, allowing to take the land into the ownership (the Decree of the President of the RF "On bringing of the land legislation of the Russian Federation to conformity with the Constitution of the Russian Federation", dated 24 December 1993), and art.212 and art.213 of the Civil Code of the RF, one can come to the conclusion that individuals may have the right to own the land in agricultural and in the non-agricultural sector of the economy, irrespective of the origins of the ownership of land, except for the land that according to the legislation, may only be in the state or in municipal ownership.

Rather important and politically intricate is the problem as to whether the subjects of the Russian Federation are allowed not to introduce private ownership of land on their territories. This question is appropriate, since according to art.72 of the Constitution of the Russian Federation and land legislation, the issues on the possession, use and disposal of the land are in the joint competence of the Russian Federation and of its subjects. Besides, the constitutions of a number of the subjects of the Russian Federation, for example of Bashkortostan and of the Republic Saha-Jakutia, consider the land as common national property of their multiethnical population.

To answer this question one should consider the following. Art.36 of the Constitution of the Russian Federation, dated 12 December 1993, affirmed that the citizens and their organisations may have the right to private ownership of land. This article is a part of a chapter on rights and freedoms of the person and the citizens which, according to art.17,

are inalienable and, according to the art.18, are of immediate applicability and, according to art.64, may not be changed otherwise than in a
way, determined by the Constitution of the Russian Federation. The
above mentioned leads to the conclusion, that every citizen of the
Russian Federation is entitled to own a land plot. In my opinion, the
restrictions in this field may concern only the categories of activities,
where the ownership on land cannot be transferred to a private person.
The constitutions of several subjects of the Russian Federation
adopted this solution. For example, art.11 of the Constitution of the
Republic of Mari El pronounces that its citizens may possess land plots
for subsidiary small-holdings, gardening and building of dwelling-
houses and sheds for household purposes. It follows from the said
article that the citizens, who embark on farming activities, cannot
possess the land plots in private ownership.

According to Moscow legislation currently in force (Regulation on
the categories of rights on the land plots in Moscow – Annex 7 to the
Resolution of the 11th session of the Council of Moscow of the 21th
session, dated 12 October 1992), citizens of the Russian Federation,
who own dwelling-houses in the Moscow area, may have the corresponding land plots in their ownership. At present a new draft law is
being prepared on the subject. According to it, private ownership on
land is allowed for private persons only in the cases, provided by the
legislative acts of Moscow.

According to the Decree of the President of the Russian Federation
"On regulation of the land market and on the development of the
agrarian reform in Russia", dated 27 October 1993, every owner of a
land plot shall be given a certificate of ownership with the mandatory
registration from a competent state institution. This certificate is a
document of the proof of the right of ownership and the basis for every
transaction with land plots.

According to art.36 of the Constitution of the Russian Federation
the owner of a land plot may possess, use and dispose of the land
according to his own discretion unless it does not damage the environment and does not infringe the interests of the third persons. On the
same time, as was mentioned earlier, the conditions and procedure of

the use of land are regulated by federal law (art.36, part 3). According to art.9 of the Constitution, the land should be used and protected, as it forms the basis for the living of the people who populate it.

The rules of the Constitution, recited above, give the reasons to conclude that the behaviour of a land owner shall conform with the requirements of the law, i.e., that the right of the ownership of land has certain limitations.

Examination of the current land and civil legislation reveals, that every power of the owner, constituting the content of the ownership, namely, the rights to possess, to use and to dispose is limited to a certain extent. The limitation of the right to possess consists in the fact, that land legislation establishes maximum limits for land plots of the ownership for every category of the economic activity and for building of the dwellings.

Land legislation imposes on the owners of the land plots the following duties besides the wide range of rights to use these plots: to use the land effectively, according to its specific purpose; to increase the fertility of the land; not to let the ecological condition be deteriorated because of the economic activity; to carry out measures for the protection of land, provided by law; while carrying out building activities, to conform to the requirements of the corresponding rules on building, on use of land, on planning and architecture, on fire safety, on sanitation and on nature protection.

By laying down these duties, for the owners of the land plots, the law guarantees a certain independence for them as well. The art.54 of the Land Code forbids the state bodies to intervene into the activities of owners connected with the use of land, except for the cases of infringement of the land legislation. If these are damages, resulting from the unlawful intervention of state bodies, there is full indemnification.

The current legislation, namely, the Decree of the President of the RF "On regulation of the land market and on the development of the agrarian reform in Russia", dated 27 October 1993, grants the owners of land plots (both private and legal persons) the right to sell, to leave land by inheritance, to mortgage, to give a lease, to invest the land plots as shares in companies, co-operatives and partnerships. According to the art.8 of the Decree the sale of the land plots with an alteration of their specific agricultural purpose into an other one, can only happen upon the decision of the corresponding executive body of the subject of the Russian Federation. The Resolution of the Government of the Russian Federation, dated 30 May 1993, introduced the Regulation on the sale of the land plots by the citizens of the Russian Federation. This regulates the sale of the land plots, designed for the subsidiary small-holdings, gardening and building of the dwelling-houses. The Resolution unambiguously mentions that the parties in the contract of sale of land plots cannot alter its specific purpose of use.

The legal regulation of the mortgage of the land plots is in a formative stage. The possibility of mortgage of the land plots as any other property is based on art.334 of the Civil Code. The article refers to the specific law on the mortgage of the land, which is not yet enacted. Temporarily the issues on mortgage are regulated by a Decree of the President of the RF "On the additional measures on the development of mortgage credits", dated 28 February 1996. According to paragraph 3 of the Decree, the buildings, including the houses and other constructions, fixed to the land, can be objects of mortgage only together with the land plot under the same contract or, if it is not possible, with the leasehold of the land plot. If the enterprise or edifice is located on a land plot with the rights of permanent use, such plot cannot be the object of mortgage.

The Decree provides for a mandatory form of contract for the mortgage, defines the content of the contract, rights and duties of the parties and deals with the issues of state registration of the rights in land in connection with the mortgage contracts. At present the mortgage of land plots is in practice not widely used in Russia.

According to art.35 of the Constitution of the Russian Federation the right of private property is protected by law; the deprivation of it is possible only upon the decision of the court. The expropriation of property for the needs of the state may take place only under condition of preliminary equivalent compensation. These rules apply also to the rights of private ownership on land.

The state ownership of land in the Russian Federation is divided between the federal property and the property of the subjects of the Federation (art.214 of the Civil Code of the RF).

According to the Decree of the President of the Russian Federation "On the federal natural resources", dated 16 December 1993, the objects of the federal property are: land plots for the needs of the military defence and security of the country, for the border guard, for the federal energy, transport and space facilities, for the operation of the nuclear power plants, for telecommunications and meteorological services, the objects of cultural and historical heritage, natural reserves as well as other objects in federal ownership. The territories of the national protection parks, national natural parks and other similar objects, enjoying the protection of the state, form a separate group of federal property.

According to the Law of the Russian Federation "On the status of the capital of the Russian Federation", dated 15 April 1993, the objects of the federal property are: the land plots in the city of Moscow, where higher bodies of the legislative and executive power of the Russian Federation are located, among them the offices of the General Public Procurator of the RF, of the Central Bank of the RF and of the Pension Fund of the RF.

According to art.215 of the Civil Code *municipal land* property is the property of the rural and urban communities as well as of other types of municipal units. The current legislation classifies the "raijons" as municipal bodies of the latter type. Thus, the legislation defines only the subjects of the municipal property. However, the criteria for the objects of the municipal property are not so clearly defined, the situation, which appears if the lack of criteria for the distinction between the objects of the municipal property and the property of the subjects of the Federation. Besides, it is impossible to make any conclusion from the analysis of the current federal legislation whether each subject of the Russian Federation has to have land in municipal ownership or whether the subjects of the Federation decide on this issue independently. In my opinion, all these problems should be clearly decided in the legislation.

Art.9 of the Constitution of the Russian Federation in addition to private, state and municipal property provides for other forms of ownership on land. Taking into consideration that the distribution of the private, state and municipal property takes place according the subjects the right on ownership: private persons, legal persons, the Russian Federation, the subjects of the Russian Federation, the municipal authorities, it would be more logical to systematize other forms of property according to the same criteria. The current federal legislation does not stipulate other subjects of the law of ownership, except the mentioned above (art. 212 of the Civil Code). In the same time, certain constitutions of the subjects of the Federation mention a new subject of the ownership on land and natural resources, the multiethnical population. It seems that this concept, made at the level of the regional legislation, requires a theoretical elaboration, namely, how the population is able to realize the rights of ownership of land in all its complexity.

5. Other rights relating to land within the Russian Federation

Besides the right of ownership the federal legislation provides for the following other rights connected with land: the inheritable right of posession (art.214 of the Civil Code), the right of the permanent use with no fixed term (art.216 of the Civil Code), an easement (art.216 of the Civil Code), the lease (art.607 of the Civil Code) and the gratuitous right of use (art.689 of the Civil Code).

Current legislation specifies neither the subjects of these rights nor their content.

Thus, by establishing an inheritable posession right and the right of permanent use with no fixed term, the current federal legislation does not throw light on their content. These rights, however, are stipulated in art.266–270 of the chapter 17 of the Civil Code. This chapter, however, will come into force only after the new Land Code has been enacted. According to art.265, the inheritable posession right of the lands under the state or municipal ownership, may be acquired by citizens in conformity with land legislation. But this right was excluded from the current Land Code by the Decree of the President of the RF "On bringing of the land legislation of the Russian Federation to conformity with the Constitution of the Russian Federation", dated 24 December 1993. This right is mentioned only in the Law of the Russian Federation "On the rights of the citizens of the RF to own as a private property and to sell the land plots for the subsidiary small-holdings, gardening and building of the dwelling-houses", dated 23 December 1992. According to art.1 of the Law the citizens, who have had at the time of the enactment of the Law in their possession the land plots in sizes not exceeding the standard limits, in all cases retain the inheritable right of posession in relation to these land plots.

According to art.266 and art.267 (chapter 17) of the Civil Code, the citizen, who has the inheritable right of posession of the land plot, has the right to posess and to use the land plot. The posessor has the right to construct buildings and other erections, acquiring the right of ownership relating to the immovable property thus created.

The legal regime for the inheritable right of posession differs substantially from the right of ownership. The holder of the land under this right can only give the land plot for a lease or for free use for a fixed time. The sale, the mortgage or any other transaction with the land, which may entail the alienation of the land plot, are not allowed.

In the similar way the Civil Code stipulates the content of the right of the permanent use with no fixed term in its art.269 and art.270. This right is even more limited than the inheritable right of posession, since the holder of the land plot can effectuate any of the transactions mentioned above only upon approval of the owner.

According to the Civil Code both private and legal persons can be the subjects of the right of the permanent use with no fixed term. It worth mentioning, that the abrogated art.12 of the current Land Code recognized as subjects of these rights only legal persons.

Taking into consideration the fact that the land plots may be allotted to private persons on the basis of the inheritable right of posession and of the right of the permanent use with no fixed term, there is a need to draw a clear line between them, which is not yet made in the current legislation. It would be logical to assume, that the right of permanent use with no fixed term cannot be inherited. If it is so, it precludes the creation of any kind of inheritable real property on the land plot under permanent use. But art.269 of the Civil Code permits the private user of the land plot to build the houses and erections, acquiring the private ownership on this real property.

In my opinion, in the new Land Code there should be an unambiguous distinction between the said two rights. It would be wise to return to the rule, established by the abrogated art.12 of the Land Code, i.e., to recognize only the legal persons the capacity to have the rights of the use of the land plots on permanent basis with no fixed term.

It follows from the comparison between the art.264 and art.268 of the Civil Code that land plots under the private ownership and land plots under the state and municipal ownership may be allotted for the permanent use. As long as part two of the Civil Code does not stipulate the issue of transfer of the property (including land) for the permanent use, the conditions of the contract on this subject can be determined by the parties in conformity with the land legislation.

Considering the situation that the rules of the Land Code on the lease of land were abrogated by a Decree of the President of the RF, for the time being the lease is regulated by the chapter 34 of the part two of the Civil Code. The art.607 provides the possibility of legislating special rules for the lease of land plots. For the time being there is no such rules at the federal level.

On the level of the subjects of the Federation, for example, in Moscow, there exists rules of sale of the leasehold on the land plots. In practice it means, that the upcoming leaseholder has to pay, in addition to the rent payment, a sum of money, equal to the market price of recent sales on leaseholds in auctions or in a tender contest. In Moscow there is the "Temporary regulation on the procedure of the allocation of the land plots for the long term lease on the basis of contest", introduced by the Resolution of the Mayor of Moscow, dated 18 December 1992, which determines the procedure for the preparation of the contest and the procedure of the contest. The main criteria for winning the contest is the price for the long term lease of a land plot.

According to art.610 of the Civil Code, a lease contract on lease is concluded for a period, provided for in the contract. At the same time, the legislation can limit maximum periods for lease of certain categories of the property. In the abrogated art.13 of the Land Code these limits were 50 years for the lease of state owned lands and 5 years for the lease of the land, owned by private persons. As far as this issue was left unregulated by the current land legislation, the business practice demonstrates that the most popular period for a long term lease is 49 years.

Regarding the allotment of the land plots for a charge free use for a fixed time, it is regulated by rules of the Civil Code (chapter 36), since the abrogation of the corresponding rules in the Land Code.

According to the art.216 of the Civil Code, one type of the rights in land is the easement. The current Land Code does not contain any rule on it. The only reference to an easement may be found in art.54, which provides, that the rights of owners, landholders, land users and leaseholders may be limited in the interests of other users of the nature in the cases, stipulated by the Land Code and by the legislation of the subjects of the Federation. However, the Land Code contains barely the rules, which limit the use of the land by owners, land users and leaseholders. Only one article mentions that land plots can be used by third parties, and it means use of tourist paths.

Chapter 17 of the Civil Code (will come in force only after the new Land Code becomes effective) it regulates in detail easements, the categories of easements, the procedure and the conditions for their foundation and termination.

6. Land rights for foreign investors

The issue of the right of ownership of land by foreign investors in the Russian Federation is quite important. It is worth mentioning that foreign investors may operate in the Russian territory like legal persons according to the Russian law, the land legislation uses the term "foreign legal person" instead of "foreign investor". Foreign private and legal persons may become owners of land plots, acquired under privatization, according to the "Procedure of the sale of the land plots in the process of the privatization of the state and municipal enterprises, extension and additional construction activities of these enterprises, as well as of the land plots, allotted for the private persons and their unions for the business activities", endorsed by the Decree of the President of the Russian Federation, dated 14 June 1992 with amendments, introduced by the Decree of the President of the RF, dated 14 October 1992. The current land legislation does not answer the question as to whether a Russian legal person, wholly owned by the foreigners, may become the owner of the land plot, if the basis of the transaction on the land would be not privatization but an ordinary purchase of land from the private owner, the state or municipality. Regarding Russian legal persons with foreign participation, they may have the right of ownership on the land plots, transferred as a part of the investment of the Russian partners into the capital of the limited liability companies, co-operatives, partnerships, according to the Decree of the President of the Russian Federation "On regulation of the land market and on the development of the agrarian reform in Russia", dated 27 October 1993 and of art.213 of the Civil Code of the RF.

Russian legal persons with foreign investments may also hold other rights connected with land, as a right of the permanent use or right to lease, in case these rights are invested into their capital. The possibility of investment of these rights as property in the enterprise was stipulated by art.66 (paragraph 6) of the Civil Code of the RF.

Despite current land legislation being silent on the issue of rights of Russian legal persons, wholly owned by foreigners, business practice shows that, as a rule, they acquire the rights of land on the basis of the long term lease of land.

7. Protection of the land rights within the Russian Federation

The current Land Code guarantees the protection of the rights of all persons who use land plots. According to art.54, any interference from the side of the state, administrative and other institutions in the activities, connected with the use of land by owners, landholders, land users and leaseholders is forbidden except in the cases of violation of land legislation.

In case of an unjustified intervention by official bodies into the activities of the use of the land, the infringed rights are to be restored following the procedure of the resolution of the disputes relating to land. All damage should be fully compensated.

This principle is confirmed in art.304–305 of the Civil Code, where the landowner or any other person with the right in land is entitled to require the elimination of all the infringements of their rights, including cases, when the infringements did not lead to the dispossession of the right to the land plot.

From the legal rules, mentioned above, the conclusion follows that the law protects the rights of the use of land plots and does not protect the right of disposal of them, for example, the rights of the owners to conclude contracts on land. Since the Land Code was adopted in 1991, when the moratorium on the sale of land existed, it is quite natural, that the protection of the rights on disposal of the land is missing in the Land Code.

The constitutional rules on the protection of landowners to dispose, to possess and to use the land plots is enshrined in the Constitution, art.36. According to it, the owner may enjoy the possession, the use and disposal of the land at his own discretion unless his actions lead to the damage of the environment or infringe the lawful interests of third parties. To put it another way, nobody can prevent the owner making transactions concerned with land plots unless it contradicts the legislation in force. According to art.131 of the Civil Code all the transactions, bringing about the transfer of the ownership on land, should be submitted for state registration and no one can be refused registration in any case the relevant law has been observed in the conclusion of the contract on the land. It would be reasonable to expect the enactment of the corresponding rules of the law on the state registration of rights on land.

It is very important for the protection of land rights, irrespective of their categories, that the law provides an exhaustive list of the grounds and specifies the procedure for losing these rights.

While the rules of art.235 of the Civil Code cover the cases of losing rights of ownership of land, the problem of termination of the other rights connected with land in the current legislation remains unsolved. The art.287 (chapter 17) of the Civil Code stipulates, that the cessation of rights on the land plots except for ownership occurs according to the rules of the land legislation. Therefore, these problems should be solved in the new Land Code. Taking into consideration, that the inheritable right of possession, the right of permanent use and the right to lease may refer to the lands under the state and municipal ownership, the grounds and the procedure of the termination of these rights should be different from the grounds and the procedure for cessation of real property ownership. In particular, it is possible to set up an administrative procedure of the confiscation of land plots in case of infringement of the land legislation, and so on.

Art.301–304 of the Civil Code has a considerable importance for the protection of property rights and other land rights. According to them, both the owners and the landholders with the rights others than ownership, have the right to demand back their property, being in unlawful possession of a third party. Additionally, the landholders with the rights others than ownership on land plots have the right of protection of their right also against the owner.

8. Dues on land

One of the main principle of the land legislation before the economic reform commenced was the principle of the free use of land. However, already in the 1970′s in the mass media the discussion on the necessity of the introduction of payment for the use of the natural resources and in particular, for the use of land has emerged. The main arguments for the introduction of the payment for the use of land was the fact, that the free use of land lead to its irrational use and created the situation, where the enterprises often held more land in their possession than it were able to use.

The payment for the use of land was introduced only in 1990 by the principles of the legislation on land of the USSR and the Republics. In the legislation of the Russian Federation the issues on the payment for the use of land are stipulated in a chapter of the current Land Code, as well as by the Law "On rent payment for land", dated 11 October 1991 with the subsequent amendments.

The purpose of the introduction of the payment for the use of land is to stimulate the rational use of land, to protect the land and to develop the new cultivated lands, to increase the fertility of the soils, to equalize the socio-economic conditions for the use of lands of different qualities, to develop infrastructure in the dwelling areas and to establish specific money funds for the activities mentioned above.

The categories of payments for the use of land are the following: the land tax, the rent payment and the normative price of the land. The landowners, the landholders and the land users pay the annual land tax. The rent payment is paid for the lease of land. The normative price of the land is used in case of purchase of the land, as stipulated by the Land Code, or in the case of a mortgage.

The Law "On payment for land" specifies the following main schemes for the estimation of the land tax for the lands of agricultural and non-agricultural purposes. The land tax on the agricultural lands is calculated according to the composition, the quality, the size and the location of the land. The average amounts of the land tax per hectare of the arable land for each subject of the Russian Federation as well as the distribution of the land tax and of the rent payment among the federal authorities and the subjects of the Federation are enacted in the specific annex to the Law. These amounts vary depending on the climate conditions of the regions. The subjects of the Russian Federation, in their turn, proceeding from the average amounts of land tax per hectare and from the evaluation of the land in the state cadastre, establish concrete rates of the land tax for the groups of arable lands, for the lands under cultivation, hayfields and pastures.

The tax for residential lands in the urban area is calculated according to average rates, according to a separate annex to the Law for the 11 economic regions of the Russian Federation. The tax for the residential lands in the resort areas is calculated using the corresponding coefficients, fixed in yet another annex to this Law mentioned above. The status of a city or of a town and its socio-cultural potential has significance in calculation of the corresponding coefficient as well.

It is worth mentioning that the Law establishes preferential taxes for private persons, living in urban areas and using the land plots for subsidiary small-holdings, gardening and the building of summer houses and garages.

The average rates of tax on the land plots within the urban areas differ depending on their location and on their significance for city planning.

The Law "On payment for land" produces a list of the objects, exempted from the payment of land tax. These are, amongst others, the following: nature preservation areas; national and dendrological parks; botanical gardens; cultural, educational, touristic and scientific institutions; institutions of fine arts; public health services; property of the veterans of the Second World War; invalids of the first and second category; who have, suffered radiation from Tchernobyl and other nuclear disasters, etc.

Private persons who engage in farming activities for the first time, are exempted from land tax for a period of five years from the moment of the allotment of land plots to them.

As the tax is fixed by law, the rent payment is determined by the lease contract. However, when the lease has for its object the state and municipal lands, the corresponding authorities decide on the basic rates of the rent payment, depending on the categories of the land plots and on the categories of the leaseholders.

The land tax and the rent payment for the state and municipal lands make a separate item in the income part of the corresponding budgets, and are used exclusively for the financing of the following objectives and activities: organization of the use of land, registering and monitoring of land plots, protection of land, increasing the fertility of the soils, construction of municipal infrastructure, etc.

While the land market price is being assessed, the legislation of the Russian Federation introduces a so-called fixed price of the land, which is to be established by the executive authorities of the subjects of the Russian Federation for lands of different categories, depending on the location of the land and other variables (Resolution of the Government of the Russian Federation, dated 15 March 1997). According to art.25 of the Law "On payment for land", the fixed price of the land is to be applied for transactions, aiming at the transfer of the ownership. In my opinion, this rule needs to be defined more clearly, in particular, it should be stated unambiguously, which categories of private and legal persons have the right to buy the state and municipal lands on a fixed and not on a free market price.

9. State administration for the rational use and for the protection of land in the Russian Federation

The state administration for the rational use and protection of land is the task of the executive authorities of the state, aimed at the creation of favourable conditions for the rational use and protection of land by all the subjects having rights on the land plots in different spheres of the socio-economic life of the society. Administrative functions of the state are twofold. On the one hand, the authorities help the subjects to use their land plots rationally, providing them with all necessary information. On the other hand, the authorities take necessary measures against subjects, who infringe the rules on the rational use and protection of land, up to the administrative deprivation of the rights on land plots, in an administrative process.

According to the current federal legislation, the main functions of the state administration of the use and protection of land are: creating and maintaining the state land cadastre, organising the land survey and the state control over the use and protection of land. One of the most important functions of state administration of the use of land is the territorial planning of the use of land, but this function is not yet regulated by law for the time being. In practice, during the last few years, the planning of the use of land was effectuated by the elaboration of the schemes of the use of land on the regional and local levels. These schemes were approved by the local and regional councils of the people's deputies. On the basis of these schemes agricultural, residential and industrial areas were established, but the detailed procedure of these schemes and their legal force has not yet been defined by law.

To a certain extent, the new draft Land Code will fill the existing gaps on the territorial planning of the use of land by introducing a specific chapter on this issue and by providing for the elaboration of the specific law on the territorial planning. The existing gaps on the federal level are filled by the subjects of the Federation. Thus, the Moscow region's Duma adopted the Law "On organization and functional zoning of the territory of the Moscow region". According to the Law, the territory of the Moscow region is divided into a number of zones with different functions (industrial, agricultural, etc.). Each zone will have its own planning scheme with detailed restrictions on the economic activities, including the use of land.

The legal foundations for the *land cadastre* were incorporated in the legislation of the USSR of the RSFSR. Today this legislation is renewed, its implementation is in the process of development. The land cadastre is needed for the creation of the land market; for its successful development the credible information of the economic and legal character of land plots is necessary. Moreover, without this information a number of activities connected with the economic use of land of federal and rregional level will be impossible to fulfil: the land legislation, namely, often refers to the information of the cadastre. For example, it is possible, in exceptional cases, to alienate the agricultural lands with the cadastre value higher than the average value in the region. These exceptions follow from the international obligations of the Russian Federation, they may be justified by the use of the mineral resources and in other cases, stipulated in the art.24 of the Land Code (this list of exceptions may be amended by the subjects of the Federation).

The current Land Code specifies the content, the goals of the cadastre and the authorities, which are competent to run the cadastre. According to art.110 of the Code, the state land cadastre systematizes the necessary data and the documents on the legal status of lands; on the division of land among the landowners, landholders, land users and leaseholders; on the different categories of lands; on the technical data and the economic value of lands.

It is mandatory to use the data of the land cadastre in cases of the planning of the use and for the protection of land, the allotment and alienation of land, deciding on the payment for land, the organization of the use of land, of the evaluation of the economic activities and other actions concerned with the protection of land.

The state land cadastre shall be carried out by the State Committee on land resources with a landsurvey. Its activities are financed from the regional budget under a unified scheme.

The procedure for carrying out the state land cadastre is stipulated in the Regulation on the procedure of the state land cadastre, approved by the Resolution of the Government of the Russian Federation on 25 February 1992. The main work on the carrying out the cadastre is done by the regional or local committees on land resources and landsurvey. These committees register the data about the objects and the subjects of the property, about the possession, use and lease of land, about the specific purposes of land plots and the regime for its use; they set up databases on lands and on their quality in the municipality (town), monitor the current status of the lands by collecting periodically the data from all the holders of the rights on land and update the cadastre.

Before the Land Code and the above mentioned Resolutions of the Government were adopted the moratorium on the land transactions had been established and the registration of these transactions had been suspended. Nowadays transactions on land are allowed. The Procedure on the purchase and sale by the citizens of the Russian Federation of land plots was adopted by the Resolution of the Government of the Russian Federation on 30 May 1993. This procedure requires the registration of these transactions with the local committees on land resources and a landsurvey.

On 21 July 1997 the President of the Russian Federation signed the Law "On the state registration of the rights on the immovable property and of the transactions with it", approved by the State Duma on 17 June 1997 and by the Federation Council on 3 July 1997. According to the Law, under the registration of the rights on the land plot an authentic registration number should be given to every land plot. The state registration of rights should be carried out on the whole territory of the Russian Federation in the Common state register on the immovable property and on the transactions with it. The state registration is the only evidence of the existence of a registered right. Once the right on the land plot is registered, it may be challenged only in court.

State registration has a public nature. The registering authority is obliged to disclose the data on any object of immovable property, including land plots, to: any private person, who identifies himself and who applies for it in writing; any legal person upon submission of its documents of incorporation and of the powers of its representative.

The state registration of the rights connected with land plots and transactions with them is carried out by state offices with the competence to register the rights on the immovable property and the transactions on it in the territory of the area, where the immovable property is located. The procedure for organizing, the administrative structure of the offices on the registration of rights and the location of these offices is determined by the subjects of the Russian Federation upon the consent of the federal office, appointed by the Government of the Russian Federation.

By specifying the detailed procedure for the registration of rights on immovable property and transactions with it, the Law contains the exhaustive list of the grounds, when the registration may be dismissed or postponed, as well as the liability for the inadequacy of the data and for the delays in its supply. The liability may include compensation for material damage to the private or legal person or to the state.

The process of carrying out the land reform in the Russian Federation and of the formation of the land market shows the lack of modern methods in carrying out the state land cadastre. Therefore the Government of the Russian Federation approved the specific Federal Programme entitled "On the establishing of the computerized system for the state land cadastre". The main purposes of the Programme are: to set up an effective machinery for the maintaining of the state land cadastre on the basis of the modern computer systems and information technologies; to assist in the setting up of the system of the state protection of the rights of landowners, landholders, land users and leaseholders; to improve the system of calculation of the amount of the land tax and other payments for the use of land, as well as to guarantee payments to the budget in time; to support the land market. One of the main activities under the Programme is the renewal of the legislative basis of the land cadastre. For the time being a new resolution of the Government of the Russian Federation relating to the maintaining of the state land cadastre is anticipated.

The next function of the state administration for the use and protection of the land resources is *state control over the possible infringements of land legislation*. Under control are: state and public bodies, legal and private persons. According to art.108 of the Land Code, state control over the use and the protection of the land is effectuated by the State Committee on the land resources and landsurvey, as well as by other institutions of the executive power. The procedure for the implementation of the state control on the use and the protection of land in the Russian Federation is approved by the Government of the Russian Federation in its Resolution, dated 23 December 1993 as well as by the

Decree of the President of the Russian Federation "On the reinforcement of the state control over use and protection of the land under the process of the land reform", dated 16 December 1993.

The institutions with the competence to effectuate the state control over the use and the protection of lands in the Russian Federation are the State Committee on land resources and landsurveys and its local branches; nature protection bodies; sanitation offices; architecture and building offices.

The executive officers of these institutions have wide powers, permitting them: to suspend any kind of building activity if it infringes land legislation; to give mandatory orders for the elimination of infringements of the land legislation; to impose fines within the limits stipulated by the legislation, etc.

Besides, the executive officers of the State Committee on land resources and landsurveys have the right to control the procedures of the contests and auctions on land and the conclusion of the transactions with land, to initiate court proceedings on the validity of the transactions with land as null and void, in case they contradict the current legislation.

A very important informative role in the state control over use and protection of land is played by the monitoring system. The art.109 of the Land Code and the Regulation on the land monitoring in the Russian Federation, approved by the Resolution of the Government of the Russian Federation, dated 15 July 1992, entitle the following institutions to carry out land monitoring: the State Committee on land resources and landsurveys, nature protection bodies with participation of the Ministry of Agriculture, planning and architecture offices, offices on the use of mineral resources and geological institutions, as well as other ministries and departments. Land monitoring is effectuated on all levels on the federal, regional and local (up to individual estates) levels.

The results of the monitoring are brought together into briefings, reports, scientific forecasts and recommendations, characterizing the dynamics of the transformations, in particular, negative transformations of the land resources.

The State Programme on monitoring of the land of the Russian Federation for the years 1993–1995 was approved by the Resolution of the Government of the Russian Federation, dated 5 February 1993. The Programme provided for the inspection of the land in different regions of Russia and for the elaboration of the plan for the prevention and elimination of the negative processes, disclosed under the monitoring. At the present time the monitoring is being processed.

The Landsurvey, as one of the function of the state administration for the use and protection of the land, implies the following: working out the prognoses and regional programmes on the protection of the land resources, making plans for the creation of new and regulation of the existing objects of the rights connected with land; elimination of the inconveniences in use and in location of the land plots; preparation of the documents confirming the rights on land; elaboration of the plans for recultivation of lands, for protection of lands from erosion and other negative processes, for improvement of the quality of agricultural lands, exploration of the virgin lands, etc (art.113 of the Land Code). All the landsurvey projects, initiated by official authorities, should be approved by the holders of the rights on corresponding land plots. These projects are financed by the budget. Landsurvey work can be initiated by the landowners, and land users and carried out at their own cost.

10. Liability for the infringement of land legislation

In case the citizens, executive officers and legal persons do not comply with the provisions of land legislation, they are liable according to civil, administrative and criminal law.

Art.125 of the Land Code, the Decree of the President of the Russian Federation "On the reinforcement of the state control over use and protection of the land under the process of the land reform", dated 16 December 1993 and the Code of Administrative liability stipulate the categories of the infringements of the land legislation which lead to the administrative liability in the form of a payment of a fine. These infringements are: taking the land plot into possession without proper authorization; pollution of land with chemical, radioactive, industrial waste and sewage; contamination of land with bacteriological and other insanitary waste; damaging or destroying of the fertile part of soil; breaking of the obligations to return in time the lands in temporary possession and to restore their conditions according to their specific purposes; designing, building and putting into operation the erections which negatively influence the condition of land; misrepresentation of the data about the condition and the use of land; non-examination by the executive officers of the claims, submitted by the private persons on the allotment of the land plots and non-disclosure of the information on the available lands; violation of the rules for the lands, designed for nature protection, therapeutic and recreational needs, for other purposes; non-rational use of the agricultural lands, non-performance of the duties on amelioration of lands and on protection of lands from wind and water erosion and other negative processes which worsen the condition of lands; violation of the regime of lands to be used for specific purpose; continuous non-payment of the taxes on land and violation of other mandatory duties connected with land.

Art.254 of the Criminal Code stipulates the criminal liability in the forms of fines, of prohibition to hold certain official positions or to practice certain activities during three years, or penitentiary work for two years for the poisoning, pollution, damage of the land by the products of industrial or other activity following the non-compliance with the instructions on use of the fertilisers, of the stimulators of growth of plants, of the pesticides and other dangerous biological and chemical substances under their storage, use and transportation that lead to the damage to the person or to the environment. The same doings, but made in the area of ecological emergency or in the area of extraordinary environmental situation, increases the liability up to three years of imprisonment or personal restraint. If the same things cause the death of a person, liability is two to five years imprisonment.

According to art.126 of the Land Code the land plots, taken into possession without proper authorization, should be returned to their due holders without compensation of the expenses, occurred during the unauthorized possession. The restoration of the land plots into condition, suitable for use as well as pulling down unlawfully erected buildings should be made by the party, liable for the infringement or at his/her own cost.

Legal and private persons have the duty to compensate for damage, caused by them as a result of the infringement of the land legislation.

11. General features of the stock of land of the Russian Federation

The stock of land of the Russian Federation consists of the following categories of lands, to each of them there is a specific chapter in the Code: agricultural lands; urban and municipal lands; industrial lands, lands for transport, telecommunications and other non-agricultural use; lands of nature protection, of natural preservation areas and other specifically safeguarded lands; lands under forest and water; reserve lands.

According to art.56 of the Land Code agricultural lands are the lands, designed for the needs of agriculture. The agricultural lands may be allotted to the following persons: to private persons for farming, subsidiary small-holding, gardening, cattle-breeding and other agricultural needs; to commercial agricultural enterprises for agricultural production; to agricultural research and educational institutions as well as for secondary schools for research and educational purposes; to non-agricultural enterprises for subsidiary agricultural holding.

Only private individuals over 18 years old, who have experience in agricultural occupation, corresponding qualification or training, have the right to receive a land plot for farming. The selection of the persons, who wish to become farmers (and have agricultural land), can be made on the basis of contest, if necessary.

The refusal of the competent authorities to allot a land plot to a person for farming activities may be disputed in court.

According to art.257 of the Civil Code, land plots for farming activities belong to family members being a joint property, unless the law or the contract provides otherwise. The Land Code and the Law "On the peasant's (farmer's) household" permit to owner, the right of ownership of a land plot, designed for farming, by one person, namely the head of the household. Irrespective of whether the land plot belongs to one person or is under the joint property of several persons, the law forbids to parcel this plot into smaller households. If the land plot is in joint property, its co-owner may receive only money compensation if he wishes to withdraw from the household.

In order to secure the necessary conditions for the use of land plots for farming, the law provides the allotment of the plots, cadastre evaluation of which, as a rule, should equal the average evaluation in the region, where the plots are allotted. If a person receives the land plot with a lower, than average, quality, he shall be given fair adjustment in the form of taxation preferences, etc.

For the time being, more than 12 millions hectares of land are owned by private persons for farming activities.

The Government of the Russian Federation approved on 16 December 1996 the Federal Programme for the development of individual and co-operative farming holdings for the years 1996–2000. The Programme provides for a number of additional measures, having as its purpose to allot more land plots to people who wish to embark on farming. Thus, a system of preferential crediting for the purchase of land plots should be developed, enabling the landholders to buy the neighbouring plots, available for sale, in the first instance. Complex measures on the rational organisation of the use of land plots, allotted for the farming activities will be taken. There are restrictions on the sizes of land plots in private ownership, but there are no restrictions on the possession of land plots which are being leased. According to certain forecasts, the number of the private farms will increase from 280 000 to 350 000 by the year 2000.

The land of the commercial agricultural enterprises is, as a rule, the joint property of their members. For the time being, more than 108 millions of hectares of agricultural land is allotted to agricultural companies and partnerships as joint property of their members.

According to the legal rules on the reorganisation of the agricultural enterprises, the private persons obtained the right of ownership on the so-called "land share", i.e., a share of the land in the possession of the agricultural enterprise. This share has only been defined mathematically; its natural equivalent is not defined. The right to obtain the land share in the reorganisation free of charge have: working employees of the collective and state farms, other agricultural enterprises, retired employees of these enterprises under condition they are living in the areas where their enterprises are located, the people, engaged in all kinds of auxiliary services in the rural area; former employees, dismissed from their jobs on the grounds of staff reduction from 1 January 1992.

The size of the land share does not depend on personal qualifications, neither on the length of employment, the personal contribution of the employees, etc. It should be calculated on the basis of the standard size of the free of charge land plot in each corresponding region. This standard size is to be calculated according to the Decree of the President of the Russian Federation "On the procedure of the calculation of the standard size of the land plots for the transfer of them into the private ownership of the citizens", dated 2 March 1992. According to the Decree, the standard share is determined by the division of the common surface of the agricultural lands of the region into the composite quantity of all employees of the region, working in agriculture, including the retired employees and the people, engaged in all kinds of auxiliary services in this region.

The distribution of land is taking place in collective and state farms under reorganisation and in the state agricultural enterprises under privatisation.

Each owner of the land share is allotted a certificate on the right of ownership. 12 millions inhabitants of the countryside became the owners of the land shares after the lands of the reorganised collective and state farms had been privatised. The owner of a land share has the right to use it in the following way.

First of all, he can get the land plot for farming, building and other types of businesses. In this case the right to receive a land share for a private person converts into the right of ownership on the permanent land plot.

Secondly, a private person can invest his land share in a company, partnership or co-operative as a payment for membership, or for a share in the capital of these enterprises.

Thirdly, the owner of the land share has the right to sell his share, use it for leasing to farmers, to agricultural enterprises, to private persons for subsidiary small-holdings, to convey it in succession or to hand it over to private or legal persons for their possession on the basis of the leasing contract. The sale and lease of land shares is widespread, for example, in the Nizhni Novgorod region, where the persons, willing to set up a farm or another agricultural enterprise, are buying land shares or taking out a lease on it.

In case the lands of the enterprise belong to a group of the private persons as their joint property, the enterprise itself may be the owner of these lands if the original owners invest their shares as a part of the capital of the enterprise. In case they only lease their land shares to the enterprise, the latter is merely a leaseholder of these shares.

According to the current Land Code, *the lands of urban communities as well as of other types of municipal units* are divided into the following categories.

The lands for building purposes are the built-up lands or the lands, designed, according to the municipal planning, for construction of the dwelling, industrial, socio-cultural, religious and other erections.

The lands of the common use are the lands, utilised for the communication purposes (marketplaces, streets, roads, strands, alleys), for socio-cultural purposes (parks, forest-parks, public gardens, beaches, avenues), places for the storage of the industrial waste and other kinds of lands, utilised for the urban necessities.

One of the category of the urban lands may also be the lands for *agricultural use*, as ploughed fields, gardens, vineyards, hayfields, pastures. The urban lands include as well *lands for nature protection, for therapeutic use, recreational, industrial lands, lands of the trans-*

port and telecommunications, lands for the military defence purpose.

A specific category of lands are *lands outside the rural and municipal territories*. These are industrial lands, lands for transport and telecommunications, for space facilities and for other purposes. These lands are allotted to enterprises, institutions and organisations for specific objectives. With a view to ensure the safety of the population and favourable conditions for the functioning of the industrial, transport and other objects, zones with special regimes may be established. The land plots of these zones cannot be alienated from the landowners, landholders, land users and leaseholders, but certain restrictive covenants can be established for them.

In the military defence zones military units, educational military institutions, enterprises and institutions of the army are located. In case of temporary needs for military exercises, certain lands may be used without alienation of the corresponding rights of the holders.

Lands of nature protection include lands of nature reserves, national and dendrological parks, botanical gardens. On these lands all kinds of activities, not connected with the research of the nature, are forbidden. In order to ensure the safe running of the nature reserves, national, dendrological parks and botanical gardens, they may be surrounded by the safeguarding zones with the prohibition of any harmful activity for the nature protection lands.

Lands for therapeutic use are lands with natural medicinal or healing properties (mineral waters, muds, etc.), beneficial for the organisation of the preventive and medical treatments. Around these lands safeguarding zones may be set up as well.

Recreational lands are used for the organisation of tourism: for camping, holiday hotels, tourist centers, etc.

On *the lands of historical and cultural significance* monuments of history and culture are located, as well as institutions of culture, related to traditional handicraft and applied art. Alienation of these lands for the needs, not connected with their primary specific purpose, is not allowed.

A specific category of land is made for *land under forest and water stocks*. The land of forest stock comprise the land, covered with forest and the land, not covered with forests, but allotted for the needs of forestry. The land of the water stock include the land, covered by water, glaciers, bogs, and does not include land of the tundra area and hydrotechnical and other man-made water systems, as well as land of the water collector network and of the channels.

All the land, which is not under the ownership, possession, use or lease, constitute *reserve land*.

In the present chapter the main concepts of the current land law of the Russian Federation were examined. However, for the time being land legislation needs to be reformed in order to comply with the requirements of the formulating market economy. Gaps in the legislation, especially, these relevant for the land market, should be filled. Particularly important are the following fields: consistent interaction of the land and civil legislation in the regulation of ownership issues and of the issues, related to other rights connected with land; formation of the legal basis for the sale of land, which should ensure the appropriate balance between private and public interests; setting up a juridical database on land legislation, and open for public inspection.

V Procedural Law in Russia
Judicial Procedures of Resolving Disputes in the Economic Field

Elena Aleksandrovna Vinogradova

1. Main branches and main sources of the procedural law in Russia

1.1. Brief review of legislation and doctrine

Traditionally, laws on organisation of judicial system and procedural codes of law have been considered sources of law of procedure.

As a result of the judicial reform of the mid-19th century in Russia, there were adopted judicial charters of November 20, 1864 that drastically changed court organisation and content of the applied rules and regulations. Those charters remained the major source of the Russian law of procedure until 1917. The charters consisted of four codes of law: 1) The court system 2) charter of civil procedure; 3) regulations on notary part; 4) charter of criminal procedure. The first two of the above mentioned charters referred to civil procedure. The first defined judicature, the second – order of considering civil cases in court and had been established mainly under the influence of the Code of Civil Procedure created in France in the early 19th century (1804) at the time of Napoleon. The content of the discussed charters is referred to again in theoretical legal discussions of these days – at the time of the cardinal reform of the Code of Civil Procedure.

However, unlike the 19th century legislature, in modern Russia there is no systematic collection of laws on the judicial system and court procedure. Systematization of the sources as well as description of the branches of the law of procedure is rather a result of a certain tradition which is reflected in special books on law – mostly textbooks and reference books. In the course of time this tradition has been changing.

At present, the most important law regulating the judicial system in the Russian Federation along with the Constitution of the Russian Federation of December 12, 1993, is a federal constitutional law "On Judicial System" put into effect on January 1, 1997.

Current procedural legislation of the Russian Federation also has several codified sources legally formulating various independent branches of the law of procedure. Among such codified sources of law of procedure are: The Code of civil procedure of the RSFSR (being applied with amendments and additions of 1997); Code of arbitration procedure (introduced into effect on July 1, 1995); Code of criminal procedure of RSFSR (adopted in 1960 and valid until now with numerous – over 500 – amendments and additions). Norms of procedural law can also be found in the number of material laws.

The administrative procedure law recognised in the doctrine as a special branch has no codified source.

The disputes of the parties participating in the economic transactions are considered by the state courts which form two independent sub-systems of the modern judicial system of the Russian Federation: state courts of general jurisdiction headed by the Supreme Court of the Russian Federation and state courts of arbitration headed by the Supreme Arbitration Court of the Russian Federation. Organisation and functioning of these two judicial sub-systems is the subject matter of this chapter.

Though several competent scholars, such as professor M. S. Shakaryan, question the independence of the law of arbitration procedure and consider it as a part of the law of civil procedure, nobody disputes independence of the law of arbitration procedure as a branch of legislation and as a research and academic discipline. The subject matter of this discipline is organisation and functioning of the state courts of arbitration system established in 1991.

Legislation on structure and functioning of the arbitration tribunals (commercial arbitration) which resolve both "domestic" and foreign economic disputes is not considered an independent branch of law of procedure. The position of this legislation as a part of law of procedure has not attracted attention of Russian specialists in procedural law.

Russian legislation in the 90s of the XX century, concerning both civil an arbitration procedure, have been characterised by high dynamics resulting from the economic and judicial reforms being implemented in the country. It explains the fact that the doctrine is lagging behind the legislation. Influence of science on the legislative development is not carried out by means of working out and publishing different kinds of fundamental proposals de lege ferenda to be accepted by legislators, but mainly by means of direct participating of the most competent Moscow scholars in the law-making process.

Comprehension of the new legislation and its practical application is reflected in the basic textbooks, teaching materials, commentaries and reference books.

1.2. General description of the main current sources of the procedural law

The most important source of the modern law of procedure is the Constitution of RF of December 12, 1993, which defined the judicial system in the state and secured such basic principles of law of procedure as adversarity and equality of the parties, right for judicial defence, administering justice only by court, independence of judges and their subordination only to law etc. These constitutional regulations have essentially defined direction and content of law of procedure reform. Besides, of great importance is a thesis from part 1, Article 15 of the Constitution of 1993 which states that the Constitution is the supreme legal source and it has direct effect in the whole Russian Federation territory. It allowed courts, first, to independently evaluate from constitutional point of view the content of a law or other legislative act regulating legal relations considered in court, and second, in case of absence of any direct indication in legislation where a concrete case has to be settled to consider such cases applying a constitutional norm which guarantees to everyone judicial defence of one's rights and freedoms in court.

Codified sources of the current law of procedure in Russia are: the Code of Civil Procedure of RSFSR (CoCP) of 1964 (with numerous amendments and additions) which regulates the procedures of civil cases in courts of general jurisdiction; the Code of Criminal Procedure of 1960 (also with numerous amendments and additions) which regulates the procedure of criminal cases in the courts of general jurisdiction; and also Code of State Arbitration Procedure(CSAP) introduced into effect on July 1, 1995, which regulates the rules applied by courts of state arbitration when resolving economic disputes.

According to Part 4, Article 15 of the Constitution of 1993, international treaties of the Russian Federation are a part of its judicial system. In the situation when an international treaty sets regulations different from those specified by the Russian law, rules of the international treaty are applied. As a legal successor of the USSR, Russia participates in the Hague Convention on civil procedure which was signed on March 1, 1954(the USSR joined the Convention in 1966).

The Convention cancelling the requirement of legalising foreign official documents which was signed in Hague on October 5, 1961, entered in force for the Russian Federation on May 31, 1992 according to the decision of the USSR Supreme Soviet of April 17, 1991.

Also, due to the fact that it is a legal successor of the USSR, Russia participates in the New York convention "On recognition and enforcement of foreign arbitration awards" of June 10, 1958.

Among the sources of law of procedure are also several multilateral treaties signed within CIS and containing rules of law of procedure. They include: Convention on legal help and on legal relations in civil and criminal cases of January 22, 1993 and Agreement on settling economic disputes of March 20, 1992.

A number of bilateral treaties/agreements on legal help and on legal relations in civil, family and criminal cases which are signed by the Russian Federation is constantly growing. In the Collection of international treaties/agreements of the Russian Federation published in 1996 one can find the texts of 41 such agreements signed among others with Azerbaidjan, Albania, Algeria, Bulgaria, Hungary, Vietnam, Greece, Georgia, Iraq, Italy, Yemen, Cyprus, China, North Korea, Cuba, Kirgizia, Latvia, Lithuania, Moldova, Mongolia, Poland, Romania, USA, Tunis, Turkmenia, Finland, Chechoslovakia, Switzerland, Estonia, Yugoslavia. The list of such agreements is constantly growing.

Furthermore, rules of procedure, especially those defining the competent court having jurisdiction for cases, are often included into the material legislative acts such as: the Family Code of RF, the Housing Code of RF, the law "On protection of consumers' rights", the patent law of RF, and many others.

A RF law "On court fees" is a source of the law of procedure since it contains the rules about the size and order of paying court fees when applying to the courts of general jurisdiction and state courts of arbitration.

Russian Federation laws "On execution procedure" and "On officers of the court" are considered to be the sources of the law of procedure which regulate the stage of the forced execution of the court judgements.

Judicial practice is not officially recognised as a source of law in Russia. However, in the doctrine there have always been expressed opposite opinions.

By the law "On the judicial system" of December 31, 1997, the Supreme Court of RF and the Supreme State Arbitration Court of RF are endowed with the right to explanation on the questions of judicial practice. Such explanations often take the form of the Supreme Court and Supreme Arbitration Court Plenary sessions resolutions. They may contain interpretation of laws and even fill the gaps in legal regulation. Not withstanding their formal value the explanations provided by the supreme judicial bodies on the problems of judicial practice are recognised as the sources of law. In any case they strongly influence the work of the lower courts.

The legal doctrine is not a source of law in Russia. We can say that until recently theoretical justification of the parties' positions in court or consideration of conceptual theses when passing court decisions did not take place. However, for the scholars involved in the formation of judicial practice, changing relations between the judicial practice and the doctrine are quite evident. The latter more and more influences the judicial practice.

1.3. Situation with the law-making activities

The tempo of adopting new codes of procedure is hardly adequate to the high dynamics of the legislation concerning court system. It can be easily explained by the fact that a code of procedure is a voluminous legislative act in which all the norms must be co-ordinated. Besides, procedural laws and especially codes must be stable and planned for a long time ahead. This is the reason why the development of the drafts of the new Code of Civil Procedure and the new Code of Criminal Procedure has been under way for several years.

A draft of the new Code of Criminal Procedure has been developed for about three years. It is well known that there were two versions of the draft prepared. The draft has been under consideration in the State Duma since the end of 1994. The urgent need in adopting a new Code of Criminal Procedure is explained, among other things, by introducing into effect a new Criminal Code of the Russian Federation on January 1 1997.

Of special interest for this chapter is the situation with the project of the new Code of Civil Procedure. The development of this project was accomplished by a working group formed at the Ministry of Justice by the decision of May 24, 1993. The working group included employees of the courts and the Ministry of Justice, representatives of civil procedure law scholars.

The first draft of the Code of Civil Procedure was ready by the end of 1994 – early 1995. It was published as a separate edition "The Code of Civil Procedure of the Russian Federation. Draft.". – M.: Ministry of Justice. 1995. According to the plan of legislative work for 1995, the draft of the Code of Civil Procedure was to be discussed in the State Duma in October 1995. For a number of reasons, including those connected with some incomplete draft laws, which the work on the project depended on, it was not submitted for consideration to the State Duma in 1995. For example, the developers had not been able to solve certain problems before the law "On the Judicial System of Russian Federation" determining courts structure in was adopted.

Work on the second draft of the Code of Civil Procedure was completed by April 1997. This draft, as well as the first one, was published as a separate edition and discussed at the international conference which was held in April 1997 in Moscow. Official information about the future of the new Code of Civil Procedure project was not available to the author of this chapter at the time of finishing the manuscript.

A code which is called in Russia the Code of State Arbitration Procedure (hereinafter CAP), regulates court procedures in state arbitration courts which were established in 1991–1992 to resolve economic disputes between organisations and citizens involved in enterpreneurship activities. In less than five years' period two Codes of Arbitration Procedure were prepared and adopted (1992 and 1995). However, we might expect that no changes will be introduced to the code of 1995, or that work on the next, third, project of the Code of Arbitration Procedure will soon begin. Opinions about the advisability of improving the 1995 Code of Arbitration Procedure are being expressed unofficially by theoreticians and practical workers.

There is also no information about the possible time of adopting a draft of the new law "On the Courts of Commercial Arbitration" which has been ready for two years. During the 1995–1996, according to the initiative and under the aegis of the Chamber of Commerce of Russian Federation a draft law "On the Courts of Arbitration" was developed. The draft law was twice (in October and December 1995) discussed at the meetings of the Council on the Courts of commercial arbitration at the RF Chamber of Commerce. The project, improved after the discussions, was submitted to the State Duma of the Federal Assembly by a group of deputies and considered by the Council of the State Duma on June 4, 1996. In October 1996 the State Duma rejected the project. At present the project is being worked on. According to the idea of its developers, it is supposed to replace two legislative acts on the Arbitration Tribunal now in force: Annex 3 to the Code of Civil Procedure of RSFSR and Temporary Regulations. Thus, in case the draft law is adopted, there will be two laws on the Court of Arbitration in force: 1) a law of July 7, 1993 "On International Commercial Arbitration"; 2) a newly adopted law "On the Courts of Commercial Arbitration in Russian Federation".

2. Organisation of the judicial system in the Russian Federation

2.1. Legislation of court system and procedure. General characteristics

The judicial system of the Russian Federation is established by the Constitution of the Russian Federation and a federal constitutional law. Such federal constitutional law (FCL) is a FCL "On Judicial System in the Russian Federation".

According to Article 4 of the FCL "On Judicial System in the Russian Federation", in the Russian Federation there are federal courts, constitutional courts and conciliating courts of the subjects of the Russian Federation.

Federal courts include:

– Constitutional Court of the Russian Federation, Supreme Court of the RF, supreme courts of the Republics, Territory/Krai and Region/Oblast courts, city courts in the cities of federal importance, autonomous region and autonomous district courts, district courts, military

and specialised courts. They constitute the system of federal courts of general jurisdiction;
- Supreme State Arbitration Court of the Russian Federation; regional federal state arbitration courts, state arbitration courts of the subjects of the Russian Federation. They constitute the system of federal state courts of arbitration.

Three supreme judicial bodies of the federal courts – Constitutional Court of RF, Supreme Court of RF, Supreme State Arbitration Court of RF – were established according to the Constitution of the Russian Federation and can be abolished only by means of making amendments to the Constitution of RF. Other federal courts are established and abolished only by means of a federal law.

Along with the FCL "On Judicial System in the Russian Federation", there were adopted two more FCLs now in force which determine organisation of the federal courts: FCL of July 21, 1994 "On Constitutional Court of the Russian Federation" and FCL of April 28 1995 "On Arbitration Courts in the Russian Federation".

A FCL about competence, procedure of establishment and functioning of the courts of general jurisdiction headed by the Supreme Court of RF has not been yet adopted. These questions are regulated by the RSFSR law of July 8, 1981 "On Judicature in RSFSR" (with further changes and additions) which is being applied in the part which does not contradict FCL "On Judicial System in the Russian Federation".

A possibility of establishing courts of the subjects of RF has been provided for in FCL "On Judicial System in the Russian Federation" for the first time. Courts of the subjects of RF include constitutional courts of the subjects of RF and justices of peace who are judges of the subjects of RF.

Thus, on the level of FCL the practice of establishing constitutional courts or committees of the constitutional supervision in the subjects of RF has been sanctioned after having been spread for some time in the subjects of RF even before the FCL was adopted.

The constitutional court of a subject of RF can be established by the subject to consider issues of consistency with the basic law of the subject of this subject's laws, of legal acts of the bodies of state power of the subject and bodies of local self-government, and to interpret the constitution (charter) of the subject of RF. The procedure of considering the issues within the competence of the constitutional court of the subject of RF is regulated by a law of the subject.

After implementation of the justice of peace system, justices of the peace will consider within their competence civil, administrative and criminal cases as the court of the first instance. Powers and proceedings of the justice of peace must be established by a federal law and a law of the subject of RF (Article 28 FCL "On Judicial System in the Russian Federation"). Information about such laws being adopted was not available by November 1997.

It should be noted that there are no specialised federal courts yet. Their establishment will be possible after adopting a special federal constitutional law.

2.2. Constitutional basis and principles of the judicial power structure and administration of justice

Justice in RF is administered only by court (Article 118 of the RF Constitution, 1993). It means that the state endowed only the state courts included in the judicial system established by the RF Constitution and FCL with the responsibility to administer justice. From the point of view of the Russian historical experience, the constitutional ban on establishing "emergency courts" is very important (Part 3, Article 118 of the RF Constitution).

Constitutional norms about the unity of the judicial system were further developed in the FCL "On Judicial System in the Russian Federation" which for the first time determined the elements of this system (see above) and provided guarantees of the unity of the judicial system. According to article 3 of this FCL, the unity of the judicial system is provided by means of:

- establishing the RF judicial system by the RF Constitution and FCL "On Judicial System in the Russian Federation";
- complying with the rules of the court procedure established by the federal laws for all federal courts and justices of the peace;

- applying by all the courts RF Constitution, federal constitutional laws, universally recognised principles and norms of the international law and international treaties/agreements of RF, as well as constitutions (charters) of the subjects of RF;
- recognising compulsory execution in the whole territory of RF of the court judgements which have entered in force;
- legislative consolidation of the uniform status of judges;
- financing federal courts and justices of peace from the federal budget.

RF Constitution of 1993, have fixed important principles of judicial power organisation based on the constitutional provision for the division of the powers and providing real independence of the judicial power from the legislative and executive branches of power. Among such principles are: independence of judges and their subordination only to law, irremovability and inviolability of judges, publicity of the court examination, financing of the courts only from the federal budget (Articles 120–124 of the RF Constitution).

The most important constitutional principles of the court procedure are: adversarity and equality of the parties (Part 3, Article 123 RF Constitution). We can say without exaggeration that the fact of making these particular principles constitutional has already resulted in cardinal changes in philosophy and rules of the civil, criminal and arbitration procedure. At the same time, the implementation of these principles in the specific norms of the procedural law and their concrete application in the courts, requires further development.

2.3. Constitutional Court of the Russian Federation. Authorities and order of their realisation

Constitutional Court of RF was established based on article 163 of the RSFSR Constitution adopted by the Congress of People's Deputies of RSFSR on May 24, 1991. It was a supreme body of constitutional supervision in RSFSR executing judicial power in the form of constitutional legal procedure. On April 21, 1992, the wording of the article was changed and the Constitutional Court was defined as "the supreme body of the judicial power for protection of the constitutional system".

According to the new RF Constitution adopted on December 12, 1993, FCL "On the Constitutional Court of the Russian Federation" was adopted which entered into force on July 23, 1994.

According to Article 3 of this FCL, the RF Constitutional Court at present is endowed with the following powers:

to resolve cases on consistency with the RF Constitution of :

– federal laws, normative acts of the RF President, of the Council of Federation, of the State Duma and of the RF Government;
– constitutions of the republics, charters, also laws and other legislative acts of the RF subjects passed on the issues within the competence of RF bodies of state power and within the joint competence of RF bodies of state power and bodies of the RF subjects
– agreements between RF bodies of the state power and bodies of the RF subjects, agreements between bodies of the subjects;
– international treaties of RF before they have entered into force;
– to solve disputes about competence:
– between federal bodies of state power;
– between bodies of RF and bodies of RF subjects;
– between the supreme state bodies of the RF subjects;
– to check on the constitutional validity of the law applied or due to be applied in the concrete case (based on the complaints about violation of constitutional rights and freedoms and on the request of the court);
– to interpret the RF Constitution;
– to make statement on complying with the adequate procedural rules in impeachment of the President with treason or other serious crimes;
– to propose legislative initiatives within competence of the constitutional court;
– to implement other powers granted by the Constitution, the federal treaties and federal constitutional laws, to exercise rights granted by the agreements concluded according to article 11 of the RF Constitution on division of the competence and powers between the bodies of the RF and bodies of the subjects if these rights are not in conflict with its legal nature and tasks of the constitutional court as a judicial body of the constitutional supervision.

The RF Constitutional Court solves exclusively problems of law. It abstains from establishing and examining the factual circumstances when they are within the competence of other courts and bodies.

Order of applying to the RF Constitutional Court, principles and rules of the constitutional court procedure are established in the second and third sections of the FCL "On the Constitutional Court of the Russian Federation" (Articles 29–110).

RF Constitutional Court consisting of 19 judges considers and re-solves cases at plenary sessions in which all the judges take part or the sessions of two chambers (accordingly 10 and 9 judges). The scope of questions to be considered at the plenary sessions and sessions of the chambers is defined in articles 21 and 22 of the FCL "On the Constitu-tional Court of the Russian Federation".

The final decisions of the RF Constitutional Court is called "resolu-tion" or "conclusion". All other decisions are called "definitions". Decisions of the RF Constitutional Court are final and without appeal. They enter into force immediately after being announced and are mandatory in the whole territory of the Russian Federation for all representative, executive and judicial bodies of state power, bodies of local self-government, enterprises, organisations, officials, citizens and their associations. Resolutions and conclusions of the RF Consti-tutional Court are to be published immediately in the official editions of the relevant RF bodies of state power.

Decision of the RF Constitutional Court has direct effect and does not require any confirmation on behalf of other bodies and officials. Legal validity of the RF Constitutional Court resolution declaring a legislative act unconstitutional cannot be overruled by the second adoption of the act. Acts or parts of the acts considered to be unconsti-tutional lose validity; RF international treaties considered to be uncon-stitutional and not yet in force cannot be ratified or implemented. Decisions of courts and other bodies considered to be unconstitutional are not subject to enforcement and must be reviewed in the cases defined by the federal law (Articles 8, 71, 78, 79 FCL "On the Consti-tutional Court of the Russian Federation").

2.4. Courts of general jurisdiction. Structure. Court instances

Before the FCL "On Judicial System in the Russian Federation" was put into effect on January 1, 1997, courts of general jurisdiction consisted of three main links:

the first link – district (city) courts;

the second link – supreme courts of the republics within RF, territory/krai (regional) courts, courts of the cities of federal importance, autonomous region courts, autonomous area courts;

the third link – the Supreme Court of the Russian Federation.

According to the FCL "On Judicial System in the Russian Federation", all above mentioned links of the general jurisdiction courts are included into the judicial system as it used to be before. However, within the competence which is to be determined in the federal law and laws of the RF subjects on the justices of peace which have not been adopted yet, the first (lowest) instance of the courts of general jurisdiction will be represented by the justices of peace. A higher judicial authority over the justices of peace in the territory of the corresponding judicial district will be district courts (Part 2, Article 21 of FCL "On Judicial System in the Russian Federation»).

Relatively independent position in the system of courts of general jurisdiction will be occupied by the military courts of the Army and the Navy which will replace the military tribunals which have been included in the system so far. They have been functioning until now according to the statute on the military tribunals in the wording of the USSR law of June 25, 1980. Article 546 (in the part which does not contradict FCL "On Judicial System in the Russian Federation»). Newly established military courts will consider within their competence cases as the courts of the first, second and third instances. A last instance for the military courts will be the Supreme Court of the Russian Federation.

In case of establishing specialised federal courts in accordance with Article 26 of the FCL "On Judicial System in the Russian Federation", these courts will supposedly occupy a special place in the system of courts of general jurisdiction. Specialised federal courts are not included in the group of courts which have the RF Supreme Court as a last instance for appeal. The RF Supreme Court is, however, endowed with the responsibility of "judicial supervision" over the specialised federal courts activity. The content and legal forms of such supervision are not yet defined by the legislation.

A specific feature of the courts of general jurisdiction in Russia consists in the fact that these courts' structure, at present including three levels and a system of the military tribunals, does not coincide with the system of judicial instances. It would be a mistake to suppose that the courts of the first level represent the first instance and the courts of the second level – the second instance etc.

According to the law, in the courts of general jurisdiction there are three instances: the first, the cassational (the second) and the "supervision" (the third) instances. In view of the subject matter of this book, the system of the court decisions review in the instances is discussed here applied to the decisions on civil cases.

At present, according to the general rule, district courts (up to the establishment of justices of peace) serve as the first judicial instance. At the same time, in the cases provided for by the legislature, functions of the first instance can be carried out by the courts of the second level as well as by the RF Supreme Court. Each of the three levels can consider cases (review the earlier decisions of these court) on the newly discovered circumstances.

A decision of the first instance court enters into legal force 10 days after its final passing, except for the cases when within these 10 days one party files an appeal («cassational appeal») to the cassational instance or when the procurator files a protest («cassational protest») against the decision of the first instance court.

Such appeals and protests are considered by the cassational instance the functions of which can be fulfilled by:
- the courts of the second level – with regard to the decisions of the district (city) courts;
- the RF Supreme Court (Judiciary Board on civil cases) – with regard to the decisions of the second level courts.

If the case has been considered in the RF Supreme Court as the first instance court, the decision enters into legal force immediately and cannot be a subject of reconsideration by the cassational instance.

The functions of the third (supervision) instance are fulfilled by:
- the Presidium of the second level court (with regard to the cassational rulings of these courts and decisions and rulings of the district courts which entered into legal force);
- The Judiciary Board on civil cases or the Judiciary Board on criminal cases of the RF Supreme Court with regard to decisions and rulings of all RF courts which entered into legal force if these decisions and rulings were not the subject of cassational review in the RF Supreme Court, as well as on the decisions of the presidiums of RF courts of the second level;
- The Presidium of the RF Supreme Court (with regard to the decisions and rulings of the Judiciary Boards of the RF Supreme Court).

In practice, it is possible to consider a case consecutively in several instances. Depending on the affiliation of the first instance court to a certain level, and on the fact if the court of the first instance decision was a subject of reconsideration in the cassational instance, the case may be considered in two, three, or even four instances. Below are some examples illustrating judicial practice of the court decisions review in instances.

Example 1. A district court has examined the case as the court of the first instance and passed a decision. Then the district court decision (the court of the first instance) can be reviewed by the Judiciary Board on civil cases of the second instance court the (cassational instance). Then, a cassational ruling of the Judiciary Board on civil cases of the second level courts can become a subject of consideration in the Presidium of the same court of the second level (supervision instance). Then, a decision of the Presidium of the second instance court can be a subject of consideration in yet one more supervision instance (Judiciary Board on civil cases of the RF Supreme Court).

Example 2. The case has been considered by the court of the second level as the court of the first instance. A decision passed by the court can be reviewed by the Judiciary Board on civil cases of the RF Supreme Court (cassational instance). A cassational ruling of the Judiciary Board on civil cases of the RF Supreme Court can be reviewed by the Presidium of the RF Supreme Court (supervision instance).

Example 3. The case has been considered by the RF Supreme Court as the court of the first instance. Since cassational review of such decisions is not allowed, the decision passed on the case can be subject to review only in the Presidium of the RF Supreme Court (supervision instance).

A number of the following examples refer to the cases when a decision of the first instance court is not submitted to the cassational instance for review and, thus, enters into legal force 10 days after its passing. For such cases a number of court instances will be different.

Example 1. The case has been considered by the district court as the first instance court. Since a cassational appeal/ protest have not been filed, the first instance court decision enters into legal force 10 days after its passing. A decision of the first instance court which has entered into legal force, can be a subject of consideration by the Presidium of the court from the second level (supervision instance). Then, a decision of the Presidium of the court from the second level (supervision instance) can become a subject of consideration in yet one more supervision instance (Judiciary Board on civil cases of the RF Supreme Court).

Example 2. The case has been considered by the court of the second level as the court of the first instance. The decision of this court has not been considered by the Judiciary Board on Civil Cases of the RF Supreme Court (cassation instance) by way of cassation. A decision passed by the court of the second level which entered into legal force can be reviewed by the Presidium of the RF Supreme Court (supervision instance).

Completing a brief survey of the review of decisions in the courts of general jurisdiction, we should emphasise that the issue of number and amount of the court instances authorities in Russia is exceptionally urgent and debatable. As an illustration of this problem, one example can be presented here: a draft of the new Code of Civil Procedure includes two versions of the sections about the cassational review: one is based on the necessity of keeping the existing three-instance system intact, the other (alternative) proposes four court instances: the first, appellate, cassational and supervision ones.

The size of the chapter does not allow us to specify the issue of the history of Russia's court instances in more detail. Therefore, readers' attention should be focused only on the lack of appellate instance in Russian courts of general jurisdiction and on the different interpretation of the term "cassational" instance in Russia with analogous name of the court instance in other countries, for example in France. Cassational instance combines features and authorities of two instances: appellate (reconsidering the case before the original decision enters into legal force, including presenting and examining new evidence), and cassational (reconsidering decision on the "point of law" but not on the "point of fact" which entered into legal force). The third instance called "supervision" is unique and only known in the Russian legislature (for more details see: paragraph 3.2. on specific features of considering cases in different instances).

2.5. State arbitration courts in the Russian Federation. Structure. Court Instances

Resolving economic disputes and other cases in the field of economy has been commissioned to the system of the state arbitration courts in RF which consists of three levels:
– the first level – state arbitration courts of the republics, territories, regions, cities of federal importance, autonomous regions, autonomous areas (hereinafter state arbitration courts of RF subjects);
– the second level – area federal arbitration courts;
– the third level – the RF Supreme Arbitration Court.

In the state arbitration courts there are four court instances: the first, appellate (the second), cassational (the third) and "supervision" (the fourth).

The functions of the first instance are fulfilled by the state arbitration courts of the RF subjects (the first level), except the cases which are to be considered by the RF Supreme Arbitration Court as the court of the first instance which considers: a) economic disputes between the Russian Federation and RF subjects; b) cases on invalidation (completely or partly) non-normative acts of the RF President, of the Council of Federation and of the State Duma as a part of the RF Federal Assembly and of the RF Government, when these acts are inconsistent with the law and violate rights and lawful interests of legal entities and citizens-entrepreneurs.

Appellate instances are also located within the state arbitration courts of the RF subjects. They consider appeals against the decisions which had been passed by the same state arbitration courts having examined the case as the courts of the first instance. An appeal can be filed within one month after passing a decision.

Decisions of the state arbitration courts of the first instance, which have not been appealed against in the appellate instance within a month after being passed and thus have entered into legal force, can be a subject of cassational appeal. Decrees of the appellate instance which enter into force immediately after being passed can also be a subject of cassational appeal. Thus, considering cassational appeals, cassational instances review the legality with regard to the decisions of the RF subjects state arbitration courts which have entered into legal force and were passed both in the first and appellate instances.

Since introducing into effect the Code of Arbitration Procedure of the Russian Federation on July 1, 1995, 10 federal regional state courts of arbitration have been established for the purpose of fulfilling functions of this cassational instance.

The fourth ("supervision") instance is the RF Supreme Arbitration Court which can review decisions and decrees of all state courts of arbitration in the Russian Federation except the Presidium of the RF Supreme Arbitration court.

Except for the cases which are subject to consideration by the Supreme Arbitration Court as the first instance court, all other cases within jurisdiction of state arbitration courts can be consecutively considered in all four court instances. If the parties do not exercise the right of appeal, the number of instances is reduced to three: the first, cassational and "supervision".

It is necessary to emphasise a different structure, number, names and competences of the state courts of arbitration and courts of general jurisdiction. The most representative example to prove this is existence of two instances of the same name – cassational – which are in fact absolutely different in essence and in competence. Unlike the courts of general jurisdiction, where cassational instance examines appeals against decisions of the first instance courts which have not entered into legal force, in the state arbitration courts this instance examines appeals against the first instance court decisions which have entered into legal force and decision of the appellation instance (the latter not being possible in the courts of general jurisdiction).

2.6. Judicial Reform: short-term perspectives

The closest steps directed at the implementation of the judicial reform will probably be adopting and enforcing federal constitutional laws and federal laws which are envisaged in the FCL "On Judicial System of the Russian Federation". Among such laws are : a federal law and laws of the RF subjects on justices of peace; FCL defining powers, order of establishing and functioning of the RF Supreme Court and other courts of general jurisdiction which are under its supervision (including military courts and specialized federal courts), as well as the RF subjects laws on establishing the constitutional courts of RF subjects.

Further measures on implementation of the judicial reform may be connected not only with the internal problems but also with the fact that Russian Federation joined the Council of Europe. Preparation of the appropriate proposals should be completed by the RF President's Council on the issues of justice improvement, which was organised according to the President's decree of October 14, 1997 (to replace the RF President's Council on Judicial Reform). According to the statute on this Council, the basic directions of its work are:

consistent implementation of the constitutional principles of organising judicial power in order to secure rights and freedoms of the person and the citizen;

elaboration of the proposals for the organisation and functioning of the judicial power in view of the Russian Federation's joining the Council of Europe;

preparation of the conceptions of the legal procedure system, as well as development of the Russian Federation legislation for judicial defence of the rights and freedoms of the person and the citizen when violated by bodies of the executive power and officials etc.

3. Basic procedural rules and institutions in the courts of general jurisdiction and in the state courts of arbitration

3.1. Jurisdiction in the courts of general jurisdiction and state arbitration courts in civil cases. Cases of conflicting jurisdiction. Means of their resolving

Defining a scope of disputes to be resolved by the courts of general jurisdiction and the state arbitration courts has a significant practical importance. Every person (either physical or legal), in the process of using the constitutional right of judicial defence, should decide correctly: state court of which of the two systems (courts of general jurisdiction or state courts of arbitration) he/she should resort to for defending the violated or disputed right protected by law.

The procedural legislation does not always give a clear answer to this question.

According to the general rule, courts of general jurisdiction consider cases on the disputes occurring from civil, family, labour, kolhoze farm legal relationship, if at least one party in the dispute is an individual citizen. Besides, these courts consider the following cases with the parties as described above: resulting from the administrative legal relationship" (listed in Article 231 of the Code of Civil Procedure and including: cases on the complaints on electorate lists; on the complaints on actions of the state bodies and officials connected with administrative punishment; on the complaints on actions of the state bodies, public organisations and officials violating rights and freedoms of citizens; on the complaints connected with denying exit visa permit from the Russian Federation or entry visa permit to the Russian Federation; other cases included into the courts jurisdiction); "cases of a special legal procedure" (listed in Article 245 of the Code of Civil Procedure and including: cases on establishing facts having judicial significance; on declaring a citizen missing and on declaring a citizen dead; on recognising a citizen incompetent or completely legally incompetent; on declaring property masterless; on defining errors in the Registry Office books on civil status; on complaints on notary actions or refusal to complete notary actions; on reinstitution of rights according to the lost documents).

During the last decade, a general approach to defining a scope of disputes to be considered by the courts of general jurisdiction has drastically changed. Before the 90's, these courts considered only disputes within their direct jurisdiction in accordance with the law. Adoption and application of the Declaration of Human Rights and Freedoms of the Person and the Citizen (on January 22, 1991) and after that of a new RF Constitution (1993), where in Article 46 "everyone is guaranteed judicial defence of one's rights and freedoms", allowed to shape such judicial practice where any disputes connected with defending rights and freedoms of a person and a citizen are within jurisdiction of court.

This rule is applied to defending the rights of the organisations (legal entities). Equal rights of the citizens and organisations for judicial defence of their rights is justified not only by the reference to Article 46 of the RF Constitution but also to other statutes of the Constitution, and in particular, to the article 8 saying that private, state, and other types of property are equally acknowledged and defended.

Furthermore, in the article 25 of the Code of Civil Procedure two groups of cases where the parties are not citizens but organisations, are classified as disputes to be considered by the courts of general jurisdiction: the disputes resulting from the contracts on direct international transport of goods by railway and by air between state enterprises and organisations, co-operative organisations, their associations, other organisations on the one side, and bodies of the railway or air transport on the other side, according to the corresponding international treaty; cases in which participate foreign citizens, stateless persons, foreign enterprises and organisations, unless otherwise provided by inter-state agreement, international treaty, or agreement of the parties.

State arbitration courts consider cases on economic disputes occurring from civil, administrative or other relationship:

between legal entities and citizens performing entrepreneurial work without establishing juridical entity and having a status of individual entrepreneur acquired in accordance with the established procedure (citizens-entrepreneurs);

between the Russian Federation and subjects of the Russian Federation, between subjects of the Russian Federation.

Among economic disputes between the above mentioned parties which are be considered by the state courts of arbitration are, for example, disputes: on changing terms of contracts or cancelling contracts; on failures to perform or on improper observance of contract obligations; on recognition of property rights; on vindication by lawful owner property from unlawful possession; on violation of proprietor's or other legal holders rights not connected with deprivation of property; on recovery of losses; on declaring invalid/void (completely or partly) of non-normative legal acts of the state bodies which are inconsistent with the laws in force and other legitimate acts and violate rights and lawful interests of organisations and/or citizens; on protection of honour, dignity and business reputation; on recognising a enforcement document in indisputable order not subject to execution; on appealing against refusal of official registration or evasion from the official registration of an organisation or a citizen within a designated period of time, or in other cases when such registration is stipulated by the law; on fining organisations and citizens by state bodies, bodies of local self-government and other bodies exercising control functions if the federal law does not stipulate indisputable order of fining; on reimbursement from the budget finances written off by the bodies exercising control functions in indisputable order with violation of law or other legislative act (section 2 of article 22 of the Code of Arbitration Procedure).

State courts of arbitration also consider other cases (not included in the concept of "economic disputes»). Among them are cases: a) on establishing facts relevant for creating, changing or cessation of rights of organisations and citizens in the field of entrepreneurial or other economic activity; b) on insolvency (bankruptcy) of legal entities and citizens-entrepreneurs.

There are two criteria of dividing jurisdiction between courts of general jurisdiction and state courts of arbitration: composition of the participants; character of the dispute.

Unfortunately, both criteria are not perfect. The size of the chapter does not allow us to give a complete list of the examples to show that courts of general jurisdiction not only consider disputes with citizens (physical persons) as participants, but also disputes with participating organisations, and state courts of arbitration not only consider disputes with involved legal entities and citizens-entrepreneurs, but also disputes with involved citizens who are not entrepreneurs and disputes in which parties do not have rights of a legal entity.

The possibility of deviation from the general rule, saying that only cases with participation of those parties which are legal entities or citizens-entrepreneurs should be within competence of the state courts of arbitration, is established in section 4, Article 22 of the Code of Arbitration Procedure.

One of the examples of application section 4 of article 22 of the Code of Arbitration Procedure (CAP) is filing an appeal against refusal in official registration of the organisations which are not legal entities and of the citizens not having a status of a citizen-entrepreneur.

One more example: filing a suit for protection of state and public interests by state bodies not being legal entities, bodies of local self-government and other bodies (Article 42 of the CAP).

Furthermore, legislature directly provides for the jurisdiction of the cases on insolvency/bankruptcy in which creditors may be represented by the citizens not having a status of a citizen-entrepreneur to the state courts of arbitration.

In conclusion some words about the jurisdiction of the disputes involving foreigners.

On the one hand, in accordance with section 6, article 22 of the CAP, from the July 1, 1995 state courts of arbitration have in their jurisdiction cases on economic disputes in the course of civil, administrative and other legal relationship not only between Russian organisations and citizen-entrepreneurs, but also "foreign organisations, organisations with foreign investments, international organisations, foreign citizens, stateless people involved in entrepreneurship, unless otherwise stipulated by the international agreement of the Russian Federation".

The current situation is assessed by some specialists as a "joint competence" of the two judicial systems, or as an "alternative jurisdiction" of the economic disputes "with a foreign element".

Other specialists claim that with enforcement of the new Code of Arbitration Procedure of the Russian Federation (July 1, 1995), a rule secured in article 25 of the Code of Civil Procedure about jurisdiction of disputes with participation of foreign organisations and organisations with foreign investments, became invalid.

In practice courts of general jurisdiction refer to article 25 of the Code of Civil Procedure, and state courts of arbitration – section 6, article 22 of the CAP of 1995. It gives the parties a possibility to choose, either to lodge a claim to the court of general jurisdiction or to the state court of arbitration.

3.2. Basic procedural rules. Civil procedure in the courts of general jurisdiction

in the first instance

Courts consider cases: a) based on suit; b) not based on suit (on the cases from administrative legal relationship and cases of special procedure).

Civil action cases are initiated by filing a plaintiff's statement of claim/petition to sue, cases from administrative legal relationship – by filing an application, and cases of special procedure – by filing a complaint.

A plaintiff's statement of claim is submitted in a written form and must contain the following information: 1) name of the court where the plaintiff's statement of claim is filed; 2) name of the plaintiff, his address and if the plaintiff is a legal entity – its location, as well as the name of his representative and his address, if the statement of claim is lodged by a representative; 3) name of the defendant, his address and if the defendant is a legal entity, its location; 4) facts on which the plaintiff grounds his claim and evidence confirming the facts stated by the plaintiff; 6) value of the claim if the claim is subject to assessment; 7) list of the documents attached to the statement of claim.

A statement of claim is signed by the plaintiff or his representative. A letter of authorisation or another document certifying authority of the representative should be attached to the statement of claim signed by the representative (Article 126 of the Code of Civil Procedure).

It should be emphasised that the Code of Civil Procedure does not contain a requirement to specify in the statement of claim a legal norm which a plaintiff grounds his claim on. In accordance with the Law of Civil Procedure, it is the court's responsibility.

The statement of claim is submitted to the court with a number of copies corresponding to the number of defendants (Article 127 of the Code of Civil Procedure). A document certifying the payment of a due court fee (see paragraph 3.3. of this chapter) is attached to the statement of claim.

A defendant has a right to join in with the counterclaim formally registered according to the rules for the statement of claim. The counterclaim is accepted: 1) if it is meant as a set-off against the original claim; 2) if sustaining the counterclaim completely or in part rules out sustaining of the original claim; 3) if there is inter-connection between the counterclaim and the original claim and their joint consideration will result in a faster and correct resolution of the dispute. (Articles 131–132 of the Code of Civil Procedure).

A judge considers a question about accepting a statement of claim individually and can reject it only in case of grounds specified in Article 129 of the Code of Civil Procedure.

The Code of Civil Procedure regulates the procedure of preparation a case for the trial which is performed by a judge individually. The tasks of such preparation are : specifying facts relevant for correct settlement of the case; determining legal relationship of the parties and of the law to comply with; specifying the parties involved in the case; determining the evidence which every party shall present in order to substantiate its allegations.

During the preparation phase the judge performs actions provided for in article 142 of the Code of Civil Procedure including the following: a) interviewing the plaintiff on the substance of the claim, explaining possible objections from the side of the defendant, suggesting submitting additional evidence, explaining to the plaintiff his legal rights and responsibilities; b) summoning the defendant if necessary, interviewing him about the facts of the case, finding out about possible objections to the claim and how these objections could be substantiated, in especially complicated cases suggesting submitting written explanations on the case, explaining to the defendant his rights and responsibilities.

Parties in the case must be informed about the court session.

Before 1992, all the cases in the first instance were considered collegially by the members of the court consisting of one judge and two People's Assessors.

At present, a judge considers cases alone when it is directly provided for in the Code of Civil Procedure(Article 113) or if the parties do not object against one judge composition before the consideration of the substance of the case started. In case of such objection, the case is considered collegially by a professional judge and two People's Assessors (Article 6 of the Code of Civil Procedure).

A case is considered by court, as a rule, at a public court session, orally and with the fixed judges membership. A session should be continuous except for the time assigned for rest. Before the end of the trial or its adjourning, the court is not entitled to consider other cases.

The court session consists of five parts: 1) preparatory part of a court session; 2) consideration of the substance of a case; 3) pleadings; 4) procurator's opinion if he participates in the case; 5) passing and pronouncing of the decision. The order of the proceedings is rather well regulated in Articles 144–190 of the Code of Civil Procedure.

A resolution of the first instance court on the substance of the case is pronounced in the form of judgement. If the trial is terminated without a decision on substance, the court adopts a judicial act called a definition.

Court resolves the case within the limits of the plaintiff's claim. However, the court can go beyond the plaintiff's claim if it is recognised necessary for defending rights and interests of the plaintiff protected by law and in other cases established by the law. (Article 195 of the Code of Civil Procedure).

Cases resulting from the administrative legal relationship and cases of special procedure are considered according to the general rules of the civil action with some specific features established for each category of such cases in chapters 22–32 of the Code of Civil Procedure.

According to the RF law of October 27 (November 30, 1995), additions have been introduced to the Code of Civil Procedure providing for special procedures: a) for releasing court order (having authority of a writ of enforcement with regard to the decree of the judge, pronounced on the creditor's claim of recovery sums of money or obtaining personal property from the debtor, not disputing the filed claim) (Chapter 11–1 of the Code of Civil Procedure); b) judgement by default which can be pronounced in case when a properly informed defendant did not appear at the court session and a plaintiff does not object against a decision being passed in his absence (Chapter 16–1 of the Code of Civil Procedure). For such procedures special periods of procedure, rules of court proceedings, and procedure of appeal have been established.

in cassational instance

Decisions of all the courts of the Russian Federation except the decisions of the RF Supreme Court can be appealed by way of cassation on behalf of the parties or individuals participating in the case. In such situations legal procedure in cassational instance is initiated by filing "a cassational appeal".

Procurator and Deputy Procurator also have a right of instituting cassational legal procedure. They lodge "a cassational protest" instead of "a cassational appeal".

A cassational appeal or protest are lodged against the decision of the court of the first instance which have not entered into legal force, which is within 10 days after passing the final decision.

A cassational appeal or protest should contain 1) name of the court to which an appeal or a protest are addressed; 2) name of the person filing an appeal or a protest; 3) indication of the decision which is being appealed against or protested and of the court which passed the decision; 4) indication of the failure of justice and a claim/request of the appellant; 5) list of the written materials attached to an appeal or a protest.

A cassational appeal is signed by the person filing it or by his representative (in the latter case a letter of attorney or another document certifying a representative's authorities should be attached to the cassational appeal). A cassational protest is signed by the procurator.

A cassational appeal or a protest is addressed to the corresponding court of cassation (see paragraph 2 of this chapter), but they are submitted to the court whose decision is being appealed against or protested. This court in its turn submits the case together with the appeal (protest) to the court of cassational instance.

A court of cassational instance verifies legality and validity of the first instance court decision within the cassation appeal. It can examine new evidence and establish new facts. The court of cassational instance examines new evidence submitted by the parties, if it admits that the evidence could not be submitted to the court of the first instance. At the same time, the court has a right to verify the lower court decision completely "in the interest of law" (Article 294 of the Code of Civil Procedure).

The parties in the case are informed about the time and place of hearing the cassational appeal. However, if such parties being duly informed about the time and place of the trial do not attend the court session, court can consider the case in their absence (by default).

Legal court proceedings in the cassational instance are defined in Articles 295–304 of the Code of Civil Procedure. The case is considered collegially by three professional judges. The parties and other participating persons and their representatives have a right to give explanations to the court and give arguments, including the ones not mentioned in the cassation appeal or protest and to submit additional materials after one of the judges has announced the description of the case.

First, speaks a person who filed a cassational appeal and his representative or procurator (in case of a cassational protest). In case of both parties appealing against the decision, the first to speak is a plaintiff. The procurator pronounces his opinion on the validity of the decision after hearing explanations of the persons participating in the case.

After hearing explanations of the persons participating in the case and procurator's opinion, the court members go to a special room for deliberations on the judicial act which is called a ruling. From the moment of its passing, this ruling enters in force and can not be appealed.

The court of cassational instance can by its ruling:
- leave the decision unchanged and dismiss an appeal;
- revoke the decision completely or in part and relegate the case for reconsideration to the court of the first instance with the same or different composition of the bench;
- revoke the decision completely or in part and drop legal proceedings or dismiss the appeal;
- change the decision or pass a new decision without submitting the case for reconsideration (if the facts relevant to the case have been established on the basis of the existing and additionally presented materials which the parties have been acquainted with) (Article 305 of the Code of Civil Procedure). In the latter case, despite the fact

that "a decision" is passed on the case, it is formally registered in the document called "a ruling".

Grounds for revoking the court decision in the cassational instance and submitting the case for reconsideration to the first instance court are the following:
- incorrect establishment of the legally relevant circumstances;
- unproved facts relevant for the case which the court considers established;
- inconsistency of the court conclusions laid down in the decision with the facts of the case;
- violation or misuse of the material laws or norms of procedural law.

However, a court decision correct with regard to the substance of the case, cannot be revoked on formal grounds alone (Article 306 of the Code of Civil Procedure).

In case of revoking a decision of the first instance court and submitting the case for reconsideration, the court of cassational lays down in its ruling instructions mandatory for the court which will reconsider the case. However, such instructions should not prejudge the issues of validity or invalidity of the evidence, the issues of advantages of some evidence over the other, and of a decision to be passed in the retrial.

in the supervision instance

Judicial acts which entered into legal force (decisions and rulings of the first instance court, rulings of the court of cassational instance, decrees of the supervision instance) can be reconsidered in exercise of a special procedure called "judicial supervision".

Supervision procedure cannot be initiated on the grounds of a complaint on behalf of a party or other persons participating in the case. Supervision procedure can be initiated only on the grounds of appeals of officials whose range is exhaustively defined in the Code of Civil procedure. Such appeals are called "protests".

The following officials have a right of filing a protest: 1) Procurator of RF, Chairman of the RF Supreme Court and their deputies (against decisions, rulings, decrees of any court in the Russian Federation except the rulings of the Presidium of the RF Supreme Court); b) chairman of the supreme court of the republic within the Russian Federation, of the autonomous region court and autonomous territory court, procurator of the republic, regions or territories, autonomous regions and territories – against the decisions and rulings of the district (city) courts and rulings of the judicial boards on civil cases of the supreme court of the republic within the Russian Federation, autonomous region court and autonomous territory court respectively.

Officials having a right of filing a protest have a right of requiring documents in civil cases from respective courts to resolve the question whether there is grounds for filing a protest by way of supervision; of suspending execution of the decision, ruling or decree which are protested against.

Court sends copies of a protest to the parties and other persons participating in the case and if necessary informs them about the time and place of the trial.

In the process of case consideration, the supervision instance examines correctness of application and interpretation of the norms of material and procedural law by the first instance courts and of cassational instance courts with regard to the materials of the case within the arguments of the protest. However, in the interests of law, the court of supervision instance can go beyond the limits of the protest.

The period of considering a protest in the supervision instance cannot exceed one month.

The supervision instance passes a judicial act which is called "decree" or "ruling" which enters into legal force immediately.

The grounds for revoking judicial act of the lower courts (decisions, rulings and decrees) in the supervision instance are the following:
– incorrect application or interpretation of the norms of material law;
– serious violation of procedural law resulting in passing unlawful decision, ruling or decree (Article 330 CCP).

As a result of consideration, the supervision instance has a right:

- to leave a decision, ruling or decree unchanged and a protest dismissed;
- to revoke the decision, ruling or decree completely or in part and relegate the case for reconsideration to the court of the first instance or to the court of cassational instance;
- to revoke the decision, ruling or decree completely or in part and drop legal proceedings or refuse to consider the appeal in substance;
- to leave one of the previously passed decisions, rulings and decrees in force;
- to revoke or change the decision of the first, cassational or supervision instance and pass a new decision without submitting the case for reconsideration in case of failure in application and interpretation of the norms of material law.

3.3. Economic disputes in the state courts of arbitration

in the first instance

Legal proceedings on the case in the first instance start with filing a statement of claim in a written form.

A statement of claim must contain: 1) name of the state court of arbitration where the statement of claim is filed; 2) names of the persons participating in the case and their postal addresses; 3) value of the claim if the claim is subject to assessment; 4) name of the defendant, his address and if the defendant is a legal entity, its location; 4) facts on which the claim is based; 5) evidence confirming the grounds for the claim; 6) calculation of the amount under dispute; 7) plaintiff's claims with the reference to the laws or other legislative acts, and in case of suing several defendants – claims to each of them; 8) information about compliance with pre-trial proceedings of settling a dispute with the defendant, when it is provided for by the federal law for a certain category of disputes or by an agreement; 9) list of the attached documents. Other information is also included in the statement of claim if it is necessary for the proper settlement of the dispute, as well as the plaintiff's petitions (Article 1102 CAP).

Attached to the statement of claim should be the documents certifying: 1) payments of the due court fees; 2) posting copies of the statement of claim and attached documents; 3) compliance with pretrial procedure of settling a dispute with the defendant when it is provided for by the federal law for a certain category of disputes or by an agreement; 4) facts that serve as a ground for the claim. If the statement of claim is signed by the plaintiff's representative, a letter of attorney is attached which certifies his authorities for filing the claim. The claim to a compel to a contract is supplied by a draft contract (Article 104 CAP).

Decision about acceptance of the statement is made by the judge who can: a) accept the statement of claim for consideration; b) reject the statement of claim (Article 107 CAP); c) return the statement of claim without consideration (Article 108 CAP). The main difference between "rejection of the statement of claim" and "returning the statement of claim" consists in procedural consequences. In case of "rejection of the statement of claim" (for example, for the reason that the dispute is not subject to consideration in the state court of arbitration) the repeated resort to such court is possible only after revoking the ruling about "rejection by the higher courts. "Returning" of the statement of claim (for example, for the reason of failure to comply with the required content and form of the statement of claim established by Article 102 CAP) does not prevent repeated resort to the state court of arbitration (after eliminating errors). Defendant has a right to submit his opinion of the statement of claim to the state court of arbitration and to file a counterclaim (Articles 109, 110 CAP).

The judge performs preparation of the case to the hearing informing interested parties about the proceedings on the case, proposing to present documents and information relevant for resolving the dispute, summoning witnesses, considering the question of ordering the expertise, taking interim measures to reconciliate the parties, taking measures to secure the claim (Article 112 CAP).

Consideration of the case takes place at the court session. According to the general rule, judge considers the case in the first instance individually. The following cases are subject to mandatory collegiate consideration by three professional judges: a) cases about annulling acts of the state bodies/agencies, bodies of self-government and other bodies; b) cases about insolvency(bankruptcy). By the decision of the Chairman of the state court of arbitration, any case can be considered collegially (Article 14 CAP). Hearing of the case is held with the fixed composition of the court. In case of replacing one of the judges in the process of the trial, it must be done in the very beginning (Article 117 CAP).

The proceedings of the trial and examination of the evidence are determined by the judge. During the session court examines the evidence on the case; listens to the explanations of the parties involved in the case, to the witness testimony, to the findings of the experts; examines documents and other material evidence.

The parties must be informed about the time and place of the hearing. If the defendant being properly informed fails to appear in court, the case can be considered by default. In case of the plaintiff's failure to appear in court after being properly informed, the case can be considered by default only if there is an application about considering the case by default (Article 119 CAP).

The case must be tried and decided within the period of two months after the statement of claim has been filed to the state court of arbitration.

When the dispute is resolved on the substance, the trial is finished by passing a decision.

For the two categories of cases special rules of procedure have been established.

Cases about insolvency (bankruptcy) are considered in accordance with the regulations of the CAP with some specific features regulated by the law on insolvency (bankruptcy) (Article 143 CAP).

Consideration of applications about establishing facts having legal importance is held according to the procedure regulated in CAP. However, the practice has worked out specific features of considering such applications. Among the legal facts which are established by the state court of arbitration, are a fact of fixtures to a building or to a plot of land as a part of property, a fact of good faith, open and continuous possession of real property as one's own property for 15 years, or other property for 5 years, a fact of organisation registration at a certain time and a certain place.

State courts of arbitration consider applications about establishing legal facts if in accordance with the law such facts result in legal consequences; if establishing of the legal fact is not connected with settling a dispute on the point of law, which is within jurisdiction of the state court of arbitration; if the appellant has no other possibility to obtain or restore proper documents certifying a legal fact; if the effective legislature does not provide for another (other than judicial) way of establishing a legal fact. All the above listed conditions in the aggregate are grounds for accepting an application about establishing a legal fact (see: decree of the Plenum of the Supreme Arbitration Court of Russia of October 31, 1996 "On application of the Code of Arbitration Procedure of RF in consideration of cases in the court of the first instance»).

in the appellate instance

Appellate procedure is initiated with filing an appeal. Such an appeal can be filed against the decision which has not entered into legal force, which is within one month after its passing by the state arbitration court of the first instance (Articles 145–147 CAP). The appeal must be considered within a period of one month after filing at the state court of arbitration (Article 156 CAP).

An appeal must include: 1) name of the state court of arbitration to which the appeal is addressed; 2) name of the appellant and persons involved in the case; 3) name of the state court of arbitration which passed the decision which is being appealed against, case number and date of passing the decision, a subject matter of the dispute; 4) demands of the appellant filing an appeal and grounds on which the appellant considers the decision incorrect with reference to the laws or legislative acts and materials of the case; 5) list of the attached documents.

An appeal is signed by the appellant or his representative. A letter of attorney certifying his authorities for appealing against judicial acts is attached to the appeal (Article 148 CAP). Certificates of court fees payments and of posting copies to other persons involved in the case, are attached to the appellate appeal (Article 148 CAP).

The appellant should send copies of the appeal and attached documents to all persons involved in the case (Article 149 CAP).

If the appeal does not meet requirements on the content and form of the appeal, it is returned by the judge without consideration (Article 151 CAP).

The case is considered in the appellate instance by three professional judges.

The procedure of the court proceedings in the appellate instance is not established in CAP. Such trial is held according to the rules of procedure for the first instance court with specific features of the appellate instance (Article 153). It means that the court proceedings are determined by court. The parties and other involved persons are informed about the time and place of the hearing, and as a rule they participate in the session, give explanations to court, ask and answer questions, announce petitions.

The appellate instance reconsiders cases based on the existing and additionally presented evidence. However, additional evidence is not accepted by court if the appellant has not proved that for objective reasons he had no possibility to present this evidence to the first instance court.

As a result of considering the case, the appellate instance has a right: 1) to leave the decision of the first instance court unchanged, and the appeal dismissed; 2) to revoke the decision of the first instance court completely and in part or pass a new decision; 3) to change the decision of the first instance court; 4) to revoke the decision in full or in part and drop legal proceedings or refuse to consider the case in substance completely or in part (Article 157 CAP).

Appellate instance can not relegate the case for reconsideration to the first instance.

Grounds for changing or revoking the decision of the first instance court are the following: 1) incomplete examination of the evidence relevant for the case; 2) unproved evidence relevant for the case; 3) inconsistency of the findings laid down in the decision of the first instance court with the facts.; 4) violation and incorrect application of the norms of material and procedural law. (Article 158 CAP).

In Part 3, Article 158 of the CAP there is a list of the procedural law violations which serve as ground for revoking a decision of the first instance court (consideration of the case by illegal composition of the court, breaking the rule about the language of the legal procedure, lack of judges' signatures on the decision, etc.) These grounds are called "unconditional" for revoking a decision of the first instance court.

A judicial act passed by the appellate instance as a result of considering the case, is called "a decree". A decree must be signed by all the judges who considered the case, and it enters in force from the moment of passing.

in cassation instance

The cassation instance verifies correctness of applying norms of material law and norms of procedural law by the courts of the first instance and by the courts of appellate instance (Article 174 CAP).

The cassational instance considers appeals («cassational appeals") against the decisions of the first instance court which have entered into legal force (decisions which have not been appealed against during one month after passing) and against the decrees of the appellate instance.

A cassational appeal can be filed within one month after the appealed decision or decree enters into legal force. Such an appeal is addressed to the cassational instance (the federal district state court of arbitration), but it is sent to this court through the state court of arbitration of the subject of RF (passing decisions and decrees subject to appeal). The state court of arbitration of the subject/unit of RF refers the cassational appeal together with the case to the proper federal district state court of arbitration (Articles 161, 163 CAP).

A cassational appeal must be considered within one month after its arriving together with the case to the federal district state court of arbitration (Article 173 CAP).

Cassation appeal should include: 1) name of the state court of arbitration to which the appeal is addressed; 2) name of the person filing an appeal and persons involved in the case; 3) name of the state court of arbitration which passed the decision or decree being appealed against, the case number and the date of passing the decision or decree, the subject of the dispute; 4) demands of the appellant and indication of the failure of justice or wrong application of the norms of material law or norms of procedural law; 5) list of documents attached to the appeal.

Reference in the cassational appeal to the unproved evidence or to the inconsistency of the findings laid down in the decision or ruling and real relations between people involved in the case, is not allowed.

An appeal is signed by the appellant or his representative. An appeal signed by the representative is supplied by a letter of attorney certifying authorities of the representative to file a cassational appeal against judicial acts. Certificates of court fees payment and of posting copies of the appeal to other persons involved in the case must be attached to the appeal (Article 165 CAP). An appellant must send copies of the appeal and attached documents to all persons participating in the case (Article 166 CAP).

If an appeal does not meet requirements on the content and form, it is returned by the judge without consideration.

The case is considered by the three professional judges.

The court proceedings in the cassational instance are not established in CAP. Such court trial is held according to the rules of procedure for the first instance court with specific features of the cassational instance (Article 153). It means that the court trial procedure is determined by court. The parties and other involved persons are informed about the time and place of the hearing, and as a rule they participate in the session, give explanations to court, ask and answer questions and announce petitions.

As a result of considering the case, cassation instance has a right: 1) to leave the decision of the first instance court or the decree of the appellate instance unchanged, and the appeal dismissed; 2) to revoke the decision of the first instance court completely or in part or pass a new decision; 3) to revoke the decision of the first instance court and the decree of the appellate instance and relegate the case for reconsideration to the instance, which passed the revoked decision, if the decision or ruling are not sufficiently justified; 4) to change the decision of the first instance court and the decree of the appellate instance; 5) to revoke the decision of the first instance completely or in part and drop legal proceedings or refuse to consider the case in substance completely or in part; 6) to leave in force one of the previously passed decisions or decrees (Article 175CAP).

Grounds for changing or revoking a decision of the first instance court or a decree of the appellate instance are violation or wrong application of the norms of material law or norms of procedural law (Part1, Article 176 CAP).

In Part 2, Article 176 CAP there is a list of violations of law of procedure that can serve as grounds for revoking decisions of the first instance court (consideration of the case by the unlawful composition of the bench, breaking the rule of the legal procedure language, lack of the judges' signatures on the decision etc.). These grounds are the same as the "unconditional" grounds for revoking decisions of the first instance court by the appellate instance.

A judicial act passed by the cassational instance as a result of the consideration of the case is called "a decree". The decree must be signed by all participating judges and it enters into legal force from the moment of passing.

by way of supervision

The decisions and decrees of all state courts of arbitration in RF (except the decrees of the Presidium of the Supreme Arbitration Court of RF) which have entered into legal force may be reviewed through "supervision". The supervision instance is represented by the Presidium of the Supreme Arbitration Court of RF.

The supervision procedure can be initiated only by means of a special application («a protest») of the officials from the Procurator's Office of RF and the Supreme Arbitration Court of RF.

The following officials have a right to file a protest:

Chairman of the Supreme Arbitration Court of RF and Procurator – General of RF against the decisions and decrees of any state court of arbitration in RF (except the decrees of the Presidium of the Supreme Arbitration Court of RF); Deputy Chairman of the Supreme Arbitration Court of RF and Deputy Procurator – General of RF against the decisions and decrees of any state court of arbitration in RF (except the decrees of the Presidium of the Supreme Arbitration Court of RF (Article 181 CAP).

Parties and other persons involved in the case have a right to apply to these officials with applications in which they request to file a protest against a decision or a decree of lower courts. An application about filing a protest may be submitted after consideration of the case in the appellate instance or cassational instance (Part 1, Article 185 CAP).

The above mentioned officials having a right to lodge a protest, after receiving such an application, require the case material from the state court of arbitration and having found grounds for filing a protest, file it (Article 184 CAP).

When considering the protest, the Presidium of the Supreme Arbitration Court of RF hears a statement of the Supreme Arbitration Court of RF judge about the facts of the case and arguments of the protests. Persons involved in the case may be summoned to the court to give explanations. Their default, though, does not prevent the case from consideration.

Grounds for changing and revoking a decision or a decree through supervision are "unlawfulness or baselessness of a judicial act" (Article 188 CAP).

The supervision instance has a right; 1) to leave the decision or the ruling of a lower court unchanged and the protest dismissed; 2) to revoke the decision or decree of a lower court completely or in part and submit the case for reconsideration; 3) change the decision on the decree or revoke if completely and pass a new decision 4) to revoke the decision or decree completely or in part and drop legal proceedings on the case or to refuse to consider the case in substance completely or in part; 5)to leave in force one of the previously passed decisions or decree on the case (Article 187 CAP).

The supervision instance has no right, submitting the case for reconsideration, to establish or consider as proved the evidence not being presented in the decision or decree under review, or rejected, to prejudge questions about validity or invalidity of the evidence, about advantage of some evidence over another, about a norm of material law to be applied and a decision or decree to be passed at the retrial.

As a result of considering protests, the Presidium of the Supreme Arbitration Court of RF passes a judicial act which is called "a decree", which enters into legal force immediately from the moment of passing. It is signed by the Chairman of the Supreme Arbitration Court of RF and within five days after its passing it is sent to the parties involved in the case.

Legal fees and expenses for court proceedings

In the effective Russian procedural legislature, a term "legal expenses" does not include expenses for the advocate or other representative of a party in court.

Court expenses consist of : 1) court fee – mandatory payment valid in the whole territory of RF; 2) costs connected with the consideration the case in court. The costs connected with the consideration of the case in court of general jurisdiction include: a) sums of money to be paid to the witnesses and experts; b) expenses connected with the examination of the evidence on the site; c) expenses to find out the defendant; d) expenses connected with the execution of the judiciary act.

According to the general rule, court expenses are referred to the persons involved in the case in proportion with the sustained claims. It means that the party for which is the judgement is to be paid for all legal expenses by the other party. If the claim is sustained in part, legal expenses are adjudged to the plaintiff in proportion to the recovered claims and to the defendant in proportion to the part of the rejected plaintiff claims.

3.4. The court fee to be paid when applying to the state courts of the Russian Federation, procedural fines and remuneration of the advocates

The size of the court fee to be paid to the federal budget for applications and appeals submitted to the courts of general jurisdiction and to the state courts of arbitration, is established in the law of RF "On the court fee" of December 1991. At present, a new wording of this law, approved by the federal law "On changes and additions to the RF law "On the court fee" of December 1995 (in view of the latest changes and additions introduced by the RF law of July 19, 1997), is used. The procedure of paying court fees is defined in the Instruction on application a RF law "On the court fee", adopted by the State Tax Service of RF on May 15, 1996.

Payers of court fees are the citizens of the Russian Federation, foreign citizens and legal entities irrespectively of the: form of property, applying with statements of claim and other applications and appeals to the courts of general jurisdiction, state arbitration courts and to the Constitutional Court of the Russian Federation.

In the state arbitration courts court fees are paid for: statements of claim; applications for declaration of insolvency (bankruptcy); applications for entry in the case as a third party, claiming independent demands on the subject matter of the dispute; applications for establishment of facts having legal importance; appellate and cassational appeals against decisions of the court of arbitration, against rulings about termination of proceedings in case, about dismissing the suit and imposition of judicial fines; applications for issuing writs of execution for enforcement of arbitration tribunal decision and in some other cases.

The amount of the court fee for statements of claim dealing with property matters is determined according to the scale which is based on the inversely proportional approach: the more the amount of the suit claim, the less percentage of this sum constitutes court fee.

Thus in case of applying with a suit to the state court of arbitration when the value of suit is below 10 mln roubles, a court fee constitutes 5 % of the value of suit but not less that the minimum payment for labour. When the value of suit is more from 10 mln roubles to 50 mln roubles, the amount of the court fee would be 500,000 rubles + 4 % of the sum above 10 mln roubles. Then, when the value of suit is from 50 mln roubles to 100 mln roubles, the amount of the court fee is 2 mln 100,000 roubles + 3 % from the sum above 50 mln roubles. In the next column of this scale, the amount of the court fee for the suits from 100 mln roubles to 500 mln roubles is determined as 3 mln 600,000 roubles + 2 % of the sum above 100 mln roubles. When the value of suit is from 500 mln roubles 1 billion, the court fee would be 11 mln 600,000 roubles + 1 % of the sum above 1 billion, but not exceeding amount equal to 1,000-fold minimum payment for labour.

In cases of applying to the courts of general jurisdiction with statements of claim dealing with property matters, the court fee is calculated according to the inversely proportional scale with lower absolute figures than those in the state courts of arbitration. Thus, the first column of the scale determines the amount of the court fee with the value of suit below 1 mln roubles as constituting 5 % of the value of suit. The last column determines the amount of the court fee with the value of suit above 500 mln roubles as constituting 1.5 % of the value of suit.

The amount of the state fee for the applications and complaints of non-property character, is determined in the law "On the court fee" in percentage or certain relation to the minimum payment for labour. For example, in case of applying to the court of general jurisdiction with an application for divorce, it is necessary to pay a court fee in the amount equal to one minimum payment for labour. For the lodged to the state court of arbitration statements of claim on the disputes occurring in the process of concluding, altering or cancelling contracts and on the disputes on annulling contracts, a court fee is paid equal to the 20-fold amount of the minimum payment for labour.

Court fee is also paid for cassational appeals (in courts of general jurisdiction), as well as for appellate and cassational appeals in the state courts of arbitration. The amount of the court fee for filing such appeals would constitute 50 % of the court fee imposed; a) for applying with the non-property applications and appeals; b) calculated from the disputed amount.

In cases when the amount of the court fee is determined in comparison with the minimum payment for labour, the amount of the minimum payment for labour should be applied as it is for one day.

According to Articles 108, 151, 168 of the Code of Civil Procedure of RF, a statement of claim (application), appellate or cassational appeal are returned to the appellant without consideration if the documents certifying payment of the court fee in due course and amount are not attached.

For foreigners applying with applications to the state courts of arbitration of RF a new practice can be of interest. According to this new practice payment of the court fee can be made on behalf of the plaintiff (appellant) by another person. In the decree of the Plenum of the Supreme Arbitration Court of RF of March 20, 1997 "On some issues of applying RF legislature on the court fee by the state courts of arbitration" (RG. 1997.22.04.1997) it is explained that in such case "court should consider that that the court fee has in fact been paid and put into federal account, and thus there are no grounds for returning the statement of claim (application) and a complaint on the motive of payment the court fee by an inappropriate person.

According to point 9 of the Instruction of the State Tax Service", "foreign persons can pay the court fee through appropriate representatives in Russia having rouble and hard currency accounts". In the appendix to this Instruction the procedure of filling out every line of the payment order for paying the court fee: "Payer", "Payer's bank", "Payee", "Payee's bank", "Purpose of payment". The Instruction determines that in case of occurring disputes subject to consideration in the state courts of arbitration of RF with participating foreign organisations and citizens, payment documents on the court fee are formally registered according to the same procedure, only in the line

"Payee's bank" it is necessary to indicate the name and requisites of the bank, serving the holder of the account of the federal budget in the place where the court of arbitration is located to which a statement of claim or any other application, appellate or cassational appeal are lodged.

Procedural fines

Both in the Code of Civil Procedure of RF and in CAP, fines – pecuniary penalties imposed by court on persons guilty in violating procedural rules are provided for. These rules are established in norms of the Code of Civil Procedure of RF (Chapter 8) and in CAP (Chapter 13). In the Russian procedural legislature such fines are called "judicial(court) fines". Judicial (court) fines are imposed only in cases and in amounts provided for in the Code of Civil Procedure of RF and in CAP. In the Code of Civil Procedure 8 cases of imposing "judicial(court) fines" are determined. For example, judicial(court) fines can be imposed by the courts of general jurisdiction basically on citizens (physical entities) or on officials from different bodies and organizations. They are collected from the personal funds of those officials (Articles 65,70, 134, 149, 160, 344, 388, 389, 390, 201, 406 of the Code of Civil Procedure).

A ruling about imposing a fine is passed and its copy is sent to the person being fined. Within 10 days after receiving a copy of the court ruling about a fine being imposed on him, a citizen or an official can ask court about revoking a fine or reducing its amount. A ruling about rejection of the request can be appealed against to the higher court instance.

State courts of arbitration as well as courts of general jurisdiction can not impose judicial(court) fines in cases which are not provided for in CAP RF. In accordance with CAP RF imposing of the "judicial(court) fines" is possible in three cases:

for non-execution of the duty to present evidence required by the state court of arbitration without a valid reason (up to 200-fold minimum payment for labour amounts);

for non-observance of measures to ensure the claim suits consisting in forbidding a defendant and other persons to commit certain actions with regard to the subject of the dispute (on the suits subject to evaluation – up to 50, and on the suits not subject to evaluation – up to 200 minimum payment for labour amounts determined by the federal law of payment for labour) (Article 76 CAP);

for non-observance of the court decision or decree about collecting money and for non-observance of the actions mentioned in the writ of execution by a person who has been endowed with the responsibility for performing these actions (up to 200 minimum payment for labour amounts determined by the federal law) (Article 206 CAP).

A question about imposing a judicial(court) fine is solved at the session of the state court of arbitration. A person in whose regard the question is considered is informed about the time and place of the session. If this person has been properly informed but failed to appear in court session, a question about imposing a fine can be considered by default. A ruling is passed according to the results of consideration of the question. An appellate or cassational appeal can be filed against the ruling on imposing a fine. Ruling about refusal to impose a fine is without appeal.

It is evident that the amount of judicial(court) fines which the state court of arbitration can apply is incompatibly less than the sums which the parties are disputing. So it can hardly be expected that the "judicial (court) fines" will be applied often and with effect. For example, in 1996 1641 applications of non-execution of court decisions and decrees were considered, and only in 152 cases fines were imposed for their non-execution.

Remuneration for the services of advocates

In the Russian Federation the interests of citizens and organisations (legal entities) in state courts may be represented not only by advocates. Both the CCP of RF and CAP RF use the general term "representative" instead of "advocate". The common rule provides that such a representative may be not only advocate, but any citizen having the letter of attorney for conducting the lawsuit, and allowed by the court considering the suit to be a representative in that particular case.

However, the procedure legislation has several exceptions from the rule mentioned above. These exceptions are stated in the articles of the CCP RF and CAP RF which determine "the persons who may not be representatives" in courts of general jurisdiction and state courts of arbitration of the Russian Federation (art. 47 of the CCP RF and art. 51 of the CCP RF respectively). Thus, persons who have not attained their majority, persons under guardianship, may not be representatives in courts.

Judges, investigators, and procurators may not be representatives in courts of general jurisdiction and state courts of arbitration. Personnel of the state courts of arbitration may not be representatives in the state courts of arbitration either. It doesn't mean that they can not appear in court as legal representatives (parents, guardians, adoptive parents), or as authorised by respective bodies.

A regulation according to which advocates may not be representatives in court in certain cases is included only in the Code of Civil Procedure of the Russian Federation (CCP RF, part 2 of article 47). There are two cases of that kind. First, the advocate who has accepted the commission of providing legal assistance with violations of appropriate bar legislation rules. Besides, persons expelled from the bar are not allowed to be representatives in court.

Before 1990-s, legal services for enterprises and organizations, including services for conducting lawsuits, were provided by advocates in legal advice offices, members of the bar of autonomous republics, regions, districts, and the cities of Moscow and Leningrad. Such services were provided constantly on the basis of contracts. Legal advice offices signed contracts with the enterprises and organizations their advocates worked with. According to the contracts, the client organization made certain regular monthly payments not personally to the advocate, but to the legal advice office the advocate belonged to, which in its turn paid the advocate. At that time the system of monthly payment for advocates from legal advice offices providing constant legal services for enterprises and organisations, was established. (See details in: M.Ju. Barschevsky. Advocate. Advocates' firm. The bar. – Moscow, 1995, p.p.100–102). Such kind of relations and ways of payment were acceptable before the beginning of 1990-s, because at that time legal assistance and legal services did not include, as a rule, conducting economic lawsuits in courts and other jurisdiction bodies.

The economical and legal reforms started in 1980-s – 1990-s quickly led to increased demand in legal services, including those for conducting lawsuits in state courts of arbitration considering economical disputes. The range of advocates and organisations providing legal services in conducting lawsuits became wider. Nowadays, these services are provided by:

– advocates from legal advice offices established in all regions previously and for many years were providing the whole range of legal services in civil and criminal lawsuits (such legal advice offices were called "traditional" ones),

– advocates from newly established legal advice offices, who as a rule do not conduct criminal lawsuits and often specialise in providing legal aid for large scale commercial projects in a certain sphere or branch of economy, as well as in conducting certain types of economical lawsuits (such legal advice offices are referred to as "alternative" ones, most of them uniting under the term "business-advocates"),

– employees of organisations often called "legal firms" with various forms of organisational structure,

– advocates working individually on the basis of licenses received according to the established procedure from the Ministry of Justice of the Russian Federation or in judicial bodies of the subjects of the Russian Federation.

In the third and fourth case, the organizations ("legal offices") and persons ("advocates") must receive a license for providing legal services issued for the term of up to three years. ('The Regulation on Licensing Paid Legal Services on the Territory of the Russian Federation', adopted by the decree of the Government of the Russian Federation, April 15, 1995. By the middle of 1997, approximately 6,000 licenses were issued. The list of "Advocates and Legal Firms of the Russian Federation" is published by Russian Judicial Publishing House according to the data base of the Ministry of Justice of the Russian Federation.

The former system of "subscription" monthly payment for the legal services of advocates proved to be unacceptable for both "alternative" legal advice offices, legal firms, individually practising advocates, and the "traditional" Bar. New approaches to payment were not established in a normative way but shaped by practice.

It is hardly possible to provide accurate and comprehensive data on all currently existing forms and ranges of payment for legal services.

Very wide-spread is the practice of signing contracts for certain type of work, e.g. conducting a lawsuit in court. Such a contract is concluded with a particular legal advice office belonging to a certain type of advocate collegium, or with an independent legal firm, and those in their turn pay a due sum of received money to the advocate conducting the lawsuit.

The payment for services provided by a legal advice office or firm in conducting a lawsuit in court is often calculated in percentage from the sum of the claim. It's a common knowledge that the honoraria of a legal advice office or firm equals 5–10 % of the satisfied statement of claim (in case the client is the plaintiff), or 5–10 % of the claim proved not due to exaction (in case the client is the defendant). By usual practice, the client pays a certain sum in advance which is not returned later. In case of a favourable decision of the court, the client pays to the legal advice office the part of honorarium which equals 5–10 % of the "won" sum minus the advance payment made before. There are no strict rules, though. In case the claim sum is very large, or very small, the honorarium may be determined not in percentage of the sum, but in a certain sum stated in the contract. Payment per hour is common, too, which varies from USD 50 to USD 300. (For details see: M.Ju. Barschevsky. Organisation and Practices of the Bar in Russia. – Moscow, 1997, p.p.246–248).

Of special interest, of course, is the question of possibility of the honorarium paid by the winning party to its representative (advocate) to be exacted from the losing side. In the CCP RF and CAP RF this question is solved in different ways.

According to the updated wording of Article 91 of the CCP RF (dated 10.10.95), "the court obliges the party that lost the suit to pay the expenses connected with the services of the representative for the side in favour of which the decision was made, in reasonable amount and considering circumstances". Until 1995, the court of general jurisdiction imposed payment of the expenses connected with the services of the advocate participating in the suit, in the amount of up to 5 % of the satisfied claim, or the portion of the claim rejected by the court, but not higher than the determined tariff.

Unlike CCP, CAP of 1995 does not contain regulations obliging the side that lost the suit to pay the expenses connected with the services of the representative, the advocate. Because of the absence of such regulations in CAP, state courts of arbitration nowadays rejects the claims of the side in favour of which the decision was made, to impose payment of the expenses connected with the services of the advocate and other representatives on the other side.

3.5. Organisation and order of execution of judicial acts (decisions, decrees, rulings)

Organisation of the execution of court decisions

For many years the mandatory execution of the decisions of both courts of general jurisdiction and state courts of arbitration, as well as other bodies, was carried out by court executors of district (city) courts of general jurisdiction.

In 1997, the Laws of the Russian Federation on the reform of the organization of the execution of the decisions of courts of general jurisdiction, state courts of arbitration, and arbitration tribunals, as well as the decisions of other bodies of jurisdiction, were adopted: the Law on court executors and the Law on executive organisation. These laws terminate functioning of court executors working at regional (city) courts of general jurisdiction and being members of staff of those courts.

It was created a special service for court execution. This consists of executors securing the functioning of the courts in execution and executors to enforce court decisions. Execution service is established by the Ministry of Justice of the Russian Federation and is incorporated into the system of bodies of that ministry.

The service of execution includes:
- the department of executors of the Ministry of Justice of the Russian Federation,
- execution service of the Department of military courts of the Ministry of Justice of the Russian Federation,
- execution services of the bodies of justice of subjects of the Russian Federation,
- local department of execution.

According to Article 25 of the Law of the Russian Federation "On executors", the Ministry of Justice of the Russian Federation was commissioned to create the executor service in 1997–1999, and have it started from January 1, 1998, and all service in full strength from January 1, 1999.

Enforcement of court decisions

According to the Law "On the Execution Procedure" of the Russian Federation, the acts (decisions, rulings, decrees) to be executed are those of state courts of general jurisdiction and state courts of arbitration, as well as other public bodies having the right of making individuals, organizations, and budgets of all levels responsible for assigning money assets or other property to other people, organizations, and budgets, or for undertaking certain activities in favor of those entities, or abstaining from certain activities.

According to article 7 of the Law "On the Execution Procedure", execution documents include:
- writs/acts of execution, issued by courts on the basis of judicial/court decisions,

- decisions of international commercial arbitration and other arbitration tribunals,
- decisions of foreign courts and courts of arbitration,
- decisions of inter-governmental bodies of the defense of human rights,
- court orders,
- certified by notary agreements on alimony payment,
- certificates of labour conflict board issued on the basis of its decisions,
- duly formulated demands of control bodies of exaction of money assets with bank's or other credit organisation's note of full or partial non-performance of the exaction due to the absence of money assets on the debtor's accounts sufficient to satisfy the claims of the claimant, unless the legislation of the Russian Federation provides a different way of executing the documents mentioned above,
- resolutions of bodies (officials) in charge of considering administrative violation of law,
- decisions of court executors,
- decisions of other bodies in cases specified by the federal legislation.

The legislation specifies time within which the execution documents may be presented for execution. For example:
- writs/acts of execution issued on the basis of judicial/court acts of courts of general jurisdiction, as well as court decrees – within three years, while those issued on the basis of court acts of courts of arbitration – within 6 months,
- writs/acts of execution issued on the basis of decisions of international commercial court of arbitration and other arbitration tribunals – within 6 months (article 14 of the federal law "On the Execution Procedure").

According to the CCP RF and CAP RF, the writ of execution is issued by the court of general jurisdiction or state court of arbitration which

made final decision (part V of CCP "execution procedure", articles
338–432, part IV of CAP "Execution of court acts", articles 197–209).
The demands of court acts may be executed:

- by court executors in charge of compulsory execution of judicial
  acts;
- tax authorities, banks, and other credit organizations, or other bodies specified in federal legislation.

The claimant may send the execution document containing claims of
court acts or acts of other bodies on exacting money assets, directly to
the bank or other credit organization, if the claimant has the information of the debtor's accounts being there and of money on those
accounts, or to the executor if he does not have information of that
kind.

Within three days after being presented execution document from
the claimant or the executor, the bank or other credit organization
providing services for the debtor's accounts, must satisfy the claims on
exacting money assets or certify full or partial non-execution of the
claims due to the absence of money on the debtor's accounts sufficient
to satisfy the claims of the claimant (article 6 of the federal law "On
court executor").

Measures of enforcement are taken by executor after having been
presented the appropriate document and after initiating execution procedure (after the expiration of the time specified by the executor for
voluntary execution).

The federal law "On the Execution Procedure" regulates specific
features of compulsory execution by means of imposing exaction on
the property of the debtor organization, the procedure of arresting and
selling the property of the debtor organization (chapter 5 of the federal
law "On the Execution Procedure").

For example, the legislation provides that in case the debtor organization has no money sufficient to pay the debt back, the exaction is
imposed on other property belonging to it by the right of ownership,
the right of economical management, or operative management (in
case of state enterprises with the exception of the property withdrawn

from economic circulation or property of limited circulation), regardless of where and at whose disposal the property currently is. The property is arrested and becomes also subject to other executive deeds specified by the law.

The arrest and sale of the property of the debtor organization is conducted in the order specified by article 53 of the federal law "On the Execution Procedure".

– first, property not involved directly in production (securities, money assets on deposit accounts and other accounts of the debtor, hard currency assets, automobiles, design items, office equipment, etc.) is sold.
– second, ready products (goods), and other material values not involved directly in production and not intended for it, are sold.
– third, real estate, raw materials, machines, equipment, and other major assets intended for use in production, are sold.

In case the executor arrests the property of the third group belonging to the debtor, the executor presents within three days a letter on the exaction of property to the federal department on bankruptcy at the State committee of the Russian Federation on management of state property, attaching the list of the arrested property and its value, and indicating the sum of claim. A copy of that letter is sent to the tax authorities controlling the payments of the debtor organization to the budgets of all levels and state non-budget funds (article 60 of the federal law "On the Execution Procedure").

4. Commercial Arbitration according to present Russian legislation

4.1. Basic legislative acts of the RF concerning domestic and foreign trade arbitration; International conventions on this area applicable in Russian Federation

At the present time there are three federal laws and other legislative acts about arbitration, namely: 1) A Decree about the arbitration – annex n:o 3 to the Code of Civil Procedure; 2) Temporary statute on the arbitration tribunal, confirmed by the decision of the Supreme Soviet of the RF 24.6. 1992.; 3) Law of the RF "On the international commercial arbitration" 7.7. 1993

The acceptance in 1992–1993 two of these three legislative acts signified the termination of the period which had started already from the beginning of 30-s of this century when arbitration was in practice not used to settle domestic disputes between citizens or organisations and the function of foreign trade arbitration was performed only two permanent arbitration tribunals (courts): Maritime arbitration commission created in 1930 and International commercial arbitration Court, created in 1932 (FTAC, today International arbitration court) by the Chamber of Commerce and Industry of the USSR (today: RF).

A special study of the practice in implementing of new legislation allows to make a conclusion that there was about 250 functioning permanent arbitration courts in Russia. In their lists on judges roughly 1500 arbitration judges were included (Information Bulletin of the Supreme State Arbitration Court of RF. 1997.N:o 8)

The Russian Federation as the legal successor of the USSR is a member of the New York Convention from 10 June 1958 "On the recognition and enforcement of foreign arbitral awards" and also a member of European convention on foreign trade arbitration (Geneva, 1961). These conventions by virtue of the article 15 of the Constitution of the RF 1993 are a part of the legal system of RF.

The functions of the state courts of general jurisdiction in recognition and enforcement in Russia the above mentioned New York convention have been regulated up to now by the Decree of the Presidium of the Supreme Soviet of USSR from june 21, 1988 "On the recognition and enforcement in the USSR of the decisions of the foreign courts and arbitration.

Moreover, by virtue of the part 4 of the article 15 of the RF Constitution, some other bilateral and multilateral international conventions on arbitration are also in force in Russia.

The Russian procedural legislation in force confirms the general rule according to which the disputes of private law being under the jurisdiction of state courts of general jurisdiction or under state arbitration courts can be settled in arbitration according to parties´ contractual provision or by virtue of special contractual document. The disputes being according to material or procedural legislation under exclusive competence of the state courts or other bodies cannot be settled by arbitration. For example, disputes in patent law, the settlement of which are conferred to the Supreme Patent Chamber (article 31 of the Patent Law 1992) cannot be settled by arbitration, neither disputes in family or labour relations (article 1 in Annex 3 to the CCP).

Considering the theme of this book one have to pay special attention to the normative acts of 1995 which contain a regulation concerning arbitration dispute settlement in auctions concerning the state own shares. The state (Federation) can sell them on credit and/or creating security in the form of lien to its shares. The third form is to sell the commission for further selling the shares. The rules of the auctions in these cases and the mandatory provisions of the contracts in the auctions are given by the Decree of the President of RF 31. 8.1995. One of the mandatory contractual provisions between the Russian Federation and debtor, lien giver or commissioner says that the disputes on the performance, alteration or repudiation of the contract have to be settled by the International commercial arbitration Court in the Chamber of Commerce and Industry of RF, if one party is foreign legal person or an enterprise with foreign investments or by the arbitration court for the settlement of economic disputes of the Chamber of Commerce and

Industry of RF, if the party is registered in a state-member of the Commonwealth of Independent States (CIS) or is a Russian legal person without foreign participation.

It is evident that there is no obligation (by virtue of legislation) to use arbitration for dispute settlement. It is noteworthy, however, that in this decree the Russian state in the relations under consideration is qualified as a subject of private law when taking part in the above mentioned auctions and thus may be a party in arbitration proceedings.

Disputes between the Russian state and investor, arising out of the agreements on the division of the products, concluded according to the article 22 of the federal law from 30.12. 1995 "On the agreements of division of the products ", may also be settled by arbitration (among others by international arbitral institutions), provided that an arbitration clause is included in the concrete agreement on the division of the products.

The law of the RF from 9.12.1991 "On the state fees" have relevance to a lot of normative acts concerning arbitration, because there is determined the amount of state fees when applying in state arbitration courts the enforcement document on the basis of the awards of arbitration in economic disputes.

Moreover, there are a lot of legislation defining the possibility to use arbitration for the settlement of various kinds of disputes or disputes between parties of various categories in economic exchange. The legislation has also defined the organisations being entitled to form permanently functioning arbitral courts (tribunals). All these laws express mostly the basic principles of arbitration, explained above and the genuine interest of the lawgiver to use the arbitration form of dispute settlement in various spheres of life.

4.2. Rules of procedure in arbitration according to the Russian legislation

The rules of arbitration procedure cover norms regulating the activity of the arbitration court. This includes starting the process, election of arbitrators (judges) in concrete disputes, the way of conducting the process and final decision making in the form of arbitration award.

The form of the process is determined by the parties directly or by referring to the arbitration rules the parties have agreed upon earlier. The violation against these rules is one of grounds justifying refusal by the enforcement authorities to enforce the arbitration award.

When defining the rules of procedure by the parties the mandatory norms of legislation concerning arbitration cannot be circumvented. These norms require inter alia that the agreement to use arbitration is made in written form and that the process must follow the principle of equality between the parties.

Non-mandatory legal norms of arbitration will be applied in concrete disputes in case the parties have not agreed otherwise. In permanent arbitration court the non-mandatory legal norms are not used in case the arbitration court has its own rules stipulating otherwise than in non-mandatory legal norms. If, on the contrary, these own rules are silent concerning certain procedural problem the non-mandatory legal norms will be applied.

If the founders of a permanent arbitration court have granted the powers to the arbitration court to settle domestic economic disputes as well as disputes arising out of foreign trade or other international economic relations, the order of procedure will be determined either according to the Temporary statute of arbitration tribunal for the settlement of economic disputes or according to the RF Law on the international commercial arbitration from 7.7. 1993. This means that the imperative norms to be applied depends on the subject of the dispute, the parties and their agreement. In some cases the imperative norms must be taken from the Temporary statute and in others from the RF Law on international commercial arbitration. The same approach is used when the applicable non-mandatory norms are concerned or the norms defining the grounds for refusal to give an enforcement document for the enforcement of the arbitration award.

The three basic laws and other normative acts contain, namely, differences in imperative and non-mandatory norms on quite important points, for example concerning the capacity of the parties to agree on the use of arbitration and procedural rules.

Thus, the Decree on the arbitration in the Annex 3 of the CCP is applicable only to the disputes between physical persons. They can give any dispute between them to the arbitration settlement excluding, however, disputes in family and labour law context. Further, individual persons can agree on the use of arbitration only in regard to already existing disputes. Agreements concerning the possible future disputes are not permitted. The enforcement of the arbitration award, not voluntarily performed, will be implemented according to enforcement document issued by the district (city) court on the jurisdictional territory of which the arbitration process has taken place. When the judge concerned studies the prerequisites of the arbitration award for enforcement document he/she pays attention to the Decree on the arbitration mentioned above.

It is quite evident that the contents of the Decree on the arbitration for the settlement of disputes between individual persons is outdated. According to general opinion of experts there are, for many years, no practice in the implementation of this Decree. No one denies the necessity to renew the regulations of arbitration between individuals. It is, however, difficult to predict the date of the acceptance of new legislation on the arbitration.

As it was mentioned earlier, determining of regulations for arbitration examination of disputes on domestic or foreign trade transactions should be first of all based on the sphere of application of the Temporary statute on the arbitration tribunal for resolving economic disputes and RF law "On international commercial arbitration".

According to Article 1 of Temporary statute and Article 23 of CAP, Temporary statute is applied in case of submitting for examination by arbitration tribunals of civil law economic disputes within jurisdiction of the courts of arbitration. Temporary statute is not effective with regard to organisation and activity of the International commercial arbitration court and Maritime Arbitration Commission at the RF Chamber of Commerce (Part 3 Article 1 of the Temporary statute).

If not otherwise provided by the agreement of the parties, Temporary statute is not applied if at least one of the parties is located in the territory of a foreign state or is an enterprise or organisation with foreign investments (Part 2 Article 1 of the Temporary statute). Therefore, in case of lack of such an agreement, cases with foreign organisations participation, organisations with foreign investments, international organisations, foreign citizens, stateless persons which are within jurisdiction of courts of arbitration, are subject to arbitration examination on the territory of the Russian Federation in accordance with the norms of the RF law "On international commercial arbitration".

According to Part " Article 1 "Sphere of Application" of the RF law "On international commercial arbitration", this law is applied to arbitration examination: a) of disputes occurring from contractual relations and other civil law relations in the process of foreign trade and other kinds of international economic ties, if a commercial enterprise at least partly is located abroad; b) disputes between enterprises with foreign investments and international associations and organisations set upon the territory of the Russian Federation, disputes between their members, as well as their disputes with other subjects of law of RF.

I would like to attract attention to some rules of the RF law "On international commercial arbitration" which have extreme practical importance for determining procedure of the arbitration examination and which are not presented in the Temporary statute on arbitration tribunal for resolving economic disputes. These rules are contained in the following articles of the RF law "On international commercial arbitration":

Article 3 "Receiving of written messages", according to which: if the parties have not agreed otherwise, any written message is considered received if it has been delivered personally, or to the commercial enterprise, according to permanent residence address or postal address; when these can not be found by reasonable inquiry, a written message is considered received if it has been sent to the last known location of the commercial enterprise, permanent place of residence or postal address of the addressee by a registered letter or by any other way which implies registration of the attempt of delivery of the message, which is considered received on the day of such delivery.

Part 2 of Article 7 "Definition and form of arbitration agreement" providing for two known from Temporary statute ways of concluding arbitration agreement: 1) by means of exchange of statement of claim and reply by the defendant in which one party asserts existence of agreement, and the other party does not object; 2) by means of reference in the agreement to the document containing arbitration clause/ reservation under the condition that the agreement has been concluded in a written form and that the reference document is a part of the agreement.

Article 11 "Appointment of arbiters" according to which if in the course of procedure agreed upon by the parties, one party does not observe the procedure; or if parties can not reach agreement in accordance with such procedure; or if the third person including organisation (permanent arbitration tribunal) does not perform some function placed on it in accordance with such procedure, any party can ask President of the RF Chamber of Commerce take necessary measures (which means to make an appointment of arbiter) unless arbitration agreement on procedure provides other means of providing such appointment.

Articles: 12 "Grounds for removing arbiters"; 13 "Procedure of arbiter removal", article 14 "Termination of arbiter's power (mandate)".

Article 16 "Right of arbitration tribunal to pass decision on its own powers" providing for a possibility to realise such a right with regard to a preliminary issue or in the decision on the subject matter of the dispute, and some others

4.3. Decisions of the arbitration tribunals. Finality of the arbitration tribunal decisions

In accordance with a Temporary statute on the arbitration tribunal for resolving economic disputes, arbitration tribunal decision is final. It follows from Article 24 of the Temporary statute according to which arbitration tribunal decision is executed voluntarily in the order and in the period set in the decision. If the period for performance has not been established, it is subject to immediate execution.

However, the assertion about final character of the arbitration tribunal decision on economic disputes is not justified with regard to cases where the state court of arbitration observing Article 26 of the Temporary statute when considering an application for issuing a writ of execution finds that this decision is inconsistent with the legislation or that it has been passed on the grounds of non-examined materials of case. In this situation the case is returned to the arbitration tribunal which has passed the decision for reconsideration.

In the RF law "On international commercial arbitration" there is no indication of the moment from which decision passed by the international commercial arbitration is considered final and thus subject to compulsory execution.

It can be supposed that if one party files petition to the state court about annulling decision of the international commercial arbitration, provided for by Article 34 of RF law "On international commercial arbitration", decision will be final after consideration and refusal to satisfy petition about annulling decision of the international commercial arbitration. In accordance with Article 6 of the same law, consideration of such petitions is placed on the courts of general jurisdiction of the subjects of Russian Federation. However, regulation of the procedural activity of courts of general jurisdiction on considering petitions about annulling decisions of the international commercial arbitration was not included in the text of the RF law of July 7, 1993 "On international commercial arbitration" or in the Code of Civil Procedure of RF which serves as major law regulating procedural activity of courts of general jurisdiction in the country.

In spite of the mentioned gap in the legislature, courts of general jurisdiction in complete accordance with Articles 6, 34 of the law "On international commercial arbitration" accept and consider petitions about annulling decisions of the international commercial arbitration. As the analysis of the Moscow city court practice showed, procedural rules of considering petitions about vacating decisions of the international commercial arbitration have been worked out by judicial practice.

For example, petition filed to the Moscow city court is considered by judge from the Judicial Board on civil cases individually. Consideration of petitions takes place in the open court session as a rule with participation of the parties which must be informed about the session.

The amount of the court fee imposed by the Moscow state court in our example is also determined by judicial practice in the same way as it is done with regard to the court fee imposed on the cassational appeals against decisions of the courts of general jurisdiction of the first instance (which is 50 % of the amount of the court fee which would be imposed on cassational appeal against decision on a similar dispute passed not by international commercial arbitration but court of general jurisdiction of the first instance). Until now, additions to the RF law of December 9, 1991 "On the court fee" (it is effective in the wording of December 31, 1995) which would establish amount of the court fee due to be paid when applying to court of general jurisdiction with an appeal about annulling decisions of the international commercial arbitration.

State courts do not satisfy petitions about annulling decisions of the international commercial arbitration in cases when one of the grounds listed in Part 2 Article 34 of the law on international commercial arbitration is present.

Existence of the grounds included in group one results in annulling decision of the international commercial arbitration if the party filing petition proves that:

– one of the parties in the arbitration agreement was to some degree incapacitated, or this agreement is ineffective according to the law which was applied, or in case of lack of such reference – according to the RF law; or

– the party was not properly informed about appointment of arbiter or about arbitration examination, or for other reasons could not present adequate explanations; or

– decision has been passed on the dispute not envisaged by the agreement or inconsistent with its conditions, or contains decrees on the issues going beyond the arbitration agreement. However, if the decrees on the issues covered by the arbitration agreement can be separated from those not covered by such an agreement, only that part of the arbitration decision can be annulled, which contains

decrees on the issues not covered by the arbitration agreement; or
- composition of the arbitration or arbitration procedure were inconsistent with the agreement between parties unless such an agreement contradicts the law "On international commercial arbitration"
  which the parties can not derogate from, or in the absence of such an
  agreement they were inconsistent with this law.

Another group of grounds for annulling decisions of the international
commercial arbitration constitute those which need not be proved by
the parties. Such grounds applied by the initiative of the state court and
are the following:
- subject-matter of the dispute can not be a subject of arbitration
  examination in accordance with the RF law;
- Arbitration decision contradicts to the public policy of the Russian
  Federation.

VI Private Law; Commercial Organisations

Vladimir Konstantinovich Andrejev

1 Intotroductory remarks on private law in Russia

Adoption of the new Civil Code of the Russian Federation (CC RF) marks a new qualitative stage in the legal regulation of Russia's economy which is gaining more and more features of market economy. The CC RF consistently presents the constitutional principles of the single economic space in the country, free flow of goods, services and financial resources, support of competition, freedom of entrepreneurship and other economic activity not prohibited by law. In the Russian Federation equally recognized and protected are private, state, municipal and other forms of property. Nobody can be deprived of property, otherwise than by court decision. Forced alienation of property for state needs can be performed only on the condition of preliminary and just compensation.

Civil legislation is based on the recognition of the equality of all the participants of the regulated relations, inviolability of property irrespective of its form, the freedom of contract, the inadmissibility of the arbitrary intrusion into private matters, and the necessity of the unimpeded exercising of civil rights and their judicial defence. The civil rights may be restricted on the grounds of the federal law and only to the extent necessary for protection of the constitutional system, morality, health, rights and lawful interests of people, for defence of the country and state security (Article 1, CC RF).

The sphere of the civil legislation has been significantly enlarged. It can be justly called a reference point in determining the boundaries of the private law. Though traditional for the Soviet civilistics concepts of property and non-property relations are used in order to characterize the entrepreneurial and other economic activity not prohibited by law and freedom of its performance, their content has been enlarged. Reinstitution in the Russian civil legislation of the immovable property concepts resulted in incorporation into it the plots of land, the earth/ mineral resources, isolated water objects which all have traditionally been part of the land law and other branches of law. These areas of legal norms mainly regulated relations of authority and subordination. Thus, land and other natural objects were totally excluded from the commercial exchange.

The laws for economic partnerships and societies of corporate foundations provide for distribution of the profit received in the course of entrepreneurial activity, recognise the rights of shareholders and members of production cooperatives. This resulted in the replacement of the relations regulated by the norms of the labour law to the ones regulated by the civil legislation. Though norms of the civil legislation are not applicable to tax and financial relations, if not otherwise provided by the legislation, in practice the influence of the CC RF can be felt even beyond its direct application. This can be seen, for example, in determining the priority of writing off the money from the taxpayer's account and satisfying the creditor's demands in the process of liquidation of a commercial organization.

The private law also includes relations among persons carrying out entrepreneurial activity or participating in it. The entrepreneurial activity is understood as any independent activity performed at one's risk and directed to systematic receiving of profit from using the property, selling goods, performing works and services by persons registered in this capacity in due legal order (Part III, p. I, Article 2, CC RF). Incorporation of regulation of entrepreneurial relations into the CC RF has significantly complicated the perception of its norms. To understand the content of the CC RF articles, each time it is necessary to determine if the regulated relations are qualified as entrepreneurial activity. If it is so, a different qualification of the CC RF norms may follow. For example, if a usual representative cannot conclude transactions on behalf of the represented person with regard to himself or other person whom he also represents (p.3, article 182, CC RF), a commercial representative, however, is endowed with a right to conclude such transactions (Article 184 CC RF). The adoption of the Entrepreneurial or Commercial Code in Russia would allow to more precisely reflect in legal norms the specific character of the activity having a systematic and risky character and being performed professionally. The practice of passing federal laws to further develop the CC RF has shown that its rule (Part II, p.2, article 3) that the civil law norms contained in other laws must be consistent with the Civil Code is not being observed. The law on the joint-stock companies in p.5, article 1 distorts the content of p.3, article 96 and p.5, article 98 of the CC RF on the specific legal status of the joint-stock societies established in the process of privatizing state and municipal enterprises. The norm of p.2, article 7 of the federal law on production cooperatives dealing with a possibility for a certain number of the cooperative members not to participate personally in its activity is not fully consistent with the rule of article 107 of the CC RF. This norm contradicts the essence of this organizational-legal form of the commercial organization.

Anyhow, the CC RF is now the foundation of the private law in Russia. It guarantees exercise of personal initiative and freedom of every citizen in achieving personal prosperity by means of using one's abilities and property.

2. Commercial organizations. General

2.1. Introductory remarks

The CC RF and other federal laws regulate the legal status of commercial organizations. The basic legal act to determine legal characteristics is the CC RF. Its Chapter 4 "Juridical persons" has entered into force since the day of the official publication of part I of the Civil Code on December 8, 1994. Dividing of juridical persons into commercial and non-commercial organizations is performed in article 50 of the CC RF on the economic grounds. A juridical person, which pursues as its main goal profit and divides it among the participants, is considered a commercial organization. Though the second feature does not apply to the unitary state enterprises whose property is indivisible and cannot be divided according to contributions (participatory shares) for ex. to the workers of the enterprise (p.4, article 113 CC RF). Discussing the first feature of the commercial organization it is necessary to keep in mind the definition of the commercial organization which can be found in, p. 1, article 2 of the CC RF.

In defining certain kinds of commercial organizations the legislator points out that partnerships perform the entrepreneurial activity (articles 69, 82 CC RF), or that participants of business societies including joint-stock companies take risk of losses connected with their activity (articles 87, 96 CC RF), or that production cooperatives are created for joint production or other business activity (article 107 CC RF), or that unitary enterprises perform activity determined by the owner (p.1, article 295 CC RF). Federal laws on joint-stock companies and production cooperatives do not clarify the provisions contained in the norms of the Civil Code. However, the first act reads that the specific features of the establishment and legal status of the joint-stock companies in the areas of banking, investment and insurance activity are defined by federal laws. In the law on banks and banking activity it is written that a credit organization is established on the basis of any form of property as an economic organization (Article 1). The list of the bank transactions named in article 5 of the above mentioned law allows to assert that it extends the concept of the entrepreneurial activity defined in the CC RF. It turns out not to be limited to the production or other economic activity. At the same time, the stock exchange which renders services directly contributing to concluding civil law contracts with securities, is established in the form of non-commercial partnerships. Though we may say that these services are not significantly different from bank transactions of credit organizations considering the fact that the latter participate in the securities market. The discussed provisions of the federal laws regulating the legal status of commercial organizations allows to conclude that the priority should be given to these special norms. A conclusion which would refute the federal law rules cannot be made on the basis of the general provisions on commercial organizations contained in part I of the CC RF. The general norms of chapter 4 "Juridical persons" can be only used for more precise interpretation of the norms, for example of the law on joint-stock companies. Replacement or canceling of the rules contained in the federal laws determining the legal status of commercial organizations is not allowed by the norms of the CC RF. The principle of supremacy of the special norms contained in the federal laws prevails. Adoption of such laws is envisaged in the CC RF.

2.2. Legal capacity of commercial organizations

Unlike the legal capacity of a citizen which means a capacity to have civil rights and bear responsibilities, the legal capacity of the juridical person in the article of CC RF is not defined in this way. But from its content we may conclude that the legal capacity is understood as a capacity to have civil rights corresponding to the goals of the juridical person's activity envisaged in its constitutive documents and liabilities connected to this activity.

The legal capacity of a commercial organization, except unitary enterprises, covers all rights and responsibilities necessary for performing any kinds of activity not prohibited by law. We can see an obvious inconsistency in defining the content of the legal capacity of the commercial organization if we compare part I and part II, p.1, article 49 of the CC RF. If in the beginning part the legal capacity is restricted by the goals of the activity stated in the constitutive documents of a commercial organization, further on (part II) nothing is said about a possible combination of rights and responsibilities respective of the activity goals. More precise are the provisions of part I of the article under consideration, since it corresponds to the rule of article 173 of the CC RF. A transaction concluded by a commercial organization which is in conflict with the goals of the activity specifically restricted in the constitutive documents may be considered invalid by court. The offered interpretation of the CC RF articles 49 and 50 makes us doubt the assertion that the commercial organization possesses the general legal capacity, as does the physical entity. The above mentioned norms prove that the legal capacity of a commercial organization is not general, but goal-oriented, being specifically defined in constitutive documents.

Such interpretation of the legal capacity of the commercial organization is supported by the rule saying that certain kinds of activities which have been listed by law can be performed by a juridical person only upon getting a special permission (license). Before this law has been passed, a decree of the Russian Federation Government of December 24, 1994«Of licensing of certain kinds of activity" was applied. This decree has been replaced by the Law "On licensing of certain kinds of activity" on September 25, 1998. If the conditions of issuing a license on performing a certain activity include the requirement to perform such an activity exclusively, the joint-stock company has no right to perform other types of activity during the term of the license validity, except for those envisaged by the license or the accompanying ones (p.3, article 2, "Law on the joint-stock companies").

The legal capacity of a commercial organization stands from the moment of its official registration. The data of the official registration and a firm name for commercial organizations are included in the state register of the juridical persons open for the public. The violation of the legal order in establishing a juridical person and inconsistency of its constitutive documents with law will result in registration refusal. A refusal to officially register the organization as well an rejection of register application may be appealed against in court (Article 51 CC RF).

Before the federal law on registration of the juridical persons is passed, the body to perform registration is a territorial executive body of public power, usually a body of local self-government. The latter often sets up a specialized registration office. Such bodies are supposed to provide proper registration of the juridical persons and to check the consistency of their constitutive documents with the existing legislation according to articles 34 and 35 of the "Law on enterprises and entrepreneurial activity".

Taxation agencies, unlike the bodies of local self-government, are not registration bodies. They keep register of enterprises for taxation purposes.

2.3. Firm name and location of the commercial organization

A firm is a name of the commercial organization. A right to a firm name means an exclusive right of a proprietor to produce or sell goods, provide works and services under the firm name. As a well-known enterprise may gain a wide range of customers due to the quality of its product, it is forbidden for other enterprises to use the same name. The choice of a firm name is not totally free for an entrepreneur. It is necessary to observe following legal rules:

The firm name of the full partnership should contain the names of all the participants and expression "full partnership", or the name of one or several participants and the words "and Co" and "full partnership" (p.3, article 69 CC RF).

The firm name of the limited partnership should either contain the names of all full partners and the word "limited partnership" or "commandite partnership" for one of the names of full partners and the words "and Co" and "limited partnership". If the firm name of the limited partnership contains the name of the investor, such investor becomes a full partner (p. 4, article 82 CC RF).

The firm name of the limited responsibility society or the additional responsibility society must contain the name of the society and the words translated as "limited responsibility" or "additional responsibility" respectively (p.2, article 87 and p.2, article 95, CC RF).

The firm name of the join-stock company should contain its name and the indication of the company form (p.2, article 96, CC RF).

The firm name of the production cooperative should contain its name and the words as "production cooperative" or "artel" (p.3, article 107 CC RF).

The firm name of the unitary enterprise (state or municipal enterprise) should contain the indication of the public body owning the property of the enterprise. (p.3, article 113, CC RF).

The juridical person, with the firm name which has been registered in due order, has an exclusive right to use it its firm name. A juridical person illegally using somebody else's registered firm name must stop using it and compensate for the losses upon the request of the legal owner of the firm name (p.4, article 54, CC RF).

The location of the commercial organization is determined as the place of its official registration if not otherwise stipulated in the constitutive documents. The firm name and location of the commercial organization should be stated in its constitutive documents.

2.4. Bodies and persons exercising legal capacity of the commercial organization

The CC RF does not provide for the term of the capacity to make legal acts on behalf of the juridical persons. A commercial organization as an association of people with its own structure cannot, as a rule, by its actions get and enjoy rights, create liabilities. From this point of view, limited responsibility societies or companies established by one person or consisting of one person, represent an extreme judicial fiction and basically fall out of the list of juridical persons characterized in article 48 CC RF as organizations. Not all organizations are labour collectives, but a juridical person, unlike a citizen, is always a collective subject of law. It is obvious that the only justification for an organization of one person is creating a possibility for a citizen (and also for a juridical person) to limit the property responsibility in the area of entrepreneurship. While for the sole entrepreneur (as well as for state and municipal units) such move is quite justified, for the commercial organization it serves as an escape from full responsibility on obligations. That is why the legislator has put a certain barrier to such a course stipulating that neither a limited responsibility society, nor a joint-stock company can have as the only participant in another business society (p.2 article 88, p.6, article 98, CC RF)

While the citizen's legal capacity to make legal acts depends on age and health, the acquisition of rights or acceptance of different responsibilities by the commercial organization is determined by the competence of its bodies according to constitutive documents. The body of a juridical person represents the commercial organization. On behalf of the latter may also act the heads of the representations and branches and other members of the commercial organization. Their actions are considered in the CC RF as the actions of a juridical person not on the grounds of law or constitutive documents, but on the grounds of the authority resulting from the authorization, or act of the authorized state agency or body of local self-government (Article 182, CC RF).

Thus, despite the identity of the achieved legal results, it should be kept in mind that the actions of the body of the juridical person on the one side and its authorized representatives on the other, are based on different legal foundations and result in different legal responsibilities. A person representing a the juridical person must act in the interests of the represented the juridical person reasonably and conscientiously. He should upon demand of the founders (participants) of the commercial organization compensate for the inflicted losses if not otherwise provided by law or agreement (p.3, article 53 CC RF). According to article 71 of the law on the joint-stock companies, members of the companies board of directors (supervisory council), director and/or management board (directorate) members are responsible only for the losses inflicted to the society by their guilty activity (inaction).

Having introduced the general concepts of the juridical person, CC RF continues with the administration of the business enterprises

In the limited (additional) responsibility societies the supreme body is the general meeting of their participants. An executive (collegiate or one-man) body is also established in such societies.

In joint-stock companies the supreme body is the general meeting of the shareholders. Companies with more than fifty participants have to have the board of directors (supervisory council) which is elected by the general meeting of the shareholders. This board appoints the members of the executive body of the society. The supreme administrative body of the production cooperative is the general meeting of its members which forms the supervisory council in the cooperative with the number of participants over fifty, as well as executive bodies (management board and/or chairperson of the cooperative).

The body of the unitary enterprise is its head who is appointed by the proprietor (state or municipality) or by the body authorized by the proprietor.

In order to determine which administrative body of the business society or production cooperative acts in the legal relationship as a body of the juridical person, it should be kept in mind that current management is carried out by an executive body which in some cases cannot represent the society without a special decision of the board of directors or another supreme body. For example, a decision of concluding a big transaction with the property being from 25 to 50 percent of the all balance assets of the company is made by the board of directors unanimously (article 79, "Law on joint-stock companies»). Quite often law treats the head of the executive body as the head of the commercial organization.

In cases provided by law a juridical person can get rights and responsibilities through its members. It concerns full and Commandite partnerships.

2.5. Organizational-legal forms of commercial organizations

The Civil Code of the Russian Federation contains a list of commercial organizations. They can be created in the form of economic partnerships and societies, production cooperatives, and state and municipal unitary enterprises (p.2 article 50). The listed forms are quite sufficient (articles 105–106). But there is some economic organizational forms which are not mentioned in the list. One of them is "small enterprise". The Federal Law "On the state support of small business in the Russian Federation" defines such enterprises as commercial organizations:

– with the share of the Russian Federation, subjects of the Russian Federation, public or religious organizations (associations), charity and other funds not more than 25 percent;
– with the share of one or more juridical persons which are not subjects of the small business not more than 25 percent;
– with the average number of employees not exceeding the following limits: in industry, construction and transport – 100 people, in agriculture and scientific technical sphere – 60 people, in wholesale trade – 50 people, in retail trade and consumer services – 30 people, in other areas and other types activity – 50 people. The average number of the small business workers for the accountable period is determined by counting all of them including those working under civil law contracts and on part-time conditions considering the real time worked, as well as the workers of the representations, branches and other separated subdivisions.

Subjects of the small business also include physical persons undertaking entrepreneurial activity without forming a juridical person. Literal interpretation of the above mentioned article of law lets us assert, however, that it concerns only economic societies with limited (additional) responsibility.

The CC RF does not include in a list of commercial organizations, financial-industrial groups or holding companies. In the federal law on financial-industrial groups a possibility of applying CC RF is not mentioned at all, though a combination of juridical persons acting as main and subsidiary societies is dealt with in the article 195 CC RF. It envisages independent legal regulation of legal norms of establishment, activity and liquidation of financial-industrial groups.

The Russian Federation President's decree of November 16, 1992 "On measures on implementation of the industrial policy of privatizing state enterprises" confirmed the temporary provision on holding companies created in the process of transformation of state enterprises into joint-stock companies. This decree contains only some norms on joint-stock companies and they were formulated without considering requirements of the CC RF.

Joint regulation of property, consumer and entrepreneurial relations in one code resulted in the situation when the entrepreneurial activity of citizens performed without forming a juridical person is regulated by the rules of the CC RF which regulates also the activity of juridical persons in the form of commercial organizations, if not otherwise provided by law, other legal acts or the nature of legal relations (Article 23, CC RF).

The used judicial technique of presenting normative materials has not always considered logical structure of legal norms and thus complicated the activity of individual entrepreneurs. If the head of the farm is considered as an entrepreneur, he is treated as a commercial organization, not the farm itself. But we can come to the opposite conclusion: since the whole farm is registered, it is considered as a commercial organization, not its head.

2.6. Reorganization of the commercial organization

We can conclude from the content of the articles 57–61 of the CC RF that there may occur termination of a juridical person activity with transfer of rights and duties in the form of legal succession to other juridical subject (reorganization) or without it (liquidation). Reorganization of the commercial organization means disappearing of the previously active subject of law in its old form without termination of its entrepreneurial activity. This latter is performed in one way or another by a new bearer of rights and duties, a new commercial organization (probably with changing the goal, object and scope of activity). Unlike liquidation, reorganization of the commercial organization implies preservation of rights and duties, property, production and technological system in reduced or enlarged form. Reorganization is always connected with legal succession, transfer of property and other rights (duties) from one terminated (changed) subject of law to another. Reorganization of a juridical person as a variety of universal legal succession, represents one form of circulation of the private law objects (p.1, article 129, CC RF).

General provisions on reorganization are contained in articles 57–60 of the CC RF and are further developed in federal laws on some commercial organizations. Merger, accession, division, separation and transformation are carried out upon decision of the founders (participants) of the commercial organization or the juridical person's body authorized to do it by the constitutive documents. Reorganization of the commercial organization in the form of division or separation to one or more juridical persons may be carried out upon decision of the competent state bodies or upon court decision. Such a right, for example is given to the federal anti-monopoly body in case when the commercial organization occupies a dominating position and has committed two or more violations of the anti-monopoly legislation (p.1, article 19, "Law on competition and restriction of monopolistic activity in commodity markets). In cases established by law, reorganization of juridical persons in the form of merger, accession or transformation may be carried out upon approval of the competent state bodies. A juridical person is considered reorganized from the moment of state registration of the newly formed juridical person except for the cases of reorganization in the form of accession. In reorganizing juridical persons in the form of accession to it of another juridical person, the former is considered reorganized from the moment of making in the state register of juridical persons an entry of terminated activity of the accessed juridical person.

In cases of merger, accession and transformation rights and duties are transferred in accordance with an endorsement act and in cases of division and separation – according to the division balance. The endorsement act and division balance must contain information on legal succession concerning all obligations and rights of the reorganized juridical persons with regard to all creditors and debtors including the obligations disputed by the parties. The endorsement act and division balance are confirmed by the founders (participants) of the juridical person or the body which has made a decision on reorganization. They are submitted along with the constitutive documents for the state registration of the newly formed juridical persons. Failure to submit along with the constitutive documents of the endorsement act and division balance or lack of provisions on legal succession in them result in refusal to register newly formed juridical persons (Article 59, CC RF).

Founders (participants) of the juridical person or the body which has made a decision on reorganization of the juridical person must inform in writing the creditors of the reorganized juridical person who have a right to demand termination or fulfillment of the obligation before time in case the juridical person is the debtor, as well as compensation of losses. The Federal Law on joint-stock companies provides that within 30 days from the date of passing a decision on reorganization of the joint-stock company, it informs its creditors about it in writing. The creditor has a right to demand from the society termination or fulfillment of the obligations before time and compensation of losses by written notification within 30 days from the date of sending by the society notification of reorganization in the form of merger, accession or transformation and within 60 days – of reorganization in the form of division or separation (article 15).

Merger of companies is considered as formation of a new company by means of passing to it all the rights and duties of two or more companies with termination of the latter according to the endorsement act. Companies participating in the merger conclude an agreement on the merger which defines the procedure and terms of the merger, as well as the procedure of conversion of the shares of each society into shares or other securities of the new company.

Accession of the company is considered as termination of one or more companies with passing all rights and duties to another company according to the endorsement act. The accessing company and the company being accessed conclude an agreement on accession which determines the procedure and terms of accession, as well as the procedure of conversion the shares of the accessing society into the shares and/or shares and other securities of the accessed company. The Russian Federation President's decree of August 18, 1996 "On measures of protection of shareholders rights and securing of the interests of the state as proprietor and shareholder" envisages that the agreement on merger or accession of the companies must determine rights of the holders of all types of shares distributed in reorganization of the newly created or still functioning joint-stock company, terms and order of exchanging shares of the reorganized companies to the distributed shares of this company, as well as the terms of such exchange including the correlation of types and par value of the distributed shares used in the process of exchange for every type of earlier issued shares of every reorganized joint-stock company and other important terms according to model agreements on merger or accession of joint-stock companies confirmed by the Federal Commission on the securities market.

Division of the company is considered as termination of the society with transfer of all rights and duties to the newly formed companies. The board of directors (supervisory council) of the reorganized company submits for consideration of the general meeting of shareholders the issues of reorganization of the company in the form of division, the order and terms of such reorganization, formation of new companies and the order of conversion of the reorganized company shares into the shares and/or other securities of the newly formed companies. The general meeting of shareholders passes a decision on reorganization of the society in the form of division by the three fourth of votes. The general meeting of shareholders of the newly formed society passes a decision on its confirmation and on the election of the board of directors (supervisory committee) (Article 18, Law on joint-stock companies).

A question of reorganization in the form of separation and in the form of transformation is treated in the same way (articles 19–20, Law on joint-stock companies).

Article 26 of the law on production cooperatives envisages that the endorsement act and division balance are confirmed by the general meeting of the cooperative. Transformation of the cooperative into the economic partnership or company may be performed by unanimous decision of its members.

2.7. Liquidation of the commercial organization

As it was earlier mentioned, liquidation of the commercial organization involves its termination without transfer of rights and duties in the form of legal succession to other persons (article 61, CC RF). This article offers two forms of liquidation of the commercial organization: the common one and the liquidation as a result of declared bankruptcy.

The commercial organization may be liquidated
1) upon the decision of its founders (participants) or its body authorized to do this by the constitutive documents for example after the expiration date of the period the commercial organization was set up for or upon achievement of the original goal;
2) upon the court decision that the organization's registration is invalid as a result of violations of law and other legal acts in the process of its formation if these violations cannot be corrected.

A commercial organization may be also liquidated upon the court decision in case of performing activity without a license, or performing a certain activity forbidden by law, as well as in case of repeated flagrant violations of law or other legal acts. A demand to liquidate a commercial organization may be submitted to court by a state agency or a body of local self-government. For example, the State Taxation Service has a right to pose questions of juridical persons liquidation if they evade from paying taxes.

The founders (participants) of the commercial organization or the body which has made a decision on liquidation must immediately inform in writing the body performing the state registration of juridical persons about it. This body will enter in the state register the information that the commercial organization is in the stage of liquidation. The founders (participants) or the body which has made a decision on liquidation of the commercial organization, appoint the liquidation commission (liquidator) in coordination with the body performing the state registration of juridical persons and fix the order and terms of liquidation. From the moment of its appointment, the liquidation commission acquires the authority to manage the commercial organization.

The liquidation commission places in printed media an announcement on liquidation of the commercial organization and on the procedure and the period for creditors' claims which cannot exceed two months from the date of the publication. The liquidation commission takes measures to find the creditors and to receive debts. It also informs the creditors about liquidation in writing. According to p.2 of article 12 of the Law on accounting, liquidation involves compulsory inventory inspection.

After the expiration of the period for creditors' claims, the liquidation commission prepares an interim liquidation balance which is then approved by the founders (participants) of the commercial organization or the body which has made a decision on liquidation in coordination with the body performing the state registration of juridical persons. The balance should contain information on the property of the organization under liquidation, a list of the creditors' claims which have been made and results of their consideration. Payment of money sums to the creditors of the commercial organization under liquidation is carried out in accordance with the interim liquidation balance.

After settling accounts with creditors, the liquidation commission prepares the liquidation balance which is confirmed by the founders (participants) of the commercial organization or the body which has made a decision on liquidation in coordination with the body performing the state registration of juridical persons. If the state enterprise under liquidation has not enough property to satisfy creditors' claims, the latter have a right to apply to court.

Commercial organizations except the state enterprises can be declared *insolvent (bankrupts)* by court decision if they are not able to satisfy creditors' claims. Declaring of the commercial organization bankrupt by court results in its liquidation. The commercial organization together with its creditors may make a decision to declare its own bankruptcy and voluntary liquidation. The grounds on which court declares the commercial organization or the individual entrepreneur bankrupt or recognizes their declared bankruptcy, as well as the procedure of liquidation are fixed by the law on insolvency (bankruptcy) (Article 65, CC RF). At present, the existing law is the law on insolvency (bankruptcy) of enterprises. Insolvency is understood as failure to satisfy creditors' claims dealing with payments for goods (works, services) including failure to provide obligatory payments to the budget and non-budget funds connected with the debtor's obligations exceeding his property or with the unsatisfactory structure of the debtor's balance. A symptom of insolvency (bankruptcy) is interruption of current payments – when a commercial organization does not satisfy or is not capable to satisfy its creditors' claims during three months from the due time of payment. By law, reorganization and liquidation measures are applied towards the debtor, as well as an amicable agreement. In case of forced liquidation of a commercial organization the bankruptcy proceeding is carried out by the state arbitration court decision. The purpose of the latter is a proportional satisfaction of the creditors' claims and pronouncing then the debtor free of debts. The procedure of distributing of the bankruptcy property mass is determined by article 30 of the Law on insolvency (bankruptcy) of enterprises. Requirements of article 64 of the CC RF should be taken into account as well. According to this article, in the process of liquidation of the commercial organization the creditors' claims are satisfied in the following order:

– first, claims of the citizens in cases when the organization under liquidation is responsible for injury to life or health by means of capitalization of the corresponding periodical payments;
– second, payments of severance benefits and payment for labour to the employees working under the labour contract and remuneration on the contracts with authors;

- third, creditors' claims on some debts, secured on the property of the debtor.
- fourth, indebtedness on compulsory payments to budget and non-budget funds (taxes etc.);
- fifth, payments to other creditors according to law.

In the process of liquidating banks and other credit institutions accumulating citizens' finances, first are satisfied the claims of the citizens being the depositors of the bank and other credit institutions (in the wording of February 20, 1996).

The Law on joint-stock companies envisages that the property left after payments to creditors is distributed among the shareholders in the following order:

- first, payments for shares to be redeemed upon shareholders' request;
- second, payments of calculated but not paid dividends on the preferred shares at the liquidation value set by the company rules;
- third, distribution of the property of the company under liquidation among the shareholders of common and all types of preferred shares.

The procedure of liquidation of production cooperatives is determined in article 27 of the Federal Law on production cooperatives.

3. Economic partnerships

The Civil Code of the Russian Federation regulates two kinds of partnerships: full and limited (Commandite).The norms of articles 69–81 are sufficient for the full partnership. Passing of new laws is not envisaged by the CC RF. Economic partnerships in the form of commercial organizations should be differentiated from the partnerships in the form of non-commercial organization, for example, the partnership of housing owners. According to the Federal Law on the partnerships of housing owners, it is a non-commercial organization, a form of association of house owners for joint management and exploitation of the real estate complex in condominium, for possession, use and disposition of the common property (within the limits fixed in the legislation).

In full partnership the participants (full partners) perform entrepreneurial activity on behalf of the partnership according to the agreement concluded among them and bear responsibility on its obligations with their own property. The full partnership as a juridical person has an incomplete character because property responsibility of the partnership on debts is not limited by the amount of the joint capital. In case when it is not sufficient, the participants of the full partnership together bear subsidiary responsibility with their property on the partnership's obligations. That is why according to p.3, article 9 of the Law on enterprises and entrepreneurial activity, the full partnership was not considered a juridical person. It had not any accounting regulations. The law on the registration fee charged from physical entities performing entrepreneurial activity and the procedure of their registration envisaged that the certificate issued upon the registration of the full partnership was the same as the one issued upon the registration of an individual entrepreneur.

Now the full partnership which functions on the basis of the constitutive agreement resembles an association of persons who according to the agreement count on making profit. It is practically possible to differentiate between the full partnership and common partnership (agreement on joint activity) only on the basis of one formal feature – whether the association of individual entrepreneurs and/or commercial organizations is a registered juridical person.

A full partnership is formed and functions on the basis of the constitutive agreement which is signed by all the participants. The constitutive agreement should determine the name of the full partnership, its location, the order of management; terms of the amount and composition of the joint capital, the amount of the participatory shares and their transfer for every participant of the joint capital, the amount, time and procedure of making contributions, the participants' responsibility for breaking obligations on contributions. As it is seen from p. 2 article 70 CC RF, practically all compulsory terms of the constitutive agreement are aimed at determination of the joint capital by the participants. The law does not determine the minimal amount of the capital as it is done in case of other economic organizations. It is not accidental, since the joint capital does not guarantee the interests of the partnership creditors which are provided by the organizational legal form of this type of the juridical person. Full partners bear responsibility on the partnership obligations with their own property.

The participants of full partnerships may be individual entrepreneurs and/or commercial organizations. The unitary (state) enterprise has no right to contribute the immovable property belonging to it by the right of economic use as a contribution into the joint capital of the partnership without the owner's approval. An individual entrepreneur or a commercial organization may be participants of just one full partnership. From the moment of concluding the constitutive agreement every partner enjoys rights and bears responsibilities with regard to other participants of the partnership. Though full partnerships have their own property in the form of the joint capital, there is also unlimited responsibility of all the partners with all their property. It significantly strengthens the enterprise credit but at the same time there is a threat for every participant to loose the property as a result of the entrepreneurial activity of another in full partnership. Such associations are only possible among a few people who know one another well and have complete mutual trust. A full partnership usually consists of two or three people and very seldom of more than four.

The management of the full partnership is carried out upon the agreement of all the participants unless the constitutive agreement provides for the cases when decisions are passed by the majority of votes. The constitutive agreement may provide for another procedure of determining the number of votes of the partnership members. Every participant even if he is not running the business has a right to get acquainted with the account books and other documentation. The refusal to endow people with this right or its restriction, even upon approval on behalf of the partnership participants, has no legal force.

The constitutive agreement of the partnership fixes if the participants jointly run the business, or certain participants are responsible for this. If there is no such provision in the constitutive agreement, any participant has a right to act on behalf of the partnership. If the partnership participants have selected one or more persons to run the business, the rest of the participants must have a an authorisation from the participants in order to conclude contracts on behalf of the partnership. The authority for running the business granted to one or more partnership participants may be terminated by court upon demand of one or more partnership participants in case of serious grounds (for example in case of failure to run the business reasonably). On the basis of the court decision, necessary changes are introduced into the constitutive agreement. A participant of the full partnership has no right to conclude contracts similar to those which constitute the subject-matter of the partnership activity without consent of other participants.

A participant of the full partnership is obliged to participate in its activity according to the terms of the constitutive agreement. First of all, he must pay at least a half of his contribution into the partnership joint capital by the moment of its registration. The rest should be paid during the period fixed in the constitutive agreement. In case of failure to fulfill this responsibility, the participant must pay the partnership 10 percent interest of the unpaid part of the contribution and compensate for the inflicted losses. The profit and losses of the partnership are distributed among the participants according to their participatory shares in the joint capital. An agreement to neglect somebody when distributing profits and losses is not allowed. The distribution of the profit is not conducted if the value of the partnership assets is less than the amount of the joint capital as a result of suffered losses.

A participant of the full partnership has a right to withdraw or transfer his participatory share in the joint capital to another participant or the third person upon the consent of other participants. The procedure of the participant's withdrawal differs depending on the fact if the partnership has been established for a certain or uncertain period. Refusal to participate in the full partnership established without indication of the period, should be announced at least six months before the factual withdrawal from the partnership. Refusal to participate before time in the full partnership established for a certain period is allowed only in case of a justifiable reason. But since according to p.2, article 77 of the CC RF an prior agreement among the participants on withdrawal from the partnership is not valid, the issue of recognizing the reason justifiable in case of disagreement among the participants should be solved in court. A participant quitting the partnership is paid the part of the partnership property corresponding to the contribution of the participant into the joint capital or upon the consent of the quitting participant he is given the property in kind. In case of the full partnership participant's death his heir can join the partnership only upon the consent of other participants, Such consent is also required for a juridical person being a legal successor of the reorganized juridical person which participated in the full partnership. An heir or a juridical person, legal successors which have not joined the full partnership have a right to be paid the part of the partnership property corresponding to the participant's share or the property in kind. In case of a person's withdrawal the shares of the remaining full partners in the joint capital increase if not otherwise provided by the constitutive agreement or another agreement among the participants. The participants of the full partnership have a right to demand in judicial order to expel a participant if a unanimous decision of the rest of the participants has been made in case of serious grounds for this (for example in case of failure to run the business reasonably). A participant who has withdrawn from the partnership fulfills the partnership obligations which have occurred before the moment of his withdrawal along with the remaining participants. This liability lasts for the period of two years from the day of the approval of the partnership annual account for the year when the participant withdrew.

If the partnership have agreed to transfer its participant's share in the joint capital or a part of it to another participant or the third person, the latter acquires in full or partly the rights which belonged to the participant who transferred the share (part of it). In the process of making a decision on such transfer the participants take into consideration business qualities of the new participant, especially in case of the third person which must be either an individual entrepreneur or a juridical person. The person who has received the share (part of it) fulfills the obligations which occurred before his joining the partnership along with the rest of the participants (p.2, article 75, CC RF).

The participant's share in the joint capital may be used to satisfy his own creditors only if he has no other property to pay debts with. The creditors of such participant have a right to demand from the full partnership to separate the parts of the partnership property corresponding the debtor's contribution to the joint capital according to the balance sheet which is prepared on the day when creditors submit their demand.

The composition of the partners changes in cases of withdrawal or death of an individual entrepreneur, in cases when he is declared missing, or having lost legal capacity, or he has been declared bankrupt. The composition also changes in case of initiating reorganization procedure with regard to the commercial organization being a partner.

A full partnership is liquidated on the grounds fixed in article 61 of the CC RF and in cases when there is only one participant left in the society. He can transform such partnership into other enterprise form within six months.

The limited (commandite) partnership is a partnership which along with the participants performing entrepreneurial activity on behalf of the partnership and responsible for the society obligations with their property, includes one or more investors who take risks of losses connected with the partnership activity within the sums of their participatory contributions and do not participate in entrepreneurial activity of the society (p.1, article 82, CC RF). The essence of the limited partnership is a combination of personal business activity of full partners with the property of the investors necessary for running the enterprise. The limited partnership is the most convenient way of attracting investments without burdening the investors with the concerns about running the business or its supervising. The last feature differs the partnership of this kind from the joint-stock company. That is why the Russian translation of "limited partnership" is "partnership based on trust".

The status of full partners participating in the limited partnership and their responsibility for the partnership obligations are determined by the above discussed rules for the full partnership. They are used as long as they do not contradict the rules of articles 82–86 CC RF.

The constitutive agreement of the limited partnership along with the information relevant for the full partnership should contain the total amount of the contributions paid by the investors. The limited partnership investor must pay his contribution into the joint capital which is confirmed by the document of participation issued to the investor by the partnership. After that the investor has a right:

1. to receive a part of the partnership profit according to his contribution to the joint capital in the order fixed by the constitutive agreement;
2. get acquainted with the yearly reports and balance sheets of the partnership;
3. in the end of the fiscal year to withdraw from the partnership and receive one's contribution;
4. transfer one's share in the joint capital or its part to the third person. The investors have a priority before the third persons concerning the right to buy a share (part of it) according to the terms and procedure provided for the transfer of the share in the share capital of the limited society to another person (p.2, article 93 CC RF).

A limited partnership is liquidated upon withdrawal of all investors. But full partners have a right instead of liquidation to transform a limited partnership into a full partnership. A limited partnership stays if there is at least one full partner and one investor left. During the liquidation of the limited partnership investors have a priority before full partners in receiving investments from the partnership property which is left after the creditors claims have been satisfied.

4. Economic society

4.1. General

Subdivisions of chapter 4 of the CC RF specify the limited responsibility society (in german: GmbH), the additional responsibility society, the (joint-stock) company, as well as subsidiary and dependent companies. Thus, economic societies can be of different types which should be taken into consideration. At the same time the joint-stock company can be of the open and closed types. In the framework of the current text we will discuss the limited responsibility society and the joint-stock company.

The limited responsibility society is considered as a society established by one or more persons. Its charter capital is divided into shares. The size of the shares is determined by the constitutive agreement and the articles of incorporation. The participants of such economic society are not responsible for its obligations and take risk of losses connected with the activity of the society within the value of the initial contributions (p.1, article 87). The contribution into the economic society may be in the form of money, securities, other things or property rights after monetary appraisal. Monetary appraisal of the contribution made by the limited responsibility society participant, is performed upon the agreement among the founders (participants). In cases envisaged by the agreement it is subject to independent expert inspection (p.6, article 66 CC RF). The legal status of the society is determined by the CC RF. And by the law on limited responsibility societies, which have been passed in February 8, 1998.

The number of the society participants cannot exceed the limit (50 participants) determined by the law on the limited responsibility societies. The participants of the economic society may include citizens and juridical persons including non-commercial organizations. Institutions financed by the proprietors/owners may also be participants of the economic societies upon the owner's consent. The society cannot have as a sole participant another economic society consisting of one person. The limited responsibility society constitutive agreement and the articles of incorporation must contain the rules of the share capital; of the participatory share sizes of every participant; of the time and procedure of making contributions; of the participants responsibility for breaking obligations to make contributions; of the composition and competencies of the society managerial bodies and the order of making decisions such as those on the issues which require unanimous vote or a qualified majority of votes, as well as other rules provided for by the law.

The size of the share capital of the limited responsibility society should not be less than the sum equal to the 100-fold amount of the minimal amount of payment for labour per month valid on the day of submitting constitutive documents for the registration (p.3, "On the provisions on the procedure of the state registration of the entrepreneurial subjects confirmed by the Russian Federation President's Decree of July 1994). At least one half of the share capital of the society should be paid by the participants by the moment of registration. The rest of the sum is to be paid by the participants during the first year of the society's activity. In case of violating this obligation the society should announce a decrease of the size of the foundation capital and register it in due order, or terminate its activity by means of liquidation. The society participants can be exempt from the obligation of making contribution to the share capital, for example by offsetting claims to the society. The share capital determines the minimal value of the society property which guarantees the creditors' interests. Decreasing of the foundation capital is allowed only after informing all the creditors who have a right to demand termination or execution of the corresponding obligations and compensation of all their losses. If after the second and any consequent fiscal year the value of net assets will be less than the foundation capital, the society should decrease of its share capital and register it in due order. If the value of assets is below the minimal amount of the share capital fixed by law, the society is subject to liquidation.

Article 91 of the CC RF enumerates the issues where the general meeting of participants has the exclusive competence. These include:

amendments to the articles of incorporation, changing its share capital; confirmation of annual profit statement and balance sheet and division of profits; formation of the executive bodies; decisions on reorganization and liquidation of the society. They cannot be passed to the executive body of the society under any conditions. The current management of the society is conducted by the executive body (collegiate or one-man). The one-man managerial body can be also elected from non-participants of the society.

The society participant has a right to transfer his share or its part to one or more participants of the society. Its alienation to a third person is allowed in case it is envisaged by the articles of incorporation. Acquisition of the share by the person, not member in the society results in the necessity for him to join the society. But this is not always consistent with the interests of the current members. Therefore, the articles may envisage prohibition of alienation. Though such prohibition is absent, the members have the right of pre-emption. If the members do not use this right within the period of time set in the articles, the share may be alienated to the third person. If the share cannot be sold to third persons and no members wants to buy it, the society must redeem the share for the real share value.

Shares in the limited responsibility society can be inherited and transferred to the legal successors of juridical entities – participants of the society unless the constitutive documents fix that such transferal is allowed only upon consent of the remaining society participants. A refusal to approve the transferal of the share results in the obligation to pay to the heirs (legal successors) of the participant a real share value or give out property in kind.

A limited responsibility society has a right to be transformed to a joint-stock company or a production cooperative.

The additional responsibility society is a variety of the limited responsibility society. Most of the rules about the latter are applied to it (p.3, Article 95,CC RF). There is one exception: in case of lack of property to satisfy the creditors' claims, the society participants can be jointly brought to property responsibility on the society debts by their personal property in the amount corresponding to the sum of contributions. In case of bankruptcy of one of the participants, his additional responsibility is divided among the rest of the society participants.

4.2. Companies

The company is an economic society joining of the capital. The share capital is divided into a number of equities. Each of them is expressed by a security – a share. The company and the limited responsibility society are similar in their legal nature – stockholders are not responsible for the society obligations and take the risk connected with the society activity only within the value of the shares belonging to them. At the same time, the structure of the share capital in the company is different from that in the limited responsibility society. The shares of one issue have the same par value, while the contributions in the limited (additional) responsibility societies may be different. The certificates fixing their belonging to the society participants are not securities. Registration of the stockholders rights by securities means that exercising and transferring rights are possible by means of shares and their transfer, while withdrawing from the company a participant cannot demand any payments or property in kind. Thus, the economic society of this type, contrary to the society of limited responsibility, fully preserves its property after the participants' withdrawal. That is why the CC RF and the Federal law on the companies regulate not only the legal status of the company, but also the rights and responsibilities of stockholders. The latter circumstance has also resulted in a considerable amount of the norms regulating the competence of the stockholders general meeting and the procedure of its convening and conducting, the competence of the board of directors (supervisory council) and the executive body. As the company directors have, in case of a great number of small shareholders, a possibility of uncontrolled use of the company property in their own interests, the law demands from the open (public) company to publish the annual report, a balance sheet, and the information of profits and losses for public notice. To provide control of the financial and economic activity of the company, the general meeting elects a revision commission. Moreover, an independent auditor annually confirms the validity of the information contained in the reports and other financial documents of the company. The audit control of the company activity must be carried out at any time upon the demand of the stockholders whose accumulative share in the share capital is over 10 percent (p.5, article 103, CC RF).

In the course of privatization of the state and municipal enterprises the company of an open type was announced as the only organizational-legal form of their transformation. Their legal status and its creation has specific features. These specific features of setting up companies in the course of privatization have been established by the laws on privatization of the state and municipal enterprises and other legal rules. Of special importance among them is the Russian Federation President's Decree of July 1, 1992 "On organizational measures to transform state enterprises and associations of state enterprises into companies" including the model articles of incorporation of the open type company. The specific features of the legal status of the companies organized by means of privatization of the state and municipal enterprises are determined by the CC RF, the law on the companies and the laws and other legal rules on privatization of these enterprises (p.3, article 96, CC RF). The law on the companies puts it more definitely – the specific features of formation and legal status of the companies in the process of privatization of the state and municipal enterprises are determined by the legal rules of the Russian Federation on privatization of the above mentioned enterprises. The specific regulation of these companies is in force from the moment of passing the decision on privatization up to the moment of alienation by the state or a municipal unit of the 75 % of the shares belonging to them within the period fixed by the privatization plan of the given enterprise (p.5, article 1).

The procedure of forming companies in the process of privatization of the state and municipal enterprises was determined before August 1997 by law and the state programs of privatization of December 29, 1991, June 11, 1992, December 24, 1993 and July 22, 1994. The RF President's Decree of July 1, 1992, determined a simplified procedure of transforming state enterprises into companies. A provision on transforming state enterprises into open companies adopted in this decree, determines that a committee on management of property considers the privatization plan, act of the property assessment and the articles of incorporation of the company prepared by the working commission on privatization and confirms them in case of their compliance with the requirements of the commercialization provisions. The approved privatization plan is a prospect for share emission. The norms of the Rules on issue and circulation of securities and on stock exchange in RSFSR confirmed by the Decision of the RF Government December 28, 1991 are applied. A committee on management of property provides transfer of shares to the respective property fund within the period determined by the privatization plan. The fund sells shares according to the state program of privatization. Share transfer is registered by means of entering changes into the shareholders register of the company. From the end of 1993 a special registrator keeps the shareholders register in case there are more than 500 shareholders – the owners of common stock.

While creating companies in the process of state enterprises privatization in some branches of industry, share holding packages of 51 %, 38 % and 25.5 % of ordinary shares (after July 1, 1994 of 51 % and 25.5 %) were fixed in federal ownership for the period up to three years. In 1996 the period for fixing the share holding packages in federal ownership was extended for the enterprises producing strategically important goods. A RF President's decree of June 10, 1994 "On some measures on providing state management of the economy" envisages the procedure of performing the functions of representing state interests by the state representatives in the privatized companies managerial bodies. They must in writing coordinate with the federal bodies of power or with the Russian fund of federal property the draft decisions of the managerial bodies which they are going to support, as well as their future voting on the draft decisions proposed by other members of the companies managerial bodies.

The law on the companies envisages that all the society shares are nominal (p.2, article 25). This imperative norm does not comply with the rules of the law on the securities market which allow issuing of bearer shares in a certain ratio to the amount of the paid share capital of the emitent according to the norms set by the Federal Commission on the Securities Market. Therefore, there is a visible contradiction between the above mentioned laws, with the priority being given to the federal law on the companies, since its adoption is envisaged in p.3, article 96 CC RF. According to the author, since the CC RF explains the concept of the bearer security (article 145), there are grounds to assume lawful providing for the bearer share in the law on the securities market. To avoid unnecessary conflicts, respective amendments should be entered in the law on the companies.

The law on the companies lacks a special chapter on the rights and responsibilities of shareholders. Such norms can be found in different chapters which complicates their application. The articles of incorporation must contain information on the number, par value, category of shares (ordinary or preference shares), types of preference shares, as well as on the shareholders rights for every share category.

Each ordinary share gives to its owner a fixed set of rights. In accordance with the articles of incorporation, a shareholder has a right to participate in the general meeting of shareholders with a right to vote on all the issues of its competence, a right to receive dividends, and in case of liquidation – a right to receive a part of the company property. In the law on the securities market a share is defined as an emitted security granting a number of property and non-property rights.

Preference shares may be of different types. Within these types their owners get the same rights and have the same par value. The articles of incorporation should define the types of the preference shares which are differentiated according to the amount of the dividends and/or the value paid in liquidation and the order of payments. According to article 32 of the law on companies shareholders of the preference shares have a right to vote, for example, in decisions on reorganization and liquidation of the company.

A share does not give a right to vote before it has been paid for. In case of incomplete payment in due time, the share goes in the company's disposal. The money and other property paid for the share are not returned.

The powers of the general meeting of shareholders are determined in article 48 of the law on the companies. The law specifies the issues referred to its exclusive competence, which include the issues entered only upon the board of directors (supervisory council) proposal. Among the questions which cannot be decided by the board of directors (supervisory council) are the questions of amendments and additions in the articles of incorporation, company reorganization and its liquidation, confirmation of the company auditor, annual reports, balance sheets, division of profits, concluding of big transactions or transactions in which the interests company executives are involved.

The board of directors competence includes issues of general management of the company except for the issues referred to the exclusive competence of the general meeting of shareholders. For example, the board of directors may increase the share capital by means of increasing par value of shares in case it possesses such a right according to the articles of incorporation or decision of the general meeting of shareholders. The articles of incorporation may grant the board of directors a right of forming an executive body and terminating its powers before time, determining remuneration and compensation. Only on the recommendation of the board of directors does the general meeting of shareholders determine the amount of remuneration and compensation paid to the members of the revision commission, the amount of payment for audit services and the amount of dividend payment and its procedure. The company board of directors members are elected by the annual general meeting for the period of one year. The meeting elects the board of directors chairman who usually chairs also at the general meeting of shareholders.

The management of the current activity of the society is carried out by the manager (general manager) or a manager (general manager) and the management board (directorate). As follows from part II, p. 1, article 69 of the law on companies, the articles of incorporation determine simultaneous functioning of both one-man and collegiate executive bodies and their competence. The competence of the executive body includes all the questions of managing the routine activity of the company. It provides for the fulfillment of the decisions of the general meeting and the board of directors. The manager acts on behalf of the company without the power of attorney. He represents the company interests, concludes contracts on behalf of the company, confirms hiring, issues orders and gives directions obligatory for all employees. Rights and duties of the manager (general manager) and the members of the management board (directorate) are determined by the law on the companies, other legal acts and employment contract concluded by each manager in the company. These contracts are signed on behalf of the society usually by the board of directors chairman. Labour legislation extends to these relations in part not contradicting the provisions of the law on the companies. The board of directors is given the decisive role in determining rights and responsibilities of the manager (general manager). The law on the companies prescribes the board of directors members, director and the members of the management board (directorate) to act in the interests of the company reasonably and in good faith. They bear responsibility before the company for the losses inflicted to the company by their guilty activity (failure to act) if other grounds and the degree of responsibility are not fixed by federal laws (article 71).

The law on the companies specifies big transactions which cannot be concluded in the process of regular economic activity. They concern directly or indirectly the property of the company (more than 25 % of the balance value) or a considerable share holding package (more than 25 % of the emitted ordinary shares). Assessment of the property being an object of a big transaction, is carried out by the board of directors according to article 77 of the law on the companies. In order to determine the market value of the company, an independent assessor(auditor) may be invited. Involving of the latter is also obligatory in case the company buys shares from shareholders when shareholders have a right to demand redemption by the company of the shares belonging to them (article 76, The law on the companies). A decision to conclude a big transaction with the object being in the form of property constituting 25–50 % of the balance value of the company assets is made by the board of directors unanimously. In case when the unanimous decision of the board of directors on conclusion of a big transaction is not reached, the issue may be submitted to the general meeting of shareholders. The latter passes a decision on the conclusion of a big transaction with the object value constituting over 50 % of the balance value of the company assets on the date of passing a decision on concluding such transaction.

A person having an intention independently or together with an affiliated person (persons) to acquire 30 % or more of distributed ordinary shares, must at least 30 days before the purchasing date send to the company a written application stating the intention to acquire the shares. After purchasing such share-holding package the person must within 30 days from the date of purchase make an offer to shareholders to buy ordinary shares belonging to them at the average price of the company shares for the last six months. The offer to the shareholders contains information about the person who has purchased 30 % or more of shares, a number and offered price of the shares to be bought, and the time of purchasing(article 80, Law on the Companies).

A person affiliation is a group of persons meeting one or more requirements:
- a person or several persons together upon their agreement have a right to dispose of 50 % of the total number of votes for the shares constituting the share capital of the company;
- among two or more persons there has been signed a contract giving a right to determine conditions of performing entrepreneurial activity or carrying out the functions of the executive body;
- a person has a right to appoint 50 % or more of the composition of the executive body and (or) the company board of directors;
- the same physical persons represent more than 50 % of the executive body and/or the board of directors of the two or more juridical persons (article 4, law on competition and restriction of monopolistic activity at commodity markets).

A necessity to refer to the affiliation of persons occurs not only in concluding big transactions, but also in revealing the interest in the society transactions. In accordance with article 93 of the law on the companies, the affiliated persons are obliged to inform the company in writing about the shares belonging to them indicating their number and category (type) within ten days after their acquisition. The company is obliged to keep record of the affiliated persons and supply a report fixed by law and other legal acts.

The following parties are considered interested in the company transactions: members of the company board of directors, executives in other managerial bodies, shareholders holding together with their affiliated persons 20 % or more of the voting shares in case the above mentioned persons, their spouses, parents, children, sisters, brothers, and all their affiliated persons:

– are parties of such transaction or participate in it as representatives or intermediaries;
– hold at least 20 % of the voting shares (stocks) of the juridical person which is a party in the transaction or is participating in it as a representative or intermediary;
– occupy positions in the managerial bodies of the juridical person which is a party in the transaction or is participating in it as a representative or intermediary (article 81, Law on companies).

Persons indicated in the above mentioned article are obliged to inform the board of directors, the audit commission and the auditor about the juridical persons in which they hold independently or together with affiliated person /persons 20 % or more of the voting shares, about the managerial bodies where they occupy positions and about the current or planned transactions they are aware about in which they may be considered interested. Requirements to the procedure of concluding a transaction in which there is an interest, are provided for in article 83 of the law on the companies. Failure to meet these requirements may result in declaring a transaction invalid.

The company provides its shareholders with an access to the documents which should be kept according to article 89 of the Law on the companies except the accountant documents and minutes of the directorate meetings. The open company must publish in the mass media available to all shareholders an annual report, a balance sheet, an account of profits and losses, a prospect of share issue (if the number of shareholders is over 500 and in case the total amount of the issue exceeds 50.000 minimum salaries), information of the general shareholders meeting, and lists of affiliated persons.

5. Production cooperatives

The production cooperative (artel) is a voluntary association of citizens in order to perform a joint economic activity. It is based on the members' personal labour or other participation and on joining together the members' property contributions. Participation of juridical persons in the activity of the cooperative may be envisaged by the constitutive documents. The law on the production cooperatives allows participation of juridical persons in their activity. The cooperative members bear subsidiary responsibility on its obligations in the amount and in the order fixed by the law on the production cooperatives and the cooperative charter. The legal status of the production cooperatives, the rights and responsibilities of their members according to the CC RF are determined by the federal laws on the production cooperatives and on the agricultural cooperation. The latter defines legal and economic foundations for creation and functioning of the agricultural production cooperatives and their associations.

The production cooperative is formed upon the decision of its founders. The number of its members must be at least five. A juridical person participates in the cooperative activity through its representative according to the cooperative charter. The cooperative charter approved by the general meeting of the cooperative members should define its firm name and location. It should also contain information on the amount of participatory contributions; on the character and procedure of making participatory contributions and cooperative members responsibility for the failure to fulfill contribution obligations; on the character and order of labour or other participation of the cooperative members in its activity and on responsibility for their failure to fulfill obligations of personal participation; on the procedure of distributing profits and losses of the cooperative activity; on the amount and terms of the subsidiary responsibility of the cooperative members for its debts; on the composition and competence of the cooperative management bodies and the procedure of passing decisions; on the order of refunding the value of the contribution or giving out respective property to the person who has terminated membership in the cooperative; on the procedure of joining to the society of the new members; on the procedure of withdrawing from the cooperative; on the grounds and procedure of expelling members of the cooperative; on the list of branches and representations of the cooperatives; on the order of reorganization and liquidation of the cooperative (article 5, Law on the production cooperatives).

Citizens of the Russian Federation and foreign citizens having achieved the age of sixteen can be members of a cooperative if they have made a contribution according to the cooperative charter. In accordance with article 27 of the CC RF a citizen having achieved the age of sixteen and having become a member of the production cooperative may be declared as having legal capacity. The number of the cooperative members having made contributions but not participating in its activity can not exceed 25 % of the number of the cooperative members who personally participate in its production activity.

The cooperative has a right to own any property except for the state or municipal property. The property is formed of the contributions of the cooperative members, profit from its activity, loans, property given as a gift by physical and juridical persons, and from other sources permitted by law. The property owned by the cooperative is divided into the members' contributions which consist of the cooperative member participatory share and corresponding part of the cooperative assets except for the indivisible fund if its formation is envisaged in the cooperative charter.

A share transfer to the citizen not being a cooperative member is allowed upon the agreement of the cooperative. Then the citizen will become a member of the cooperative. A cooperative member must pay at least 10 % of the participatory contribution by the moment of the cooperative official registration. The rest of the share is paid within a year after the official registration. The assessment of the contribution is carried out at the time of the cooperative formation on mutual agreement of the cooperative members. When new members join the cooperative, the assessment is carried out by the commission appointed by the cooperative board. The assessment of the participatory contribution exceeding 250 minimum salary for labour fixed by law must be carried out by an independent expert.

The cooperative profit is divided among its members according to their personal participation and on the amount of the participatory contribution. Among the cooperative members not participating personally in the production activity the profit is divided according to their contributions (article 12, law on the production cooperatives).

The supreme managerial body of the cooperative is the general meeting of its members which unlike the general meeting of shareholders has a right to consider any issue and pass decisions on any issue dealing with the cooperative formation and activity. The exclusive competence of the general meeting includes:

- confirming the cooperative charter and making amendments in it;
- determining basic guidelines of the cooperative activity;
- accepting new cooperative members and expelling cooperative members;
- determining the amount of the participatory contribution, the amount and order of making the cooperative profits, determining ways of their usage;
- formation of the supervisory committee and termination of its members' authority;
- election of the cooperative audit commission (auditor), termination of its members' authority;
- confirming annual reports and balance sheets, opinions of the audit commission (auditor);
- distribution of the cooperative profits and losses;
- formation and liquidation of the cooperative branches and representations, passing rules on them;
- making decisions on the cooperative participation in economic societies and partnerships and its joining unions (associations).

The cooperative charter may also refer other issues to the exclusive competence of the general meeting.

Every cooperative member irrespective of the amount of the initial contribution has one vote in the process of passing decisions by the general meeting of the cooperative members. The general meeting is empowered to pass a decision if at least 50 % of the total number of the cooperative members are present at the meeting. Decisions are passed by the simple majority of votes if not otherwise stipulated by the law on the production cooperatives or the cooperative charter.

A supervisory committee is formed in the cooperatives with the number of members over 50. The committee oversees the activity of the executive bodies and solves other problems referred to its competence by the cooperative charter. A supervisory committee member cannot be a managing board member or the board chairman.

The cooperative executive bodies perform the routine management of the cooperative activity. The managing board is elected of the cooperative members for the period fixed by the charter in the cooperative with the number of members over 10. The board headed by the cooperative chairman manages the cooperative performance during the period between the general meetings of the cooperative members. The cooperative chairman is elected by the general meeting of the cooperative members. If a supervisory committee has been elected, the cooperative chairman is confirmed by the general meeting of the cooperative members upon recommendation of the supervisory committee. The powers of the cooperative chairman are determined by the cooperative charter. Within these powers the chairman acts on the behalf of the cooperative, represents the cooperative in the bodies of state power, in the bodies of local self-government and different organizations, disposes of the cooperative property, signs contracts and releases power of attorney, opens the cooperative accounts in banks and other credit organizations, hires and fires employees, issues orders and regulations obligatory for the cooperative members and employees (article 17, Law on the production cooperatives).

The bodies of state power and local self-government contribute to the cooperatives development, for example, by means of introducing tax privileges, priority supplying of cooperatives with non-living premises with the right of their redemption, access to state purchasing orders etc. Introduction of any restrictions of the cooperatives rights compared to other commercial organizations in terms of participation in privatization of the state and municipal property is not allowed. Cooperatives have a right for all benefits and privileges fixed by the legislation for the subjects of small business.

Expelling of the cooperative members is allowed upon the decision of the general meeting of the cooperative members in case the member failed to make a contribution in due time, or if the member does not fulfill his responsibilities imposed on him by the cooperative charter, and in other cases envisaged by the cooperative charter. A member of the supervisory committee or of the cooperative executive body can be expelled from the cooperative upon the decision of the general meeting of the cooperative members in the connection of his membership in a similar cooperative. The decision on expelling a cooperative member can be appealed against in court.

6. State and municipal unitary enterprises

This organizational-legal form of commercial organizations has been undergoing most radical changes in the process of the economic reform. The right of full economic freedom exercised by state and municipal enterprises from January 1, 1991 has been significantly restricted. Previously, according to the RSFSR property law, the rules of the property right were applicable to state and municipal enterprises with certain reservations. Now, according to the CC RF, property independence of state and municipal enterprises has been reduced to their disposition of the movable property and that of fiscal/public enterprises to the right of operational management. There is an opinion that "presence in our property system the juridical persons ("enterprises" and "institutions") which are not owners of their property but act as its independent participants, is a direct result of the transitional period and of preserving certain elements of state economy in it". Such opinions do not consider a specific character of the Russian economy in which the state and municipal sector should contain at least 40–60 % of the total production of goods, works and services due to climatic, geographical and other factors. A social factor should also be taken into account. It is necessary to re-establish to a certain extent the powers of labour collectives which they previously possessed according to the USSR law on the state enterprise (association). The rights and responsibilities of the workers of the unitary(state or municipal) enterprises are regulated by the norms of the labour law, rather than by those of the civil law, which is typical for the economic partnerships and companies.

Restriction of the state and municipal unitary enterprises rights started at the time of their accelerated privatization. In the RF President's Decree of May 23, 1994 "On the reform of the state enterprises" it was prescribed to terminate beginning from 1994 the establishment of new federal state enterprises with affiliated state property on the basis of the full economic freedom. Because of the restricted number of the federal state enterprises under liquidation it was necessary to set up economic institutions – fiscal plants, fiscal factories and fiscal enterprises with affiliated property of the liquidated federal state enterprises on the basis of operational management. The decree determined the grounds for passing a decision on liquidation of the state enterprise, such as lack of profit during the last two years, improper usage of the federal finances and others. Fiscal plants set up on the basis of the liquidated enterprises and being their legal successors had no right to establish subsidiaries or to act as founders of the enterprises, institutions and organizations without approval of the RF Government.

A unitary enterprise is regarded as a commercial organization not endowed with the ownership of the property in their use. The property of the state or municipal enterprise cannot be distributed to contributions (shares) including the enterprise employees. If the unitary enterprise has made a contribution to the economic society, the received profit cannot be distributed among the enterprise workers and will become the property of the enterprise as a whole.

The charter of the state and municipal unitary enterprise should contain additionally to common for any juridical person information, the data on the subject matter of its activity and its goals. The unitary enterprise is the only commercial organization exercising civil rights and duties directly connected with the activity indicated in the charter. The property apportioned to the unitary enterprise at the moment of its formation, results, products and profits of using the property in its economic management, as well as the property acquired by the enterprise according to the contract or on other grounds, is the property of the respective state or municipality.

Unitary enterprises can possess the property affiliated to them by the owner on the basis of economic or operational management (federal fiscal enterprises). The unitary enterprise based on the economic management is established upon the decision of the authorized state body or the body of local self-government. According to the Decree of the Russian Federation Government of February 10, 1994 "On delegating authorities of the Russian Federation Government concerning management and disposition of the objects of federal property", all the decisions on establishment and liquidation of the state enterprises being in state ownership, are passed by the government on the basis of the joint decision of the State Property Committee, RF Ministry of Economy and the federal body of the executive power responsible for the coordination and regulation of the activity in the respective branch (field of administration). Decisions on establishment and liquidation of the federal enterprises are to be agreed with the bodies of the executive power of the subjects of the Russian Federation on which territory they are located.

A constitutive document of the unitary enterprise is its charter approved by the ministry, state committee, federal state service or body of executive power of the RF subject, or by the local self-government body. The amount of the charter fund of the unitary enterprise must be at least equal to the 1000-fold amount of the fixed minimum salary for labour per month. Before the state registration of the enterprise based on the right of economic management, the charter fund must be fully paid by the owner. The unitary enterprise may establish as a juridical person another unitary enterprise (subsidiary enterprise) by means of transferring to it a part of its property under its economic management. The founder confirms the charter of the subsidiary enterprise and appoints its head.

The owner of the enterprise property is not responsible for the obligations except for the cases when the bankruptcy of the unitary enterprise has been caused by the directions of the owner.

The unitary enterprise based on the right of operational management is established in cases stipulated by the law on state and municipal unitary enterprises (it has not been adopted yet), upon the decision of the RF Government on the basis of the property being in federal ownership (article 115, CC RF).

The constitutive document of the federal fiscal enterprise (enterprise of operational management) is its charter confirmed by the RF Government. The decree of the RF Government of August 12, 1994 "On confirming the Model Rules on the fiscal plant (factory) established on the basis of the liquidated federal state enterprise" stipulates that the respective federal body of the executive power confirms the fiscal enterprise charter, appoints and relieves of his position its leader, and passes a decision on performing by the fiscal enterprise independent economic activity. Such a decision is passed in the form of an order and defines the specific kinds of goods (works, services) to be produced.

Before adopting the law on the state and municipal unitary enterprises RF Government Decree of October 6, 1994 has been applied. The decree confirms the procedure of planning and financing the activity of fiscal plants (factories). It stipulates that the productive and economic activity of the federal fiscal enterprise is performed according to the plan-order and the plan of the enterprise development. The enterprise has, moreover, a right to perform independent economic activity allowed by the respective authorized body. The relations of the fiscal enterprise with suppliers and customers are based on the contract. Financing connected with fulfilling the plan-order and the plan of the enterprise productive and social development, with the measures on mobilization, maintenance of the non-productive objects is carried out from the profits from selling goods (works, services). When it is not sufficient, the fiscal enterprise is financed from the federal budget. The fiscal enterprise submits a report on its use of this money, as well as on the utilization of the amortization deductions to the respective body of the executive power. The Russian Federation bears subsidiary responsibility on the obligations of the fiscal enterprise when its property is not sufficient. The fiscal enterprise may be reorganized and liquidated upon the decision of the RF Government.

VII Contract Law

Ljubov Vasiljevna Andrejeva

1. General provisions on contracts

1.1. The concept of contract in entrepreneurship and its legal regulation

A contract is an agreement between two or more parties concerning establishing, changing, or discontinuing civil rights and obligations (Civil Code of the RF, art. 420, paragraph 1).

As opposed to the contracts concluded by people in everyday life, contracts in entrepreneurial sphere have specific features, that is why in the Civil Code of the RF some rules regulating concluding, carrying out, and responsibility for not carrying out contracts in entrepreneurship, are different from the rules regulating similar issues in contracts concluded between citizens.

The concept of entrepreneurial contract is based on the concept of entrepreneurial activity stated in Article 2 of the Civil Code of the RF. It is defined as independent, at one's own risk, activity aimed at systematic profit from using property, selling merchandise, performing work, or providing services by entities registered in manner specified by the law.

Thus, parties or one party of an entrepreneurial contract must be entrepreneurs. It may be both an entrepreneurial organization and a person conducting entrepreneurial activities without being a legal entity. The aim of concluding entrepreneurial contracts is gaining profit.

The role of contracts in the period of transition to market economy in Russia has significantly changed. Formerly, the contract was subordinate to the plan, and in contract parties had to specify the figures (quantity of goods, terms of delivery, etc) which had been provided in the plan. Now, contract is the only document regulating relations between entrepreneurs, and there are no plan regulations.

The basic principle of regulating contracts is the principle of freedom of the contract, stated in Art. 421 of the Civil Code of the RF. It means that legal entities and physical persons are free to conclude contact, they decide themselves whether to conclude it or not. Obligatory concluding of contracts is not acceptable except for several cases mentioned in the legislation.

Contract concluded by its parties does not have to be specified in the Civil Code of the RF. Parties may conclude contracts both specified and not specified in the Civil Code of the RF.

The terms of a contract are determined by the parties except for cases when a certain condition is provided by the law or any other legislative act.

Another principle stated in the Civil Code of the RF is the priority of the law over the contract. The contract must meet the rules, obligatory for both parties, declared by the law or other legislative act current at the moment of signing of the contract. A contract or a transaction that does not meet the law or other legislative acts is considered void, as a rule.

In case when after the contract is concluded, a law is adopted which formulates for the parties obligatory rules different from those valid at the moment of signing of the contract, the terms of the contract remain valid, except for cases when the law specifies that it is relevant for contracts signed before the law was adopted, that is when the law as an exception from the general rule has reverse power. (art. 422, CC RF)

Requirements of the law or other legislative act may be of dispositive character, which means that while concluding a contract the parties may exclude application of these requirements or establish terms different from those provided by the act. Dispositive norms are applied unless the agreement of parties specifies different terms. If there is no agreement of parties, the contract is ruled by the dispositive norm.

Thus, for example, the general rule is that the risk of accidental destruction or damage of the merchandise passes to the buyer after the seller is considered to have fulfilled his duties of delivering the merchandise to the buyer according to the law or the contract (paragraph 1, art. 459, CC RF). But, as this norm is of dispositive character, the contract may contain different regulations.

The main source of regulating contract relations is the Civil Code of the RF. Other federal laws, though they are on the same level with the CC RF, must agree with CC RF (p. 2, art. 3, CC RF).

Other normative acts regulating contracts are the Decrees of the President of the RF, which must not contradict the CC RF, and the resolutions of the Government of the RF. The resolutions of the Government may be issued on the basis or for the implementation of the CC RF and other laws, as well as the decrees of the President of the RF (p.4, art. 3, CC RF).

Ministries and other federal bodies may issue acts regulating contract relations, too, but only in the cases and within the limits determined by the CC RF, other laws, decrees of the President and the resolutions of the Government, that is in cases they are commissioned (p. 7, art. 3, CC RF).

Among other sources regulating contract relations one might mention the customs and traditions of business, not quite widespread in entrepreneurship. They are traditional and widely used in a certain sphere of entrepreneurship rules of conduct not specified by the legislation, regardless of whether it had been stated in a certain document or not (art. 5, CC RF). If they contradict norms obligatory for the parties, or the contract, they are not used.

International agreements have a priority over civil legislation. If an international agreement of the RF requires rules different from those envisaged by the civil legislation, the rules of the international agreement are used (art.7, CC RF). This is confirmed by art. 5 of the federal law dated July 15, 1995. "On international agreements of the Russian Federation".

1.2. Main contract constructions

The CC RF contains several articles on contract constructions formerly unknown in Russian legislation (Public contract, contract of accession). Other constructions (preliminary contract, contract for the benefit of a third party, etc) had been envisaged by the former legislation, but the CC RF has a number of rules regulating them in a different way.

A characteristic feature of a *public contract* is that one of the parties is a commercial organization, which by the nature of its activity has to provide services to everyone who applies for them (retail trade, public transportation, supplying energy, etc).

In business, commercial organizations providing public services are usually natural monopolies. They don't have right to give preference to a certain party while concluding a public contract, except for cases envisaged by the law or other legislative acts. A commercial organization does not have right to refuse to conclude a public contract, if there is a possibility of providing customer with the respective merchandise, services, or doing certain work for him. Refusal to conclude a public contract is considered in court.

Terms of public contracts, like the price for merchandise, services, and work, are established the same for all customers, except for the cases when certain groups of customers have benefits according to the law.

In cases envisaged by the law, the Government of the RF has a right to issue regulations obligatory for parties while concluding and carrying out a public contract (typical contracts, regulations). Thus, it is the Government of the RF and not the Ministries, as before, that has the right to issue typical contracts. Terms of public contracts contradicting the rules set by the Government of the RF are considered void.

Another new type of contract included into the CC RF is the *contract of accession* (art. 428).

This construction is used in the legislation of western countries. While concluding this type of contract, the party providing merchandise, service, or work, designs a set standard form used in signing specific contracts. The other party has a right to conclude a contract by joining the proposed draft contract as a whole without discussing specific terms.

The party that has joined the contract has a right to demand discontinuing or changing the contract, if it proves that it didn't know or didn't have to know that the concluded contract, though does not contradict the law or other legislative acts, but deprives it of the rights usually provided by such type of contracts, excludes or limits the responsibility of the other party for violating the obligations, or contains any other terms obviously burdening for the party that has joined the contract, and which it would not have accepted if it had had an opportunity to participate in defining the terms of the contract.

According to the resolution No 1445 of the Government of the RF dated December 30, 1994, the following contracts have to be concluded as contracts of accession: contracts for the delivery of natural gas between the deliverers and the customers or gas distributing organizations, and between gas distributing organizations and the customers.

Preliminary contract had been included in the former Basic civil legislation of the USSR and the republics. However, the CC RF has changed several rules regulating this construction.

According to a preliminary contract, the parties take the responsibility of concluding in future a contract of property transaction, performing work, or providing services (main contract) under the conditions stated in the preliminary contract (art. 429, CC RF).

The Code sets strict requirements for the form of a preliminary contract. It has to be signed in the form established for the main contract, and if the main contract form is not set, in written form. If the regulations on the form of the preliminary contract are not followed, the contract becomes void.

Preliminary contracts must contain the terms concerning the subject of the main contract and other relevant conditions. The time of concluding the main contract is established by the parties in the preliminary contract. If it is not set, the main contract has to be concluded within a year after the preliminary contract is signed.

The CC RF contains a rule demanding the obligatory concluding of the main contract. If one party refuses to sign it, the other party has a right to apply to the court demanding obligatory signing of the main contract.

Obligations set in the preliminary contract remain valid during the time within which the parties must sign the main contract. In case the main contract is not signed or one of the parties does not ask the other party to conclude the main contract, the obligations are annulled.

Preliminary contracts are not widely used in business yet. In practice, parties sign such documents as intentions agreements, memoranda, etc, that do not imply obligatory signing of the main contract in future.

The main difference between these documents and preliminary contracts is that they have no legal force and contain only moral obligation of the parties to sign a contract in future.

A contract for the benefit of a third party is a type of contract where the parties agree that a debtor has the responsibility not before the creditor but before a party stated or not stated in the contract which has a right to require the performing of the obligations for its benefit (art. 430, CC RF). Thus, the third party gets the priority right of demanding compared with the creditor's demands. The latter may use this right only in case the third refuses its right and if it does not contradict the law, other legislative acts, and the contract.

The debtor has a right to argue the demands of the third party with arguments he could have used against the creditor. Besides, after the third party informs the debtor that it is going to use its right according to the contract, the parties can not discontinue or change their contract without the agreement of the third party, unless a different regulation is envisaged by the law, other legislative acts, or the contract.

The contract may specify that its several parts are determined by model terms developed for contracts of a certain kind and published (art. 427, CC RF).As opposed to the typical contracts containing imperative obligatory norms, model terms are only of a recommendation character.

Model terms may be formulated as an model contract or other document containing these terms. While concluding a contract, parties may make use of the model contract as a whole, or some parts of it, or develop the terms of the contract themselves.

As an example one can mention the form of a state contract adopted as a supplement to the Regulations on state contracts for purchasing products for the federal needs, adopted by the resolution of the government of the RF, dated June 26, 1995, No 564, "On the realization of the federal law 'On delivery of products for federal and state needs'".

If the contract does not contain references to model conditions, such model conditions may be used for the relations of the parties as expressing the traditions of business if they meet the requirements set for them.

Parties may also conclude contracts containing elements of various types of contracts provided by the law or other legal acts (so called "*mixed contracts*").

Before the CC RF was adopted, the mixed contract was regulated by the rules of the contract which dominated it. Thus, for example, common were contracts of delivery with supplied raw material, they combined elements of delivery and contract work. They were regulated by the rules of delivery contracts.

According to the new rule stated in paragraph 3, art. 421, CC RF, the relations of parties in respective parts of a mixed contract are regulated by the rules of the contracts elements which are contained in the mixed contract, unless a different solution follows from the agreement of the parties or the essence of the mixed contract.

1.3 Concluding a contract

A contract is considered concluded if the parties have achieved agreement (in a required form) in all essential issues of the contract (p.1, art. 432, CC RF).

Essential issues are the conditions concerning the subject matter of the contract, conditions mentioned in the law or other legislative acts as essential or necessary for that type of contracts, as well as all conditions one of the parties required agreement on.

Legal significance of the essential conditions is that in case of absence of one of them the contract is not considered concluded. An essential condition of a contract is that on its subject matter. Besides, various other conditions may be called essential in the law and other legal acts for a certain type of contract. Moreover, essential are the conditions which, though not mentioned in he law as such, are insisted upon by one of the parties.

The form of a contract is regulated by the rules set for transactions, unless a specific form is determined for contracts of that type (p.1, art.434, CC RF). The law allows concluding a contract by the agreement of its parties in a form which is not required of contracts of that type according to the law. In this case the contract is considered concluded after it is shaped in the determined form (p.1, art. 434, CC RF).

Most contracts in business are concluded in written form.

As a rule, a contract is concluded by making a document signed by the parties. However, the CC RF allows concluding a written contract by means of exchanging documents by mail, telegraph, teletype, telephone, email, and other means providing a way to make sure the document comes from the contract party (p.2, art. 434).

The law and other legislative acts, as well as the agreement of the parties, may set forth additional requirements the form of the contract must meet (using a certain stationery form, seal, etc) and consequences of not abiding by them. In case the consequences are not determined, the consequences of not abiding by a plain written contract form are used, that is impossibility for the parties in case of a conflict to refer to witnesses for the confirmation of the transaction and its terms (p.1, art.

162, CC RF). The parties, however, have a right to provide written evidence and other kinds of evidence. In cases stated directly in the law or the contract of the parties, failure to abide by a plain written form of a contract leads to the voidness of the transaction (for example, foreign trade transactions), p.2, 3, art. 162, CC RF.

Transactions must be certified by notary in cases specified by the law or agreed upon by the parties even if the law does not require it for transactions of that kind (art. 163, CC RF).

For some kinds of transactions the law requires state registration. These are transactions with land and other real estate in cases and in the ways specified in art. 131, CC RF. The federal law "On state registration of the rights for real estate and for transactions with it" which became effective on January 30, 1998, states that state registration is required for the rights of property and other proprietary interests for real estate and for transactions with it, except for the rights for air and sea vessels, boats of inland navigation, and space objects. These rights are to be registered in the Single State Register of rights. State registration is here only evidence of registered rights.

The law may require state registration of transactions with movable property of certain types (art. 164, CC RF).

The Civil Code also determines the consequences of failure to abide by the notary form and the requirements of the law for state registration of a transaction. Such transaction is considered null and void since the moment of concluding (p.1, art. 165, CC RF).

Thus, for example, for a contract of selling an enterprise the law requires a written form single document signed by the parties and state registration of the contract. Non-compliance with these rules results in the nullity of the contract.

However, if one party has fully or partly completed a transaction requiring notary certifying, while the other party is trying to avoid such certifying of the transaction, the court has a right on the request of the former party to accept the transaction effective, and in this case notary certifying is not necessary (p.2, art. 165, CC RF).

If one party is avoiding state registration of a transaction, the court has a right on the request of the other party to pass a decision on registering the transaction. The transaction in this case is registered according to the decision of the court (p. 3, art 165, CC RF).

Commercial organizations, except for unitary enterprises and other kinds of organizations specified by the law, according to art. 49, CC RF, have a *general legal capacity*, it means that it is able to conclude any contracts that do not contradict the law.

They can not, however, enter into contract if they do not have an appropriate license for the respective activity(when it is needed), or if the transaction contradicts the goals set in the articles of association of the organization (art. 173, CC RF).

The contract is concluded by one party's sending an *offer* to the other party and the other party's *acceptance*.

The law has certain requirements for offers and acceptances.

An offer to enter into a contract must be clear, it must express the intention of the offering party to enter into a contract with the addressee who is to accept the offer. The offer must contain the basic terms of a contract. It must be addressed to one or several definite persons (art. 435, CC RF). The Code also provides for a public offer, which is an offer containing all essential terms of the contract and which expresses the will of the offering party to enter into a contract under the specified conditions with any party that responds (art. 437, CC RF).

The offer binds the offering party after it is received by the addressee. Being received by the addressee, it becomes irrevocable, it means it can not be withdrawn within the term set for its acceptance, unless other conditions are specified by the offer itself or follow the essence of the offer or the circumstances in which it was made (art. 436, CC RF).

The acceptance is considered effective if it is complete and unconditional (p.1, art. 438, CC RF). If the person agrees to enter into the contract under different conditions rather than those specified in the offer, such response is considered a refusal and at the same time a new offer (art. 443, CC RF).

No response is not considered acceptance, unless it follows from the law, business customs, or previous business relations of the parties (p.2, art. 438, CC RF). However, activities aimed at abiding by the terms set in the offer within the time set for acceptance (shipment of merchandise, doing the work, paying the necessary sum of money, etc) are considered acceptance, unless the opposite is specified by the law, other legislative acts, or the offer (p.3, art. 438).

This new rule was introduced into the Civil Code, because often in response to an offer concrete activities are undertaken to meet the terms specified in the offer. Such activities are treated as acceptance now.

The offer may contain the time for acceptance, then the contract is concluded if the offering party receives the acceptance within the specified time period (art.440, CC RF).

When the written offer does not specify the time for reply, the contract is considered concluded if the acceptance is received by the offering party within the time set in the law or other legislative documents, and if it is not set, then within time reasonably necessary for an answer (art 441, CC RF). Reasonably necessary time is the time necessary for a letter (a cable, etc) to be delivered both ways.

The contract is considered concluded at the moment the offering party receives the acceptance. If according to the law concluding a contract requires also transfer of property, the contract is considered concluded after the property is transferred. A contract requiring state registration is considered concluded after the registration unless the law provides different conditions (art. 433, CC RF).

The Civil Code contains also a rule concerning the place of concluding a contract. If the place is not specified in the contract, the contract is recognized as concluded in the place the physical person lives or the legal entity is located (art. 444).

In certain cases the law requires obligatory concluding of a contract, as an exception from a general principle of freedom of contract (for example, concluding of a public contract, concluding the main contract according to the preliminary contract, etc). The Civil Code, art. 445, provides the way and timing of an obligatory contract.

Besides the general rules for concluding contracts, the code establishes rules for organizing and holding auctions for concluding contracts (art. 447–449).

1.4. Authority to conclude a contract

The question who has the authority to sign a contract on the behalf of a legal entity is very important, as the contract signed by a person without authority may be pronounced void.

Thus, for example, the court of arbitration pronounced void one contract between a company and a bank, because the contract was signed by the general manager of the company with the exceeding of authority determined by the articles of association (Courier of the Higher Court of Arbitration of the RF, 1996, No 11, p. 73). So, when concluding a contract one should check the authorities of the person signing it. Restrictions on certain kinds of transactions may be set in the articles of association of a company, or established by the law. Thus, the federal law "On joint stock companies" sets certain regulations for the procedure of concluding contracts in which certain groups of people might be interested (people from administration bodies, stockholders having 20 or more percent of voting shares of the company, etc). Decisions on concluding such contracts are taken by the board of directors or the general meeting of the stockholders (art.82, 83).

Unitary companies don't have a right to enter into contracts involving real estate without the agreement of the owner (p.2, art. 295, CC RF).

Heads of company subsidiaries (branches and representative offices) must conclude contract on the behalf of a legal entity according to the authority set in the Regulations on the subsidiary, and to the letter of authority issued by the company.

Quite often contracts are concluded by the representatives of organizations (art. 182, CC RF). The authority of the representative must be set in the letter of authority. If the contract requires notary certification, the letter of authority for the contract must be also certified by the notary, except for the cases provided by the law (p. 1, art. 185, CC RF). A representative can not conclude a contract on the behalf of a person he is representing with regard to himself. An exception is a commercial representation office (art. 164, CC RF). A commercial representative is a professional entrepreneur constantly and on his own acting as a representative when concluding contracts. For his work he receives payment. He has a right to represent in one contract both parties, the seller and the buyer, the client and the contractor. The consent of the parties or legislative provision is required in such a case. In this case the commercial representative must represent the interests of both parties.

1.5. Fulfillment of contract obligations and responsibility for their violation

Obligations must be fulfilled properly according to the terms of obligation and the requirements of the law, other legislative acts, and in case of absence of any such requirements, according to the customs of business (art. 309 CC RF).

The Civil Code sets the general rule that a party can not unilaterally refuse to fulfill obligations. However, this rule does not cover obligations connected with entrepreneurial activities. Entrepreneurs have a right to state in the contract the right for unilateral refusal to fulfill obligations and unilateral change of the conditions of an obligation, unless something different is implied by the law or the contents of the obligation (art. 310, CC RF).

Proper fulfillment of an obligation means it is done to the right person, in due time, in the right place, in the right manner, by the right persons.

The law allows the possibility of debtor's delegating the fulfillment of obligations to a third party, unless the law, other legislative acts, the conditions and the contents of the obligation imply personal responsibility of the debtor to fulfill the obligation. The creditor then must accept the fulfillment of the obligation by a third person (p.1, art. 313, CC RF).

A third party being in danger of losing its right for the property of the debtor (the right of lease or bailment, etc) as a result of the creditor's charging the property, may satisfy the creditor's demands on its own expense without the debtor's consent. In that case the creditor's rights are passed to the third party, according to the rules of the Civil Code (p. 2, art. 313, CC RF). Thus, a lessee may satisfy the creditor's demands in case of the latter's charging the lessor's property, and in this case he will receive the creditor's rights.

If an entrepreneurial obligation involves several debtors or several creditors, the responsibilities of the debtors, as well as the demands of the creditors, are collective (p.2, art.322, CC RF), unless the law, other legislative acts, or the terms of the obligation state differently.

The time for fulfilling the obligation may be set in the contract, otherwise it is a reasonable time after the start of the obligation. In case the time is determined by the moment of demand, the debtor must satisfy that obligation within 7 days after the creditor demands the fulfillment of the obligation, unless different time is implied by the law, legislative acts, terms of the obligation, customs of business turnover, or the essence of the obligation (art. 314, CC RF).

Anticipatory fulfillment of obligations connected with entrepreneurial activities is justifiable only in cases when anticipatory fulfillment is provided by the law, other legislative acts, terms of the obligation, the customs of business or the essence of the obligation (art. 315, CC RF).

Of great importance are the rules set in the Civil Code for counter fulfillment of obligations by one of the parties (art. 328, CC RF). Counter fulfillment is one party's fulfillment of obligations dependent, according to the contract, upon the fulfillment of obligations by the other party. Thus, a delivery contract may envisage that the delivery of the product is done after prepayment by the buyer. If the party can not fulfill the obligation (does not pay for the product in our example), or if it is obvious that the obligation won't be fulfilled in due time (buyer's inability to pay), the party responsible for the counter fulfillment has a right to suspend the fulfillment of its obligation (delivery of the product), or refuse to fulfill the obligation and demand payment of damages. In case of partial fulfillment of obligation, the party responsible for the counter fulfillment has a right to suspend the fulfillment or refuse to fulfill the obligation in the part corresponding to the unfulfilled obligation. Thus, in case of partial prepayment, the contractor has the right to deliver not all the product, but partly, in proportion with the prepayment.

However, the contract or the law may contain different rules.

If the counter fulfillment of the obligation is done in spite of the other party's not fulfilling its obligations which had been set in the contract, that party must fulfill its obligation. Thus, if the contractor delivers products in spite of the absence of payment, the buyer must pay it.

Legal means of payment in Russia is the ruble (p.1, art. 140, CC RF). Using foreign currency and payment documents in foreign currency in payment of obligations is accepted only in cases provided by the law, on conditions provided by the law, and in manner provided by the law (p.3, art. 317, CC RF). These rules imply that the requirement of providing payment documents in rubles (p.1, art. 317). However, as inflation protection measure, there is a rule that the payment document may say that it is to be paid in rubles, the sum being equivalent to a certain sum in foreign currency or in conventional units (ECU, "special rights of borrowing", etc), in that case the sum due to be paid in rubles is calculated according to the official exchange rate of the respective currency or conventional units for the day of payment, unless a different rate or different rate date is determined by the law or the agreement of the parties (p.2, art. 317, CC RF).

The Civil Code contains rules concerning the place of the fulfillment of the obligation (art. 316), and the rights of the debtor at the time of fulfilling the obligation to demand the proof that the fulfillment is being accepted by the creditor himself or a person authorized by law (art. 312). The risk of consequences of not demanding that proof is let with the debtor. It means that in case of an argument, the debtor may find it difficult to prove that he has fulfilled the obligations.

The Civil Code states the following ways of *securing the fulfillment of the obligation*: penalty, lien, withholding the debtor's property, surety, bank guaranty. The list is not exhaustive and both the law and the contract may set some other ways (p.1, art. 329, CC RF). Securing obligations, except for property are considered additional to the main obligation. As a rule, they are set by means of written agreements. Their voidness does not imply voidness of the main obligation. However, voidness of the main obligation results in voidness of its securing obligation, unless the law sets a different rule (p. 2, 3, art. 329, CC RF). An exception is the bank guaranty, which is independent of the main obligation it is securing (art. 370, CC RF). It means that if the main obligation is void, bank guarantee is still effective.

Quite thorough legal regulation of different ways of securing obligations and choosing the most suitable way while concluding a specific contract help to reduce negative consequences in case of the debtor's failure to fulfill the obligations connected with the main contract.

In case of not fulfilling or improper fulfilling the obligations, the debtor must compensate the creditor's losses (p.1, art. 393, CC RF). Losses mean real damage, that is real expenses the person whose rights have been violated has made or will have to make in order to regain the violated right, loss or damage of his property, and lost profit, that is income not gained which the person would have gained in normal conditions if his right had not been violated (art. 15 CC RF).

When the losses are counted, prices are taken as existed in the place of due fulfillment of the obligation on the day of voluntary fulfillment the creditor's demands, or, if the demand was not satisfied by the debtor, on the day of bringing a suit against him. The court may satisfy the demands of the creditor using prices on the day of passing judgement (p.3, art. 393, CC RF).

When determining the lost profit, one takes into account the measures taken by the creditor in order to gain it, and the preparatory work he has done (p.4, art. 393, CC RF).

If the law or the contract determines a penalty for not fulfilling an obligation, the general rule says that losses are compensated in the part not covered by the penalty (so called discount penalty). The law or the contract may set different proportion of the losses and the penalty: when only penalty is to be paid but not the losses ("exceptional penalty"), when full losses may be paid on top of the penalty ("penalty fine"), when the creditor may decide whether to demand the penalty or the losses ("alternative penalty") (art. 394).

For the first time the Civil Code sets special responsibility for not fulfilling money obligations. Such violations as unlawful holding of somebody else's money assets, evading returning of the money, late paying back, or illegal acquiring or saving somebody's money have become quite widespread.

In case of any of these violations, the debtor is obliged to pay interest which is determined by the bank interest rate on the day of satisfying the obligation or its part in the area the creditor lives. When the debt is extracted by court, the court may satisfy the creditor's demand with the consideration of the bank interest rate on the day of making the claim or the day of passing the resolution. These rules are applied unless the law or the contract determines different interest. Losses the creditor suffers may be demanded in the amount surpassing the interest for using somebody else's assets (p.1, 2, art. 395, CC RF).

Interest for using somebody else's money is charged up to the day when the money is returned to the creditor, unless the law, other legislative acts, or the contract set a shorter term for interest charging (p.3, art. 395, CC RF).

The Civil Code now treats differently the issues of real, natural fulfillment of obligations. In case of inappropriate fulfillment of an obligation, the debtor besides paying the penalty and covering the losses has to fulfill the obligation in product, unless the law and the contract state differently. If the debtor has not started fulfilling the contract, paying the penalty and the losses release him from fulfilling the obligation in product (art. 396).

In case the debtor does not fulfill certain kinds of obligations (producing and delivering a thing, performing work, rendering service) the creditor has a right to ask a third party to fulfill the obligation in reasonable time or for reasonable pay, the creditor may also fulfill it himself, if the law, other legislative acts, the contract or the essence of the obligation does not imply different rules. Then the creditor demands that the debtor pay the expenses and other losses (art. 397).

For improper fulfillment of an entrepreneurial obligation the law sets strict responsibility up to force major, that is extreme and unavoidable circumstances under the given conditions (floods, fires, wars, etc). Unavoidable circumstances don't include though the absence of certain goods on the market that are necessary for the fulfillment, the debtor's lack of necessary money, or the violation of obligations by the debtor's counter agents (art. 401, CC RF). The rule concerning strict responsibility is dispositive, the law or the contract may set different rules. However, laws prohibit entering into agreements on excluding the responsibility for intentional breaking of obligations. Such agreements are considered null and void (p.4, art. 401, CC RF).

1.6. Change and discontinuation of the contract

First of all, a contract may be altered or discontinued on consent of the parties, unless the Civil Code, other laws, or the contract provide different regulations (p. 1, art. 450, CC RF).

On the demand of one of the parties the contract may be altered or discontinued by the decision of the court in case of a significant violation of the contract by the other party, in case of significant breaking of obligations, and in other cases mentioned by the Civil Code, other laws, or the contract.

Changing of circumstances is considered significant if they have changed to such extent that if the parties could have rationally expected it they would not have entered into the contract or would have signed it on considerably different terms (p.1, art. 451, CC). A contract may be discontinued by the decision of the court on the demand of the interested party in case the following conditions are present simultaneously:

1. At the moment of signing the contract the parties assumed that this change of circumstances would not occur;
2. The change of circumstances has occurred due to reasons the interested party could not eliminate though being appropriately careful and cautious;

3. Carrying out the contract without changing its conditions would so much distort the proportion of material interests of the parties supposed by the contract and would cause such damage for the interested party that the party would lose considerable part of what it had a right to gain signing the contract;
4. Traditions of business or the essence of the contract don't imply that the risk of the change of circumstances is taken by the interested party.

Changing the contract by the decision of the court is done in exceptional cases when the discontinuing of a contract contradicts public interests or results in damage for both parties considerably surpassing the expenses necessary for carrying out the contract under conditions changed by the court (p. 2, 4, art. 451, CC RF). For example, when in spite of considerable growth of prices it is necessary to complete the construction of a project for people's needs, etc.

The Civil Code sets the procedure for altering and discontinuing a contract (art. 452).

The moment from which the obligations are considered altered or discontinued depends on whether the contract was altered or discontinued voluntarily or by court decision. In the first case the obligations are considered altered or discontinued since the moment the parties conclude an agreement about it, unless the agreement or the manner of altering the contract state differently. In the second case it is the moment when the decision of the court comes into legal force (p.3, art. 453, CC RF).

Parties can not demand the return of what had been done by them according to the obligation before the moment of altering or discontinuing of the contract, unless the law or the agreement of the parties state differently (p. 4, art. 453, CC).

If the basis for the altering or discontinuing of the contract was considerable violation of it by one of the parties, the other party can demand compensation of the damage caused by the altering or discontinuing of the contract (p. 5, art. 453, CC).

2. Particular kinds of contracts

2.1. Delivery of merchandise

Delivery contracts (in Russian: postavka) are regulated by § 3, chapter 30 of the Civil Code. Regulations of § 1 "General concepts of sale and purchase"(in Russian: kupla-prodaza) of that chapter are applied unless the rules of § 3 on delivery contracts state differently. This contract is considered as a separate kind of sale and purchase contract characterized by long term relations of the parties.

According to a delivery contract, the delivering party accepts the obligation to deliver in due time produced or purchased merchandise to a buyer or user with entrepreneurial purpose, not connected with personal, family, or similar use (art. 506, CC). Delivery contracts are concluded only in entrepreneurial practice.

The supplier party may be the producer of the merchandise or an intermediary selling organization buying merchandise in order to resell it. The supplier is a commercial organization or an individual entrepreneur working without forming a legal entity. The buyer party is usually an entrepreneur.

The basic terms of this kind of contract that have to be agreed upon when signing the contract are usually the terms of long term relations, e.g. time of delivery, compensation for not fully delivered merchandise, delivery procedure, etc.

Delivery may be carried out in separate lots, and their time of delivery may be specified in the contract in various ways (quarterly, monthly, etc). If the time is not specified by the contract, the merchandise must be delivered in equal lots monthly, unless the laws, other legislative acts, the essence of the obligation, or the business customs imply differently (p.1, art. 508, CC RF).

Besides the time of delivery, the contract may specify the schedule of shipments (decade, daily, hourly, etc) (p.2, art 508).

Anticipatory delivery may be possible in case of the buyer's consent. If the anticipatory delivery of merchandise is accepted by the buyer, the merchandise is referred to as part of the delivery due in the next period (p.3, art. 508, CC RF). If the buyer on a legal grounds rejects the merchandise provided by the supplier, he is obliged to provide the safety of the merchandise and immediately notify the supplier. The regime of responsible storage is set in art. 514, CC RF.

The delivery of merchandise may be done both to the buyer party of the contract, and to the person specified in the contract as recipient. In the latter case the buyer must give the supplier directions for delivering the merchandise to the recipients, delivery orders. Their contents and the time of sending them to the supplier are determined by the contract. If the time of sending is not set by the contract, the delivery order must be sent to the supplier at least 30 days before the period of delivery. If the delivery order is not provided, the supplier can either refuse to carry out the contract or demand the payment for the merchandise. Besides, he can demand compensation of the damage caused by not providing the delivery order (art. 509, CC RF).

Delivery of merchandise is carried out by means of transportation determined by the contract and on terms provided by the contract. The contract may provide for the receiving of the merchandise by the buyer (recipient) at the location of the supplier (collection of the merchandise). The procedure of the collection is determined in Article 515, CC RF).

In case the contract does not specify the type of transportation and the terms of delivery, the supplier has the right to choose the type of transportation, unless the laws, other legislative acts, the essence of the obligation, or the business customs imply differently (art. 510, CC RF).

The Civil Code contains a rule according to which the merchandise not delivered in one period of delivery must be provided by the supplier in the next period within the period of validity of the contract, unless the contract states differently (p. 1, art. 511, CC RF).

In case supplier delivers merchandise to several recipients, the goods delivered to one of the recipients over the quantity stated in the contract or the delivery order, do not compensate the merchandise not delivered to other recipients. The contract may set other rules concerning that. The customer may refuse to accept the merchandise if the shipment is late, unless the contract specifies differently. However, the merchandise delivered earlier than the supplier is notified, must be accepted and paid by the customer (art. 511, CC RF).

In the contract the parties agree upon the assortment of merchandise due for compensating. Unless the contract has other provisions, the supplier must supply all the shortage in the assortment in the period set for the delayed supply (p. 1, art. 512, CC RF). Supply of a certain type of merchandise over the quantity specified in the contract does not make up for the shortage in delivery of other types of merchandise from the same assortment. The shortage should be provided, except for the cases when such a supply was made upon written consent of the customer (p. 2, art. 512, CC RF).

Customer (recipient) must do everything necessary for accepting the merchandise according to the contract: examine, check the quantity and quality, report the defects found, etc. The duties of the customer (recipient) of the merchandise concerning accepting of the merchandise are specified in article 513, CC RF.

Another important duty of the customer is payment for the merchandise. The procedure and forms of payment are specified in the contract, in case the contract does not specify the terms, the payment is made by money orders (p. 1, art. 516, CC RF). Payment for the merchandise may be made by the recipient of the merchandise and not the buyer, and if the former did not pay or unfoundedly refused to pay for the merchandise, the supplier has the right to demand payment from the buyer (p. 2, art. 516, CC RF).

The buyer must return reusable packaging and packing materials that contained the merchandise, the time and procedure of the return are set by the law, other legislative acts, or the contract. Other packaging and packing materials are to be returned to the supplier only in cases specified by the contract (art. 517, CC RF).

In case of delivery of merchandise of inappropriate quality, the supplier can promptly replace it with the appropriate quality merchandise. Otherwise, the Civil Code gives the buyer a wide range of rights. He can demand from the seller lowering the price, correction of the merchandise defects in reasonable time, or compensation for its expenses connected with correcting the merchandise defects (p. 1, art. 475, CC RF). In case of considerable non-observance of quality requirements (irremovable defects, or defects that can not be removed without disproportionate expenses or time expenditure, or defects revealed continuously and occurring after their removal or the removal of similar ones) the buyer has the right to either refuse to fulfill the contract and demand the return of the money paid, or to demand the replacement of the bad quality merchandise with the merchandise matching the contract (p. 2, art. 475, CC RF).

The Civil Code contains a rule guaranteeing the right of the buyer, in case of failure to fulfill his demands of improving the non-sufficient delivery of the merchandise or providing the whole range of merchandise, to acquire the non-delivered merchandise from another party and make the supplier liable to pay all the necessary and reasonable expenses connected with their acquisition. The buyer has the right to refuse to accept merchandise of inappropriate quality or incomplete delivery, and if that merchandise was already paid for, he can claim the return of the money until the defects are removed, the delivery completed, or merchandise replaced (art. 520, CC RF).

Unilateral refuse to fulfill the contract of delivery (fully or partly) or unilateral modification of the contract is acceptable in case of serious violation of the contract by one party. Violation on the supplier's part is considered serious if delivered merchandise is of inappropriate quality and the defects can not be removed in time acceptable for the buyer, or in case of repeated failure to comply with the time of delivery of the merchandise. The following violations are considered serious on the buyer's part: repeated failure to provide payment on time, or repeated failure to collect the merchandise.

The time of discontinuing or altering the contract is set in the notice sent by one party to the other one, or otherwise is agreed upon by the parties. In case the time is not set, the regulation of the Civil Code is applied according to which a contract is considered discontinued or altered upon receiving by one party the other party's notice of unilateral refusal to fulfill the contract fully or partly (art. 523, CC RF).

Material responsibility for violating the contract of delivery is set according to the general rules on responsibility determined by Civil Code.

New are the rules set by the Civil Code on the calculation of the damage caused by discontinuing a delivery contract (art. 524 CC RF). These damages are not covered by the general term "losses", determined by art. 115 of the CC RF. Their characteristic features are simpler ways of calculation and absence of necessity to prove them.

If in case a contract is annulled due to a violation of an obligation by the supplier, and as a result the buyer purchased the merchandise from another supplier at a higher but reasonable price, he can demand that the supplier pays the damage, the difference between the price set in the contract and the price of the purchase.

The supplier can demand payment of the damage, the difference between the contract price and the price of purchase, if within reasonable time after the annulling of the contract due to the buyer's violation of his obligations, the supplier sold the merchandise at a price lower than that specified by the contract.

If after the annulling of the contract no transaction was made to substitute for it, a party can demand covering the damage as the difference between the price set in the contract and the current price for the moment of the annulling of the contract. The Civil Code determines what price is to be considered as current. It is the price required for similar merchandise in comparable circumstances in the place where the merchandise was to be passed to the buyer. If there is no current price in this place, one can use the price current in another place that can be a reasonable substitute, the difference in transportation cost must be taken into account. The aggrieved party may have other damages specified in art. 15 CC RF, they are to be covered too.

2.2. Delivery of merchandise for state needs

New in the Civil Code is paragraph 4, chapter 30, regulating deliveries of merchandise for state needs. These transactions are also regulated by a number of laws and other legislative acts: Federal law dated December 13, 1994, "On delivery of merchandise for state needs", Federal law dated December 2, 1994, "On purchase and delivery of agricultural products, raw materials and food for state needs", Federal law dated December 29, 1994, "On Federal material reserve", Federal law dated November 24, 1995, "On federal defense order", etc. These laws are applied in cases when §4 of chapter 30 does not provide regulations.

In cases of delivery of merchandise for state needs the rules of delivery contracts are applied, unless the rules of the Civil Code provides differently.

State needs are defined as demands of the Russian Federation or subjects of the Russian Federation, provided at the expense of budget and non-budget sources of financing (art. 525, CC RF). Deliveries of merchandise for state needs are done to meet the demands of the state in merchandise essential for solving most important tasks of life provision, defense and state security, realization of federal purpose programs and international programs in which the Russian Federation participates.

The procedure of developing and realization of federal and international programs in which Russia participates, is determined by the decision of the Government of the Russian Federation dated June 26, 1995.

Federal purpose programs are adopted by the Government of the Russian Federation. Most important federal purpose programs receive the status of presidential programs. According to the decree of the President of the Russian Federation, a special Fund for presidential programs was created. It mobilizes non-budget financial means for the realization of presidential programs.

Responsible for federal purpose programs and other state needs are state orderers confirmed by the Government of the Russian Federation. They hold a competitive selection of suppliers, determine definite recipients of the merchandise, agree with them upon the assortment of the merchandise delivered for state needs.

As a result of the competition the supplier is chosen who offers optimal terms for the fulfillment of the state order for supplying merchandise for state needs.

State contract is signed on the basis of the order made by the state orderer and accepted by the supplier (performer) (p. 1, art. 527, CC RF).

Signing contracts for the delivery of merchandise for state needs is voluntary. Exceptions are set by the law, the necessary condition is compensation of all losses the state orderers may have connected with fulfilling the state contract (p. 2, art. 527, CC RF). Losses are not compensated for government enterprises only (p. 3, art. 527, CC RF).

Thus, entering into state contracts is obligatory for suppliers-monopolists, unless these contracts result in losses caused by the production of the merchandise. State contracts may be obligatory for government enterprises.

According to a state contract for the supply of merchandise for state needs, the supplier is obliged to pass the merchandise to the state orderer, or to another party by the latter's decision, and the state orderer is obliged to provide payment for the delivered merchandise (art. 528). The procedure and time for concluding these contracts are set in article 528, CC RF.

Supplies of merchandise for federal needs may be performed either directly on the basis of the concluded state contract or according to contracts of supplying merchandise for federal needs. In the latter case the orderer, according to the signed state contract, within 30 days after the day of signing the contract, notifies the supplier and the buyer about the assigning the supplier for the buyer. This notification is the basis for signing a contract of delivery of merchandise for federal needs (p. 1, art. 529, CC RF.

The procedure and time of sending a draft delivery contract for federal needs, considering it and signing it, as well as settling disagree-ments, are determined in p. 2–5, article 529, CC RF. In case of failure to settle a disagreement while concluding a contract, or in case of the supplier's refusal to enter into a contract, the dispute is considered in court.

The buyer has a right to refuse totally or partly to accept the merchandise listed in the assignment notification, and to refuse to enter into contract for their delivery. The state orderer must be promptly informed, and within 30 days after that he either sends to the supplier a notification about assigning another buyer, or sends him loading orders indicating the recipient of the merchandise, or informs him about his consent to accept the merchandise and pay for it. If the state orderer fails to fulfill these obligations, the supplier has a right either to demand that the orderer accepts the merchandise and pays for it, or sell the merchandise and charge the state orderer with paying the expenses connected with the sale (art. 530, CC RF).

In the Procedure of preparing and signing state contracts for buying and delivery of merchandise for federal needs, adopted by the decision of the Government of the Russian Federation on June 26, 1994, the following conditions of the state contract are called essential: its subject matter (parameters of the product, its name, assortment, quantity, quality), price of the state contract, time of its fulfillment, rights and duties of the parties. In the supplement to the document there is an approximate form of a state contract for buying and delivery of merchandise for federal needs.

The fulfillment of state contracts in cases when the delivery is made directly to the state orderer or, according to his loading orders, to another party (recipient), is regulated by the rules of delivery contracts (art. 531, CC RF). In these cases the payment is made by the state orderer, unless the state contract specifies another payment procedure (p. 2, art. 531, CC RF).

If the delivery of the merchandise is done on the basis of a delivery contract, payment is made by the buyers, unless the state contract specifies another procedure. The state orderer is recognized as the guarantor of the obligation of the buyer. The price of the merchandise is set in the state contract (art. 532, CC RF).

In order to encourage the supplier to fulfill his obligations appropriately, he may be granted tax benefits, beneficial credits, and other benefits provided by the laws on deliveries of merchandise for federal needs.

In cases specified in the law, the state orderer can fully or partly refuse to accept merchandise the delivery of which is envisaged by the state contract. But he has to compensate the losses the supplier may suffer, as well as the losses of the buyer if the refusal to accept the merchandise resulted in discontinuing or changing the contract of delivery of merchandise for federal needs (art. 534, CC RF).

The state orderer also has to compensate the losses of the supplier connected with the fulfillment of the state order. Otherwise, the supplier can refuse to fulfill the state contract and demand compensation for the losses connected with the breaking of the state contract. In this case, after the breaking of the state contract, the supplier has a right to fulfill the contract of delivery for state needs. The losses of the buyer in this situation of the supplier's refusal, are covered by the state orderer (art. 533, CC RF).

Material responsibility and the size of sanctions for various violations of obligations connected with the state contract are determined by the laws on the delivery of merchandise for state needs.

2.3. Contract of sale of an enterprise

It is a new kind of contract provided by the Civil Code. It is regulated by p. 8, chapter 30, CC RF. The rules concerning selling real estate are applied to it as different rules are not provided by p. 8.

According to the contract of sale of an enterprise, the seller is obliged to convey the whole enterprise as a complex of property to the possession of the buyer, except for those rights and obligations that the seller does not have rights to convey to other parties (p.1, art. 559, CC RF).

According to art. 132, CC RF, an enterprise is considered as a complex of property and is recognized as real estate. Separate regulation of real estate sales and enterprise sales is caused by the specific character of this contract, because besides buildings, equipment, and other belongings, the seller's rights and obligations are to be conveyed too. The rights of the seller may be divided into two categories: those due to be conveyed, unless the contract specifies differently (the right for a brand name, trade mark, service mark, and other means of individualizing of the seller, his merchandise, work, and services, as well as belonging to him on the basis of a license the rights of using such means of individualizing). The rights received by the seller on the basis of a license to perform certain activities are not due to be conveyed, unless the law or other legislative acts specify differently. Conveying to the buyer as a part of the enterprise the obligations that the buyer can not fulfill due to the absence of such a license, does not relieve the seller from respective obligations before the creditors. In case of failure to fulfill such obligations, the seller and the buyer bear collective responsibility (p.2, 3, art. 559, CC RF).

The contract must state definite contents and price of the enterprise being sold, determined after a complete inventory of the enterprise.

Before signing the sale contract, the parties must prepare and consider the inventory act, accounting balance, auditor's certificate on the contents and price of the enterprise, and the list of all debts (obligations) included into the contents of the enterprise, indicating the creditors, and the character, size and terms of their demands (art. 561, CC RF).

These documents must be attached to the contract which is made as a single document signed by both parties. Failure to comply with the form of the contract of sale of an enterprise results in its voidness.

The contract of sale of an enterprise is due to state registration (art. 560, CC).

An essential condition of such a contract besides the subject of the contract is the price of the enterprise. In this case the rule on price in the contract of sale of real estate is applicable (art. 555, CC RF). In case the contract does not specify the price of the enterprise, it is considered incomplete.

The sale of the enterprise is accompanied by passing the rights of the seller to the buyer, and readdressing to him the debts, which requires the creditors' consent. That is why the Civil Code (art. 562) contains rules on obligatory written notifying the creditors about the sale of the enterprise. If this rule was not followed, the creditor has a right within one year to bring a suit demanding annulment or advance fulfillment of the obligations and the seller's covering all losses connected with it, or considering the contract of sale of the enterprise void completely or partly.

The same demands may be made by the creditor within three months' term after receiving the notification about the sale of the enterprise, in case he does not agree with passing the debts from the seller to the buyer.

The seller and buyer bear collective responsibility for the debts included into the enterprise and passed to the buyer without the creditors' consent.

Conveying of the enterprise by the seller to the buyer is done by the conveyance act, including the information about the contents of the enterprise, notifying the creditors, the defects of the property, and the list of property not conveyed because of its loss (art. 563, CC RF).

The law specifies the consequences of conveying an enterprise with defects. The buyer has a right to demand reducing the price of the enterprise if the conveyance act contains information about defects found at the enterprise or about losses of property, as well as in case of passing with the enterprise the debts of the seller that were not listed in the contract or the conveyance act, unless the seller proves that the buyer knew about those debts at the moment of concluding the contract.

The seller, upon receiving the notification of the buyer about the defects of the property or absence of its parts, may promptly change the defected property or provide the missing property.

The enterprise is considered conveyed to the buyer after the conveyance act is signed by both parties. After that moment the risk of accidental destruction or damage of the property passed with the enterprise belongs to the buyer (p. 2, art. 563, CC RF). However, the moment of conveying the enterprise to the buyer does not coincide with the moment of his receiving the right of ownership of the enterprise. The right of ownership is passed to the buyer after the state registration of that right. As a rule, the right of ownership is passed to the enterprise and is to be registered by the state after the conveyance of the enterprise to the buyer.

VIII Private International Law of Russian Federation

Elena Vitaljevna Kabatova

1. Definition and subject matter of private international law

I think it would be justified to say that never before the private international law (PIL) played such a role in Russia as today. Cardinal changes taking place in Russian economy and politics significantly influenced the approaches in PIL of Russia. "Opening" Russian economy to the foreign capital, on one hand, and participating of Russian citizens and different kinds of legal entities in foreign economic relations, on the other, demanded profound changes in legislation governing this sphere. From the beginning of 90s a lot has been done in this connection: many new legislation acts have been adopted, such as Fundamentals of Civil Legislation 1991, Law on Foreign Investments 1991, two parts of the new Civil Code 1994, Family Code 1995, etc., in which new approaches and ideas were reflected.

Traditionally governing of PIL matters in Russia was included in civil legislation, such as the Fundamentals of Civil Legislation and Civil Procedure, Civil Code, Family Code and other specific acts (such as Trade Maritime Code, Air Code, etc.), as opposed to some countries where special PIL Laws were adopted. Until recent changes there were 13 articles on PIL in the Civil Code 1964, 10 articles in the old Family Code 1969 (which was called the Code of Marriage and Family), 6 articles in the Fundamentals of Civil Procedure and some two or three articles in specific acts. It means that some 30 articles governed the huge sphere of PIL. It is clear enough that this regulation became insufficient in new conditions. The main problem was certainly not the quantity of articles, but old approaches, worked out in a quite different society. The aim of that legislation was to apply the Russian (at that time Soviet) law as often as possible and minimise the application of the foreign law.

The modern situation in Russia demanded to review radically old rules and work out new ones that could be adequate in new conditions. Except new acts that have already been mentioned above there are still a lot being in the process of working out. The most important of them is the third part of the Civil Code (two of which have already been adopted), which contains the section "Private International Law". The draft of this section was published in 1996 so that it could be discussed widely. There are 40 articles in it; the authors of the draft analysed and used in their work the latest doctrines and concepts in the sphere of PIL, both on national and international level.

Another factor that influenced PIL greatly was disintegration of the USSR and creating the Commonwealth of Independent States (CIS). It led to appearing several independent states, citizens and legal entities of which were connected with each other in different ways. This situation also demanded new approaches – the main task in this connection is to try to keep united legal space on the territory of the former USSR.

According to Russian doctrine PIL governs different kinds of civil relationships with the foreign element. The latter could be i) foreign subject (e.g. foreign party to a contract), ii) an object, in connection with which civil relationships are being created, is situated abroad (e.g. inherited property is situated abroad), iii) civil relationships are connected with legal fact that take place abroad (e.g. the tort takes place abroad). All issues connected with the international civil procedure, such as jurisdiction, recognition and enforcement of foreign judgements and arbitration awards, also belong to PIL.

The Russian doctrine was never unanimous on the definition and the subject matter of the PIL. There are three main concepts on the issue. According to the first one the PIL is a part of the national law, the second – part of the international law, the third – PIL encompasses the norms of national and international law. The doctrines are presented in different courses on PIL, but it could be said that most specialists on PIL matters adhere to the first doctrine.

Another disputable question is whether substantial norms as well as conflict norms should be included in PIL. More detailed consideration to this problem will be given in para. 2.

2. Legal sources of private international law

It is considered traditionally that there are four main legal sources in PIL: i) national legislation, ii) international treaties, iii) court and arbitration practice, iv) usages. In different countries these sources play different role and in some cases are not recognized as sources at all. For instance, in Russia court and arbitration practice legally is not a source of PIL, but I will still say a few words about it to show its peculiar role. As it was mentioned above most specialists on PIL in Russia believe the PIL to be a part of the national law, and I undoubtedly support this opinion; it explains why the first group of sources I start with is national legislation.

i) National legislation.

a) Constitution 1993

The main legal source, which forms the basis for the whole legal system of Russia is the Constitution 1993. In connection with PIL article 62 of the Constitution should be mentioned. Paragraph 3 of this article states that foreign citizens and stateless persons enjoy rights and bear responsibilities equal to those of Russian citizens unless otherwise is established by the federal law or international treaty of the Russian Federation. This rule, called national regime, is traditional for the Russian legislation. The exceptions, mentioned in the article, partly could be found in other articles of the Constitution, partly in the USSR Law on legal status of foreign persons in the USSR 1981 (this act is still in force until a new one is adopted) and other federal acts that deal mostly with different professions.

Absolutely new and very important is paragraph 4 of article 15 of the Constitution, which runs as follows: widely recognized principles and norms of international law and international treaties of the Russian Federation constitute a part of its legal system. If the rules established by international treaty of the Russian Federation differ from those contained in the Russian law the rules of the treaty are applied. Actually only the first sentence of this paragraph is new, while the second reflects well established rule, which was included and remains in most important legislative acts.

Introduction of this article to the Constitution cannot be overestimated. It means that now courts or other public agencies are entitled to apply directly the norms of international law, though the problem of direct or indirect application of such norms is quite disputable in Russia, and not only in Russia. The article states that two types of norms are included in the Russian legal system – i) widely recognized principles and norms of international law and ii) international treaties of Russia. Certainly, the application of the first type might be of some difficulty since there is no such an international act which states all recognized principles and norms. In each case courts or other public bodies would have to decide whether this or that principle or norm could be considered as widely recognized, taking into account all circumstances and evidences and international documents as well.

b) Fundamentals 1991

Another legal source is Fundamentals 1991, namely its last part "Capacity of foreign citizens and legal persons. Application of the civil laws of foreign states and of international treaties". This part of the Fundamentals contains main conflict rules concerning application of foreign law, legal capacity of foreign persons, law of ownership, limitation of actions, transactions and power of attorney, obligations arising from foreign trade transactions, from the causing injury, inheritance law, etc.

c) Family Code 1995

Recently adopted Family Code 1995 (came into force March 1,1996) also contains whole part governing family relationships with participation of foreign citizens and stateless persons. It includes 12 articles dealing with conclusion and dissolution of marriage, spouses personal property and non-property rights and obligations, establishing and contesting fatherhood, parents' and children's rights and obligations, alimony, adoption, etc. Main difference between this Code and old one is that old conflict rules in most cases provided for the application of Russian (then Soviet) law. New conflict rules meet new tasks set by our new situation and meet requirements of the new level of international co-operation.

d) Other acts

Number of conflict rules are contained in different special acts, e.g. Fundamentals of Civil Procedure 1961, Trade Maritime Code 1968, Air Code 1997. Though traditionally, as it was already mentioned, conflict rules are contained in the Civil Code and other acts several attempts were undertaken to work out and adopt a law on private international law. The first attempt to codify PIL was undertaken in 50s, the second – in 1989–90. The last version was widely discussed by specialists, who underlined the necessity to enlarge and modernize

PIL regulation. However, it happened neither in 50s, nor in 90s. Nevertheless the problem remained and recently another draft appeared, but this time it was not a law on PIL. Preparing the new civil legislation is close to its completion and now the last, third, part is being worked out – the part that traditionally contained conflict rules. The efforts spent on the last draft of the law on PIL were not wasted, on the contrary, the draft was used almost totally in the draft of the third part of the Civil Code. Thus the long standing dispute on codifying Russian PIL was decided in favour of traditional including conflict rules in the civil legislation after their substantive revision. I think it would be quite appropriate to say a few words about it here.

PIL in the draft of the 3d part of the Civil Code

The section consists of three chapters – chapter 68 "Generals", chapter 69 "Persons", chapter 70 "Law applied to property and personal non-property relationships" – that contain 40 articles (comparing to 15 articles in corresponding section of the Fundamentals of Civil Legislation). Chapter 68 includes 10 articles and only their titles give the idea of what problems are considered there: qualification, determination of the content of the foreign law, public order clause, renvoi, effects of evasion from proper applicable law, etc.

The first article of the section, 1233, contains the new rule, introduction of which into Russian legislation could show the recognition of modern doctrines in the sphere of private international law. I mean the second paragraph of the article which says that if it is impossible to determine the applicable law, the law most closely connected with civil relationships should be applied. Many national legislations and international conventions contains nowadays such a conflict rule. Most recent and well known examples are the Laws on Private International Law in Switzerland 1987, Austria 1978, International Convention on the law applicable to contract obligations 1980, Convention on law applicable to contracts of international sale of goods 1986, etc.

International co-operation in different spheres inevitably led to working out flexible conflict rules which could make it possible to take into consideration all circumstances of a concrete dispute and find reasonable and just decisions. Rigid conflict rules that establish one possible approach do not always give such possibility. The problem is being actively discussed since 30s, and the essence of the problem could be formulated as follows: rigid conflict rules do not always lead to just and reasonable result that could satisfy all parties to a dispute. The reality demanded creating new or changing old rules that would absorb more nuances of practical situations. The most famous case in which this problem arose was held in 1963 in the USA – Babcock v. Jackson case. The facts were as follows: in 1960 Miss Babcock and her friends Mr. and Mrs. Jackson, residents of New York, left in Mr. Jackson's automobile for a weekend trip to Canada. Some hours later in the province Ontario Mr. Jackson who was driving lost control of the automobile: the car went into the stone wall and Miss Babcock was seriously injured. After she returned to New York she brought a suit against Mr. Jackson in New York court. Jackson denied the charge relying on an Ontario Statute which provided no liability of a driver for injures sustained by passengers in the vehicle.

Traditional conflict rule is that the tort is governed by the law of the place of the tort. However it was considered that this case had greater connection with New York – all parties were from New York, the trip commenced and ended in New York. The connection with Ontario was casual. Application of classic conflict rule lex loci delicti in this case would have led to unjust and unreasonable result. It was decided that the law of the place of injury was not always inevitably applied. This case illustrated that classic conflict rules do not always successfully govern civil relationships with foreign element. Since then many classical approaches in private international law were reconsidered and now national legislation acts and international agreements contain different kind of new flexible conflict rules, such as the law of the place with which the relationships have the most close connection, the law of the place where the performance most important to a contract is rendered, etc.

Until recently Russian private international law consisted mostly of rigid and unequivocal conflict rules. The draft clearly demonstrates withdrawal from such approach. The reasons for the past and present situation in PIL are too evident and closely connected with the processes that take place in Russia now.

Next article of the draft governs one of the most complicated problem in private international law – problem of qualification. It is well known that similar definitions and terms that are used in the law of different countries sometimes have different content. One of the examples that is often given in this connection is the term "limitations", which in the Continental law is related to material law, and in countries of Common law – to the procedural law. Since a court usually would apply its own procedural rules, the application of limitation will depend on its qualification – as material or procedural term.

Property law, place of conclusion of a contract, the capacity to acquire civil rights and obligations, movable and immovable property, etc. – all these terms that are widely used in conflict rules have different meaning in different legal systems and should be defined in every case. There are several ways of solving this problem, e.g. the terms can be defined or qualified according to the law of the court or the law of the country of the foreign element in civil relationship.

The most widely recognized theory of qualification according to the law of the court that entertain the concrete case could not be used in the USSR as it was shown by prominent scholar L. Lunts, because of the essential difference between two legal systems – socialist and capitalist. For instance, the qualification of the term "property" would have led to quite different results if defined according to the former Soviet law, and in these cases more general definitions were used to govern civil relations with foreign element.

Cardinal changes that took place in the Russian society and economy diminished the distinctions among terms used in conflict rules of different countries. The distinctions that are left are more of legal and not political or economic character. It made it possible to include in the draft the approach that is recognized in many countries – qualification according to the law of the country where the court sits.

It is also proposed to regulate the situation where the qualification according to lex fori does not help – either because of its difficulty or because there is no such term in the law of the court country. Paragraph

2 of the article 1224 establishes that in this case the foreign law should be applied.

Article 1228 is titled "Public order". In current legislation such clause is formulated as follows: foreign law is not applied if its application would contradict the basic principles of the Soviet system" (art 568 of Civil Code of RSFSR 1964). The same definition was included in the draft of the Law of private international law which was discussed in 1990. It was outlined during the discussion that words "basic principles of Soviet system" have more political than legal meaning and that it is better to use the language of international co-operation in order to be understood in the world community. The Fundamentals 1991 made it better (art. 158) by diminishing the political "aspect" of the article that made it sound as practically standard public order clause. Article 1228 of the draft of the Civil Code in fact repeated that in Fundamentals: "Foreign law is not applied if its application would contradict the basic principles of the legal order (public order) of the Russian Federation".

Article 1230 deals with no less important problem – problem of renvoi, which is along with qualification one of the most difficult problem in private international law. The specialists all over the world during centuries made numerous attempts to solve it. Renvoi is an inevitable result of applying foreign law which contains conflict rules that may refer back to initial law or to the law of the third country. If the reference to the foreign law is understood as the reference to the whole legal system of a concrete state including its conflict rules then the problem of renvoi appears – they may refer back or to the law of the third country. For example, this problem occurred when an English person who lived in Belgium died. His heirs contested the will. According to the Belgian conflict rules the will should be drawn up according to the law of the citizenship of a testator, which in this case meant English law. But English conflict rule states that the will should be made in compliance with the laws of the residence, i.e. Belgian law. Whether accept the renvoi or not – the question that is answered differently in different countries and in different times and each point of view can be proved quite convincingly.

In the Soviet doctrine of private international law attitude towards the renvoi was in general positive. The main reason for that was the intention to enlarge the application of the Soviet law. There was no general rule on the issue, but concrete rules concerning concrete questions, both in national law and international treaties.

However lately another tendency shows itself. For example, General Conditions of Sale among socialist countries, which were first adopted in 1968 and then periodically amended, contains an article that states: the reference to the law of the country of the seller means the material law. The Law on International Commercial Arbitration 1993 restricts the application of renvoi. Article 28 establishes that any reference to the law of any country should be construed as the reference to its material law, and not to conflict rules. It means that the problem of renvoi does not arise in contractual relationship and other civil relationship connected with foreign trade and other international economic co-operation.

The draft of the Law on private international law states that renvoi does not applied if there is an agreement between parties on applicable law and if parties' intention on applicable law can be determined on the basis of their contract.

It is interesting to note that if in the draft of the Law on private international law the renvoi is recognised with several exceptions, in the draft of the Civil Code the renvoi is excluded with certain exceptions. The article 1230 says: any reference to foreign law in accordance with the rules of this section should be considered as reference to material and not conflict law of the corresponding state, unless otherwise provided by this article.

The second part of the articles establishes that renvoi can be accepted in following four cases:
- in determining personal law (art.1233),
- in determining foreign citizens' and stateless persons' capacity to acquire civil rights and obligations (art.1235),
- in determining the name of foreign citizens and stateless persons (art. 1236).
- in establishing custody (art.1239).

All these exceptions are connected with the personal status of natural persons. It means that after the adoption of the third part of the Civil Code the renvoi and the reference to the law of the third country will not be applied to contractual and non-contractual civil relationships, that meets the modern tendency and approaches in private international law.

Article 1233 of the draft of the Civil Code "Personal Law" governs the determining the personal law of a natural person. There is no such general rule in the current legislation. Its introduction facilitates the definitions of such terms connected with natural persons as their capacity to acquire civil rights and obligations, establishing custody, etc.

There are no essential changes concerning legal entities in the Draft – as the current legislation the Draft states that the legal capacity is defined according to the law of the place where a legal entity is founded. There is only one additional rule about organizations that are not legal entities according to foreign law (art.1242). The conflict rule provided for such organisations equals to that for the legal entities (art.1243) – it refers to the law of the state where the organization is founded.

The importance of the article 1245 "Participation of the state in civil relationships" cannot be overestimated. The necessity to govern all problems that arise in connection with the state's participation in civil relationships is too evident today. It was clear already in the beginning of 90s – Fundamentals 1991 contain article 25 "State participation in civil relationships" which certainly could not solve the problem and provided the adoption of the law on state immunity and its property. It is not yet done. Absence of the law cannot be substituted even partly by the doctrine since there is no unanimous opinion among Russian scholars on the issue.

There are two well known doctrines on the matter – the doctrine of absolute immunity and functional immunity. Legislation and judicial practice of many countries accepted the latter doctrine, several international treaties also reflected the doctrine of functional immunity. Traditionally Soviet scholars were strictly against any possibility of restricting state immunity, but lately certain changes are taking place.

All these circumstances make the article 1245 very important, though it should be understood that one article does not solve the whole problem. The article contains characteristics of a transaction with state participation which make it a civil transaction. Legislation acts in different countries and international treaties give examples of different approaches to the definition of such a transaction and the article 1245 could be considered as a compromise. There are three main characteristics which should be taken into consideration while determining the nature of a transaction with the participation of a state:

− a state makes a transaction not as a sovereign,
− nature of a transaction,
− purpose of a transaction.

Future application of the article by the courts will not be an easy task but it will enrich the practice of considering the problem of state participation in civil relationships.

It is interesting to follow the development of the will autonomy clause in Russian legislation − clause according to which parties to a contract are entitled to choose the applicable law. Article 566 of the Civil Code 1964 established the concrete conflict rule in the sphere of foreign trade and, at the very end of the article, provided that parties had right to choose applicable law to their contract. Article 166 of the Fundamentals 1991 starts with the autonomy clause. The draft of the Civil Code contains separate article 1254 titled "Choice of the Law by Parties". The following should be underlined in this article: it states that the applicable law may be determined, in the absence of the parties agreement, from the terms of the contract and all relative circumstances.

Determining the real intention of the parties concerning applicable law when parties do not include such clause in the contract is not easy task. Legislation and judicial practice of many countries dedicate much attention to this problem what circumstances should be taken into consideration, how the terms and conditions of a contract should be interpreted, etc. Russian legislation for the first time includes such a norm which proves that modern approaches, recognized in the world, become a part of the Russian legal system.

The authors of the draft could use the rules from the Convention on Law applicable to contracts of international sale of goods, signed in the Hague in December 22, 1986 which established that the parties agreement on applicable law should be clearly expressed or drawn from terms of a contract and parties behaviour, taken in the whole.

Any international convention is a result of studying different experience, national and international, and working out a compromise acceptable by different countries. Including the rules that are contained in international treaties and conventions into national legislation shows the will of national legislators to bring national legislation closer to international standards. There are many evidences of that kind in the draft of the Civil Code, and article 1254 is one of such examples.

Paragraph 4 of the article 1254 entitles parties to determine applicable law to a part of a contract. It could lead to applying different laws to different parts of a contract. Many Russian scholars treat such possibility negatively and future discussions on the Draft will show whether such clause will remain in it.

Will autonomy clause was also added by retroactive force of such clause – analogous rule can be found in the Switzerland Law on private international law 1987.

Article 1255 "Law applicable to a contract in the absence of parties' agreement" to large extent repeat the article 166 of the Fundamentals 1991. But there is the new rule concerning contracts not mentioned in the article – in this case the law of the state where the party, that render performance most important to a contract, resides or has its place of business. If it is impossible to determine such law, then the law most closely connected with a contract should be applied.

Both these conflict rules are quite new for Russian private international law. Such flexible rules give the court while entertaining a case the possibility to take into consideration all relative circumstances and render the most fair and reasonable decision. Such rules can be found in the codifications of private international law in many countries, e.g.

Switzerland, Austria, Hungary, etc., as well as in international instruments.

Several words should be said about article 1259 "Obligations which arise from the causing injury", since it contains new rule comparing with the current legislation. Article 566 (4) of the Civil Code 1964 established two main conflict rules concerning obligations arising from causing injury: 1) lex loci delicti, 2) Soviet law – if parties to a tort that occurred abroad are Soviet citizens. The same rule was included in the Fundamentals 1991. No changes were proposed in the draft of the Law on private international law.

Only the second rule was objected. It is well known that the reference to the law of the state of the common citizenship of the parties to a tort is quite usual in the modern private international law. That is why the approach – common citizenship – should remain, but it seemed logic to formulate this rule in a more general form: to determine applicable law in torts where the parties have common citizenship as the law of the state of that citizenship, and not only for Russian citizens. Paragraph 2 of article 1259 proposes more general formulation of the rule but still it is restricted by the torts that occur abroad. It runs as follows: rights and liabilities from obligations that arise from causing injury abroad, if parties are the citizens or legal entities of the same state, are determined by the law of that state.

ii) International treaties

International treaties play very important role for PIL since they contain many PIL norms, both conflict and substantial. Their role increased greatly after the adoption of the new Constitution of Russia 1993. It was already mentioned, that article 15 of the Constitution made the customs and norms of the international law and international treaties of the Russian Federation the part of the Russian legal system. Active role of Russia on the international arena – treaties with the Commonwealth of Independent States (CIS), joining Council of Europe, etc. – attaches new significance to this kind of legal sources, unknown before. It put new task before judges of national courts and employees of state agencies, connected with the application of norms of international treaties in their practice. It is not an easy task. It demands full information of international treaties in which Russia participates, as well as of widely recognised norms and customs of international law, skills to apply them in concrete cases. Many examples are already given by the practice of the Constitutional Court, especially in the sphere of human rights.

Among different kinds of international treaties those with the CIS countries are of special importance because of the close ties of the citizens and legal entities of these countries. In 1993 the Convention on Legal Aid and Legal Relationships in Civil, Family and Criminal Matters was signed by CIS countries. The Convention governs the delivery of different kind of legal aid by the organs of contracting parties, personal statutes of the citizens, recognition of marriage in one state if concluded in another, property relationships, inheritance, recognition and enforcement of court judgements, etc. Beside this convention the CIS countries signed other multilateral and bilateral treaties in different spheres.

Russia participates (as the USSR legal successor as well) in great number of international conventions, worked out by different international organisations – United Nations and its different commissions, the Hague Conference on Private International Law, International Bank for Reconstruction and Development, etc. Among UN conventions at least one should be mentioned – Convention on Contracts for the International Sale of Goods, signed at Vienna in 1980 (Vienna Convention). Russia participates in this convention since 1991. Most Russia partners in international trade also ratified Vienna convention, including such CIS countries as Ukraine, Belarus, Moldova and Georgia.

iii) Usages

Russian legislation and doctrine positively considers the application of usages. Usages are usually defined as rules which are consistently and constantly applied for a long time. It is always rather problematic to say whether this or that usage is "constantly applied for a long time", that is why it is often defined in concrete cases. Several Russian legislation acts provide for applying usages, e.g. art.59 of Fundamentals of Civil Legislation states, that a court or arbitration while interpreting a contract takes into consideration among other things "usages of business turnover". In art. 75 of the same act it is established, that if there is no fixed price for sold goods, it is considered that they were sold for the price customarily charged at the time of conclusion of the contract for such goods sold under comparable circumstances. In the Law of Russian Federation on International Commercial Arbitration 1993 (art.28) it is said that the arbitration renders an award with consideration of the contract terms and trade usages, applied to the transaction.

In international trade most usages are codified in digests, the most known of which is INCOTERMS, prepared by the International Chamber of Commerce. INCOTERMS are regularly amended and updated; the last edition thereof is that of 1990. This document is often used in the practice of International Commercial Arbitration Court at the Russian Federation Chamber of Commerce and Industry (see below), either because parties of a contract referred to INCOTERMS or due to arbitration initiative.

As to the court and arbitration practice, I should note here that though legally it is not considered as PIL source it still plays certain role in PIL. But before explaining that, some terminology clarifications are needed. The problem is that term "arbitration" has two meanings:

- system of state arbitration courts entertaining disputes between legal entities (as opposed to ordinary courts entertaining disputes with participation of citizens; arbitration and ordinary courts form the judicial system of the Russian Federation);
- tribunals formed mostly at Chambers of commerce or other social organisation for quicker and more effective considering cases (often called in Russian as tretejskiy court – third party courts). Parties to the dispute usually choose the arbitrators, who consider the case in accordance with the Rules of this tribunal. There are two types of

tribunals: 1) permanently functioning institution and 2) arbitration ad hoc. Important condition for referring a dispute to such tribunal is a special arbitration clause which is included into a contract or signed separately. Main permanent functioning tribunal in Russia, considering cases with "foreign element", i.e. in the sphere of PIL, is International Commercial Arbitration Court at the Chamber of Commerce and Industry of the Russian Federation; main legislation act that governs the operation of this tribunal is the Law of Russian Federation on International Commercial Arbitration 1993 and its Rules 1995.

At the same time state arbitration courts now play more significant role in PIL than before. According to art. 22 of the Arbitration Procedural Code 1995 such courts entertain disputes between legal entities and citizens-entrepreneurs of the Russian Federation and foreign organizations, organizations with foreign investment, international organizations, foreign citizens and stateless persons, carring out entrepreneurial activity. Recognizing the ambiguous and misleading meaning of the term "arbitration" the specialists offered to rename state arbitration courts into commercial or trade courts. Meanwhile to avoid misunderstanding one should bear in mind dual meaning of this term in Russian.

The practice of arbitration courts (both state and tretejskiy) plays certain role in PIL. For instance, in considering concrete cases in the International Commercial Arbitration Court, mentioned above, arbitrators while interpreting legal norms can take into account previous awards. The judges of state arbitration courts also indirectly use the previous practice, observing the Decrees of Supreme Arbitration Court Plenum, which are worked out on the basis of concrete arbitration cases and are obligatory for all judges.

3. Subjects of private international law

The subjects of PIL are: 1) citizens and stateless persons, 2) legal entities and 3) state. I will consider each of these categories of subjects, dividing them into subcategories: 1a) foreign citizens and stateless persons in the Russian Federation and 1b) citizens of the Russian Federation abroad, 2a) foreign legal entities in the Russian Federation and 2b) Russian legal entities abroad, 3a) foreign state in Russia and 3b) Russia as a party to civil relationships abroad.

3.1. Citizens and stateless persons

1a. Foreign citizens and stateless persons in the Russian Federation

Main legislation acts governing legal status of foreign citizens and stateless persons in the Russian Federation are the Constitution 1993, law "On Citizenship in the Russian Federation" 1991, law "On Legal Status of Foreign Citizens in the USSR" 1981, law "On Refugees" 1993, Civil Code of the Russian Federation. Some specific aspects of foreigners entry into and stay on the territory of Russia are governed by special normative acts, e.g.

- entry of foreigners to Russia:

  i) Federal Law "On Exit from the Russian Federation and Entry into the Russian Federation" 1996,
  ii) Rules on Foreigners Stay in the USSR, introduced by Cabinet of Ministers Decree 1991,
  iii) Law "On State Duty" 1991, etc.;

- foreigners' rights, limitations and prohibitions on professional occupations:

i) Federal Law "On Communication" 1995,
ii) Law "On Insurance" 1992,
iii) Fundamentals of Legislation of the Russian Federation on Citizens' Health Protection" 1993,
iv) Commercial Maritime Code 1968,
v) Law "On Private Detective and Protection Activity" 1992, etc.;

– limitations on foreigners' participation in agencies of state power:

i) Federal Constitutional Law "On Referendum" 1995,
ii) Federal Law "On Elections of President of Russian Federation" 1995,
iii) Law "On Judges Status in Russian Federation" 1992, etc.

Definition of a foreign citizen and a stateless person can be found in the Law "On Citizenship in Russian Federation" 1991: a foreigner is a person, possessing foreign citizenship and having no Russian Federation citizenship. A stateless person according to this law is a person possessing no Russian Federation citizenship and having no evidence of possessing other state citizenship.

Changes in Russian society, opening of its economy for foreign capital, withdrawal of many administrative prohibitions for foreigners' entry and stay in Russia caused significant increase of number of foreigners that come and stay in Russia nowadays. Citizens of CIS countries also became "foreign" on the territory of Russia. Legislation on legal status of foreigners and the scope of rights granted to them depends to great extent on the goal of a state – to increase or decrease their presence on its territory. The more a state is interested in foreigners' presence, the less limitations it establishes for them in its legislation.

The main principle governing foreigners' status in Russia is the principle of national regime, which can be found in different legislation acts. For instance, in the Law "On Legal Status of Foreign Citizens in the USSR" article 3, titled "Principles of legal status of foreign citizens in USSR", states: "Foreign citizens enjoy same rights and freedoms and bear same liabilities as citizens of the USSR, unless otherwise is provided for by the Constitution, present law and other acts of soviet legislation". The same principle is included in the Constitution, art. 62:"Foreign citizens and stateless persons enjoy in the Russian Federation rights and bear liabilities equal to those of the citizens of Russian Federation, unless otherwise is provided for by the federal legislation or international treaty of the Russian Federation". It is easy to understand that minimum restrictions are imposed on foreigners in the sphere of private law and maximum – in public law.

Article 160 of the Fundamentals of Civil Legislation 1991 specifies general principle stated in the Constitution. In the first paragraph of the article, titled "Foreigners' and stateless persons' capacity to have civil rights and obligations and to perform legal acts" it is stated: "Foreigners and stateless persons enjoy same capacity to have civil rights and obligations in the USSR to the same extent as do soviet citizens. Individual exceptions may be established by legislative acts of the USSR". In the second paragraph of the same article it is said that foreign citizens' capacity to perform legal acts is determined by the law of the state of their citizenship. The stateless persons' capacity to perform legal acts is determined by the law of the state where they have permanent residence (para.3, art.160).

It should be explained what the capacity to have civil rights and to perform legal acts means according to the Russian legislation. Definitions of these terms are found in the Civil Code of the Russian Federation. Article 17 of this act states that the capacity to have civil rights and bear liability is accorded equally to all citizens and arises at the moment of birth and terminates with death. The examples of civil rights and obligations citizens can have are given in article 18 of the Civil Code: to own, inherit and bequeath property, to carry out entrepreneurial and other activity, not forbidden by law, to set up legal entities, make any transactions that do not contradict law, to have copyrights, etc. The list of civil rights and obligations cannot be final since the sphere of civil relationships develops constantly and any limitation could be an obstacle in its development. Establishing equal capacity for foreign and Russian citizens means that foreigners may enjoy the same rights mentioned in article 18.

Citizens' capacity to perform legal acts defined in article 21 of the Civil Code as the citizen's capacity through his own acts to acquire and enjoy civil rights, to create civil obligations for himself and to execute them. This capacity arises in full upon citizen's majority, i.e. when a person reaches the age of 18 years.

According to art. 160 of the Fundamentals there are different conflict norms for i) the capacity to have civil rights and obligations and ii) the capacity to acquire civil rights and obligations: the first is determined by the Russian law, the second – by the law of the state of the foreigners' citizenship(or the law of permanent residency in case of a stateless person).

i) Citizens' legal capacity to have civil rights and obligations

Equal capacity to have civil rights means that foreigners may on the territory of Russia enjoy rights and bear obligations unknown in their own states and may not have rights and obligations, established in his state but unknown in Russia. For instance, in some countries a married woman may not conclude certain transactions without the consent of her husband. Such restriction is unknown in Russia because there is the constitutional principle of legal equality of men and women in Russian legislation. It means that such married woman might conclude a transaction in Russia that she could not have made at home. The opposite is also correct: a foreigner may not exercise the rights, stated in the law of his country but unknown in Russia.

It was already mentioned that there can be certain exceptions from the national regime if provided for in a federal law. Most examples of such exceptions are in the sphere of state and public law. For example, the legislation establishing conditions of setting up different state agencies are not applied to foreigners as a rule. Another exception concerning professions is included in the Fundamentals of the Legislation of the Russian Federation on Notariat 1993: only citizens of Russia can be notaries in Russia.

In certain rare cases the Government of the Russian Federation may impose retaliatory restrictions upon citizens of those states in which special restrictions exist on the rights of Russian citizens (art.162 of the Fundamentals of the Civil Legislation).

ii) Citizens' capacity to acquire civil rights and obligations

As it was said above, foreign citizens' capacity to acquire civil rights and obligations, which include performing legal acts and to creating legal rights and liabilities is usually determined by the law of their citizenship (lex patriae). This rule, adopted in most countries, is connected with the fact that the full majority arises at different age in different states. But there are two important exceptions to the principle lex patriae that should be mentioned. If a foreigner under age concludes a contract on the territory of the Russian Federation, he cannot refer to his minority and require dissolution of the contract and relief of losses – in this case Russian law is applied. This exception was formulated in the doctrine and then included into the legislation act – Fundamentals (para.4, art.160). It was decided that contrary rule could have led to misuse of rights and limit commercial relationships. The second exception is connected with torts. In case of injury caused on the territory of Russia, Russian law is applied to foreign citizens' capacity to perform legal acts (para.4, art.160 of the Fundamentals).

In most international treaties of the Russian Federation citizens' legal capacity to acquire civil rights and liabilities is determined by the law of their citizenship. For instance, article 23 of the Convention on Legal Aid and Legal Relationships on Civil, Family and Criminal Cases 1993 signed by CIS countries states that the citizen's capacity to perform legal acts is determined by the legislation of the state of his citizenship. Same capacity of stateless persons is determined by the law of the state of their permanent residence.

1b. Citizens of Russian Federation abroad

Legal status of citizens of the Russian Federation is determined by the Russian law and the law of the state of their residence. A lot depends on the legislation of this or that foreign state and international treaties of the Russian Federation.

According to the Constitution and the law "On Citizenship" 1991 of the Russian Federation its citizens enjoy the protection of Russia wherever they reside. Usually legal status is defined equally to that in Russia: capacity to have civil rights is determined by the law of state of residence and capacity to perform legal acts – by the law of citizenship. In order to know exact status of Russian citizens in this or that country it is necessary to address its legislation on foreigners' status.

3.2. Legal entities

3.2a. Foreign legal entities in Russia

i) Foreign legal entities status

The main principle for foreign legal entities in Russia is national regime, which equals foreign and Russian legal persons on the territory of Russia; number of limitations to national regime are provided for to protect certain spheres, e.g. banking and insurance. Another regime is called regime of most favored nation usually included in international treaties. This regime equals all foreign legal persons among themselves and as a rule is formulated as follows: legal persons of the contracting party enjoy the same regime that is provided for or will be provided for legal persons from the third countries.

Status of foreign legal entities in Russia is governed by Russian legislation and international treaties of the Russian Federation. One of the most important questions that arises in connection with foreign legal entities is their "nationality". The term "nationality" is used to legal persons by analogy with natural persons in order to determine the law that governs internal legal person affairs: whether the concrete organisation is recognised as a legal person, way of its formation, liquidation, etc., i.e. its legal capacity. Russian doctrine and legislation states that the factor determining the nationality of legal persons is the place of its setting up. In para.1 of article 161 of the Fundamentals we read: legal capacity of foreign legal entities is determined by the law, where such entity is founded.

In international treaties of the Russian Federation the same principle is mostly used: para.3 of art. 23 of the mentioned Convention on Legal Aid of CIS countries 1993 establishes that legal capacity of legal person is determined by legislation of the state, according to which laws it is founded. At the same time another principle in determining nationality of legal persons is used in international practice – e.g. in the Treaty between the USSR and Poland on Legal Aid and Legal Rela-tionships for Civil, Family and Criminal Cases 1957 (which is still in force and Russia is a legal successor of the USSR in this treaty) it is stated that legal capacity of legal persons is determined by the law of the state, on the territory of which it is situated. Thus two principles for determining nationality of foreign legal persons are used in Russia – place of setting up and place of residence.

ii) Legal capacity of foreign legal entities in Russia

What concrete rights do foreign legal entities enjoy in Russia? This question is governed by several legislation acts, such as Civil Code, the Law on Foreign Investments 1991, Statute on Procedure of Founding and activity in the USSR of Foreign Firms', Banks' and Organisations' Representations 1989, Law on Banks and Banks' Activity in the Rus-sian Federation 1990, Law on Currency and Currency Control 1992, Law on Insurance 1992, etc.

Civil Code in para.1 of article 2 states that rules established by the Code are applied to relationships with foreign citizens and foreign legal persons, unless otherwise is provided for in the federal law. The main principle of the Russian civil legislation is contained in art.1 of the Civil code, which runs as follows: civil legislation is based on equality of participants of civil relationships, inviolability of property, freedom of contract, inadmissibility of arbitrary interference in private affairs, judicial protection of violated rights, etc. It is further stated in the article that civil rights may be limited only on the basis of federal law for protecting constitutional system of the country, moral, health, legal rights of other persons and national security. These principles, enumerated in the opening articles of the Civil Code, are equally applied to foreign persons, both natural and legal.

The Statute on Procedure of Founding and Activity in the USSR of Foreign Firms', Banks' and Organisations' Representations 1989 was put into force by the Decree of the Council of Ministers N 1074 dated 30 November 1989. Para.1 states that foreign firms, banks and organisations may set up their representations on the basis of a special permission given by Ministry of Foreign Economic Relations or Chamber of Commerce and Industry, or Ministry of Maritime Fleet, or Ministry of Civil Air Fleet, depending on the character of its activity. Additional Government Decrees of 1990 and 1991 entitled Ministry of Justice, Ministry of Finance and Ministry of Railways to issue such permissions. A firm applying for the permission should be well known in its country and on the world market and co-operate with Russian organisations.

The permission is given as a rule for three years, provided that this period may be prolonged. The permission contains following information: the goal of setting up a representation, terms and conditions of its activity, validity term of a permission, number of foreign employees. According to art. 14 of the Statute a representation should terminate its activity, in particular, upon expiring of the term of a permission, liquidation of the firm, that set up a representation, the decision of the ministry that issued a permission if the representation violates the terms and conditions of its activity, decision of a foreign firm itself.

Another legislation act that should be mentioned here is the Law on Foreign Investments 1991 which governs rights of foreign legal persons to invest in Russia. Investments may be carried out in different ways:
- to acquire a part of Russian enterprise,
- to set up a new enterprise wholly owned by a foreign person,

- to set up a branch of a foreign legal person,
- to acquire shares, obligations and other securities according to Russian legislation, etc.

Part II of the Law is dedicated to general conditions of foreign investments, which mostly coincide with those applied and recognised in international practice. Article 6 states that foreign investments on the territory of the Russian Federation enjoy full legal protection and the regime for foreign investors may not be worse than that for Russian legal entities. Foreign investments cannot be nationalised, unless it is performed for national public interests with payment of compensation. The sum of compensation should be equal to real cost of the investment and should be paid in investment currency or other currency, accepted by the foreign investor (art.8).

In articles 10 and 11 two other types of guarantees are included: guarantee for transfer currency abroad and for reinvesting Russian currency on the territory of Russia. Special article regulates entertaining investment and other disputes of foreign investors. Part 1 of article 9 states that investment disputes including those connected with amount and way of payment of compensation are considered in Supreme Court or Supreme Arbitration Court, unless otherwise is provided for in an international treaty of the Russian Federation.

Foreign investors disputes with state agencies, Russian legal persons connected with their commercial activity are entertained in courts of the Russian Federation or in arbitration (tretejskiy) court if parties so agreed. International treaties may provide for applying to international agencies for settlement of disputes.

This article obviously needs to be amended since there is no clear definition of investment and other disputes that makes it rather vague and uncertain (for more details see para. 5"Foreign Investments").

Enterprises may be set up partially or only with foreign capital in the form of any commercial society or a partnership envisaged in article 50 of the Civil Code: joint-stock company (art.96–104), limited responsibility company (art.87–94), company with additional responsibility (art.95), full (art.69–81) and limited partnerships (art.82–86). The

Civil Code provided for adoption special laws on joint-stock companies and limited responsibility companies. The first one was adopted
by State Duma in November 1995 and put into force in January 1996,
the second one is being worked out now.

Enterprises with foreign capital should be registered according to
the Government Decree N 26 of 28 November 1991 and other federal
and regional acts, which are replenished periodically. Due to the volume of the investment and economic sphere the registration is made
into the state agency defined to register concrete investment.

3.2b. Russian legal persons abroad

Practically any Russian legal entity is entitled to participate in foreign
trade activity, as opposed to previous times when only very limited
number of special agencies could conclude foreign trade and other
international transactions. Legal status of Russian organisations is
defined partly by Russian law, partly – by the law of a state, where
such organisation carries out its activities. Still a lot depends on conflict rules of a concrete country. If legal status of foreign legal entities
is determined by law of the state of its incorporation, then Russian law
is applied to Russian legal entities. If other connecting factors are used,
e.g. place of main administrative office or place of performing its
activity, then foreign law may be applied to legal status of Russian
legal persons.

The status of Russian legal persons also depends on international
treaties in which the regime of most favoured nation is usually granted
to them.

3.3. State as a party to civil relationships

State becomes more and more active in the sphere of civil relationships
lately. In practice it means that a state concludes different kind of civil
transactions with foreign legal and even natural persons, e.g. a contract
concluded by a state agency with a foreign firm or issue of state
obligations that are sold on the territory of a foreign state, etc. It is

quite evident that such transactions differ from those concluded by individuals or legal persons first of all due to such characteristic of a state as sovereignty which means no person can sue a foreign state or enforce court decision without state's consent. But in civil relationships any party wants to be protected and guaranteed in case of other party violation of its obligations, even if the other party is a state. This problem became especially important in 50s, when developed countries started to invest capital in developing countries. Refusal of developing countries sometimes to fulfil their obligations as regards to foreign firms-investors caused problems. The necessity to solve them led to appearing the doctrine of functional state sovereignty.

This doctrine, as opposed to absolute sovereignty, is very well known nowadays and is reflected in legislation and practice of many states. In the USSR the attitude towards functional sovereignty was strictly negative. According to soviet scholars no limitations of the state sovereignty could be recognized no matter what actions or transactions were carried out by state. But today the situation is being slowly changed. To great extent it is connected with profound economic changes that take place in Russia, more close connections with countries that adopt the doctrine of functional sovereignty (e.g. USA, Great Britain), necessity to protect Russian legal persons abroad and participation of foreign capital in Russian economy.

Different Russian scholars adhere different opinions on the issue and this "struggle of opinions" is reflected to some extent in legal literature, but after the publication of the draft of the chapter "Private International Law" in the third part of the Civil Code the dispute lost to certain extent its importance. It was mentioned above that special article 1245 titled "State's participation in civil relationships with the foreign element" was included, in which the doctrine of functional sovereignty was reflected. Though there might be some amendments and changes in the text of the draft, but it is hardly imaginable that this article will be substantially changed or excluded.

4. Foreign trade transactions

There is no legal definition of a foreign trade transaction in Russian legislation. In the doctrine under foreign trade transactions different contracts connected with the transfer of goods and services across the border are understood, such as contract of sale, lease, commission, deposit, etc., parties to which are from different states. In Russian special literature now the term "foreign economic transactions" is used instead of "foreign trade transactions" in order to underline that not only sale contracts are meant. But I will still use the term "foreign trade transactions" for the sake of better English translation ("foreign economic transactions" sounds somewhat weird in English) and because sale contracts are the most widespread contracts in the sphere of foreign economic relations.

4.1. Form of a foreign trade transactions

Article 165 of the Fundamentals states that the form of a foreign trade transaction, concluded by Russian legal and natural persons, regardless of the place in which it is concluded, is determined by Russian legislation. Russian legislation establishes two forms of concluding transactions: oral and written (art.158 of Civil Code); the latter one could be with or without notarization, i.e. simple or notarial written form. A transaction that is performed at the time of its conclusion may be concluded orally unless otherwise provided by the law or parties' agreement. Article 161 of the Code provides what type of transactions require simple written form, e.g. contracts concluded by legal entities, between legal entity and a citizen, contracts between citizens in case the price of a contract is not less than 10 times higher of fixed minimum salary. Failure to observe simple written form leads to different legal consequences:
1) a law or parties agreement may determine that failure to observe simple written form causes transactions to be invalid (para. 2, art.162 of Civil Code),

2) in the absence of such clause in law or parties agreement, the failure
to observe simple written form deprives the parties in case of a
dispute of the right to rely on oral testimony to confirm the conclusion of the transaction and its terms, however, they can use written
and other evidence (para.1, art.162).

It means that transactions concluded with violation of simple written
form will be invalid only if it is so provided in a law or parties
agreement.

The form of a foreign trade transaction is determined in para. 3
art.162 of Civil Code – it is a simple written form. In the same
paragraph the law says that failure to observe simple written form of a
foreign trade transaction causes its invalidity. This is an example of
how law establishes the consequences of failure to observe a form of a
transaction.

Until recently the question of foreign trade transactions' form was
quite disputable. Civil Code 1964 determined that foreign trade transactions should be concluded in written form with observance the
procedure for signing such transactions. The procedure was established in Decree of Council of Ministers 1978 and required two signatures from the soviet part of a transaction. Failure to observe not only
the form, but the procedure for signing foreign trade transactions
caused the invalidity of such transactions.

The Fundamentals 1991 did not mention the procedure for signing
foreign trade transactions, only their form, but since the Decree 1978
was still formally in force there was no clarity on the issue: should
foreign trade transactions be recognised invalid if there was only one
signature instead of two under the transaction, concluded by Russian
person. Some specialists believed the requirement for two signatures
was still valid, others considered that the requirement should not be
applied since the Fundamentals did not mention it, that the requirement
for two signatures was established in 30s and was already archaic now.

After Civil Code adoption the problem was clarified: article 162
stated that the foreign trade transaction should be concluded in a
simple written form. No additional requirements are mentioned. The

requirement for a simple written form of a foreign trade transaction concluded by a Russian person should be observed no matter where such transaction is made. Accession of the USSR in 1991 to International Convention on contracts for the international sale of goods, made in Vienna in 1980, demanded special reservations connected with the form of such contracts.

Article 11 of the Convention states that a contract of sale need not be concluded in or evidenced by writing and is not subject to any other requirement as to form. Legislation of many countries (not only of Russia) demands written form of foreign trade transactions. In order to increase number of future participants of the Convention article 96 was included in its text: a contracting state whose legislation requires contracts of sale to be concluded in or evidenced by writing may at any time make a declaration in accordance with article 12 that any provision of article 11, article 29, or part II of this Convention, that allows a contract of sale or its modification or termination by agreement or any offer, acceptance, or other indication of intention to be made in any form other than in writing, does not apply where any party has his place of business in that state. Russia, as well as Argentina, Belorussia, Hungary, Lithuania, Ukraine, Chile, Estonia, made such reservation.

4.2. Applicable law

Russian legislation states that in determining the applicable law in the sphere of foreign trade the principle of autonomy of will is used. It means parties to a contract are entitled to determine what law should be applied to their relationships. According to para. 1 of article 166 of Fundamentals, rights and obligations of parties to a foreign trade transaction are governed by the law chosen by parties at the moment of conclusion of a contract or by their subsequent agreement. There are no limitations to that principle in Russian law.

In case parties fail to determine the applicable law article 166 provides several conflict rules depending on the type of a contract. Article states: in the absence of parties' agreement providing applicable law, the law of that country is applied where the following party of

a contract has its place of habitual residence or of main activity:
seller – in contract of sale,
lessor – in lease contract
depositee – in contract of deposit
commission agent – in commission contract
agent – in contract of agency
carrier – in contract for carriage
insurer – in insurance contract
creditor – in credit contract, etc.

There are more than 10 different types of contract mentioned in the article. What should be noted is that two conflict rules included in article 166 are imperative – concerning setting up an enterprise with foreign investment and contracts made in auctions, competitions and stock exchange.

Contracts of setting up an enterprise with foreign investment are governed by the law of the state where such enterprise is set up (para.3 of art. 166). Since this rule is obligatory, parties may not provide different one. If parties setting up in Russia an enterprise with foreign investment provide in their contract another conflict rule on the matter, it will be null and void according to the Russian law and article 166 will be applied.

Contracts made in auctions, competitions and stock exchange are governed by the law of the country where the auction or competition take place or where the stock exchange is situated (para.4 of art.166). This rule is not unusual – auctions, competitions and stock exchanges have there own obligatory rules which might differ from those of another law. In order to escape this conflict, the law, governing auctions, competitions and stock exchange are always applied.

It is practically impossible to provide all kinds of contracts parties may conclude in practice. This situation is taken into consideration in para. 5 of article 166. It says that contracts not mentioned in the article are governed by the law of the state where the party that render the performance that is characteristic of the contract, has its habitual residence or its main place of business. Such conflict rule that is quite usual nowadays for many countries appeared for the first time in Fundamentals 1991 and its application might be rather difficult for Russian courts or arbitration, but its inclusion in Russian legislation proves cardinal changes in private international law of Russia, that "absorb" the most reasonable modern approaches in this sphere. The novelty of Russian regulation is especially clear when compared with the previous one (Fundamentals of Civil Legislation 1961) that provided the only one conflict rule in the sphere of foreign trade: rights and obligations of parties to a foreign trade contract were governed by the law of the place where it was concluded, though the parties could provide otherwise. In practice parties (state foreign trade organisations) very rare "provided otherwise" and practically all foreign trade contracts were concluded in Moscow which led to applying Soviet law in most cases.

5. Foreign investments

Foreign investments is rather new sphere in Russian economy and, as a result, in Russian legislation. First legal acts on the matter were adopted in 1987 and the main law titled "The Law on Foreign Investments" came into force in 1991. However very soon it became clear that the Law needs many alterations and amendments: since then the USSR collapsed, new sovereign states appeared instead of former union republics, market relations are being developed. Rules governing foreign investments are also contained in legislation regulating tax, bank, currency, insurance, etc. issues.

While working out special legislation on foreign investments few global problems should be taken into consideration. First – it is necessary to create economic and legal regime that might "attract" foreign investor. Second – it is necessary to keep real competition among foreign and national investors. And maybe the most difficult problem – whether the special law on foreign investments is needed. Despite the adoption of the Law the disputes on all these questions continue.

Today it is evident that the Law 1991 is quite obsolete and a draft of new one is being worked out and discussed in the Russian Parliament. And still there is no unanimous opinion whether such law should be adopted. The main principle for foreign investors established in the Law is the principle of national regime. If so it would be logical to apply national legislation to foreign investors without adopting special acts. Most countries do not have any legislation act on foreign investments and apply their national legislation governing commercial relationships. This problem is to be decided and the results remain to be seen, though it should be noted here that most specialists in Russia believe special legislation is still needed: the experience of many countries shows that during complex period of transaction economy foreign investors need additional legislation for their protection.

Legislation on foreign investments comprises several laws and many presidential and governmental decrees, regulations of different agencies. The main act is the Law on Foreign Investments 1991, that consists of 7 chapters, 42 articles, containing definitions of the foreign investor and foreign investment. It also establishes guarantees and protection for a foreign investor, settlement of disputes, procedure of setting up and liquidation of enterprises with foreign investments, acquisition of shares and other securities and land by foreign investors, their rights in free economic zones. This Law was already mentioned above, but here I will give more detailed analyse thereof.

According to article 1 of the Law following persons may be foreign investors:
- foreign legal persons,
- foreign citizens, stateless persons, soviet citizens permanently residing abroad, provided they are registered as entrepreneurs in the state of their citizenship or permanent residence,
- foreign states,
- international organisations.

Foreign investment is defined as any kind of property and intellectual property that are invested by foreign investors in entrepreneurial activ-

ity for receiving profit (art.2). Next article describes possible forms of investing:
- participation in national enterprises,
- setting up new enterprises,
- acquisition of enterprises, shares, securities and other property,
- acquisition of rights to use land and other natural resources, etc.

The most important second chapter is dedicated to guarantees and protection of foreign investments. Article 6 establishes national regime for foreign investors, that was already mentioned above. However article provides that certain withdrawals from national regime can be established by the Law. The problem is that the Law does not contains such withdrawals and foreign investor does not have enough information what spheres of Russian economy is partly or wholly closed for him. The present draft of the Law on Foreign Investments contains lists of such spheres, but the adoption of this law will take time.

Article 7 provides guarantees from expropriation and illegal actions of state agencies and their employees. The article states that the expropriation may be carried out only in exceptional cases, provided for in a law, for the purposes of public interest and accompanied by payment of prompt, adequate and effective compensation. The expropriation can be effectuated in three forms:
- nationalisation,
- requisition,
- confiscation.

According to article 243 "Confiscation" of Civil Code of the Russian Federation, the property can be appropriated without compensation from its owner only in cases prescribed by law, by virtue of court decision as a penalty for a crime or another violation of the law. Requisition is an appropriation of property from its owner by the state in case of natural disaster, epidemic and other circumstances of extraordinary character in the manner prescribed by law with paymen of compensation (art.242 of Civil Code). Nationalisation is defined in article 235 of Civil Code as appropriation of persons' property by state carried out by virtue of law with payment of compensation of property cost and losses.

The fourth part of article 7 of the Law on Foreign Investments provides that foreign investors are entitled to compensation of losses, including lost profit, that occurred as a result of illegal action or inaction of state agencies or their employees.

Article 8 gives more details on the terms and manner of payment of compensation and losses. Compensation that is paid in case of nationalisation or requisition should be equal to real cost of nationalised or requisited property which is determined as of the date immediately before the date on which it became publicly known the nationalisation or requisition was taken or is going to take place. Compensation should be paid without delay in currency in which the initial investment was effectuated or any other currency accepted by the foreign investor. If a foreign investor sustains losses that occurred as a result of illegal action or inaction of a state agency or its employees then compensation should be paid by that agency.

Article 9 of the Law deals with one of the most important for foreign investor issue – settlement of disputes. Article distinguishes two types of disputes:
– investment disputes and
– other disputes.

First type of disputes which is not defined (it is just mentioned that disputes arising from the payment of compensation fall under the category of investment disputes) are considered in Supreme Court or Supreme Arbitration Court, unless otherwise is provided by international treaty.

Other disputes include following kinds of disputes of foreign investors:
– with state agencies,
– with enterprises, social organisations and other Russian legal persons,
– among foreign investors and enterprises with foreign investments,
– between partners of an enterprise with foreign investment with the enterprise itself.

Such disputes are to be settled in ordinary courts, in state arbitration courts or in arbitration (tretejskiy) courts, provided there is an arbitration agreement between the parties.

In connection with this article several things should be mentioned. In international practice an "investment dispute" means a dispute between a foreign investor and a host state. Usually such disputes concern payment of compensation, taxation, customs, labour issues, etc., i.e. any violation by a state its obligations towards foreign investor. In the Russian Law only disputes arising from payment compensation are mentioned that makes the term "investment disputes" rather vague.

What makes it even more vague is the second part of the article, which says that disputes of foreign investors with state agencies are entertained in ordinary court or arbitration, or state arbitration. More clear and distinct formulation of investment disputes is evidently needed in the law.

As it was mentioned a foreign investor has three alternatives in case a dispute arises:

1) according to article 25 of the Civil Procedure Code 1964 (it should be noted that the new Civil Procedure Code is now being worked out) ordinary courts may entertain disputes with participation of foreign citizens and foreign legal persons, unless otherwise is provided by international treaty or parties' agreement. In this case a foreign investor can as a rule file a suit in the ordinary court that is situated where the defendant has his place of residence. A suit to a legal person may be filed in the court that is situated where the office or property of such legal person is (art. 117 of the Civil Procedure Code).

2) article 22 of Arbitration Procedural Code 1995 also establishes the possibility for a foreign investor to apply to state arbitration courts. The principle that defines concrete state arbitration court where a foreign investor may file a suit, is the same as in the previous paragraph – place where the defendant is situated.

3) arbitration (tretejskiy) court.

Ordinary courts never played more or less important role in entertaining disputes with foreign investors – lack of special experience of judges of district or city ordinary courts made foreign investors seek for another alternatives. Most such disputes nowadays are entertained in arbitration (tretejskiy) courts, the most famous of which is International Commercial Arbitration Court at the Chamber of Commerce and Industry of Russian Federation. In any case foreign investors are free to choose any alternative because all mentioned legislation acts so provide.

Articles 10 and 11 establish guarantees to convert and transfer abroad Russian currency and its use on the territory of Russia.

Chapters III and IV govern the activity of the enterprises with foreign investments. At the moment of adopting this Law legislator believed that foreign investments in Russia should be carried out mostly in the form of founding enterprises with foreign investments. That is why so much attention in the Law was dedicated to such enterprises – their foundation, registration, liquidation, etc. It should be also noted that the Law was adopted long before the new Civil Code came into force, where many aspects of legal persons activity are considered in detail. Besides, in 1995 special law on joint stock companies was worked out, which covers issues connected with this form of a legal person. It means that new law on foreign investments that is in the process of working out now should not contain articles governing enterprises with foreign investment, but only provide general regime for foreign investors, who in certain cases if they wish may establish an enterprise with foreign investment.

Last three chapters of the Law – V, VI and VII – are dedicated to very important rights of foreign investors: acquiring shares and other securities, including shares of privatised enterprises (chapter V), acquiring rights to use land and other property rights (chapter VI), rights to invest in free economic zones (chapter VII). Unfortunately many articles in these chapters refer to special legislation acts, that are not yet adopted, e.g. Land Code, Law on Free Economic Zones.

Besides the Law many other normative acts govern foreign investments, first of all Presidential decrees and Governmental regulations.

There are several reasons for such situation:
- traditionally in Russian Federation many subordinate acts were adopted to implement and apply a law,
- insufficiency of the Law for the changed economic situation,
- appearing new problems connected with foreign investments that could not be taken into consideration at the moment of the adoption of the Law.

Among such subordinate acts the following may be mentioned: Presidential decrees N 1466 dated September 27, 1993 "On improving the work with foreign investments", that introduced so-called "grandfather clause", N 73 dated January 25, 1995 "On additional measures for enlisting foreign investments in the sphere of material production", Governmental regulation N 1102 dated November 2, 1993 "On liberalisation of foreign economic activity", etc. These and other normative acts, not mentioned here, were needed for adequate governing of foreign investments.

The Law on Sharing Production Agreements 1995 should be also mentioned here. The first act concerning sharing production agreements was adopted in 1994 – it was Presidential decree on agreements of sharing production. Though the decree established the parties to such agreements – on the part of Russian Federation they should be signed by the Government of the Russian Federation and the Supreme authority of the subject of the Federation – and other issues, it did not define the legal nature of the agreement. In international practice such agreements are considered to be an independent-work contract, i.e. civil law contract, in which a foreign investor is a contractor and a Host state is a customer. In the decree the elements of civil and administrative law were not distinguished properly that led to many confusions in practice.

The Law clearly states that such an agreement is a civil law contract. Article 2 provides: The production sharing agreement (hereinafter the Agreement) shall be an agreement under which the Russian Federation shall grant to the subjects of entrepreneurial activities (hereinafter the Investor) on a chargeable basis and for a specified period exclusive rights to prospect for, explore and extract mineral raw materials in the subsoil plot specified in the agreement and to perform operations connected therewith, whereas the investor shall undertake to perform at his own expense and risk the aforesaid operations. The agreement shall determine all necessary terms and conditions connected with the subsoil use including terms and conditions of and procedure for sharing the extracted products between the parties to the agreement in accordance with the provisions of this Federal Law.

Besides it establishes the procedure for conclusion agreements, rights and obligations of the parties to the agreements, guarantees for investors, mechanism of settling disputes, etc. Article 23 is a very important one for foreign investors: it says that the agreements with foreign citizens and foreign legal persons may include the waiver of the state from judicial immunity, immunity in respect to the preliminary security of the claim and enforcement of the court and \or arbitration decision. This article shows one of possible ways of settling the problem of state immunity when a state is involved in entrepreneurial activity.

However, the Law provides that before its coming into force two conditions should be fulfilled (para. 3, art.2 and art. 26): current legislation should be brought into conformity with the Law and the list of fields to which the Law applies should be prepared. Lists of such subsoil plots should be submitted to the State Duma by the Government of the Russian Federation and representative authorities of the subjects of the Russian Federation in whose territories corresponding subsoil plots are located and established by federal laws. Neither one is yet done.

Generally it may be said that the Law on Foreign Investments in Russia played positive role at the moment of its adoption – it established worldly recognized principles that are applied in the sphere of foreign investments, i.e. national regime, nationalisation with payment of compensation, different kinds of guarantees to foreign investors, etc. But during 6 years, that passed since the adoption of the Law, brought essential and profound changes in the Russian economy which demand quite new and modern legislation act. Hopefully soon the new

Law on Foreign Investments will be worked out that will meet the requirements of the modern economic situation.

6. Torts in private international law

After foreign trade transactions, the regulation of torts that occur in the sphere of private international law plays the most important role. It is explained by two reasons:
– torts are always unexpected and unforeseeable
– applicable law usually is not chosen by parties.

Conflict rules in the sphere of torts were formulated long ago and sounds almost equally in many countries. The main principle – lex loci delicti – runs as follows: rights and obligations of the parties of tort are governed by the law of the place where the tortious act is committed. However during last three or four decades substantial changes occurred in this sphere which led to formulating new conflict rules in the sphere of torts, less rigid than classic one. Main innovation was connected with the situation where the tortfeasor and the injured party had their residence in the same state or were the citizens of the same state. It was decided that in this case the claims based on the tortious act should be governed by the law of this state. Practically all new codifications or practice in the sphere of private international law in different countries reflected this approach.

In the USSR legislation the tort conflict rule appeared in 1977. By amendment to the Civil Code 1964 the following article was introduced in the last chapter of the Code: "Rights and duties of the parties under obligations arising from the causing injury are determined by the law of the country where an act or another occurrence which provided the basis for claiming damages took place.

Rights and duties of the parties under obligations arising from causing injury abroad if the parties are Soviet citizens or Soviet organisations are determined by the Soviet law.

Foreign law is not applied if an act or another occurrence which provides the basis for claiming damages is not unlawful under Soviet law".

The same article was included in the Fundamentals 1991 (art.167) and is still in force up till now. The first part of the article establishes common principle used in the sphere of torts – lex loci delicti. The second part is most interesting and most disputable. As it was mentioned above modern approaches in torts containing the foreign element, often determine applicable law as the law of common citizenship or residence of the parties. The same approach is reflected in the Fundamentals, but partly: this approach can be used only to Russian citizens as parties to a tort that occurred abroad. To be logic the same approach should be applied to foreigners as well: if citizens from one state are the parties of a tort that occurred on the territory of Russia the law of their state should be applied to the claims arising from such tort. It is clear enough that the article should be formulated in a more general form, connecting the common citizenship or residence of a tortfeasor and injured party with the law of the state of this citizenship or residence.

As it was shown above the draft of the chapter "Private International Law" in the third part of the Civil Code" contains more general norm (art.1259) – it permits the applying the law of common citizenship of the parties of a tort but only if such tort occurs abroad. However it should be noted that the general principle – lex loci delicti – remains the same.

IX Legal Regulation of Foreign Trade Relations in Russian Federation

Marina Petrovna Bardina

1. Introduction

The legal regulation of foreign trade relations as well as of the other parts of Russian economy has undergone radical changes during the latest years. As in other spheres, the changes were directed at the abolishment of the administrative methods of regulations which caused the stagnation and then crises in the Russian economy. The dissolution of CMEA and later the dissolution of the USSR strengthened these crises in the field of foreign trade.

The reform of foreign trade system was launched in the former USSR in 1986 and was aimed at the demonopolisation of the foreign trade, which for the long years of the Soviet regime was based on the state monopoly. Russia actively continued the reform process in the foreign trade. The reforms are considered to be carried out at accelerated rate and to pass above of the other fields of the economy, bringing side by side with positive results new problems to be solved.

At the present time the regulation of the foreign trade is based on rather new legal foundations, which will be reviewed in this chapter. In the first section the regulation of the foreign trade will be analysed. This includes the survey of the principles and methods of the state regulation of the foreign trade, the characteristics of the participants of the foreign trade activity in Russia after the abolishment of the monopoly of the foreign trade, an overview of the currency regulation and of the strengthening of the state currency control of export-import control to prevent the illegal escape of the capital from the country. The analysis of the public regulations of the foreign trade is followed by a brief description of the international law aspects of the regulations. The attention is paid to the process of the accession of RF to the World Trade Organisation, to the development of the legal bases for the regulation of the foreign trade relations between Russia and European Union and the main goals which RF hopes to achieve by participating in the multilateral legal regulation of the international trade.

2. State regulation of foreign trade activity

2.1. General characteristics of the legal sources of the state regulation of foreign trade

In carrying out the reform on liberalisation of the foreign trade activity in RF numerous legal acts on different issues were adopted, which very often were in a short time replaced by again new acts. Such development of regulation by different blocks without a general basis caused instability and uncertainty of the legal regime. There was an urgent need for the law of a general character which could constitute the foundation for the development of the legal regulation. The situation was significantly improved on October 15, 1995 when the law "On State Regulation of Foreign Trade Activity" (referred later as "SRFTA") was adopted. The law summarised the development of the regulation and introduced innovations necessary for the present situation. It constitutes the fundamentals of the regulation of the foreign trade at the present time and is the basis for the further development of the legislation in this field. The normative acts adopted on the field of the foreign trade by different state organs have to correspond to its provisions. Thus the system of regulation is created.

Parallel to this law of general character, the laws on different methods of regulation should be mentioned, such as the law "On Customs Tariff" of May 21, 1993, the Customs Code of June 18, 1993, the law "On Currency Regulation and Currency control" of October 9, 1992. Some laws on special matters contain also rules concerning the different aspects of the state regulation of the foreign trade, for example in such as the law "On Certification of Goods and Services". But still a great part of the regulation in this field is covered not by federal laws but by normative acts of different legal nature, in particular RF Presidents Decrees (on the most important matters), RF Government Resolutions, Orders of the Ministry of Foreign Economic Relations (MFER) and Instruction and other acts of State Customs Committee (SCC).

Meanwhile some new federal laws in this field are in the process of elaboration and adoption.

2.2. Principles of the state regulation of foreign trade activity

The principles of the state regulation of the foreign trade activity are outlined in the law SRFTA. The main group of the principles (united by the key word "the unity") ensure the integrity of the single economic area on the territory of the Russian Federation in compliance with the Constitution of Russia. These principles are: the unity of the foreign trade policy as a part of the foreign policy of RF; the unity of the state system for the regulation of the foreign trade activity and supervision over its enforcement; the unity of the export control policy; the unity of the customs territory of RF. To ensure this unity, the law provides special detailed articles on matters within the reference of RF in the field of foreign trade, on matters within joint competence of RF and its subjects, on competence of RF subjects and on co-ordination of foreign trade activity of RF subjects in respect of matters within the joint competence.

To keep the direction strictly towards market economy, among the main principles of the law is the priority of economic measures in state regulation of foreign trade activity. To prevent illegal administrative measures the law provides the principle of the exclusion of unjustified intervention of the state and its organs in foreign trade activity, exclusion of damage to its participants and to the economy of the Russian federation as a whole. Two of the main principles determine the legal regime for the participants of the foreign trade activity: equality of the participants of foreign trade and non-discriminatory treatment and the protection of the rights and legitimate interests of the participants in foreign trade activity by the state.

2.3. Participants of foreign trade activity

For many decades in the former USSR the regime of state monopoly of foreign trade granted the exclusive right to participate in foreign trade activity only to the state foreign trade organisations. One of the first and the most important results of the reform of the foreign trade in the former USSR was providing for the producers of the exported goods a direct access to the foreign market. Since April 1989 the right of the direct export-import transactions was granted to all enterprises, amalgamations of production co-operatives and other organisations whose products, services and other activities were competitive at the foreign market. The organisations intending to participate in foreign trade contracts had to be registered at the Ministry of Foreign Trade as the participants of the foreign trade activity – to fill in the registration form to get the registration number and the registration certificate. Though the system was somewhat bureaucratic, it gave an opportunity for thousands of Soviet organisations to move to the foreign market. This situation was the starting point for the reforms in RF after the dissolution of the USSR.

Russia continued the process of the reforms with the well-known RF President Decree of November 15, 1991 "On liberalisation of foreign trade activity on the territory of RSFSR". To stimulate the foreign trade activity, the decree granted the right of being engaged in foreign trade activity without special registration for all the enterprises registered on the territory of Russia. Such openness of the market required developed state regulation. Exports were regulated by quantitative restrictions and licensing, but in practice these measures occurred to be insufficient to prevent the active export of the goods.

At the beginning of the reform process in 1992, the domestic prices of some goods were significantly lower than the prices of the same goods in the world market. This was the case with some important raw materials and fuel. The full liberalisation of the trade of these products would have caused emptying of the domestic markets, which would have had catastrophic effects on the national economy. To limit the export of these goods, the RF president decree of June 14, 1992 "On Export of Strategically Important Raw Materials" was adopted. The decree introduced a list of "Strategically Important Materials" (SIRM). The SIRM-list in 1992 included 15 groups of goods, which in practise formed the main part of the Russian exports (fuel and electric power, oil products, wood processing and pulp and paper products, ferrous and non-ferrous metals, mineral acids, apatite concentrate). In 1993, fish and fish products and marine products were added to the list, while separate kinds of timber and paper products were excluded.

Since 1 of July 1992 the SIRM-exports could be carried out only by the enterprises registered in MFER as the special exporters – so-called "specexporters". The list of SIRM-products was to some extent wider than the list of the goods under the quantitative restrictions and licensing but on the whole it coincided with the main types of Russian exports. Thus though all business entities had direct access to the world market, the SIRM-list and the registry of special exporters limited the participants of the significant part of the foreign trade activity. This system of special exporters and strategically important materials was abolished on 25 of March 1995 by RF President Decree "On the Main Principles of Carrying out of Foreign Trade Activity in Russian Federation".

According to the Law on State Regulation of Foreign Trade Activity

(SRFTA) all Russian persons have a right to engage in the foreign trade activity with the exception of cases provided by the legislation of RF. For example, at present a special legal capacity to perform trade transactions on armaments and military equipment has been established by state exclusively for separate commercial organisations.

Under the SRFTA, a Russian person can either be a legal person established in accordance with the legislation of RF, which is permanently located on the territory of RF, or a natural person who permanently or predominantly resides on the territory of RF and is registered as an individual entrepreneur. So the right to be engaged in foreign trade activity is in practise granted to all Russian juridical and physical persons. Thus the most important reform, which was already introduced in a number of previous acts during the years of opening the highly monopolised system of foreign trade got a full and detailed regulation in the law.

According to SRFTA, the Russian participants of foreign trade activity may on voluntary bases form associations and other unions according to sectoral, territorial and other principles. Such associations may be formed to protect the interests of their members, to represent their common interest, to raise the efficiency of exports and imports, to prevent unfair competition and to develop foreign trade relations.

As a matter of fact the exporters started to unite on the production basis into voluntary independent non-governmental non-commercial associations at the beginning of 1990's before the law SFRTA was adopted. The problem became actual when after the demonopolisation of the foreign trade numerous Russian exporters moved to foreign markets. The concern was expressed that they, while competing against other Russian exporters, could level down the world prices. This was what happened to the world prices for fish, metals, timber and some commodities. It provoked negative reactions on part of some countries. To prevent the dropping of price level, Russian exporters began to take measures. For example, 77 leading timber exporters formed a union, which was registered in October 1992; at the same time a Council of manufacturers and exporters of ferrous metals was also registered. In 1994 All-Russian Association of Fisheries Enterprises, Entrepreneurs and Exporters was established, as well as the Union of Oil Exporters of Russia and others. To establish interaction between with these associations, the Council of Branch Associations of Manufacturers and Exporters was founded under MFER in August, 1994. Under the RF Government Instruction of June 25 of 1995, MFER keeps a register of branch unions of manufacturers and exporters of RF. The associations elaborate recommendations for their members, render assistance and support to exporters in their activities on foreign markets. Some associations are also formulating certification system for their member to guarantee the reliability of the exporters in the world market. Associations also have and develop contacts to international associations in the same field.

These associations are important for the promotion of the penetration of the Russian exporters to the world market. On the other hand, the process of establishing such mighty associations could quite evidently seriously restrict the development of free competition. To prevent unfair competition, the above-mentioned Instruction of RF Government provides, that the RF State Antimonopoly Committee jointly with MFER supervises over the strict observance of the antimonopoly law requirements in establishing of branch association as well as over the observance of the activities of these associations. The same problem is taken on account on SFRTA, which provides that the associations shall not be used to monopolise and divide the domestic market, to restrict the competition of the non-members of these associations, to discriminate in any way Russian or foreign persons on the dependence of a membership in such association, nor to restrict business practises on foreign markets. It is noteworthy that the relevant provisions, which prevent infringement of competition by such associations are contained in the RF law "On competition and restriction of monopolistic activity at the commodity markets".

The Law SFRTA gives also a possibility to state to conclude foreign trade contracts directly. Contrary to the years of state monopoly, the Law provides that the Russian Federation, Russian Federation subjects and the municipalities shall directly carry out foreign trade activity only in cases provided by the federal constitutional laws, federal laws and other regulatory acts of RF subjects. Thus the conclusion of foreign trade contracts by the state is conducted only in exceptional cases.

The law includes a provision on trade missions of RF. Trade missions are state organs representing and protecting abroad the interests of RF relating to foreign trade activity. Considering the changes in participants of the foreign trade activity at the present time, the law stipulates that the trade missions shall not refuse to provide information and advisory services for Russian participants of foreign trade activity for example on grounds of their form of ownership, place of registration or the amount of charter capital. Later on the functions of the trade missions have been changed by the RF Government Decision on 26th of August, 1996 "On Reorganisation of the Russian Trade Missions Abroad". The aim of the decree was to optimise the control of the RF foreign economic ties with due account of the present trade and economic relations between RF and certain countries and existing budget funds for financing of the Russian trade missions. In 36 countries representations were transformed to Trade Counsellor offices of Russian Embassies. The total number of trade missions was reduced to 47 from the 130 in 1995. It was planned to retain about 20 trade missions in the countries with a traditionally large volume of mutual commodity turnover and in the other countries to establish trade representative bureaux or trade counsellor officers at the embassies. This reorganisation was explained by the decrease of international trade, by the reduction of the number of the state foreign organisations of MFER (about 20), by the growth of the number of private business entities (the biggest of them have their own representative offices abroad).

In case of a foreign state adopting measures, which infringe on economic rights of the Russian federation, its subjects, municipalities or persons, the law provides some response measures for the Government of RF. Such measures shall be introduced in accordance with the generally recognised norms of international law and within such limits as may be necessary for effective protection of the economic interests of the infringed party.

The opening of Russian economy led to a significant enlargement of the number of the foreign business entities at the Russian market. The law SRFTA envisages that foreign persons shall carry out foreign trade activity in the RF in compliance with the legislation of Russian federation. Under the law, the foreign persons are: 1) the legal persons or organisations of other legal forms whose civil legal capacity is determined in accordance with the legislation of the foreign state where they have been established; 2) natural persons – foreign nationals whose legal capacity and competence are determined in accordance with the legislation of the foreign state whose citizens they are, and stateless persons, whose civil competence is determined in accordance with the legislation of the foreign state wherein these persons permanently reside. No special permission for carrying out foreign trade activity in RF is required. In principle the foreign business entities enjoy national treatment; except for cases especially provided in the federal legislation, they have the same legal rights and obligations as the Russian participants of the foreign trade activity.

Under the law foreign legal persons are entitled to open representative offices on the territory of RF, which may carry out foreign trade activity only on behalf of these legal persons with the observance of the federal laws and other legal acts of the RF. To open a representative office a special permission is required. On this occasion, an act from the former USSR legislation is still in force – that is the Decree N 1074 of 30 November, 1989 of the USSR Council of Ministers. Under this decree, such permission is granted by the respective accrediting body depending on the nature of the business of the foreign firm. The foreign company interested in establishing a representative office shall submit an application in writing to the respective accrediting body, wherein it shall state the purpose for which it requires to open a representation, describe its business activities and give a detailed information on business relations with Russian organisations and about concluded agreements and commercial deals. The application shall be accompanied by official documents, enlisted in the decree.

Recently, as a result of the raising of the import custom tariff, the foreign firms have begun to prefer the joint venture as a legal form of activity at the Russian market.

2.4. Methods of regulation of the Foreign Trade Activity

According to SRFTA, the state foreign trade policy shall be carried out through customs-tariff regulation and non-tariff regulation (in particular establishing quotas and licensing) of foreign trade activity. To ensure the stability of the regulations, it is stressed, that foreign trade restrictions established by the state organs of Russian Federation or its subjects, other than ones regulated by the Federal laws or regulations, are not permitted; nor are the interventions on the foreign trade activity by the said organs.

Customs tariff regulation of foreign trade activity

Because in the former USSR the foreign trade was a state monopoly, customs tariff could not have the traditional function as an economic instrument of export-import regulation. After the market-oriented reforms were launched in the USSR in 1991, the law on Customs Tariff and the Custom Code were adopted, which, however, were in many aspects determined by the administrative methods of regulation. The parts of these laws, which did not contradict to the new Russian legislation, remained in force in RF after the dissolution of USSR until the adoption of new Customs Code and the law on Customs Tariff in 1993. These 1993 laws constitute the legal basis of the present RF customs tariff regulation. In addition to the provisions of these laws, numerous legal acts have been adopted, mainly by the RF Government and the State Customs Committee (SCC).

In SFRTA, customs tariff regulation is put on the first place in the description of regulation methods. The goals of the application of a customs tariff are stipulated in the law – the protection of the domestic market of RF and the stimulation of the progressive structural changes in the economy of RF. It is provided that export and import custom tariffs shall be established in accordance with the federal laws and international treaties of RF.

At the beginning of the process of the foreign trade liberalisation, on 1 of January 1992, RF government abolished the import tariff, but on July 1, 1992 re-introduced the interim import tariff, which has undergone many changes since then. The export tariff was also introduced in 1992, and during the first two years it covered three quarters of the Russian exports. The reason for applying the export tariff was the lower level of domestic prices compared to the world market prices; besides it was also used for fiscal goals.

The liberalisation of the export regulation was continued by the reduction of the goods for which the export duties were applied and by the reduction of the export duty rates. The export duties were abolished in RF on April 1, 1996 by the RF Government resolution "On Abolishment of the Export Customs Duties" for all the goods except oil and gas, the duties of which were abolished on July 1, 1996.

Thus the export tariff is not applied in Russia at the present time, but the import tariff has become the main instrument of the import regulation, and has been constantly increased. One reason for the present high import tariff rate is the fiscal needs; the abolishment of the export rates caused budget losses, which had to be compensated by raising import tariffs. Import tariffs are also being used as protective measures. The average tariff rate at the moment is about 15 percent. This is substantially higher than in the member countries of the WTO, and customs tariff level is one of the main issues to be discussed at the negotiations on the access of RF to WTO.

The majority of the import tariff charges in Russia are *ad valorem* duties. Also specified duty rates and compound duty rates are being used in some cases. The import tariff consists of three columns. The basic rate is applied for the goods from the countries, which are granted the MFN – treatment (Most Favoured Nation -treatment). The rate for the goods from the countries, which enjoy preferential treatment, is 75 % of the basic rate. The third column is for the goods from the countries, which are not granted the MFN treatment, and for the goods of unknown origin. Rate for these goods is double the basic rate.

The order of customs valuation according the Law on Customs Tariff is entirely based on the principles embodied in Art VII of the

GATT-agreement. The principles on determining the country of origin are also in compliance with the practice at the world market.

It should be mentioned that the special chapter of the Code contains an exhaustive list and the order of granting privileges in paying the customs tariff.

Import duties are paid either in rubles, or if the payer has chosen so, in freely convertible currency. The conversion of foreign currency into the rubles is made at the rate of the Central Bank of RF effective on the day of acceptance of the customs declaration.

To allow the protection of domestic markets by customs tariff regulation, the Law "on Customs Tariff" contains special, antidumping and compensatory duties. These duties are temporarily applied to goods brought to the territory of RF after an investigation conducted in conformity with RF law. These methods will be considered more thoroughly in the section on safeguard measures.

Quantitative Restrictions on Export and Import

In the first years of the reform of foreign trade in USSR, quantitative restrictions were widely used; they covered about 70 % of the exports and 6 % of the imports. The acute shortage of goods at the domestic market was the main reason for such system. In the contrast to the usual market practice the regulation was directed mainly to exports but not to the imports of goods to protect the national market not from the international competition but from the export of goods necessary for the country. Russian federation inherited this situation with the same peculiarity as in the former USSR: the administrative methods were directed towards restricting the export of the goods of paramount importance for the Russian economy. The liberalised regime for imports was necessary to compensate the deep recession in production and shortage of goods, and to promote the competition at the highly monopolised domestic market. When the reform process proceeded, the development of customs tariff regulation made it possible to renounce the system of quantitative restrictions. In RF President Decree of May 23, 1994 the quantitative restrictions and licensing were abolished since July 1, 1994 for all kinds of goods (with the exemption of export in accordance with obligations out of international treaties and the goods for which the special procedure of export was established) and since January 1, 1995 for oil and oil products.

Under the SRFTA, export and import shall be carried out without quantitative restrictions. However, quantitative restrictions may be imposed by the RF Government in exceptional cases for the following purposes:

- to safeguard national security of the Russian Federation;
- to fulfil international obligations of the Russian federation with a due account of the state of the domestic market;
- to protect the domestic markets of RF in cases provided by the SRFTA

As an example of the export of the goods within quotas may be mentioned textile products (until recently), black metals, aluminium to the EU member countries in accordance with the commitments provided in relevant international treaties. Quotas are used for observance of international obligations of RF when it is necessary to follow quotas introduced by the foreign countries for Russian exports (for example, exports of ammonium nitrate and articles of steel and rolled steel). The quota fixing as a protective measure will be considered in the part on safeguard measures.

To ensure the stability of the relations and the interests of the partners of the foreign trade, the acts of RF Government introducing quantitative restrictions on export and import shall be adopted and published no later than three months before these restrictions come into force.

As a rule, quotas and licenses shall be distributed through competition or auctioning or by actual performance of export and/or import operations until the quota is used. The priority will be given to the manufacturers by the MFER. In competitions and auctions, all legal entities shall have equal rights and opportunities. The law includes a special provision that there shall be no limitations on the number of bidders participating in such competitions and auctions, nor it is allowed to discriminate participants on the grounds of the form of ownership, the place of registration or the market share. These rules have been specified in RF Government Resolution "On holding competitions and auctions on sale of quotas when introducing quantitative restrictions by the Russian Federation" of October 31, 1996. The resolution included the establishment of Interdepartmental Commission on holding competitions and auctions on sale of export and import quotas.

Export Control

SRFTA allows export control to protect the national interests of RF in foreign trade activities involving armaments, military hardware and dual-purpose goods and to ensure observance of international obligations of the Russian federation with respect to non-proliferation of mass-destruction weapons and technologies for the production thereof. The list of the goods, which are under export control, is determined by the decrees of RF president on the recommendation of the RF Government. Such decrees shall become effective no earlier than three months after the date of their official publication.

State Monopoly

According to SRFTA, RF may introduce state monopoly on the export and/or import of various kinds of goods. The list of good subject to state monopoly shall be determined only by federal laws. State monopoly shall be based on licensing of export or of import of the goods. The licenses shall be issued by MFER exclusively to the state unitary enterprises. These enterprises are obliged to carry out the export and import transactions on the basis of such principles as non-discrimination and fair commercial practice. Attention should be paid to the serious consequences of violation of state monopoly – the transaction concluded in violation of state monopoly shall be null and void. MFER is entitled to require application of the consequences of invalidation of a null and void transaction in accordance with a procedure laid down by the Civil Code of RF.

Safeguard Measures

The opening of the domestic markets left the national manufacturers without any protection against dumping or unfair competition of the foreign producers. Because of this, the introduction of safeguard measures in the SRFTA is of special importance. At the time of the adoption of the law, the protective function of the law was of a paramount significance for the foreign trade liberalised at an accelerated rate.

The Law provides that if goods of some kind are imported in such large quantities or on such terms and conditions that substantial damage is done, or there is a threat of such damage being done, to manufacturers of similar or directly competing goods on the territory of RF the RF Government shall in accordance with the generally recognised norms of international law have a right to take protective measures. These measures may be taken in the form of quantitative restrictions or special increased customs duties to a degree and for a period necessary to eliminate or prevent substantial damage.

The safeguard measures shall be introduced on the decision of RF Government. It shall be taken on the basis of the report of MFER as a summary of the results of investigation. This investigation is carried out at the request of RF Government and/or in response to an application of an execution body of RF subject, a manufacturer or an association of manufacturers, whose total output of a similar kind of goods directly competing with imported goods accounts for more than 50 % of the total domestic output of the goods. The goal of the investigation is to establish the presence of substantial damage or a threat thereof, and the presence of an objective cause and effect relationship between the growth of imports, and the presence of substantial damage or thereof. It is stipulated that the investigation is to be conducted within two months from the date of the application.

At the request of RF Government, MFER shall notify the foreign state bodies that the investigation was launched. In this note MFER indicates the goods, proof of substantial damage or a threat of it from the import of these goods, the suggested measures and the time of their introduction. MFER will express readiness for consultations on these matters. The procedure for the introduction of safeguard measures must be published.

The introduction of safeguard measures was discussed in connection with the balance of trade of textiles between EU and RF. The first complications in this sphere appeared at the end of 1994 after the negotiations on the new agreement on trade of textile products (to replace the agreement of 1993) were not successful. Instead it was decided to preserve in force the 1993 agreement for the year 1995. Russia claimed, that in this agreement, the access of the Russian textile to the EU market was seriously restricted – the quota fixed for textile from RF to EU market was 140 million ECU, while the quota of EU textile to RF market was 580 million ECU. The counter-argument by the EU was that Russian exporters did not fully utilise the given quota, and thus the quota was not too small. RF suggested to refuse from quota-fixing in the trade of the textile products, but EU did not accept it. In 1996 the RF Governmental Commission on Safeguard Measures came to a decision that it would be rational to introduce restrictive quotas on the import of textile from EU. As an economic argument, there was adduced the difficult situation in the national textile industry with the convincing proof of a decline in the production and its profitability. It should be mentioned that the quota-fixing in the textile sphere does not contradict any international practice, it is not in the sphere of the general regime of the world trade. Russia held the inequality and the asymmetry of the trade balance as unacceptable. The negotiations on new agreement failed, and since January 1, 1997 each party regulates the trade of the textile on its own direction. There is no bilateral legal basis anymore between RF and EU in the field of textile trade.

Another sphere, were safeguard measures have been applied, is the import of alcohol (spirits). This was due to the massive imports, which led to reduction of domestic production to 80 %; many Russian producers were on the point of bankruptcy. In 1993 – 1995 the share of domestic production at the internal market was reduced from 82 % to 30 – 40 %. Since January 1, 1997 RF Government adopted resolution, which established import quotas for vodka and ethyl alcohol. Since

January 1, 1997, vodka and ethyl alcohol may be imported only on the license issued within the fixed quota. The import quotas are to be sold at the auctions, and a special Commission was set up for this purpose.

The mentioned cases were not the only where the need of protective measures arose. After the SRFTA became in force, the possibility to apply protective measures drew attention of the domestic producers in RF, which initiated investigations concerning import of some other goods.

The provision on safeguard measures in the SRFTA and already mentioned provisions of the Law "On Customs Tariff" on anti-dumping and compensatory duties constitute the legislative basis for the traditional protection of the domestic market. To create the necessary legal regulation for effective application of all mentioned protective measures, a RF Government Commission "On Safeguard Measures in Foreign Trade" was created, and an order of MFER "Regulations of Carrying Out of Investigation Preliminary to the Introduction of the Protective Measures" of January 21, 1995 was adopted. The next step expected to be taken soon in this field is the adoption of the Law "On Protection of Economic Interests of Russian Federation in Foreign Trade".

Bans and Restrictions on Export and Import

According to SRFTA, RF may in accordance with federal laws and international treaties impose bans and restrictions on export and/or import of goods, services, results of intellectual activity, proceeding from the national interests. The list of the grounds for such bans and restrictions is rather traditional. They include: maintenance of public morals; law and order; protection of life and health of people, of flora and fauna and of the entire environment; preservation of the cultural heritage of the people of RF; prevention of unlawful exportation; avoidance of depletion of non-renewable mineral resources if the measures aimed thereat are adopted simultaneously with the restriction of the appropriate domestic production and consumption; safeguarding of the national security of the Russian federation; protection of the external financial position and maintenance of the balance of payment of the Russian federation.

It is provided that federal laws on bans and restrictions shall take effect not earlier than 30 days from the date of their official publication.

Technical, Pharmacological, Sanitary, Veterinary, Phytosanitary and Ecological Standards and Requirements with Regard to Imported Goods

It is widely acknowledged now, that the introduction of technical requirements for imported goods is regarded as the most serious protective measure. In accordance with SRFTA, the goods brought into the territory of RF shall conform to the technical, pharmacological, sanitary, veterinary, phytosanitary and ecological standards and requirements effective in RF.

The legal basis of the standardisation in RF is determined by the law "On Standardisation" of July 10, 1993 (now in version of the Federal Law of January 27, 1995). The state standards are effective after registration in the State Committee of Standards, Metrology and Certification of RF (Gosstandart).

Certification of the goods and services for confirming of their correspondence to the stated standards and requirements was introduced in RF in accordance with the law "On Consumer Protection" of September 7, 1992 (now in version of Federal Law of January 9, 1996). The obligatory certification covers the goods and services where the life and the health of a human being and the ecology depends on such goods and services. Other products may be certified on voluntary bases in accordance with the requirements agreed by the seller and the buyer.

The lists of the goods liable to obligatory certification in RF has been constantly enlarged. The lists of the goods effective at present are confirmed by the order of State Customs Committee of RF of August 14, 1996 N 496 (in version of 31.01.1997) "On Application of the lists of the goods, subject to obligatory certification imported to the customs territory of RF". The lists are formed in accordance with the Brussels nomenclature of the goods.

The procedure of certification is regulated by the Federal Law "On Certification of Products and Services" of June 10, 1993 (now in version of December 27, 1995) and by other regulatory acts of RF. In accordance with the law "On Certification..." in the terms of contract liable under the legislative acts of RF to obligatory certification there shall be provided the availability of a certificate and the mark of correspondence confirming the correspondence to the established requirements. The certificates and the certificates on their acknowledgement are to be submitted with the customs declaration to get the permission on the import of the production into the territory of RF.

The main provisions on certification of imported goods are contained in the special document "The Procedure of the Import on the Territory of RF of the Goods Subject to Obligatory Certification" affirmed by order of SCC of RF and of Gosstandart on June 15, 1994 N 599. This document provides that the certification of imported goods is to be carried out by the Russian organs accredited in Gosstandart on certification, or by foreign organs on certification if their certification and the mark of correspondence are acknowledged in RF. As an example of such foreign certificates may be mentioned the following: certificates DIN GOST TUV (Gesselschaft für Zertifizierung in Europa GmbH), certificate of the organ accredited by an international organisation of certification, in which RF has joined (for instance IECG, IECEE), and a certificate of the organ of certification of the country of the exporter.

The law "On Certification..." forbids the advertising of goods subject to obligatory certification, which do not have the label of the certificate. This was developed in the Federal Law "On Advertising" of July 18, 1995.

SRFTA outlines the special cases when the import of goods into the territory of RF shall be banned. They are: failure to conform to the standards and requirements effective in RF; the case when the goods are not provided with the necessary certificate, marking or symbol in cases provided for by legislative acts; or if the goods are forbidden for use as dangerous consumer goods and if the goods have defects dangerous for consumers. Such goods shall be sent back or destroyed on the basis of a certificate made out by independent experts of the Chamber of Commerce and Industry of RF.

The regulation on the requirements regarding to the imported goods is constantly developed in Russia, and is becoming stricter. This illustrated by such documents as RF Government Resolution "On Measures of Protection of Consumer Market from Bringing of Imported Goods of Bad Quality" of July 12, 1996 N799 or RF Government Resolution "On Marking of the Goods and Production on the Territory of Russia by the Marks of Correspondence Protected from Falsification" of May 17, 1997, which also is addressed to the imported goods.

Stricter requirements are also provided for the information about the imported goods, In accordance with RF Government Resolution of December 27, 1996 N869 with the amendments of July 14, 1997 all imported foodstuffs must have information on a concrete point given in Russian. In accordance with RF Government Resolution "On measures of ensuring information in Russian on no-food goods brought to the territory of Russian Federation" of August 15, 1997 since July 1, 1998 the sale of non-food goods without required information on the territory of RF is forbidden.

At present the regulation in this sphere, mainly in standardisation and certification, is at the point of some changes, which are prepared by Gosstandart in accordance with the requirements of the Agreement "On technical barriers in trade of WTO"

3. Requirements of currency legislation obligatory for the accounts in foreign trade relations

Currency regulation constitutes an important aspect of the regulation of the foreign trade relations. The basic provisions, which are to be taken into consideration in this field are provided in the law "On Currency Regulation and Currency Control". Its provisions are complemented by numerous legal acts, mainly of the Central Bank of RF as the main organ of currency legislation, adopting normative acts of obligatory force.

When outlining the main provisions of the law "On Currency Regulation…", it is necessary first of all to mention the division of all currency transaction into two groups: the current currency transactions and currency transactions related to the movement of capital. Current currency transactions include, in particular in the sphere of foreign trade relations, the transfers into the RF and from RF of foreign currency for payments without delay for the export and import of goods, works and services and for the settlements pertaining to credits for export and import transaction for a period up to 180 days; receipt and granting of financial credits for a period up to 180 days. Currency transactions related to the movement of capital include, in particular, direct investment and portfolio investments, granting and obtaining postponement of payment for a period more than 180 days for the export and import of goods, work and services; granting and obtaining financial credits for a period more than 180 days; all other currency transactions that are not current currency transactions.

As it may be seen, the main criterion for the classification is the time of the transfer of money – 180 days.

Different currency operations are regulated under different legal regime. Current currency transactions are conducted by the residents without restrictions. Currency transactions related to the movement of capital are conducted by the residents in the order established by the Central Bank of RF, and by the licences of Central Bank. Therefore in case when the transfer of currency payment for the exported goods exceeds the period of 180 days and in case when the import of goods to RF exceeds the period of 180 days after the date of prepayment, the current currency transactions are transformed to currency transactions related to the movement of capital. They exit the category of transactions operated without restrictions, and enter the category of transactions for which the residents need the license of the Central Bank.

Another basic provision for the accounts states, that the residents may have foreign currency accounts in the authorised banks – the banks which have obtained the license for the execution of currency transactions. Foreign currency obtained by resident enterprises shall be credited to their accounts in the authorised banks unless otherwise provided by the Central Bank of RF. Residents may have foreign currency accounts outside RF only on the conditions established by the Central Bank – on the license of Central Bank. Thus only in such cases the currency revenue may be transferred to the account of the Russian contractual counterpart in a foreign bank.

Third, transactions concluded in violation of the provisions of the law "On Currency Regulation" (in particular the mentioned provisions) are declared null and void. The law provides the rules on strict liability for the violation of the stated requirements (for example, to recover in favour of the state, the entire proceeds of the transactions are declared null and void under the present law). It should be mentioned that in the new version of the law, which is expected to be adopted, the special attention was paid to the provisions on liabilities.

The Development of Currency Control over Foreign Trade Transactions

The reviewed requirements of the law "On Currency Regulation" are directed at prevention of the illegal escape of currency from the country, which actually began parallel with the liberalisation of the foreign trade. Foreign trade transactions became the main channel for the illegal outflow of currency by such means as non-return of the payment for the exported goods, prepayment for the fictitious imported goods, abuse of barter contracts, setting the contract prices low in export and overstating the contract prices in import etc. However, the law "On Currency Regulation" created the legislative bases but not the effective mechanism for the currency control over the movement of currency in foreign trade transactions. To achieve this goal, a number of special acts were adopted in this field, which step by step created the mechanism of currency control.

First of all, currency control was introduced over the repatriation of currency revenue to Russia from export of goods. This was introduced since January 1, 1994 for the goods included in the list of SIRM, and since March 1, 1994 it was spread to the export of all nomenclature of exported goods. The currency control was introduced by the Instruction N 19 of the Central Bank and the State Customs Committee of October 12, 1993 "Regulations of carrying out of currency control over repatriation to RF of currency revenue for the export of goods". The Instruction provided for the mechanism to ensure the strict observance of the obligation of the exporter to credit the foreign currency, which he obtains for the exported goods to his account in the authorised bank, where the currency revenue must come from the foreign importer. The exporter and the bank form the passport of the transaction where the terms of the transaction are envisaged in brief. The bank which signs the transaction is obliged not only to render services in the sphere of accounts, but also to carry out the function of a currency control agent and to control the repatriation of currency revenue. To identify the sums of revenue, the exporter informs the importer that he has to note in the payment documents the requisites of the contract or the passport of the contract. The custom bodies require the passport of the contract parallel with all other documents, obligatory under Russian legal acts for customs declaration. Custom bodies verify the compliance of the terms of the passport to the provisions of the customs declaration. Customs bodies also perform the function of the control. The instruction N 19 provides for the liability for non-observance of its requirements by the exporter and by the authorised bank.

The currency control in the field of import transactions was introduced since January 1, 1996 by the joint Instruction of the Central Bank of RF and the State Customs Committee of RF "On the procedure of currency control of well-founded payments in foreign currency of imported goods" of July 26, 1995 N30. The mechanism of the currency control of the import transactions is actually a mirror reflection of the mechanism of the export control. The passport of the transaction is the basic document for the control by the authorised bank through which the importer transfers the foreign currency payment for the imported goods and by the customs bodies.

The system of the currency control was developed by the RF President Decree N 1209 of August 18, 1996 "On State Control of Barter

Transactions" and by RF Government Resolution of October 31, 1996 N 1300 "On Measures on the State Regulation of Foreign Trade Barter Transactions". The control has to ensure the import of the goods, works, services and the results of intellectual activity equivalent to the cost of the exported goods, works and services. The passport of the barter transaction is the basic document for the control but the mechanism of the control has some peculiarities determined by the complicated character of these types of foreign trade transactions.

As a part of a state control of foreign trade it is necessary to mention the pre-custom expertise on the correspondence of the price and the quantity and quality of the exported goods. According to Resolution of RF Government of March 21, 1996 N 298, the expertise is not obligatory, but the commission of MFER for consideration of the application of the exporters on valid non-receiving or delay in receiving of currency revenue will consider such applications only if the certificate of pre-customs expertise is submitted.

Reviewing the state control, the Order of registration of foreign trade contracts as means of currency control execution of July 2, 1996, should also be mentioned. The order provides the procedure of foreign trade contracts registration of recommendatory character (as distinct from the previous obligatory registration of the contract of SIRM). This procedure covers all types of foreign economic contracts valued over 50 000 US dollars and is fulfilled by the MFER via its representatives in Russian regions. The registration of a recommendatory character is of special importance for application of the exporters on valid non-receiving of currency revenue in time or in a full amount.

The regulation in the sphere of currency and export control is in the process of development and strengthening, but still may be considered too complicated and consisting of too numerous acts and carrying out of too numerous bodies.

4. Problems of the accession of the RF to multilateral international legal regulation of the foreign trade

One important aspect of the legal regime is the participation of the country in the international agreements and the international organisations in this field. Russia, as a successor of the USSR, inherited the legal bases of the regulation of the foreign trade relations, created by the numerous agreements of the former USSR. Russia continued the activity directed at integration into the world economy system, launched by USSR in the years of reforms; negotiations on joining GATT/WTO and the development of the co-operation and the conclusion of agreements with the European Union. These items will be reviewed in this chapter.

4.1. Accession to the World Trade Organisation

In order to return to the world market on equal terms, it is important for RF to participate in the multilateral legal mechanism created by GATT/WTO. USSR took part in negotiations on creation of International Trade Organisation at the end of 1940's, when the basis of the world trade system was set up. But the socialist system, based on the central planning, made the actual participation of the USSR in the multilateral system based on market economy principles impossible. For many years, the USSR was out of the activities of the GATT on liberalisation of the foreign trade regime. The need to participate in the GATT became actual when the reforms on foreign trade regulation began. In 1990 the USSR got the status of the observer in the GATT. In 1992 this status was inherited by RF. In June, 1993 Russia applied officially for full-pledged membership in the GATT. The completion of the Uruguay round on multilateral trade negotiations resulted in the establishment of WTO, where the GATT became its integral part, and RF government submitted its application with an official request for accession to WTO. The Special Interdepartmental Commission on

GATT including the representatives of 50 ministries and organisations was transformed into the Commission on WTO. In March 1994 RF submitted to GATT the memorandum on the foreign trade regime in the country, which was the starting point for practical negotiations. Later Russia submitted answers for more than 1500 additional questions, which were put by the WTO member countries. RF also submitted the materials on the regulation of the trade of services, the trade aspects of the investing policy, and the trade aspects of the rights of intellectual property, which were the new spheres of the multilateral regulation, adopted at the conclusion of Uruguay round. The negotiating process on joining WTO during the years 1995–1997 concentrated on the discussion of the regime of foreign trade in Russia. The next step will be bilateral and multilateral negotiations on concrete terms of the accession. The package of tariffs of RF will be discussed (Russia submitted its initial offer on tariff rates in February 1998), as well as the opening of the domestic market of Russia for WTO members – the entrance ticket, which the country usually has to get for free accession to the world market. The initial obligations have to concern customs tariffs on the goods; protection of agricultural production (domestic support, tariff protection, export subsidies); obligations in the field of access to the market of services (insurance, banking) – the most sensitive for Russia.

Certainly it is not an easy task for Russia to join the system, which was formed during dozens of years by regular mutual concessions of the countries. Besides, it is considered to be rather problematic for RF to open the domestic market for free competition of the goods and services, to minimise the custom tariff taking into account the difficult transitional period of the economy. RF needs step by step guidance of most difficult obligations, and these problems will be discussed during the negotiations. It is widely supported view that the accession to WTO is not regarded as an end in itself but as an opportunity to improve the terms of trade for RF at the world market. Entering into the multilateral trade system, the rules of which regulate 90 per cent of the international trade, would provide more favourable access for Russian exporters to the world market; this is the main goal of the accession.

Quite evidently, the main principles of WTO, such as most favoured nation treatment and the national regime, are important for RF. The system of dispute settlement existing within the frames of WTO is also of special interest of RF. It may be expected that full membership of Russia in WTO would facilitate solution to such problem as the discrimination in trade on the part of western countries still considering Russia to be a country with non-market economy. On the other hand, bringing the foreign trade regulations of Russia in conformity with the WTO rules would ensure WTO-member countries more favourable, and secure access to the enormous Russian market.

4.2. Development of the legal bases for co-operation between Russia and the EU

The development of the legal basis for economic co-operation with EU is of special importance for RF. European Union has become the principal trading partner of RF. The share of EU in the total Russian trade turnover in 1996 was as high as 40 %. The initiative legal basis for economic co-operation was the Trade and Co-operation agreement of the USSR and EC signed in December 1989. The drastic changes at the beginning of 1990's made the agreement quickly out-dated. The dissolution of the USSR and the emergence of newly independent state made it necessary to review the EU-Russia economic relations. EU and Russia started negotiations on a new agreement in 1992, and on June 23, 1994 on the island of Corfu EU and Russia signed the Agreement on Partnership and Co-operation (PCA). This agreement, however, includes provisions, which are not within sole competence of EC, and thus had to be ratified by the parliaments of each EU member country. The ratification process took a long time, and PCA-agreement finally came into force in December 1, 1997. To gain some progress earlier, an Interim Agreement on Trade and Trade Related Matters, which includes the provisions of PCA, which belong to the competence of EC, was negotiated, and it became in force on February 1, 1996 (after delays caused by political reasons, mainly because of EU's disapproval for the Russian actions in Chechnya). The interim agreement replaced the trade provisions of the 1989 agreement.

PCA is based on art. 113 and art. 235 of the Rome treaty as a classical trade and economic co-operation agreement of EU; thus it is not an "association agreement" like the so-called Europe-agreements EU concluded with the countries of Central Eastern Europe, which are based on the art. 238. This means that PCA is not aimed at as far-reaching integration as the Europe-agreements.

PCA is based on the principles of equality and non-discrimination. It provides for a permanent dialogue in the sphere of commercial policy. It is aimed to support the RF efforts in development of market economy and Russia's gradual integration into the wider economic co-operation in Europe. It also objects at creation of necessary conditions for establishing in the future a free trade area between RF and EU; it is left to be seen if such area is created in the near future. Agreement also includes co-operation in all spheres of economic relations – trade of goods and services, movement of capital and working force, and establishment of companies.

For the first time in international agreements of RF, PCA includes direct references to the main provisions of the GATT. Art. I of the Title III "Trade in Goods" provides that the parties shall accord to one another the general most-favoured-nation treatment described in art. I, paragraph 1 of the GATT. This provision spreads MFN-regime to RF till it joins to WTO. MFN-treatment grants all privileges or advantages given by RF or EU to the goods of the third countries also to the goods from EU and RF.

For Russia there are additional exceptions concerning the MFN which allows Russia before joining WTO to not to spread MFN-regime on privileges given to the countries of former USSR. RF may also apply a special regime to the import of the goods under the agreements on credits, technical and humanitarian interaction concluded with the third countries.

For Russian exporters, the MFN-treatment in accordance with GATT means non-discriminatory attitude in carrying out of the procedures of customs clearance, and that the minimum rates of the Single Customs Tariff are applied to the goods from Russia.

According to the PCA the products of the territory one Party imported into the territory of the other party shall not be subject, directly or indirectly, to internal taxes or other internal charges in excess of those applied directly or indirectly to the domestic products. The national regime is also applied for internal regulation in EU and RF concerning purchase, sale, transportation, distribution and use of imported goods. For example the tariffs for carriage of the goods on the territory of EU shall be the same for Russian and EU goods.

Under PCA EU shall fully abolish the quantitative restrictions, except for some textile and steel products, for import from RF. It should be also mentioned that before RF becomes a contracting party to GATT/WTO, EU and Russia shall hold consultations in Co-operation Committee on their import tariff policies, including changes in tariff protection. That means that RF preserves the right to change customs tariffs under the condition of such preliminary consultations.

The liberalisation of mutual trade does not prevent RF and EU the right to apply safeguard measures when it is necessary. Safeguard measures in PCA are provided in full compliance with the GATT provisions. Where any product is being imported into the territory of the Parties to the PCA in such increased quantities and under such conditions as to cause or threaten to cause substantial injury to domestic producers of like or directly competitive products the Party, which is concerned may take appropriate measures in accordance with the procedure and conditions determined in PCA.

Of special importance for RF in developing legal basis for trade relations with EU is the protection of the interests of Russian exporters in the field of antidumping practises. In EU the application of antidumping measures is not considered to be discriminatory; measures are introduced towards different countries, and in case of Russia, concern insignificant part of Russian exports from the viewpoint of EU – 0,3 per cent of mutual trade turnover. Until April 1998, Russia was considered by EU to be state-trading country – not a market economy – and this might have had some negative effects when considering application of anti-dumping measures. In determination of dumping of the products of a state-trading country, the reduction of the price of the exported goods is not proved by the real conditions of the terms of forming of the prices. Instead, as a meter for the right price level, prices of similar products from a market-economy country with a same GNP as Russia are being used. This may have naturally caused unjust treatment towards Russian products, when natural advances and conditions of Russian producers are not taken into account. The PCA -agreement was expected to improve this situation, since in the preamble of the agreement, Russia is not considered to be a state trading country, but a country with an economy in transition.

Coming into force of PCA, as well as membership in WTO, is expected to remove protectionist barriers on the way of Russian exporters to the world market.

KIKIMORA PUBLICATIONS

Series A

Temkina, Anna (1997): Russia in Transition: The Case of New Collective Actors and New Collective Actions. ISBN 951-45-7843-0

Мустонен, Петер (1998): Собственная его императорского величества канцелярия в механизме властвования института самодержца 1812–1858: К типологии основ имперского управления. ISBN 951-45-8074-5

3 Rosenholm, Arja (1999): Gendering Awakening : Femininity and the Russian Woman Question of the 1860s. ISBN 951-45-8892-4

4 Lonkila, Markku (1999): Social Networks in Post-Soviet Russia: Continuity and Change in the Everyday Life of St. Petersburg Teachers. ISBN 951-45-8911-4

Series B

Vihavainen, Timo ja Takala, Irina (red.) (1998): В семье единой: Национальная политика партии большевиков и ее осуществление на Северо-Западе России в 1920–1950-е годы. ISBN 5-230

Granberg, Leo (ed.) (1998): The Snowbelt: Studies on the European North in Transition. ISBN 951-45-8253-5

Sutela, Pekka (1998): The Road to the Russian Market Economy: Selected Essays 1993–1998. ISBN 951-45-8409-0

4 Törnroos, Jan-Åke & Nieminen, Jarmo (eds.) (1999): Business Entry in Eastern Europe: A Network and Learning Approach with Case Studies. ISBN 951-45-8860-6

5 Miklóssy, Katalin (toim.) (1999): Syitä ja seurauksia: Jugoslavian hajoaminen ja seuraajavaltioiden nykytilanne: seminaari 8.4.1999, Helsinki. ISBN 951-45-8861-4

Винников, Александр (1998): Цена свободы. ISBN 5-89739-002-9

Лебина, Н. Б. (1999): Повседневная жизнь советского города : нормы и аномалии : 1920 и 1930 годы. ISBN 5-87516-133-7, 5-87940-004-0

8 Lejins, Atis (ed.) (1999): Baltic Security Prospects at the Turn of the 21st Century. ISBN 951-45-9067-8

9 Komulainen, Tuomas & Korhonen, Iikka (ed.) (2000): Russian Crisis and Its Effects. ISBN 951-45-9100-3

10 Salminen, Ari & Temmes, Markku (2000): Transitioteoriaa etsimässä. ISBN 951-45-9238-7

11 Yanitsky, Oleg (2000): Russian Greens in a Risk Society: A Structural Analysis. ISBN 951-45-9226-3

13 Oittinen, Vesa (ed.) (2000): Evald Ilyenkov's Philosophy Revisited. ISBN 951-45-9263-8

14 Tolonen, Juha (ed.) (2000): Legal Foundations of Russian Economy. ISBN 951-45-9276-X

15 Kotiranta, Matti (ed.) (2000): Religious Transition in Russia. ISBN 951-45-9447-9

16 Kangaspuro, Markku (ed.) (2000): Russia: More different than most. ISBN 951-45-9423-1

Orders:
Aleksanteri Institute
P.O.Box 4
00014 University of Helsinki
Telephone +358-9-191 24175
Telefax +358-9-191 23822
E-mail: kikimora-publications@helsinki.fi